THE PHILOSOPHY OF HORROR

THE PHILOSOPHY OF HORROR

or

PARADOXES OF THE HEART

NOËL CARROLL

ROUTLEDGE · New York & London

Published in 1990 by

Routledge
An imprint of Routledge, Chapman and Hall, Inc.
29 West 35 Street
New York, NY 10001

Published in Great Britain by

Routledge
11 New Fetter Lane
London EC4P 4EE

Library of Congress Cataloging in Publication Data

Carroll, Noël (Noël E.)
    The philosophy of horror.

    Includes index.
    1. Horror in literature. 2. Horror tales—History
and criticism. 3. Horror films—History and criticism.
I. Title.
PN56.H6C37   1989   809'.916   89-10469
ISBN 0-415-90145-6
ISBN 0-415-90216-9 (pbk.)

British Library Cataloguing in Publication Data

Carroll, Noël
    The philosophy of horror.
    1. Arts. Special subjects. Horror
I. Title
704.9'4

    ISBN 0-415-90145-6
        0-415-90216-9 (pb)

Dedicated to Sally Banes

Contents

Acknowledgments

Undoubtedly, my parents, Hughie and Evelyn Carroll, inadvertently gave birth to this treatise by telling me not to waste my time and money on horror books, magazines, comics, TV shows, and movies. In a final act of filial defiance, I, a middle-aged baby-boomer, have set out to prove to them that I was gainfully employed all along.

My thinking about horror really began to assemble itself when Annette Michelson and I taught a course in horror and science fiction at New York University. Annette soldiered the science fiction half of the course, while the gooier parts of the terrain became my lot. Annette was, and has continued to be, very helpful in the development of my theory. She suggested casting my notions about horrific biologies in terms of fusion and fission, and, as well, she has continually pressed me, with regard to my skepticism about contemporary film theory, to take the paradox of fiction seriously. Though my solutions to her questions may not be what she expected, I hope they are at least intriguing.

Early on, two philosophers—both of them horror addicts—abetted me in the conviction that pursuing this topic could be interesting. Judith Tormey and I spent an exhilarating drive to Mexico together, boring everyone else in the car while we swapped favorite monster stories. Jeff Blustein read my earliest attempts in horror theory with the analytical rigor and the enthusiasm only a fellow horror buff can appreciate.

The late Monroe Beardsley also read my nascent efforts at horror theory. He wondered aloud how I could be interested in this stuff. But then he addressed my hypotheses with what could only be thought of as arcane counterexamples. Sheepishly, he explained his estimable expertise in the field by saying that he had had to squire his sons through the fifties horror movie cycle, and that he just happened to remember some of the films (in amazing detail, I would add).

My interest in horror gradually turned into academic papers, delivered at the University of Southern California, the University of Warwick, the Museum of the Moving Image, LeMoyne College, Cornell University,

New York University, and the University of Iowa. Each audience provided challenging comments—of special note are those of: Stanley Cavell, Ed Leites, Karen Hansen, Richard Koszarski, Johnny Buchsbaum, Stuart Liebman, Allan Casebier, Jim Manley, Bruce Wilshire, Susan Bordo, the late Irving Thalberg Jr., Stephen Melville, Mary Wiseman, Ken Olsen, Nick Sturgeon, Anthony Appiah, David Bathrick, Cynthia Baughman, Murray Smith, Dudley Andrew, Henry Jenkins, Kristin Thompson, Berenice Reynaud, and Julian Hochberg.

Much of the initial writing of this book began during a sabbatical at Wesleyan University. Early discussions with Kent Bendall—one of the most precise and yet imaginatively open philosophers it has been my privilege to know—gave me important clues for solving what I call the paradox of fiction. Long talks with Chris Gauker, over several extremely pleasant dinners, helped me clarify my position. Ken Taylor and especially Philip Hallie, whose pioneering work on the philosophy of horror in his book *The Paradox Cruelty* served as an exemplar, listened to my theories with a critical attentiveness that was generous, and always supportive and instructive. Phil was even willing to go to a number of movies with me and to discuss them afterwards (something only someone who works on the genre of horror can realize is a gesture of unstinting companionship).

Michael Denning, Nancy Armstrong and Leonard Tennenhouse provided many useful suggestions about correspondences between my research and contemporary literary studies. Betsy Traube, transcending her aversion to my topic, made many pertinent recommendations about relevant anthropological literature. Khachig Tololyan who, among his many accomplishments, runs one of the world's great clipping services, kept me constantly on top of my subject. And Jay Wallace, who read drafts of the first two chapters with immense care, supplied me with copious criticisms and suggestions. On more than one occasion, Jay showed me how I could modify my claims judiciously and still make my points. Both his unalloyed interest and his arguments have made significant differences in this book. It was wonderful to have been his colleague.

Francis Dauer, Annette Barnes, John Fisher, Dale Jamieson, George Wilson, Arthur Danto, George Dickie, John Morreall, Richard Moran, Terry Irwin, Laurent Stern, Paul Guyer, Alex Sesonske, Daniel Banes, Jennefer Robinson, Susan Feagin, Gary Iseminger, Roy Gordon, and Myles Brand listened to, or read my hypotheses, and made comments which I found important to consider. Joe Margolis, across a number of conversations, showed me the need to make several distinctions I had ignored, as well as pointing me toward some authors of whose work I had been uninformed. Richard Shusterman, after reading my essay "The Nature of Horror," alerted me to Peter Lemarque's seminal and more advanced writings on the very type of theory of fictional objects that I was attempting to develop.

Tony Pipolo and Amy Taubin, both of whom see and read everything, gave me "front-line" reports on every novel, film and video that I hoped to accommodate in my theory. If their sensibilities outstrip my formulas, I hope they can nevertheless see some of their sensitivities worked into my descriptions.

David Bordwell, David Konstan, and Peter Kivy read the entire manuscript. Each made provocative criticisms and useful suggestions. David Bordwell showed me how I needed to clarify the distinction between my theory and reigning psychoanalytic models in the humanities today, as well as correcting some (there weren't *that* many) of my film-historical errors. David Konstan made sentence-by-sentence remarks, many of which I have incorporated; those I have bypassed, I suspect, I have so done at my own peril. Peter Kivy not only copy-edited the manuscript, but made many penetrating philosophical comments about the content. However, above all, it is to Peter that I owe, due to his work in the philosophy of music, the insight of the applicability, in general, of the theory of the emotions to questions in the philosophy of art.

Special thanks are due to William Germano who, it can be said, first had the thought that such a book could be written. In the course of a conversation on other matters, he indicated that he would "love" (his word) a proposal for a book on the philosophy of horror from me. I would not have thought of it otherwise. The rest is history (destiny?).

I have dedicated this book to my wife, Sally Banes. She courageously accompanied me on my many forays to cinemas and theaters all over the world for the sake of my "research." She patiently waited while I perused innumerable bookstalls any time we went to a grocery store, a pharmacy, or a department store outlet. Her own work on the fairy tale also afforded me an extremely useful complement to my theorizing about horror. Sally has read every draft of this project and provided endless comment: grammatical and logical; stylistic and conceptual. If such a book is a labor of love, it is also a labor of lovers. And I have been blessed with a lover willing to make my project her own.

So many smart and talented people have told me so much. If there are flaws remaining in this text, it only shows that I'm a bad listener.

Introduction

Context

For over a decade and a half, perhaps especially in the United States, horror has flourished as a major source of mass aesthetic stimulation. Indeed, it may even be the most long-lived, widely disseminated, and persistent genre of the post-Vietnam era. Horror novels seem available in virtually every supermarket and pharmacy, and new titles appear with unsettling rapidity. The onslaught of horror novels and anthologies, at present at least, is as unstoppable and as inescapable as the monsters they portray. One author in this genre, Stephen King, has become a household name, while others, like Peter Straub and Clive Barker, though somewhat less known, also command large followings.

Popular movies, as well, have remained so obsessed with horror since the box office triumph of *The Exorcist* that it is difficult to visit your local multiplex theater without meeting at least one monster. The evidence of the immense output of horror movies in the last decade and a half is also readily confirmed by a quick estimate of the proportion of the space in the neighborhood video store that is turned over to horror rentals.

Horror and music explicitly join forces in rock videos, notably Michael Jackson's *Thriller,* though one must also remember that the iconography of horror supplies a pervasive coloration to much of MTV and the pop music industry. The Broadway musical smash of 1988, of course, was *Phantom of the Opera,* which had already seen success in London, and which inspired such unlikely fellow travelers as *Carrie*. On the dramatic side of theater, new versions of horror classics have appeared, such as Edward Gorey's variations on *Dracula,* while TV has launched a number of horror or horror-related series such as *Freddy's Nightmares.* Horror figures even in fine art, not only directly, in works by Francis Bacon, H.R. Giger, and Sibylle Ruppert, but also in the form of allusions in the pastiches of a number of postmodern artists. In short, horror has become a staple across contemporary art forms, popular and otherwise, spawning vampires, trolls, gremlins, zombies, were-

1

wolves, demonically possessed children, space monsters of all sizes, ghosts, and other unnameable concoctions at a pace that has made the last decade or so seem like one long Halloween night.

In 1982, Stephen King speculated—as many of us do at the end of every summer—that the present horror cycle looked as though it were coming to an end.[1] But, as of the writing of this introduction, Freddy—in his fourth, lucrative reincarnation—is still terrorizing the scions of Elm Street, and a new collection by Clive Barker, entitled *Cabal,* has just arrived in the mail.

At first, the present horror cycle gained momentum slowly. On the literary side, it was presaged by the appearance of Ira Levin's *Rosemary's Baby* (1967) and Fred Mustard Stewart's *The Mephisto Waltz* (1969) which prepared the way for best-selling entries like Tom Tryon's *The Other* (1971) and William Peter Blatty's blockbuster *The Exorcist* (also 1971).[2] The mass reading market that was secured, especially by *The Exorcist,* was then consolidated by the appearance of such books as Ira Levin's *The Stepford Wives* (1972), Stephen King's first published novel, *Carrie* (1973), Robert Marasco's *Burnt Offerings* (1973), Jeffrey Konvitz's *The Sentinel* (1974), and King's *Salem's Lot* (1975). Of course, horror literature— by masters such as Richard Matheson, Dennis Wheatley, John Wyndham, and Robert Bloch—was continuously available prior to the appearance of these books. But what seems to have happened in the first half of the seventies is that horror, so to speak, entered the mainstream. Its audience was no longer specialized, but widened, and horror novels became increasingly easy to come by. This, in turn, augmented the audience looking for horror entertainments and, by the late seventies and eighties, a phalanx of authors arose to satisfy that demand, including: Charles L. Grant, Dennis Etchison, Ramsey Campbell, Alan Ryan, Whitely Strieber, James Herbert, T.E.D. Klein, John Coyne, Anne Rice, Michael McDowell, Dean Koontz, John Saul and many others.

As the reader will undoubtedly recognize immmediately, the novels listed above were all made into movies, often very successful movies. Most important in this respect, it almost goes without saying, was *The Exorcist,* directed by William Friedkin and released in 1973. The success of this film, one speculates, not only acted as a stimulant to movie production but also made horror more attractive to publishers. For many who were horrified by the film, in consequence, sought out the novel, thereby acquiring a taste for horror literature. The relation between the horror film and horror literature has been quite intimate during the current horror cycle—both in the obvious sense that often horror films are adapted from horror novels, and in the sense that many of the writers in the genre were deeply influenced by earlier horror movie cycles—to which they refer not only in interviews but within the texts of their novels as well.[3]

Of course, the immense influence on the film industry of *The Exorcist's* success is even more evident than its impact on the literary marketplace. As well as putting in place the recurring themes of possession and telekinesis, *The Exorcist* (the movie) was immediately followed by a slew of copycats, including *Abby, Beyond the Door, La Endemoniada* (a.k.a. *Demon Witch Child*), *Exorcismo,* and *The Devil's Rain.* At first it looked as though the genre would dissipate in the flood of lackluster imitations. But in 1975, *Jaws* rocked the movie market, reassuring filmmakers that there was still gold left to be mined in horror. When the reaction to *Jaws* (and its derivatives) seemed to flag, along came *Carrie* and *The Omen.* And then, in 1977, *Star Wars,* although not a horror film, opened the door to outer space, thereby eventually admitting the likes of *Alien.* Each time the health of the genre seemed threatened, suddenly it would revive. The genre seems immensely resilient. This indicates that at present the fantasy genres, of which horror is a leading example, are continually worth trying when producers think about what to make next. The result has been a truly staggering number of horror titles. And, as well, we now have before us a generation of accomplished film directors many of whom are recognized specialists in the horror/fantasy film, including: Steven Spielberg, David Cronenberg, Brian De Palma, David Lynch, John Carpenter, Wes Craven, Philip Kaufman, Tobe Hooper, John McTiernan, Ridley Scott, and others.

In emphasizing the large numbers of horror films produced in the last decade and a half, I do not mean to imply that horror films were not accessible in the sixties. However, such films were somewhat marginal; one had to stay on the lookout for the latest offerings of American International Pictures, William Castle, and Hammer Films. Roger Corman, though beloved of horror connoisseurs, was not a figure of wide repute; and late-night classics like George Romero's *Night of the Living Dead* enjoyed primarily an underground reputation. The series of blockbusters, starting with *The Exorcist,* changed the position of the horror film in the culture, and, I would submit, also encouraged the expansion of the publication and consumption of horror literature.

Of course, the markets for horror literature and film did not spring from nowhere. The audience, one would imagine, comprised primarily baby-boomers. These audiences, like a large number of the artists who came to specialize in horror, were the first post-war generation raised by TV. And one would hypothesize that their affection for horror, to a large extent, was nurtured and deepened by the endless reruns of the earlier horror and sci-fi cycles that provided the repertoire of the afternoon and late-night television of their youth. This generation has, in turn, raised the next on a diet of horror entertainments whose imagery suffuses the culture—from breakfast cereals and children's toys to postmodern art—and which supply an impressive proportion of the literary, cinematic and even theatrical output of our society.

It is within this context that the time seems especially propitious to initiate an aesthetic inquiry into the nature of horror. The purpose of this book is to investigate the horror genre philosophically. But though this project is undeniably prompted and made urgent by the ubiquitousness of horror today, insofar as its task is philosophical it will attempt to come to terms with general features of the genre as manifested throughout its history.

A Brief Overview of the Horror Genre

The object of this treatise is the horror genre. However, before developing my theory of that genre, it will be helpful to provide a rough historical sketch of the phenomenon I intend to discuss. Following the lead of many commentators on horror, I will presume that horror is, first and foremost, a modern genre, one that begins to appear in the eighteenth century.[4] The immediate source of the horror genre was the English Gothic novel, the German *Schauer-roman,* and French *roman noir.* The general, though perhaps arguable, consensus is that the inaugural Gothic novel of relevance to the horror genre was Horace Walpole's *The Castle of Otranto* in 1765. This novel carried on the resistance to neo-classical taste initiated by the preceding generation of graveyard poets.[5]

The rubric *Gothic* encompasses a lot of territory. Following the fourfold classificatory scheme suggested by Montague Summers, we can see that it subsumes the historical gothic, the natural or explained gothic, the supernatural gothic and the equivocal gothic.[6] The historical gothic represents a tale set in the imagined past without the suggestion of supernatural events, while the natural gothic introduces what appear to be supernatural phenomena only to explain them away. Ann Radcliffe's *Mysteries of Udolpho* (1794) is a classic of this category. The equivocal gothic, such as Charles Brockden Brown's *Edgar Huntley: or, the Memoirs of a Sleepwalker* (1799), renders the supernatural origin of events in the text ambiguous by means of psychologically disturbed characters. The explained gothic and the equivocal gothic presage what nowadays are often called the uncanny and the fantastic by literary theorists.

Of greatest importance for the evolution of the horror genre proper was the supernatural gothic, in which the existence and cruel operation of unnatural forces are asserted graphically. Of this variation, J.M.S. Tompkins writes that "the authors work by sudden shocks, and when they deal with the supernatural, their favorite effect is to wrench the mind suddenly from skepticism to horror struck belief."[7] The appearance of the demon and the gruesome impalement of the priest at the end of Matthew Lewis's *The Monk* (1797) is the real harbinger of the horror genre. Other major achievements in this period of the development in the genre include: Mary Shelley's *Frankenstein* (1818), John Polidori's *The Vampyre* (1819), and Charles Robert Maturin's *Melmoth the Wanderer* (1820).

Already by the 1820s, horror stories began to provide the basis for dramatizations. In 1823, *Frankenstein* was adapted for the stage by Richard Brinsely Peake under the title of *Presumption: or, the Fate of Frankenstein* (a.k.a. *Frankenstein: or, the Danger of Presumption* or *Frankenstein: A Romantic Drama*). Thomas Potter Cooke played the monster as well as playing Lord Ruthven in adaptations of Polidori's *The Vampyre*. On occasion, adaptations of the two stories would be presented as double bills, perhaps calling to mind the way in which the two myths function to kick off both the horror movie cycle of the thirties and the golden age of Hammer Films. Alternative versions of the Frankenstein story were popular in the 1820s, including *Le Monstre et le Magicien, Frankenstein: or, The Man and the Monster,* as well as numerous satirical deviations that inadvertently herald the shenanigans of Abbott and Costello.[8] The ballet stage also explored horrific themes in the *divertissement* of the dead nuns in Giacomo Meyerbeer's opera *Robert le Diable* (Filippo Taglioni, 1831), and in such ballets as *La Sylphide* (Filippo Taglioni, 1832), *Les Ondines* (Louis Henry, 1834) *Giselle* (Jean Coralli and Jules Perrot, 1841), and *Napoli* (August Bournonville, 1844).

Horror continued to be written during the period between the 1820s and the 1870s, but it was eclipsed in importance in the culture of the English-speaking world largely by the emergence of the realist novel. From the 1820s to the 1840s, *Blackwood's Edinburgh Magazine* kept the gothic fires burning by publishing short fictions by William Mudford, Edward Bulwer-Lytton, and James Hogg, while in the later 1840s, the popular imagination was gripped by *Varney the Vampire: or, The Feast of Blood,* a serial novel in 220 chapters by Thomas Prest,[9] and *Wagner, the Wehr-wolf* by George William MacArthur. In America, Edgar Allen Poe followed the lead of *Blackwood* and, in fact, wrote a piece entitled "How to Write a *Blackwood* Article."[10]

Generalizing about his period, Benjamin Franklin Fisher writes:

> The significant trend in horror tales of this period mirrored developments in the greater Victorian and American novels then emerging into a solidly artistic and serious genre. There was a shift from physical fright, expressed through numerous outward miseries and villainous actions to psychological fear. The inward turn in fiction emphasized motivations, not their overt terrifying consequences. The ghost-in-a-bedsheet gave way, as it did literally in Charles Dickens's *A Christmas Carol,* to the haunted psyche, a far more significant force in the "spooking" of hapless victims.[11]

Along with Poe's work, Fisher would appear to have in mind here the gothic atmospherics in the works of Hawthorne, Melville, and the Brontes. However, the figure of the period who may have made the greatest direct contribution to the horror genre proper might be Joseph Sheridan Le Fanu, who in his stories frequently placed the supernatural amidst the world of everyday life, where the persecution of ordinary, innocent victims, (rather than gothic overreachers) was closely observed and received the kind of psychological elaboration that would set the tone for much of the ensuing work in the genre.

Le Fanu's *In a Glass Darkly* (1872) ushered in a period, that lasted into the 1920s, of major accomplishment in the ghost story. Masterpieces in this form, generally in a short-story format, flowed from the pens of Henry James, Edith Wharton, Rudyard Kipling, Ambrose Bierce, Guy de Maupassant, Arthur Machen, Algernon Blackwood, Oliver Onions, and others.

Classic novels of horror—later adapted and readapted for stage and screen—were produced in this time span, including: Robert Louis Stevenson's *The Strange Case of Dr. Jekyll and Mr. Hyde* (1887), Oscar Wilde's *The Picture of Dorian Grey* (1891) and Bram Stoker's *Dracula* (1897). H.G. Wells, usually associated with science fiction, also produced horror and ghost stories from the turn of the century onwards. And other esteemed, though less well-known, horror authors of this fecund period were: Grant Allen, Mrs. Riddell, M.P. Shiel, G.S. Viereck, Eliot O'Donnell, R.W. Chambers, E.F. Benson, Mrs. Campbell Prael, and William Clark Russell.

According to Gary William Crawford, in contrast to the *cosmic* strain in the works of masters of the preceding generation (like Blackwood, Machen, and Onions), the English horror story after World War I took a realist and psychological turn in the work of Walter De La Mare, L.P. Hartley, W.F. Harvey, R.H. Malden, A.N.L. Munby, L.T.C. Rolt, M.P. Dare, H. Russell Wakefield, Elizabeth Bowen, Mary Sinclair, and Cynthia Asquith.[12] However, the *cosmic* wing of horror writing was kept alive in America by Howard Phillips Lovecraft (1890–1937), who stood at the center of the writers working for the pulp periodical *Weird Tales*. Lovecraft was a prodigious writer, churning out not only reams of stories, but also a treatise entitled *Supernatural Horror in Literature* and a vast correspondence through which he advanced his particular aesthetic of horror. Partly due to this correspondence and to his support of aspiring writers, Lovecraft enlisted a loyal following of authors and imitators, such as Clark Ashton Smith, Carl Jacobi, and August Derleth. Robert Bloch also began his career in the Lovecraft tradition of cosmic horror which continued to influence the genre until long after World War II.[13]

After World War I, the horror genre also found a new home in the nascent art of the cinema. Horror films in the style that has come to be known as German Expressionism were made in Weimar Germany and some, like F.W. Murnau's *Nosferatu,* have become recognized horror masterpieces. Prior to the current horror movie cycle, the history of film witnessed several other major spurts of creativity in the horror mode: an early thirties cycle, which was started by Universal Studios and which movie makers attempted to resuscitate in the late thirties and early forties with an eye to younger audiences; the spate of adult horror films produced in the forties by Val Lewton at RKO; the horror/sci-fi cycle of the early fifties, which inspired the Japanese Godzilla industry of the mid-fifties, as well as an attempt to revive the cycle in America again in the latter part of the decade.

These films, seen either in theaters or on TV, tutored a baby-boom audience in a taste for horror, which in the sixties could be sustained by marginal matinees of the output of AIP, William Castle, and Hammer Films.[14] The classic horror film myths often sent horror-hungry adepts to their literary sources, as well as to less elevated reading material such as *Famous Monsters of Filmland* (founded in 1958). And the products of "fantastic" television, like *The Twilight Zone,* encouraged an interest in writers such as Charles Beaumont, Richard Matheson, Roald Dahl, and the short-story tradition from which they sprang. Thus, by the early seventies, an audience was ready for the next—i.e., the present—horror cycle.

This rough history of the horror genre circumscribes broadly the body of work about which the present treatise attempts to theorize. My thumbnail sketch of the genre earmarks, I think, what many would be disposed pretheoretically to include in the genre. In the course of theorizing about the genre, some of the works in this more or less naive view of the history of horror will have to be reclassified. Several of the works mentioned above will drop out of the genre when the genre is subjected to theoretical regimentation. However, I think that the philosophy of horror evolved in the course of this book will, in the main, characterize *most* of what people are disposed pretheoretically to call horror; if it cannot, the theory is flawed. That is, though I don't expect to capture every item in the preceding canned survey of the genre, if my theory misses too many of them, it is off the mark.

A Philosophy of Horror?

This book announces itself to be a philosophy of horror. The very concept may perplex many. Who ever heard of a philosophy of horror? It is not the sort of listing that one finds in a college bulletin or in the publicity catalogues of academic presses. What in the world could one intend by the strange phrase: "a philosophy of horror"?

Aristotle opens the first book of his *Poetics* with these words: "My design is to treat of poetry in general and of its several species; to inquire what is the proper effect of each—what construction of a fable, or plan, is essential to a good poem—of what, and how many, parts each species consists; with whatever else belongs to the same subject matter. . . ."[15] Aristotle does not fully realize this outline in the text that survives. But he does offer us a comprehensive account of tragedy in terms of the effect it is supposed to bring about—the catharsis of pity and fear—with respect to the elements, particularly the plot elements, that facilitate this effect: that tragic plots have beginnings, middles, and ends in the technical sense that Aristotle applies those notions, and that they have reversals, recognitions, and calamities. Aristotle isolates the relevant plot elements in tragedy, that is, with attention to the way in which they are designed to cause the emotional response whose provocation Aristotle identifies as the quiddity of the genre.

Taking Aristotle to propose a paradigm of what the philosophy of an artistic genre might be, I will offer an account of horror in virtue of the emotional effects it is designed to cause in audiences. This will involve both the characterization of the nature of that emotional effect and a review and an analysis of the recurring figures and plot structures employed by the genre to raise the emotional effects that are appropriate to it. That is, in the spirit of Aristotle, I will presume that the genre is designed to produce an emotional effect; I will attempt to isolate that effect; and I will attempt to show how the characteristic structures, imagery, and figures in the genre are arranged to cause the emotion that I will call *art-horror*. (Though I do not expect to be as authoritative as Aristotle, it is my intention to try to do for the horror genre what Aristotle did for tragedy.)

A philosophical dimension of the present treatise not found in Aristotle's work is my concentration on certain puzzles that pertain to the genre—what I call (in my subtitle), stealing a phrase from certain eighteenth-century writers, "paradoxes of the heart." With respect to horror, these paradoxes can be summed up in the following two questions: 1) how can anyone be frightened by what they know does not exist, and 2) why would anyone ever be interested in horror, since being horrified is so unpleasant? In the course of the text, I will attempt to show what is at stake in posing these questions. And, I will also advance philosophical theories which I hope will vaporize these paradoxes.

The style of philosophy employed in this book is what is often called Anglo-American or analytic philosophy. However, a word of warning is useful here. For although I think it is accurate to say that this book is written in the tradition of analytic philosophy, it is important to note that my method is not exclusively a matter of what is sometimes called conceptual analysis. For a number of reasons, I, like many other philosophers of my generation, distrust the strict division between conceptual analysis and empirical findings. Thus, in this book, there is conceptual analysis interwoven with empirical hypotheses. That is, there is a mix of philosophy, construed narrowly as conceptual analysis, and what might be called the theory of horror, i.e., very general, empirical conjectures about recurring patterns in the genre. Or, to put it yet another way, this philosophy of horror, like Aristotle's philosophy of tragedy, contains both conceptual analysis and very general, empirically grounded hypotheses.

I have already claimed Aristotle as a precedent. My project could also be likened to those of eighteenth century theoreticians, like Hutcheson and

Burke, who sought to define such things as the beautiful and the sublime, and who wished to isolate the causal triggers that gave rise to these feelings. And in the very early twentieth century, Bergson attempted a similar investigation with respect to comedy.

All of these references, however, including the implicit functionalism that I share with all these authors, undoubtedly makes the present project sound exceedingly old-fashioned. So here it is important to emphasize the ways in which the present study offers new approaches to philosophical aesthetics.

Philosophical aesthetics in the English speaking world has come to be preoccupied with two central problems: what is art and what is the aesthetic? These questions are good questions, and they have been addressed with admirable sophistication and rigor. However, they are not the only questions that philosophers of art can ask about their domain, and the obsession with answering them has unduly constrained the ambit of concern of contemporary aesthetic philosophers. Questions about art and the aesthetic should not be abandoned; but more questions, whose answers may even suggest new angles on the issues of art and the aesthetic, are advisable, lest the field become a rut.

Recently, philosophers of art have wanted to alleviate the overly constricted configuration of the field by looking at the special theoretical problems of individual arts, by returning to older questions of the aesthetics of nature, and by re-situating traditional questions about art within broader questions about the function of symbol systems in general. The present attempt at a philosophy of horror is part of this effort to widen the purview of philosophical aesthetics. Not only should the special problems of artforms be reconsidered; but the special problems of genres that cross artforms should be re-evaluated as well.

One of the most interesting attempts to broaden the perspective of philosophical aesthetics in recent years has been the emerging study of art in relation to the emotions, a research project that unites the philosophy of art with the philosophy of mind. One way to read the present text is to regard it as a detailed case study in this larger enterprise.

Moreover, philosophical aesthetics tends to track what might be thought of as high art. It is either oblivious to or suspicious of mass or popular art. One reason for this is that mass and popular art gravitate toward the formulaic, and aestheticians often presume a Kantian-inspired bias that art, properly so called, is not susceptible to formula. The present treatise offends this view doubly: 1) in considering mass art as worthy of the attention of philosophical aesthetics, and 2) in not being cowed into agreeing that the realm of art lacks formulas. Offending against both these views simultaneously is obviously interconnected, and intentional.

This book is divided into four chapters. The first chapter proposes an account of the nature of horror, specifically with respect to the emotion, art-horror, that the genre is designed to engender. This chapter not only offers a definition of horror, which it attempts to defend against predictable objections. It also tries to isolate recurring structures that give rise to the emotion of art-horror, along with a historical conjecture about why the genre emerged when it did.

The second chapter introduces the first of our paradoxes of the heart—namely, the paradox of fiction. Applied to the horror genre, this is the question of how we can be frightened by that which we know does not exist. But the problem, here, is more general. For those who believe that we can only be emotionally moved by what we know is the case, it is not only a mystery as to why we are frightened by Count Dracula but also why we are angered by Creon in Sophocles' *Antigone*. This is the most technical chapter in the book; those who have no liking for philosophical dialectics may wish to merely skim it, if not skip it altogether.

The third chapter is a review of the most characteristically recurrent plots in the genre, including extensive discussion of interrelated plot formations such as suspense and what contemporary literary critics call the fantastic. This is the most empirically developed part of the book; those who are interested primarily in philosophical dialectics may wish to skim it, if not skip it altogether.

The last chapter deals with our second paradox of the heart—indeed, the paradox for which the writers John Aikin and his sister Anna Laetitia Aikin (Barbauld) originally coined this lovely phrase in the eighteenth century. It is the question of why, if horror is as it is described in the earlier chapters, anyone would subject themselves to it. Call this the paradox of horror. Normally, we shun what causes distress; most of us don't play in traffic to entertain ourselves, nor do we attend autopsies to while away the hours. So why do we subject ourselves to fictions that will horrify us? It is a paradox of the heart, one I hope to accommodate in concluding this treatise.

Moreover, after resolving this paradox, I hope to say why the horror genre is as compelling nowadays as it is. This part of the book is not part of the philosophy of horror proper. But, on the other hand, we would probably never have noticed that a philosophy of horror was worth contemplating had we not been engulfed by the genre in its contemporary form.

I have referred to this book as a treatise for its parts are systematically related. The account that I offer of the nature of horror is fleshed out by an investigation of horrific plotting and its related formations. Likewise, my accounts of the nature of horror and of horror narration are material, in different yet concerted ways, to the answer I give to what was called the paradox of horror in the preceding paragraph. Moreover, the theory I champion in the second chapter of the book, called the *thought theory* of our response to fiction, pertains to my hypotheses about the paradox of horror, because it offers an operational construction of what authors grope at with notions like "aesthetic distance." Thus, the parts of the book are interconnected. However, no pretension is made in the direction of claiming that this is an exhaustive account of the genre. There are many more topics for future research that I have left untouched.

In some ways this book is very different from what has preceded it. The usual approach to characterizing the horror genre —from H.P. Lovecraft to Stephen King, by way of numerous academic critics—is to offer a series of very general ruminations about horror in chapter one, and then to detail the evolution of the genre historically through the examination of examples. There is nothing wrong with that approach. But I have attempted to reverse it, by initially suggesting a narrative of the form in the expectation that an organon can be developed to comprehend it.

Despite all the peregrination and animadversion called for by introductions to and executions of academic exercises of this sort, I have had a hell of a good time writing this book, and I hope some of that rubs off on the reader.

1

The Nature of Horror

The Definition of Horror

Preliminaries

The purpose of this book is to develop a theory of horror, which is conceived to be a genre that crosses numerous artforms and media. The type of horror to be explored here is that associated with reading something like Mary Shelley's *Frankenstein,* Algernon Blackwood's "Ancient Sorceries," Robert Louis Stevenson's *The Strange Case of Dr. Jekyll and Mr. Hyde,* H.P. Lovecraft's "The Dunwich Horror," Stephen King's *Pet Sematary,* or Clive Barker's *Damnation Game;* and it is also associated with seeing something like the Hamilton Deane and John Balderston stage version of *Dracula,* movies such as James Whale's *Bride of Frankenstein,* Ridley Scott's *Alien,* and George Romero's *Dawn of the Dead,* ballets like Michael Uthoff's version of *Coppelia,* and operas/musicals like Andrew Lloyd Webber's *Phantom of the Opera.* The relevant sort of horror can also be found in fine art, as in the work of Goya or H.R. Giger, in radio programs such as the *Inner Sanctum* and *Suspense* of yesteryear, and in TV series like *Night Stalker,* or *Tales from the Darkside.* We shall call this "art-horror." Generally when the word "horror" is used in what follows, it should be understood as art-horror.

This kind of horror is different from the sort that one expresses in saying "I am horrified by the prospect of ecological disaster," or "Brinksmanship in the age of nuclear arms is horrifying," or "What the Nazis did was horrible." Call the latter usage of "horror," *natural horror.* It is not the task of this book to analyze natural horror, but only art-horror, that is, "horror" as it serves to name a cross-art, cross-media genre whose existence is already recognized in ordinary language. This is the sense of the term "horror" that occurs when, for example, in answer to the question "What kind of book is *The Shining?*," we say a horror story; or when we find programs are advertised in the *TV Guide* as "halloween horror shows" or when the blurb on

12

Diana Henstell's *New Morning Dragon* proclaims it to be "The chilling new novel of horror."

"Horror," as a category of ordinary language, is a serviceable concept through which we communicate and receive information. It is not an obscure notion. We manage to use it with a great deal of consensus; note how rarely one has cause to dispute the sorting of items under the rubric of horror in your local video store. The first part of this chapter can be construed as an attempt to rationally reconstruct the latent criteria for identifying horror (in the sense of art-horror) that are already operative in ordinary language.

In order to avoid misunderstanding, it is necessary to emphasize not only the contrast with *natural horror* but also to stress that I am referring narrowly to the effects of a specific genre. Thus, not all that might be called horror that appears in art is art-horror. For example, one might be horrified by the murder in Camus's *The Stranger* or the sexual degradation in de Sade's *The 120 Days of Sodom*. Nevertheless, though such horror is generated by art, it is not part of the phenomenon I am calling "art-horror."[1] Nor shall it refer to the frequent response of people of limited experience to much avant-garde art.

"Art-horror," by stipulation, is meant to refer to the product of a genre that crystallized, speaking very roughly, around the time of the publication of *Frankenstein*—give or take fifty years—and that has persisted, often cyclically, through the novels and plays of the nineteenth century and the literature, comic books, pulp magazines, and films of the twentieth. This genre, moreover, is recognized in common speech and my theory of it must ultimately be assessed in terms of the way in which it tracks ordinary usage.

Of course, horrific imagery can be found across the ages. In the ancient Western world, examples include the story of the werewolf in Petronius' *Satyricon,* of Lycaon and Jupiter in Ovid's *Metamorphoses,* and of Aristomenes and Socrates in Apuleius' *The Golden Ass.* Medieval *danses macabres,* and characterizations of Hell such as the *Vision of St. Paul,* the *Vision of Tundale,* Cranach the Elder's *Last Judgment,* and, most famously, Dante's *Inferno* also feature examples of figures and incidents that will become important to the horror genre. However, the genre itself only begins to coalesce between the last half of the eighteenth century and the first quarter of the nineteenth as a variation on the Gothic form in England and related developments in Germany.[2] (The reason for this particular periodization of the genre will, I believe, become clearer as my exploration of the nature of the genre progresses, and an explanation of why horror waits to be born until the eighteenth century will be attempted in the concluding section of this chapter.[3])

Moreover, it must also be noted that though my emphasis is on genre, I shall not respect the notion that horror and science fiction are absolutely discrete genres. The putative distinction here is often advanced by connoisseurs of science fiction at the expense of horror. For them, science fiction explores grand themes like alternate societies or alternate technologies whereas the horror genre is really only a matter of scarefying monsters. Defenders of science fiction, for example, are wont to say that what generally passes for science fiction in movies is really merely horror—a series of exercises in the art of the bug-eyed monster such as *This Island Earth, Invaders from Mars* (both versions), and *Alien Predators.*[4]

That monsters are a mark of horror is a useful insight. However, it will not do the work to which aficionados of science fiction delegate it. Even in the case of movies, there are cases, such as *Things to Come,* that meet the supposed standards of true science fiction. But, more importantly, the defenders of science fiction protest too much. Not all of what we are prone to call science fiction is preoccupied with high thoughts about alternate technologies and societies. The late John Wyndham's *The Midwich Cuckoos, The Kraken Wakes, The Day of the Triffids,* and *Web* all seem to be straightforwardly science fiction on any unprejudiced view, though *interest in them centers on* monsters. Of course, the science fiction pundit doesn't deny that there are monsters in science fiction, but only that they play second fiddle to the imagination of alternate technologies and/or societies. But this seems to fly in the face of the facts—not only in the case of Wyndham, but also those of H.G. Wells's *The War of the Worlds* and Brian Aldiss's, Nebula award-winning *The Saliva Tree.* As these examples suggest, much of what we pretheoretically call science fiction is really a species of horror, substituting futuristic technologies for supernatural forces. This is not to say that all science fiction is a subcategory of horror, but only that much is. Thus, in my examples, we will freely move between what is called horror and what is called science fiction, regarding the boundary between these putative genres as quite fluid.

I plan to analyze horror as a genre. However, it should not be assumed that all genres can be analyzed in the same way. Westerns, for example, are identified primarily by virtue of their setting. Novels, films, plays, paintings, and other works, that are grouped under the label "horror" are identified according to a different sort of criteria. Like suspense novels or mystery novels, novels are denominated horrific in respect of their intended capacity to raise a certain *affect.* Indeed, the genres of suspense, mystery, and horror derive their very names from the affects they are intended to promote—a sense of suspense, a sense of mystery, and a sense of horror. The cross-art, cross-media genre of horror takes its title from the emotion it characteristically or rather ideally promotes; this emotion constitutes the identifying mark of horror.

Again, it must be underlined that not all genres are identified in this way. The musical, either on stage or on film, is not tied to any affect. One might think that musicals are by nature light and charming, in the fashion of *Me and My Girl.* But, of course, this is not the case. Musicals can pretend to tragedy (*West Side Story, Pequod, Camelot*), melodrama (*Les Miserables*), worldliness (*A Chorus Line*), pessimism (*Candide*), political indignation (*Sarafina!*), and even terror (*Sweeney Todd*). A musical is defined by a certain proportion of song and perhaps usually dance and can indulge any sort of emotion, the implicit argument of *The Band Wagon* (that it is always entertaining) notwithstanding. The horror genre, however, is essentially linked with a particular affect—specifically, that from which it takes its name.

The genres that are named by the very affect they are designed to provoke suggest a particularly tantalizing strategy through which to pursue their analysis. Like works of suspense, works of horror are designed to elicit a certain kind of affect. I shall presume that this is an emotional state, which emotion I call art-horror. Thus, one can expect to locate the genre of horror, in part, by a specification of art-horror, that is, the emotion works of this type are designed to engender. Members of the horror genre will be identified as narratives and/or images (in the case of fine art, film, etc.) predicated on raising the affect of horror in audiences. Such an analysis, of course, is not a priori. It is an attempt, in the tradition of Aristotle's *Poetics,* to provide clarificatory generalizations about a body of work that, in everyday discourse, we antecedently accept as constituting a family.

Initially, it is tempting to follow the lead of the defenders of science fiction and to differentiate the horror genre from others by saying that horror novels, stories, films, plays, and so on are marked by the presence of monsters. For our purposes, the monsters can be of either a supernatural or a sci-fi origin. This method of proceeding distinguishes horror from what are sometimes called tales of terror such as William Maginn's "The Man in the Bell," Poe's "The Pit and the Pendulum," and "The Telltale Heart," Bloch's *Psycho,* Tryon's *The Other,* Michael Powell's *Peeping Tom,* and Alfred Hitchcock's *Frenzy,* all of which, though eerie and unnerving, achieve their frightening effects by exploring psychological phenomena that are all too human. Correlating horror with the presence of monsters gives us a neat way of distinguishing it from terror, especially of the sort rooted in tales of abnormal psychologies. Similarly, by using monsters or other supernatural (or sci-fi) entities as a criterion of horror, one can separate horror stories from Gothic exercises such as Radcliffe's *Mysteries of Udolpho,* or from Charles Brockden Brown's *Wieland, or the Transformation,* or from Washington Irving's "The Spectre Bridegroom," or from thirties' shudder pulps such as the stories found in *Weird Tales* where suggestions of other-worldly beings were often introduced only to be explained away naturalistically.[5] Likewise the theatrical genre of the *Grand Guignol,* comprising works like Andre De Lorde's *The System of Dr. Goudron and Professor Plume,*[6] will not figure as horror on this accounting; for though gruesome, *Grand Guignol* requires sadists rather than monsters.

However, even if a case can be made that a monster or a monstrous entity is a necessary condition for horror, such a criterion would not be a sufficient condition. For monsters inhabit all sorts of stories—such as fairy tales, myths and odysseys—that we are not inclined to identify as horror. If we are to exploit usefully the hint that monsters are central to horror, we will have to find a way to distinguish the horror story from mere stories with monsters in them, such as fairy tales.

What appears to demarcate the horror story from mere stories with monsters, such as myths, is the attitude of characters in the story to the monsters they encounter. In works of horror, the humans regard the monsters they meet as abnormal, as disturbances of the natural order. In fairy tales, on the other hand, monsters are part of the everyday furniture of the universe. For example, in "The Three Princesses of Whiteland," in the Andrew Lang collection, a lad is beset by a three-headed troll; however, the writing does not signal that he finds this particular creature any more unusual than the lions he had passed earlier. A creature like Chewbacca in the space opera *Star Wars* is just one of the guys, though a creature gotten up in the same wolf outfit, in a film like *The Howling,* would be regarded with utter revulsion by the human characters in that fiction.[7]

Boreads, griffins, chimeras, baselisks, dragons, satyrs, and such are bothersome and fearsome creatures in the world of myths, but they are not unnatural; they can be accommodated by the metaphysics of the cosmology that produced them. The monsters of horror, however, breach the norms of ontological propriety presumed by the positive human characters in the story. That is, in examples of horror, it would appear that the monster is an extraordinary character in our ordinary world, whereas in fairy tales and the like the monster is an ordinary creature in an extraordinary world. And the extraordinariness of that world—its distance from our own—is often signaled by formulas such as "once upon a time."

In his classic study *The Fantastic,*[8] Tzvetan Todorov classifies the worlds of myths and fairy tales under the heading of "the marvelous." Such realms do not abide by scientific laws as we know them but have their own laws. However, though I admire Todorov's work and though I am obviously influenced by it, I have not adopted his categories because I want to draw a distinction within the category of supernatural tales between those that indulge art-horror and those that don't. Undoubtedly, Todorov and his followers[9] would attempt to get at this distinction by means of the notion of the fantastic/marvelous—stories that entertain naturalistic explanations of abnormal incidents but conclude by affirming their supernatural origin. Horror, it might be argued, falls under the label of the fantastic-marvelous. However, though this might be right as far as it goes, it does not go far enough. For the category of the fantastic-marvelous is not tight enough to give us an adequate picture of art-horror. A film such as *Close Encounters of the Third Kind* fits into the classification of fantastic-marvelous but is beatific rather than horrific.[10] The concept of the fantastic-marvelous, that is, doesn't zoom in on the particular affect that the horror genre is predicated upon. Even if horror belongs to the genus of the fantastic-marvelous, it constitutes a distinctive species. And it is that species with which we are concerned.

As I have suggested, one indicator of that which differentiates works of horror proper from monster stories in general is the affective responses of the positive human characters in the stories to the monsters that beleaguer them. Moreover, though we have only spoken about the emotions of characters in horror stories, nevertheless, the preceding hypothesis is useful for getting at the emotional responses that works of horror are designed to elicit from audiences. For horror appears to be one of those genres in which the emotive responses of the audience, ideally, run parallel to the emotions of characters. Indeed, in works of horror the responses of characters often seem to cue the emotional responses of the audiences.[11]

In "Jonathan Harker's Journal," in *Dracula,* we read:

As the Count leaned over me and his hands touched me, I could not repress a shudder. It may have been that his breath was rank, but a horrible feeling of nausea came over me, which do what I would, I could not conceal.

This shudder, this recoil at the vampire's touch, this feeling of nausea all structure our emotional reception of the ensuing descriptions of Dracula; for example, when his protruding teeth are mentioned we regard them as shudder-inducing, nauseating, rank— not something one would want either to touch or be touched by. Similarly, in films we model our emotional response upon ones like that of the young, blonde woman in *Night of the Living Dead,* who, when surrounded by zombies, screams and clutches herself in such a way as to avoid contact with the contaminated flesh. The characters in works of horror exemplify for us the way in which to react to the monsters in the fiction. In film and onstage, the characters *shrink* from the monsters, contracting themselves in order to avoid the grip of the creature but also to avert an accidental brush against this unclean being. This does not mean that we believe in the existence of fictional monsters, as the characters in horror stories do, but that we regard the description or depiction of them as unsettling virtue of the same kind of qualities that revolt someone like Jonathan Harker in the preceding quotation.

The emotional reactions of characters, then, provide a set of instructions or, rather, examples about the way in which the audience is to respond to the monsters in the fiction—that is, about the way we are meant to react to its monstrous properties. In the classic film *King Kong,* for example, there is a scene on the ship during the journey to Skull Island in which the fictional director, Carl Denham, stages a screen test for Ann Darrow, the heroine of the film within the film. The offscreen motivations that Denham supplies his starlet can be taken as a set of instructions for the way both Ann Darrow and the audience are to react to the first apparition of Kong. Denham says to Darrow:

> Now you look higher. You're amazed. Your eyes open wider. It's horrible Ann, but you can't look away. There's no chance for you, Ann—no escape. You're helpless, Ann, helpless. There's just one chance. If you can scream—but your throat's paralyzed. Scream, Ann, cry. Perhaps if you didn't see it you could scream. Throw your arms across your face and scream, scream for your life.

In horror fictions, the emotions of the audience are supposed to mirror those of the positive human characters in certain, but not all, respects. In the preceding examples the characters' responses counsel us that the appropriate reactions to the monsters in question comprise shuddering, nausea, shrinking, paralysis, screaming, and revulsion. Our responses are meant, ideally, to parallel those of characters.[12] Our responses are supposed to converge (but not exactly duplicate) those of the characters; like the characters we assess the monster as a horrifying sort of being (though unlike the characters, we do not believe in its existence). This mirroring-effect, moreover, is a key feature of the horror genre. For it is not the case for every genre that the audience response is supposed to repeat certain of the elements of the emotional state of characters.

If Aristotle is right about catharsis, for example, the emotional state of the audience does not double that of King Oedipus at the end of the play of the same name. Nor are we jealous, when Othello is. Also, when a comic character takes a pratfall, he hardly feels joyous, though we do. And though we feel suspense when the hero rushes to save the heroine tied to the railroad tracks he cannot afford to indulge such an emotion. Nevertheless, with horror, the situation is different. For in horror the emotions of the characters and those of the audience are synchronized in certain pertinent respects,[13] as one can easily observe at a Saturday matinee in one's local cinema.

That the audience's emotional responses are modeled to a certain extent on those of the characters in horror fictions provides us with a useful methodological advantage in analyzing the emotion of art-horror. It suggests a way in which we can formulate an objective, as opposed to an introspective, picture of the emotion of art-horror. That is, rather than characterizing art-horror solely on the basis of our own subjective responses, we can ground our conjectures on observations of the way in which characters respond to the monsters in works of horror. That is, if we proceed under the assumption that our emotional responses as audience members are supposed to parallel those of characters in important respects, then we can begin to portray art-horror by noting the typical emotional features that authors and directors attribute to characters molested by monsters.

How do characters respond to monsters in horror stories? Well, of course, they're frightened. After all, monsters are dangerous. But there is more to it than this. In Mary Shelley's famous novel, Victor Frankenstein recounts his reaction to the first movements of his creation: "now that I had finished, the beauty of the dream vanished and *disgust* filled my heart. Unable to endure the aspect of the being I had created, I rushed out of the room, unable to compose my mind to sleep." Shortly after this, the monster, with an outstretched hand, wakens Victor, who flees from its touch.

In "Sea-Raiders," H.G. Wells, using the third person, narrates Mr. Frison's reaction to some unsavory, glistening, tentacled creatures: "he was horrified, of course, and intensely excited and indignant at such *revolting* creatures preying on human skin." In Augustus Muir's "The Reptile," MacAndrew's first response to what he takes (wrongly) to be a giant snake is described as the "paralysing grip of *repulsion* and surprise."

When Miles, in Jack Finney's *Invasion of the Body Snatchers* first encounters the pods, he reports "At the feel of them on my skin, I lost my mind completely, and then I was tramping them, smashing and crushing them under my plunging feet and legs, not even knowing that I was uttering a sort of hoarse meaningless cry—'Unhh! Unhh! Unhh!'—of fright and animal disgust." And in Peter Straub's *Ghost Story,* Don makes love to the monster Alma Mobley and suddenly senses "a shock of concentrated feeling, a shock of revulsion—as though I had touched a slug."

The theme of visceral revulsion is also evident in Bram Stoker's "Dracula's Guest," originally planned to be the first chapter of his seminal vampire tale. The first-person narrator tells how he was awakened by what commentators take to be a werewolf. He says:

> This period of semi-lethargy seemed to remain a long time, and as it faded away I must have slept or swooned. Then came a sort of *loathing, like the first stage of seasickness,* and a wild desire to be free from something, I know not what. A vast stillness enveloped me, as though the world were asleep or dead—only broken by the low panting as of some animal close to me. I felt a warm rasping at my throat, then came a consciousness of the awful truth, which chilled me to the heart and sent the blood surging up through my brain. Some great animal was lying on me and now licking my throat.

Stevenson's Mr. Hyde also evokes a powerful physical response. In the report of his running down the little girl, Hyde is said to induce loathing on sight. This is not simply a moral category, however, for it is connected with his ugliness which is said to cause one to sweat. This bodily sense of revulsion is further amplified when Enfield says of Hyde:

He is not easy to describe. There is something wrong with his appearance; something displeasing, something down-right detestable. I never saw a man I so disliked, and yet I scarce know why. He must be deformed somewhere; he gives a strong feeling of deformity, although I couldn't specify the point. He's an extraordinary looking man, and yet I really can name nothing out of the way. No, sir; I can make no hand of it; I can't describe him. And it's not for want of memory; for I declare I can see him this moment.

Indescribability is also a key feature in Lovecraft's "The Outsider." The narrator in this case is the monster himself; but the monster, a recluse after the fashion of Kaspar Hauser, has no idea of what he looks like. The situation is one in which he encounters a mirror without initially realizing that the reflection is his own. And, he says:

As I approached the arch I began to perceive the presence more clearly; and then, with the first and last sound I ever uttered—a ghastly ululation that revolted me almost as poignantly as its noxious cause—I beheld in full, frightful vividness the inconceivable, indescribable, and unmentionable monstrosity which had by its simple appearance changed a merry company to a herd of delirious fugitives.

I cannot even hint what it was like, for it was a compound of all that is unclean, uncanny, unwelcome, abnormal, and detestable. It was the ghoulish shade of decay, antiquity, and desolation; the putrid, dripping eidolon of unwholesome revelation; the awful baring of that which the merciful earth should always hide. God knows it was not of this world—or no longer of this world—yet to my horror I saw in its eaten away and bone-revealing outlines a leering, abhorrent travesty on the human shape; and in its mouldy, disintegrating apparel an unspeakable quality that chilled me even more.

I was paralysed, but not too much to make a feeble effort toward flight; a backward stumble which failed to break the spell in which the nameless, voiceless monster held me. My eyes bewitched by the glassy orbs which stared loathsomely into them, refused to close; though they were mercifully blurred, and shewed the terrible object but indistinctly after the first shock. I tried to raise my hand to shut out the sight, yet so stunned were my nerves that my arm could not fully obey my will. The attempt, however, was enough to disturb my balance; so that I had to stagger forward several steps to avoid falling. As I did so I became suddenly and agonisingly aware of the nearness of the carrion thing, whose hideous hollow breathing I half fancied I could hear. Nearly mad, I found myself yet able to throw out a hand to ward off the foetid apparition which pressed so close; when in one cataclysmic second of cosmic nightmarishness and hellish accident *my fingers touched the rotting outstretched paw of the monster beneath the golden arch.*

I did not shriek, but all the fiendish ghouls that ride the nightwind shrieked for me as in that same second there crashed down upon my mind a single fleeting avalanche of soul-annihilating memory. I knew in that second all that had been; I remembered beyond the frightful castle and the trees, and recognized the altered edifice in which I now stood; I recognized, most terrible of all, the unholy abomination that stood leering before me as I withdrew my sullied fingers from its own.

Horrific creatures seem to be regarded not only as inconceivable but also as unclean and disgusting. Frankenstein's laboratory, for example, is described as "a workshop of filthy creation." And Clive Barker, the literary equivalent of the splatter film, characterizes his monster, the son of celluloid, in the story of the same name, thusly:

[Son of Celluloid]. "This is the body I once occupied, yes. His name was Barberio. A criminal; nothing spectacular. He never aspired to greatness."

[Birdy]. "And you?"

"His cancer. I'm the piece of him which did aspire, that did long to be more than a humble cell. I am a dreaming disease. No wonder I love the movies."

The son of celluloid was weeping over the edge of the broken floor, its true body exposed now it had no reason to fabricate a glory.

It was a filthy thing, a tumor grown fat on wasted passion. A parasite with the shape of a slug, and the texture of raw liver. For a moment a toothless mouth, badly molded, formed at its head end and said: "I'm going to have to find a new way to eat your soul."

It flopped into the crawlspace beside Birdy. Without its shimmering coat of many technicolors it was the size of a small child. She backed away as it stretched a sensor to touch her, but avoidance was a limited option. The crawlspace was narrow, and further along it was blocked with what looked to be broken chairs and discarded prayer books. There was no way but the way she'd come, and that was fifteen feet above her head.

Tentatively, the cancer touched her foot, and she was sick. She couldn't help it, even though she was ashamed to be giving in to such primitive responses. It revolted her as nothing ever had before; it brought to mind something aborted, a bucket case.

"Go to hell," she said to it, kicking at its head, but it kept coming, its diarrheal mass trapping her legs. She could feel the churning motion of its innards as it rose up to her.

More recently, Clive Barker has described the by-blows in *Weaveworld* in these terms:

The thing lacked a body, its four arms springing straight from a bulbous neck, beneath which clusters of sacs hung, wet as liver and lights. Cal's blow connected, and one of the sacs burst, releasing a sewer stench. With the rest of the [by-blow] siblings close upon him, Cal raced for the door, but the wounded creature was fastest in pursuit, sidling crablike on its hands, and spitting as it came. A spray of saliva hit the wall close to Cal's head, and the paper blistered. Revulsion gave heat to his heels. He was at the door in an instant.

Later it is said that the very thought of being touched by such creatures is sickening.

Since horrific creatures are so physically repulsive, they often provoke nausea in the characters who discover them. In Lovecraft's "At the Mountains of Madness," the presence of the Shoggoths, giant, shape-changing, black, excremental worms, is heralded by an odor which is explicitly described as nauseating. In *Black Ashes,* by Noel Scanlon, touted as "Ireland's answer to Stephen King,"[14] the investigative reporter Sally Stevens vomits when the nefarious Swami Ramesh changes into the demon Ravana who has been described as hideously and terrifyingly ugly, his face blackened, his fingers talons, his teeth fanged, his tongue scaled and, in all, giving off a smell of putrefaction.

Emotionally, these violations of nature are so fulsome and revolting that they frequently produce in characters the conviction that mere physical contact with them can be lethal. Consider the dream portent that Jack Sawyer encounters in *The Talisman* by King and Straub:

> some terrible creature had been coming for his mother—a dwarvish monstrosity with misplaced eyes and rotting, cheesy skin. "Your mother's almost dead, Jack, can you say hallelujah?" this monstrosity had croaked, and Jack knew— the way you knew things in dreams—that it was radioactive, and that if it touched him he would die.

What examples like this (which can be multiplied endlessly) indicate is that the character's affective reaction to the monstrous in horror stories is not merely a matter of fear, i.e., of being frightened by something that threatens danger. Rather threat is compounded with revulsion, nausea, and disgust. And this corresponds as well with the tendency in horror novels and stories to describe monsters in terms of and to associate them with filth, decay, deterioration, slime and so on. The monster in horror fiction, that is, is not only lethal but—and this is of utmost significance—also disgusting. Moreover, this combination of affect can be quite explicit in the very language of horror stories; M.R. James writes in "Canon Alberic's Scrap-book" that "The feelings which this horror stirred in Dennistoun were the intensest physical fear and the most profound mental loathing."[15]

The reports of characters's internal reactions to monsters—whether from a first-person, second-person (e.g., Carlos Fuentes's *Aura*), or an authorial point of view—correspond to the more behavioral reactions one can observe in theater and cinema. Just before the monster is visualized to the audience, we often see the characters shudder in disbelief, responding to this or that violation of nature. Their faces contort; often their noses wrinkle and their upper lip curls as if confronted by something noxious. They freeze in a moment of recoil, transfixed, sometimes paralyzed. They start backwards in a reflex of avoidance. Their hands may be drawn toward their bodies in an act of protection but also of revulsion and disgust. Along with fear of severe physical harm, there is an evident aversion to making physical contact with the monster. Both fear and disgust are etched on the characters' features.

Within the context of the horror narrative, the monsters are identified as impure and unclean. They are putrid or moldering things, or they hail from oozing places, or they are made of dead or rotting flesh, or chemical waste, or are associated with vermin, disease, or crawling things. They are not only quite dangerous but they also make one's skin creep. Characters regard them not only with fear but with loathing, with a combination of terror and disgust.

In the attempted-abduction scene in James Whale's movie version of *Frankenstein,* we see—in the background of a medium shot—the monster steal into the bedroom behind Dr. Frankenstein's prospective bride. As she paces to a door screen–right the monster follows her. Suspense builds. The monster growls. As she turns, the camera cuts in for a close-up. She raises her hand nearly to her eye and shrieks. The gesture suggests both an attempt to cover her eyes and a withdrawal of her hand from the vicinity of the monster, both in order to assure that he will neither grab it nor that she will touch him. After a close-up of the monster, we return again to this shot, which then yields to a medium shot where the bride backs away from the monster and toward the camera. She gathers her dress toward herself as she shrinks from the creature. Clearly, this is, in part, done so that the monster will not step on the train of the dress. But at the same time, it reinforces the feeling of her nearly hysterical desire to avoid contact with the creature. At the end of the sequence, Dr. Frankenstein and his confederates find the bride; apparently, she has fainted and is in some kind of delirium, signaled both gesturally and verbally. The very sight of the monster seems to have de-ranged her temporarily.

For an example from theater, we realize at the end of the second act of *The Dybbuk,* by S. Anski, that the bride, Leye, is possessed by a dybbuk. A frail (she's been fasting) virgin, she suddenly speaks in a strange masculine voice. The moment is one of horror—the presentation of a compound sexual being—and now *de rigeur* in possession films (such as in *The Exorcist* where the girlchild Regan speaks with the deep and aged voice of the demon).

According to the stage instructions in the text, the character who approaches this unnatural composite is supposed to do so while *shuddering.* To shudder, of course, is to suffer a convulsive tremor. But, more specifically, it is to shake as a result of extreme cold, or fear, or repugnance and disgust. Since the climate is irrelevant at this point in the play, the gesture is not to be read as a response to the weather. Rather, the shuddering of the character, which cues or at least reinforces the audience's response, is connected with abhorrence and fear. That is, the actor's body is meant to tremble in such a way that the quivering communicates extreme disgust as well as dread.

On the Structure of the Emotions

From this preliminary inventory of examples, it is possible to derive a theory of the nature of the emotion of art-horror. But before setting out that theory in detail, some comments need to be made about the structure of emotions. I am presupposing that art-horror is an emotion.[16] It is the emotion that horror narratives and images are designed to elicit from audiences. That is, "art-horror" names the emotion that the creators of the genre have perennially sought to instill in their audiences, though they, undoubtedly would be more disposed to call this emotion "horror" rather than "art-horror."

Furthermore, it is an emotion whose contours are reflected in the emotional responses of the positive human characters to the monsters in works of horror. I am also presuming that art-horror is an occurrent emotional state, like a flash of anger, rather than a dispositional emotional state, such as undying envy.

An occurrent emotional state has both physical and cognitive dimensions. Broadly speaking, the physical dimension of an emotion is a matter of felt agitation. Specifically, the physical dimension is a sensation or a feeling. An emotion, that is, involves some kind of stirring, perturbation, or arrest physiologically registered by an increase in heartbeat, respiration, or the like. The word "emotion" comes from the Latin "emovere" which combines the notion of "to move" with the prefix for "out." An *emotion* originally was a *moving* out. To be in an emotional state involves the experience of a transition or migration—a change of state, a moving out of a normal physical state to an agitated one, one marked by inner movings. To be an occurrent emotion,[17] I want to claim, involves a physical state—a sense of a physiological moving of some sort—a felt agitation or feeling sensation.

In respect to art-horror some of the regularly recurring sensations, or felt-physical agitations, or automatic responses, or feelings are muscular contractions, tension, cringing, shrinking, shuddering, recoiling, tingling, frozenness, momentary arrests, chilling (hence, "spine-chilling"), paralysis, trembling, nausea, a reflex of apprehension or physically heightened alertness (a danger response), perhaps involuntary screaming, and so on.[18]

The word "horror" derives from the Latin "horrere"—to stand on end (as hair standing on end) or to bristle—and the old French "orror"—to bristle or to shudder. And though it need not be the case that our hair must literally stand on end when we are art-horrified, it is important to stress that the original conception of the word connected it with an abnormal (from the subject's point of view) physiological state of felt agitation.

In order to be in an emotional state, one must undergo some concomitant physical agitation, registered as a sensation. You could not be said to be angry unless your negative evaluation of the man standing on your foot were accompanied by some physical state, like being "hot under the collar." A computer with a radar tracking system might be able to printout "Enemy missiles are headed at this base." But it could not be in the emotional state of fear; it lacks, metaphorically speaking, the "fleshy" hardware for that. It does not feel the agitations that go with fear of imminent destruction. If one could imagine such a computer to be in any mental state, it would be a pure cognitive state not an emotional one. For an emotional state requires a felt physical dimension. Characters like the Vulcans in *Star Trek* are said to lack emotions precisely because they do not undergo the physical perturbations and feelings that humans experience along with their reactions of aversion and approval.

However, though in order to qualify as an emotional state, a state must correlate with *some* physical agitation, the specific emotional state one is in is not determined by the kinds of physical agitations one is suffering. That is, no specific physical state represents a necessary or sufficient condition for a given emotional state. When I am angry, my blood runs cold, whereas when you are angry, your blood boils. In order to be an emotional state some physical agitation must obtain, though an emotional state will not be identified by being associated with a unique physical state or even a unique assortment of physical states.

What is being denied in the preceding paragraph is the notion that emotions are identical with certain feeling states or feeling qualities—that anger, for example, is a certain feeling, a physical agitation with a perceptibly distinctive sensation or quality. Just as we are thought to identify something as sweet by virtue of the uniquely discernible sensation it occasions, on the view rival to our own, anger has a uniquely discernible quality, a flavor, if you will, whose very feel or taste enables us to recognize we are angry. Call this approach the *qualia* or feeling view of the emotions.[19] But this approach is surely insupportable.

When I'm afraid my knees shake with a tingling sensation while when Lenny is afraid his mouth feels dry. And to complicate matters, when crestfallen my mouth goes dry while Lenny has that tingling sensation in his knees. Nancy, on the other hand, has a dry mouth and wobbly legs whenever she feels grateful. These different feelings, that is, can be correlated with different emotional states in different people. Indeed, these feelings might occur when the subject is not in an emotional state at all. We could administer a drug to someone, perhaps even to Nancy, which would render her mouth dry and her legs wobbly. But I doubt that we would be willing in those circumstances to say that Nancy is grateful. For as we've stated the case, to whom is she grateful and for what?[20]

Moreover, it should be evident that the feelings that accompany emotions not only vary from person to person, but also may vary within a single subject on different occasions. The last time I was frightened my muscles tightened but the time before that my muscles went limp. The *qualia* view of the emotions appears to entail that when I am in an emotional state I need only look inward to determine which emotional state I am in by attending to whatever pattern of feeling is dominant. However, this won't work, because the feelings that accompany given emotional states vary wildly, because a given feeling may attend a great diversity of emotional states, and because I might discern a familiar pattern of physical feeling where there is no emotion. Indeed, if we restrict our introspection exclusively to matters of inner movement, we are unlikely to attach our feelings, understood as physical feelings, to any emotional states.[21]

No specifiable, recurring feeling or package of feelings can be worked into neccessary or sufficient conditions for a given emotion. That is, to summarize the above arguments, in order to be an emotional state some physical agitation must obtain, though an emotional state will not be identified by being associated with a unique physical feeling state or even a uniquely recurring pattern of physical feelings.

What then identifies or individuates given emotional states? Their cognitive elements. Emotions involve not only physical perturbations but beliefs and thoughts, beliefs and thoughts about the properties of objects and situations. Moreover, these beliefs (and thoughts[22]) are not just factual—e.g., there is a large truck coming at me—but also evaluative—e.g., that large truck is dangerous to me. Now when I am in a state of fear with regard to this truck, I am in some physical state—perhaps I involuntarily squeeze my eyes shut while my pulse shoots up—and this physical state has been *caused* by my cognitive state, by my beliefs (or thoughts) that the truck is headed at me and that this situation is dangerous. My eyes closing and my pulse racing could be associated with many emotional states, e.g., ecstasy; what makes my emotional state fear in this particular case are my beliefs. That is, cognitive states differentiate one emotion from another though for a state to be an emotional one there must also be some kind of physical agitation that has been engendered by the presiding cognitive state (comprised of either beliefs or thoughts).

To illustrate the point here, it may be helpful to indulge in a science-fiction-like thought experiment. Imagine that we have advanced to the point where we can stimulate any sort of physical agitation by applying electrodes to the brain. A scientist observing me nearly run over by the truck in the preceding paragraph notes that when fearful my eyes clamp shut by reflex and my pulse quickens. She then arranges her electrodes in my brain so as to raise these physical states in me. Would we wish to say that, under these laboratory conditions, I am afraid. I suspect not. And the theory outlined above explains why not. For in the laboratory, my physical states are caused by electrical stimulation; they are not caused by beliefs (or thoughts) and, specifically, they are not caused by the kinds of beliefs that are appropriate to the emotional state of fear.[23]

We can summarize this view of the emotions—which might be called a cognitive/evaluative theory—by saying that an occurrent emotional state is one in which some physically abnormal state of felt agitation has been caused by the subject's cognitive construal and evaluation of his/her situation.[24] This is the core of an emotional state, though some emotions may involve wants and desires as well as construals and appraisals. If I am afraid of the approaching truck, then I form the desire to avoid its onslaught. Here the connection between the appraisal element of my emotion and my desire is a rational one, since the appraisal provides a good reason for the want or the desire. However, it is not the case that every emotion links up with a desire; I may be saddened by the realization that I will die some day without that leading to any other desire, such as, for instance, that I shall never die. Thus, though wants and desires may figure in the characterization of some emotions, the core structure of emotions involves physical agitations caused by the construals and evaluations that serve constitutively to identify the emotion as the specific emotion it is.

Defining Art-Horror

Using this account of the emotions, we are now in a position to organize these observations about the emotion of art-horror. Assuming that "I-as-audience-member" am in an analogous emotional state to that which fictional characters beset by monsters are described to be in, then: I am occurrently art-horrified by some monster X, say Dracula, if and only if 1) I am in some state of abnormal, physically felt agitation (shuddering, tingling, screaming, etc.) which 2) has been *caused* by a) the thought: that Dracula is a possible being; and by the evaluative thoughts: that b) said Dracula has the property of being physically (and perhaps morally and socially) threatening in the ways portrayed in the fiction and that c) said Dracula has the property of being impure, where 3) such thoughts are usually accompanied by the desire to avoid the touch of things like Dracula.[25]

Of course, "Dracula," here, is merely a heuristic device. Any old monster X can be plugged into the formula. Moreover, in order to forestall charges of circularity, let me note that, for our purposes, "monster" refers to any being not believed to exist now according to contemporary science. Thus, dinosaurs and nonhuman visitors from another galaxy are monsters under this stipulation though the former once existed and the latter might exist. Whether they are monsters who are also horrifying in the context of a particular fiction depends upon whether they meet the conditions of the analysis above. Some monsters may be only threatening rather than horrifying, while others may be neither threatening nor horrifying.[26]

Another thing to note about the preceding definition is that it is the evaluative components of the theory that primarily serve to individuate art-horror. And, furthermore, it is crucial that two evaluative components come into play: that the monster is regarded as threatening *and* impure. If the monster were only evaluated as potentially threatening, the emotion would be fear; if only potentially impure, the emotion would be disgust. Art-horror requires evaluation both in terms of threat and disgust.

The threat component of the analysis derives from the fact that the monsters we find in horror stories are uniformly dangerous or at least appear to be so; when they cease to be threatening, they cease to be horrifying. The impurity clause in the definition is postulated as a result of noting the regularity with which literary descriptions of the experiences of horror undergone by fictional characters include reference to disgust, repugnance, nausea, physical loathing, shuddering, revulsion, abhorrence, abomination, and so on. Likewise, the gestures actors on stage and on screen adopt when confronting horrific monsters communicate corresponding mental states. And, of course, these reactions—abomination, nausea, shuddering, revulsion, disgust, etc.—are characteristically the product of perceiving something to be noxious or impure.[27] (With regard to the impurity clause of this theory, it is persuasive to recall that horrific beings are often associated with contamination—sicknesses, disease, and plague—and often accompanied by infectious vermin—rats, insects and the like.)

It should also be mentioned that though the third criterion about the desire to avoid physical contact—which may be rooted in the fear of funestation—seems generally accurate, it might be better to consider it to be an extremely frequent but not necessary ingredient of art-horror.[28] This caveat is included in my definition by means of the qualification "usually."

In my definition of horror, the evaluative criteria—of dangerousness and impurity—constitute what in certain idioms are called the formal object of the emotion.[29] The formal object of the emotion is the evaluative category that circumscribes the *kind* of particular object the emotion can focus upon. To be an object of art-horror, in other words, is limited to particular objects, such as Dracula, that are threatening and impure. The formal object or evaluative category of the emotion constrains the range of particular objects upon which the emotion can be focused. An emotion involves, among other things, an appraisal of particular objects along the dimensions specified by the emotion's operative evaluative category. Where a particular object is not assessable in terms of the evaluative category appropriate to a given emotion, the emotion, by definition, cannot be focused on said object. That is, I cannot be art-horrified by an entity that I do not think is threatening and impure. I may be in some emotional state with respect to this entity, but it is not art-horror. Thus, the formal object or evaluative category of the emotion is part of the concept of the emotion. Though the relation of the evaluative category to the accompanying felt physical agitation is causal, the relation of the evaluative category to the emotion is constitutive and, therefore, noncontingent. It is in this sense that one might say that the emotion is individuated by its object, i.e., by its formal object. Art-horror is primarily identified in virtue of danger and impurity.

The evaluative category selects or focuses upon particular objects. The emotion is directed toward such objects; art-horror is directed at particular objects like Dracula, the Wolfman, and Mr. Hyde. The root of the term "emotion," as we noted above, comes from the Latin for moving out. Perhaps, we can read that playfully and suggest that an emotion is an inner moving (a physical agitation) directed outward (toward) a particular object under the prompting and guidance of an appropriate evaluative category.

Much of the next chapter will be concerned with the ontological status of the particular objects of art-horror. However, by way of preview, some comment may be helpful now. The problem with discussing the particular object of the emotion of art-horror is that it is a fictive being. Consequently, we cannot construe "particular object" here to mean something like a material being with specifiable space-time co-ordinates. The Dracula who art-horrifies us doesn't have specifiable space-time co-ordinates; he doesn't exist. So what kind of particular object is he?

Though this will be clarified and qualified in the next chapter, for the time being let us say that the particular object of art-horror—Dracula, if you will—is a thought. Saying that we are art-horrified by Dracula means that we are horrified by the thought of Dracula where the thought of such a possible being does not commit us to a belief in his existence. Here, the thought of Dracula, the particular object that art-horrifies me, is not the actual event of my thinking of Dracula but the content of the thought, viz., that Dracula, a threatening and impure being of such and such dimensions, might exist and do these terrible things. Dracula, the thought, is the concept of a certain possible being.[30] Of course, I come to think about this concept because a given book, or film, or picture invites me to entertain the thought of Dracula, that is, to consider the concept of a certain possible being, viz., Dracula. From such representations of the concept of Dracula, we recognize Dracula to be a threatening and impure prospect, one which gives rise to the emotion of art-horror.

In Descartes's "Third Meditation," he draws the distinction between what he calls objective reality and formal reality. The objective reality of a being is the idea of the thing *sans* a commitment to its existence. We can think of a unicorn without thinking that unicorns exist. That is, we can have the idea or concept of a unicorn—i.e., a horse with a narwhal horn—without thinking that that concept applies to anything. A being that has formal reality exists; that is, its idea is instantiated by something that exists. In this mode of speech, Dracula might be said to have objective reality but not formal reality. Twisting Descartes's vocabulary somewhat, we can say that the particular objects of art-horror, our Draculas, are objective realities (but not formal realities).

The use of the notion of impurity in this theory has caused misgivings in two different directions. Commentators, hearing my lectures on this theory, have worried that it is too subjective (in the contemporary rather than the Cartesian sense above), on the one hand, and too vague on the other. In the remainder of this section, I will take up these objections.

The charge of subjectivity involves the fear that the emphasis on disgust in the theory is really a matter of projection. It goes something like this: Carroll is a delicate sort of guy whose toilet training was probably traumatic. He hasn't actually done any empirical research into the reception of works of horror by audiences. He doesn't know that they find horrific monsters disgusting and impure. At best, he's identified his own reaction by introspection and projected it onto everyone else.

However, the method that I have adopted to isolate the ingredients of art-horror is designed to blunt charges of projection. I am interested in the emotional response that horror is *supposed* to elicit. I have approached this issue by assuming that the audience's responses to the monsters in works of horror are *ideally* intended to run parallel to and often to be cued by the emotional responses of the relevant fictional characters to monsters. This presupposition, in turn, enables us to look to works of horror themselves for evidence of the emotional response they want to engender. I have not depended on introspection in fastening on disgust and impurity as part of the emotion of art-horror. Rather, I found expressions and gestures of disgust as a regularly recurring feature of characters's reactions in horror fictions.

It is true that I have not done any audience research. Nevertheless, that does not entail that the theory has no empirical base. Rather, the empirical base is comprised of the many stories, dramas, films, etc., that I reviewed in order to track how fictional characters react to the monsters they encounter. I believe that my hypotheses about art-horror can be confirmed by, for example, turning to the descriptions of character reactions to the monsters in horror novels and checking them for the recurring reference to fear and disgust (or the strong implication of fear and disgust).

Whether art-horror is supposed to involve impurity, then, can be corroborated by scanning works of horror in order to see whether or not disgust and suggestions of impurity are regularly recurring features. Moreover, there may be another way to bolster the claims of my theory. For the theory, as stated above and in terms of some of the structures to be discussed below, can be used to create horrific effects. That is, one can use this theory as a recipe for making horrific creatures. The theory, of course, is not an algorithm that guarantees success by the blind application of rules. But it can be used to guide the construction of fictive beings of the sort that most of us would agree are horrific. The capacity of the theory to facilitate simulations of horror, then, may argue for the sufficiency of the theory.

Again, the object of my study concerns the emotional response that works of art-horror are supposed to elicit. This is neither to claim that all works of horror succeed in this matter—*Robot Monster,* for example, borders on the ridiculous—nor that every audience member will report that they are horrified—one can imagine macho teenagers denying that monsters disgust them, claiming instead that they are amused. I am not preoccupied with the actual relations of works of art-horror to audiences, but with a normative relation, the response the audience is supposed to have to the work of art-horror. I believe that we are able to get at this by presuming that the work of art-horror has built into it, so to speak, a set of instructions about the appropriate way the audience is to respond to it. These instructions are manifested, by example, in the responses of the positive, human characters to the monsters in horror fiction. We learn what is to be art-horrified in large measure from the fiction itself; indeed, the very criteria for what it is to be art-horrified can be found in the fiction in the description or enactment of the human character's responses. Works of horror, that is, teach us, in large measure, the appropriate way to respond to them.[31] Unearthing those cues or instructions is an empirical matter, not an exercise in subjective projection.

Even if I can avoid the charge of projection, it might still be argued that the notion of impurity employed in my definition of art-horror is too vague. If a work of horror does not explicitly attribute "impurity" to a monster, how can we be satisfied that the monster is regarded to be impure in the text? The concept of impurity is just too fuzzy to be of use.

But perhaps I can relieve some of these anxieties concerning vagueness by saying something about the kinds of objects that standardly give rise to or cause reactions of impurity. This, moreover, will enable me to expand my theory of art-horror from the realm of definition to that of explanation, from an analysis of the application of the concept of art-horror to an analysis of its causation.

In her classic study *Purity and Danger,* Mary Douglas correlates reactions of impurity with the transgression or violation of schemes of cultural categorization.[32] In her interpretation of the abominations of *Leviticus,* for example, she hypothesizes that the reason crawling things from the sea, like lobsters, are regarded as impure is that crawling was a defining feature of earthbound creatures, not of creatures of the sea. A lobster, in other words, is a kind of category mistake and, hence, impure. Similarly, all winged insects with four legs are abominated because though four legs is a feature of land animals, these things fly, i.e., they inhabit the air. Things that are interstitial, that cross the boundaries of the deep categories of a culture's conceptual scheme, are impure, according to Douglas. Feces, insofar as they figure ambiguously in terms of categorical oppositions such as me/not me, inside/outside, and living/dead, serve as ready candidates for abhorrence as impure, as do spittle, blood, tears, sweat, hair clippings, vomit, nail clippings, pieces of flesh, and so on. Douglas notes that among the people called the Lele, flying squirrels are avoided since they cannot be categorized unambiguously as either birds or animals.

Also, objects can raise categorical misgivings by virtue of being incomplete representatives of their class, such as rotting and disintegrating things, as well as by virtue of being formless, for example, dirt.[33]

Following Douglas, then, I initially speculate that an *object* or *being* is impure if it is categorically interstitial, categorically contradictory, incomplete, or formless.[34] These features appear to form a suitable grouping as prominent ways in which categorizing can be problematized. This list may not be exhaustive, nor is it clear that its terms are mutually exclusive. But it is certainly useful for analyzing the monsters of the horror genre. For they are beings or creatures that specialize in formlessness, incompleteness, categorical interstitiality, and categorical contradictoriness. Let a brief inventory carry this point for the time being.

Many monsters of the horror genre are interstitial and/or contradictory in terms of being both living and dead: ghosts, zombies, vampires, mummies, the Frankenstein monster, Melmoth the Wanderer, and so on. Near relatives to these are monstrous entities that conflate the animate and the inanimate: haunted houses, with malevolent wills of their own, robots, and the car in King's *Christine*. Also many monsters confound different species: werewolves, humanoid insects, humanoid reptiles, and the inhabitants of Dr. Moreau's island.[35]

Or, consider the conflation of species in these descriptions of the monster in Lovecraft's "The Dunwich Horror": "Bigger'n a barn . . . all made o' squirmin ropes . . . hull thing sort o' shaped like a hen's egg bigger'n anything, with dozens o' legs like hogsheads that haff shut up when they step . . . nothin' solid abaout it—all like jelly, an' made o' sep'rit wrigglin' ropes pushed clost together . . . great bulgin' eyes all over it . . . ten or twenty maouths or trunks a-stickn' aout all along the sides, big as stovepipes, an'a-tossin' an' openin' an' shuttin' . . . all, with kinder blue or purple rings . . . an' Gawd in Heaven—that haff face on top!. . . ." And: "Oh, oh, my Gawd, that haff face—that haff face on top of it . . . that face with the red eyes an' crinkly albino hair, an' no chin, like the Whateleys . . . . It was a octopus, centipede, spider kindo' thing, but they was a haff-shaped man's face on top of it, an' it looked like Wizard Whateley's, only it was yards an'yards acrost. . . ."

The creature in Howard Hawks's classic *The Thing* is an intelligent, two-legged, bloodsucking carrot. Now that's interstitial. Indeed, the frequent resort to referring to monsters by means of pronouns like "It" and "Them" suggests that these creatures are not classifiable according to our standing categories.[36] Moreover, this interpretation is also supported by the frequency with which monsters in horror are said to be indescribable or inconceivable. Recall our previous examples from Stevenson and Lovecraft, or movie titles like *The Creeping Unknown;* while sometimes Frankenstein's creation is referred to as the "monster with no name." Again, the point would appear to be that these monsters fit neither the conceptual scheme of the characters nor, more importantly, that of the reader.

Horrific monsters often involve the mixture of what is normally distinct. Demonically possessed characters typically involve the superimposition of two categorically distinct individuals, the possessee and the possessor, the latter usually a demon, who, in turn, is often a categorically transgressive figure (e.g., a goat-god). Stevenson's most famous monster is two men, Jekyll and Hyde, where Hyde is described as having a simian aspect which makes him appear not quite human.[37] Werewolves mix man and wolf, while shape changers of other sorts compound humans with other species. The monster in King's *It* is a kind of categorically contradictory creature raised to a higher power. For It is a monster that can change into any other monster, those other monsters already being categorically transgressive. And, of course, some monsters, like the scorpion big enough to eat Mexico City, are magnifications of creatures and crawling things already ajudged impure and interstitial in the culture.

Categorical incompleteness is also a standard feature of the monsters of horror; ghosts and zombies frequently come without eyes, arms, legs, or skin, or they are in some advanced state of disintegration. And, in a related vein, detached body parts are serviceable monsters, severed heads and especially hands, e.g., de Maupassant's "The Hand" and "The Withered Hand," Le Fanu's "The Narrative of a Ghost of a Hand," Golding's "The Call of the Hand," Conan Doyle's "The Brown Hand," Nerval's "The Enchanted Hand," Dreiser's "The Hand," William Harvey's "The Beast With Five Fingers" and so on. A brain in a vat is the monster in the novel *Donovan's Brain* by Curt Siodmak, which has been adapted for the screen more than once, while in the film *Fiend Without a Face* the monsters are brains that use their spinal cords as tails.

The rate of recurrence with which the biologies of monsters are vaporous or gelatinous attests to the applicability of the notion of formlessness to horrific impurity while the writing style of certain horror authors, such as Lovecraft, at times, and Straub, through their vague, suggestive, and often inchoate descriptions of the monsters, leaves an impression of formlessness. Indeed, many monsters are literally formless: the man-eating oil slick in King's short story "The Raft," the malevolent entity in James Herbert's *The Fog* and *The Dark,* in Matthew Phipps Shiel's *The Purple Cloud,* in Joseph

Payne Brennan's novella "Slime," in Kate Wilhelm's and Ted Thomas's *The Clone,* and the monsters in movies like *The Blob* (both versions) and *The Stuff.*[38]

Douglas's observations, then, may help dispel some of the fuzziness of the impurity clause of my definition of art-horror. They can be used to supply paradigmatic examples for the application of the impurity clause as well as rough guiding principles for isolating impurity—such as that of categorical transgression. Furthermore, Douglas's theory of impurity can be used by scholars of horror to identify some of the pertinent features of the monsters in the stories they study. That is, given a monster in a horror story, the scholar can ask in what ways it is categorically interstitial, contradictory (in Douglas's sense), incomplete, and/or formless. These features, moreover, provide a crucial part of the causal structure of the reaction of impurity that operates in the raising of the emotion of art-horror. They are part of what triggers it. This is not to say that we realize that Dracula is, among other things, categorically interstitial and that we then react, accordingly, with art-horror. Rather that monster X is categorically interstitial causes a sense of impurity in us without our necessarily being aware of precisely what causes that sense.[39]

In addition, the emphasis Douglas places on categorical schemes in the analysis of impurity indicates a way for us to account for the recurrent description of our impure monsters as "un-natural." They are un-natural relative to a culture's conceptual scheme of nature. They do not fit the scheme; they violate it. Thus, monsters are not only physically threatening; they are cognitively threatening. They are threats to common knowledge.[40] Undoubtedly, it is in virtue of this cognitive threat that not only are horrific monsters referred to as impossible, but also that they tend to render those who encounter them insane, mad, deranged, and so on.[41] For such monsters are in a certain sense challenges to the foundations of a culture's way of thinking.

Douglas's theory of impurity might also help us to answer a frequent puzzle about horror. It is a remarkable fact about the creatures of horror that very often they do not seem to be of sufficient strength to make a grown man cower. A tettering zombie or a severed hand would appear incapable of mustering enough force to overpower a co-ordinated six-year-old. Nevertheless, they are presented as unstoppable, and this seems psychologically acceptable to audiences. This might be explained by noting Douglas's claim that culturally impure objects are generally taken to be invested with magical powers, and, as a result, are often employed in rituals. Monsters in works of horror, by extension, then, may be similarly imbued with awesome powers in virtue of their impurity.

It is also the case that the geography of horror stories generally situates the origin of monsters in such places as lost continents and outer space. Or the creature comes from under the sea or under the earth. That is, monsters are native to places outside of and/or unknown to the human world. Or, the creatures come from marginal, hidden, or abandoned sites: graveyards, abandoned towers and castles, sewers, or old houses—that is, they belong to environs outside of and unknown to ordinary social intercourse. Given the theory of horror expounded above, it is tempting to interpret the geography of horror as a figurative spatialization or literalization of the notion that what horrifies is that which lies *outside* cultural categories and is, perforce, unknown.[42]

The theory of art-horror that I am advancing has not been derived from a set of deeper principles. The way to confirm it is to take the definition of the nature of art-horror, and the partial typology of the structures that give rise to the sense of impurity along with the fission/fusion model to be developed below, and to see if they apply to the reactions we find to the monsters indigenous to works of horror. In my own research, though admittedly informal, these hypotheses, so far, have proved rewarding. Moreover, these hypotheses seem worthwhile candidates for more rigorous attempts at corroboration than I have the training to pursue; that is, perhaps the definition could be tested by social psychologists. Furthermore, the definition of horror, the discussion of impurity, and the fission/fusion model might be used by authors, filmmakers, and other artists to generate horrific images. The degree to which the theory provides a reliable guide to making or simulating monsters would be a further test of its mettle.

*Further Objections and Counterexamples to
the Definition of Art-Horror*

I have hypothesized that art-horror is an emotional state wherein, essentially, some nonordinary physical state of agitation is caused by the thought of a monster, in terms of the details presented by a fiction or an image, which thought also includes the recognition that the monster is threatening and impure. The audience thinking of a monster is prompted in this response by the responses of fictional human characters whose actions they are attending to, and that audience, like said characters, may also wish to avoid physical contact with such types of things as monsters. Monsters, here, are identified as any being not now believed to exist according to reigning scientific notions.

This account of art-horror obviously depends on a cognitive-evaluative theory of the emotions. Such theories, of course, have been confronted by counterexamples. For instance, it is said that we are in emotional states while dancing and that this is a matter of rhythm and physiology rather than of cognition and evaluation. I am disposed to think that if we are in an emotional state when dancing, then that has to do with our evaluation of the situation:

our evaluation, for example, of what the dance stands for, commemorates, or celebrates; or our evaluation of our bond with our partner, or the larger community of dancers, or our audience, or our relation with the accompanying musicians, or even with the music itself. Or the evaluation might have to do with ourselves, with the joy that comes from judging that we dance well, or from appreciating being co-ordinated and active, i.e., recognizing the dance as a mark of our own well-being. That is, if we are in an emotional state while dancing, it seems attributable to many sorts of evaluative beliefs. Simply being in a rhythmically induced, trance-like state, directed at no object, does not seem to me to be an emotional state.

However, even if I am wrong here, it does not seem that such counterexamples show that there are no cognitive-evaluative states with respect to emotions. If successful, they would only establish that not all emotional states are cognitive-evaluative ones. This would leave room for the possibility that some emotional states are of the cognitive-evaluative sort. And, of course, I would hold that art-horror is one of these.

This move, though, invites the response that, like the putative dance emotion, shock is a rhythmically induced, nonevaluative emotion, and that art-horror is really a variety of shock. I would not want to deny that shock is often involved in tandem with art-horror, especially in theater and cinema. Just before the monster appears, the music shoots up, or there is a startling noise, or we see an unexpected, fast movement start out from "nowhere." Consider the end of the first act of the non-horror play *Deathtrap* by Ira Levin when the supposedly dead, aspiring writer bursts into the living room and gives the wife a heart attack. We jump in our seats, and perhaps some scream. If the fiction in question is of the horror genre, when we then recognize the monster, that scream of shock gets extended and applied as a scream of horror. This is a well-known scare tactic.

However, horror is not reducible to this sort of shock. For this technique is also found in mysteries and thrillers (like *Deathtrap*) where we don't feel horror at the gunman who suddenly steps out of the dark. This variety of shock does not seem to me to be an emotion at all, but rather a reflex, though, of course, it is a reflex that is often linked with the provocation of art-horror by the artisans of monster spectacles. And, anyway, it must also be stressed that one can feel art-horror without being shocked in the reflex sense of the term.[43]

Some theorists attack the cognitive-evaluative approach to the emotions by claiming that insofar as it requires an object, it cannot be a general theory of the emotions, because there are some emotions, like neurasthenia, that do not have objects. This is a challenge to the comprehensiveness of cognitive-evaluative theories; however, again, even if the theory does not accommodate every emotion, it may still apply to art-horror. To level the objectless emotion theory at this characterization of horror would require showing either that all emotions are objectless or that art-horror is. But no one has done that yet.[44]

My position with respect to art-horror requires that the emotion be focused upon monsters where those are understood to be creatures not countenanced by contemporary science. But this may prompt some to say that the theory is too narrow. Aren't movies like *Orca* and the *Jaws* series, and novels like Gaston Leroux's *The Phantom of the Opera* and John Farris's *Nightfall* examples of art-horror? But do they have monsters in the requisite sense? Sharks, even very big ones, exist in the case of the *Jaws* movies, and the villains in the novels cited are humans even if they are psychopaths, a phenomenon readily acknowledged by contemporary science.

The problem with these types of counterexamples, which are legion, is that though nominally the antagonists belong to our everyday world, their presentation in the fictions they inhabit turn them effectively into fantastical beings. Ostensibly whales, sharks, and men, they acquire powers and attributes above and beyond what one would be willing to believe of living creatures. Erik, a.k.a. the Phantom of the Opera, whose medical afflictions ill-match his strenuous hyperactivity, also appears, at times, to have powers of virtual invisibility and omniscience. He seems capable of being anywhere at will. Of course, many fictional characters have exaggerated attributes. But the exaggerated attributes of the Phantom are expressly played for supernatural effect of the awe-inspiring variety. He is described as a ghost and a corpse, and he carries off inexplicable feats that seem magical.

Likewise Angel, the psycho in *Nightfall*, is portrayed as an unstoppable, mute, relentless force of nature. He is said to be inhuman. The character Anita, his estranged wife, says: "Angel's not that big, but then again he isn't really human. Just what he is, I don't know." Nor does Anita intend to say that her husband, like so many others, is a monster metaphorically speaking; she means people to take her literally. If one is tempted to categorize a novel like *Nightfall* as horror, I think that it is because sentences like the one quoted, together with descriptions of Angel's willfulness, inscrutability, and powers, rhetorically move us to regard Angel as an inhuman creature.

Similar observations can be made about creatures like Orca. This is a whale that can track humans down, figure out the relation of gas and fuel pumps, and on the basis of that inference and some other observations, burn down a harbor. Likewise, the sharks in the *Jaws* series seem too smart and innovative to be sharks, while, like Orca, the creature in the last installment is capable of carrying out long term projects of revenge way beyond the mental capacities of its species. Indeed, the shark in these films manages to kill about as many humans in a single summer as all the actual sharks in the world do in a year. These are not the creatures of marine biology but fantasy.

In general, where the antagonistic creatures in films and novels that we are prone to classify as horror appear to be ostensibly on the list of presently existing beings, a brief look at the manner of their presentation most often quickly reveals they are preternatural: the killer bees in Curtis Harrington's film of the same name have made Gloria Swanson their queen, while the vampire bats in Martin Cruz Smith's novel *Nightwing* are connected to apocalyptic Hopi legends and prophecies that the reader is supposed to take seriously; in the concluding pages of that novel the burning bats and smoke become a giant wraith which speaks to the hero Youngman.

On the other hand, the eponymous dog in King's *Cujo* is just a dog, and this leads me to think that the book, though not unrelated to horror, is not a pedigreed example of the genre. Rather, it belongs to the more amorphous categories of the thriller or of suspense. Of course, this is not a criticism of King. For the concept of horror, as I am using it, is descriptive rather than prescriptive.

However, even if I have succeeded above in deflecting the major types of counterexamples, the very procedure of concocting a definition of art-horror and testing it against counter-instances may seem dubious to many readers. They might feel that art-horror is not the sort of thing that can be captured by definitions in terms of sets of necessary and sufficient conditions. Insofar as art-horror is a constructed kind, not a natural kind—an artistic genre rather than a natural phenomenon—it may be argued that it is not susceptible of the type of tight definition I propose. Rather it is a concept with fuzzy and perhaps developing boundaries. It supports myriad border cases that cannot be ruled in or out of the genre except by fiat.

Nevertheless, even if horror is such an open concept, exercises in framing it in terms of necessary and sufficient conditions are still useful, especially in understanding the genre. It may be true that a sharp line cannot be drawn between art-horror and its neighbors because its boundaries are somewhat fluid. But a theory such as the one proposed—based on extrapolations from paradigm cases—may still enhance our grasp not only of horror itself, but also of its contesting neighbors.[45]

For even if the proposed theory of horror is not invulnerably comprehensive, it does offer at least a clear picture of the central or core cases of art-horror. If there are contesting counter-cases that the theory does not accommodate, the theory may yet be useful in illuminating those examples by showing, in terms of the theory itself, how intuitions that these counter-instances should count are motivated.

Consider the case of Hitchcock's *Psycho*. One could imagine the claim that it ought to be regarded as an example of horror. But, of course, my theory does not count it as such, because Norman Bates is not a monster. He is a schizophrenic, a type of being that science countenances (though only self-deceptively, the film suggests). But there appear to be many reasons to regard *Psycho* as a horror film. There is the imagery of the old dark house, and the drama of corridors. The story is set in a lonely place, off the beaten track, where the appearance of a single woman unleashes forces of sexual assault, murder, and incest. As well, various of the narrative structures (e.g., the build-up to the final manifestation of the nefarious creature), the shock tactics (sudden movements and Bernard Herrmann's unnerving, shrieking strings), the imagery (e.g., the skeleton), and even the lighting are suggestive of horror films. With so many correspondences, am I not just standing on ceremony in refusing to accept it as an example of horror?

Perhaps. But more interesting from the point of view of the informativeness of my theory is the fact that on the basis of it, I can explain why it is that viewers are so tempted to think of *Psycho* as a horror film. For even if Norman Bates is not a monster technically speaking, he does begin to approximate the central features of art-horror as I have developed them. That a madman with a butcher knife is threatening needs no comment. But, as well, Norman Bates, in virtue of his psychosis, resembles the impure beings at the core of the concept of art-horror.

He is *Nor-man:* neither man nor woman but both. He is son and mother. He is of the living and the dead. He is both victim and victimizer. He is two persons in one. He is abnormal, that is, because he is interstitial. In Norman's case, this is a function of psychology rather than biology. Nevertheless, he is a powerful icon of impurity, which is, ultimately, why I submit that commentators are prone to classify *Psycho* as a horror film. By developing a core theory of horror, consequently, we place ourselves in a position to identify the crucial features of a figure like Norman Bates that lead people to align him with the figures of horror. Whether in the long run we count *Psycho* as horror may be a matter of decision. Nevertheless, by developing a definition of the core cases of horror, we place ourselves in a position to explain what it is about figures like Norman Bates that tempts people to classify him as horrific. That is, possessing a core theory of horror has explanatory advantages.

The explanatory advantage of this core theory of horror can also be illustrated by its ability to handle bizarre cases. A recent example is David Cronenberg's remake of *The Fly,* perhaps the gooiest version of the Beauty and the Beast legend ever made. This film has all the trappings of a horror film, including a monster. But classifying it as a horror film as such, without qualification, seems not quite right. It fails to capture an essential difference between this film and the rest of the genre. The theory of horror offered here can explain that difference.

The fly figure in this film is undeniably impure. Not only is he a grotesque man/insect; his behavior is disgusting. He digests food externally in a way that resembles vomiting. He would appear to be the very paradigm of the horrific object and yet for much of the film he is not. Why?

The horrific object is a compound of threat and impurity. However, for much of the film the fly monster is not threatening. He has a girlfriend, who, as we have argued, cues our response to the fly, and until the end of the film, at least, she does not feel threatened by the fly. Rather, she remains concerned. Likewise, for most of the film, the audience, via the agency of the girlfriend, emotionally responds to the fly in terms of disgust tinged with sympathy and care. This does change during the denouement when the fly becomes dangerous to all concerned. But the curious affect that suffuses much of this film can be pinpointed according to our theory by virtue of the way in which the creature is presented as not horrific due to the girlfriend's sense of security vis-à-vis the fly. She is patently disgusted by his malady, as we are; but her concern for him leads her to attempt to get past this, and I think the ideal audience does as well.[46]

One immensely successful, recent author whose work is sometimes classified as horror is V.C. Andrews. Her books, like *Flowers in the Attic,* as well as its sequels and prequels, concern hidden incest. Clearly, what is taken to be unnatural here is unnatural and repulsive from a moral standpoint. From my perspective, this is an extreme extension of genre, one I would be prone to reject. But I think that many, who do not explicitly advocate a theory of art-horror like the one offered here, would also be uncomfortable about including the *Flowers in the Attic* series in the genre. A novel like John Coyne's *Hunting Season,* on the other hand, where the progeny of generations of incest are quite literally monstrous and disgusting is a better candidate for inclusion in the genre.

I have examined the charge that my use of the concept of monsters in my theory of horror is too narrow. But it might also be claimed that it is too broad. If monsters are beings whose existence is denied by contemporary science, then isn't the comic book character Superman a monster? This seems not only ungrateful, given everything Superman has done for us, but also wrong if we think of monsters as beings so ugly as to frighten us, i.e., as beings somehow grotesque. But Superman, on the contrary, could be thought of as exemplifying certain ideals of male beauty.

But, of course, the sense of "monster" that I am using does not necessarily involve notions of ugliness but rather the notion that the monster is a being in violation of the natural order, where the perimeter of the natural order is determined by contemporary science. Superman is not compossible with what is known of the natural order by science. He may at a later date become so, as knowledge of other planets and galaxies advances, but I wouldn't bet on it.[47]

Strategically, I have taken monsters as a genus and then attempted to identify horrifying monsters as a species therein, a species upon which the emotion of art-horror focuses. I have taken the capacity to instill a sense of danger and impurity to be that which differentiates horrifying monsters from all other monsters. In this, care had to be exercised to make sure that the differentiating features of horrifying monsters in fact differentiated them from monsters in general. That is, I had to assure that the definition was not circular in the sense that concepts like danger and impurity were already built into the concept of the monster. My concept of monsters in general must be independent of evaluations in terms of danger and impurity, if the definition is to be effective. Thus, I opted for a conception of monsters as beings that do not exist according to the lights of contemporary science. Neither impurity or danger figure necessarily in this conception.

In construing monsters in this way, certain ordinary uses of the notion have been ignored. For example, monsters need not be ugly or grotesque. But two points need to be made here. First, ugliness does not seem to be a necessary mark of monsters even in ordinary language. Dracula as played by Frank Langella and the Wandering Jew in William Harrison Ainsworth's "The Spectre Bride" would appear to be quite handsome (monstrosity and impurity may be more than skin-deep). Second, the notion that we employ—of the monster as something outside the natural order (as dictated by science)—is also in accord with the ordinary usage, and I suspect is even more central than usage based on the outward aspect of beings.

Of course, the problems with cases like Superman are rendered even more complex because monsters in everyday speech are often thought of in terms of morality. A monster can be a being who is extremely cruel and/or evil. And Superman is such a nice man. However, I think that for our purposes we can regard this particular use of "monster" as a form of moral condemnation which is basically metaphorical. For there are lots of monsters who are good guys: E.T., Ariel, and The Swamp Thing in the D.C. comic book serial.

Lastly, the emphasis on monsters throughout this discussion should make it clear that my theory of art-horror is what might be called entity-based. That is, my definition of horror involves essential reference to an entity, a monster, which then serves as the particular object of the emotion of art-horror. Notice, in other words, that I have not taken *events* to be among the primary objects of art-horror.[48]

This may strike some readers as problematic. For if one picks up an anthology of horror stories, one notes that some of the stories lack monsters, impure or otherwise. Mysterious, unnerving, preternatural events instead seem to be the object of the peculiar emotions that such stories appear designed to provoke.

In Robert Louis Stevenson's "The Body Snatcher," there is no monster. The emotional twist that comes at the end of the story arises when the two grave robbers—Fettes and MacFarlane—realize that the corpse in the grave they have just desecrated has, after a flash of darkness, turned into the corpse of Gray, someone whom Fettes had dissected and whom Macfarlane had probably murdered some time before. The unhinging appearance of Gray—seeming to come out of nowhere—is a kind of supernatural revenge, a cosmic pang of conscience, but it does not involve anything remotely resembling a monster.

There are, of course, many stories like this: Guy de Maupassant's "Who Knows?," in which the narrator's furniture inexplicably disappears and reappears; Richard Matheson's "The Edge," in which Donald Marshal, gradually and with mounting anxiety, appears to learn that he is a *doppelganger* from a parallel universe; David Morrell's "Mumbo Jumbo" where the reader is led step by skeptical step to the point at which one is supposed to conclude that the pagan statue actually is the source of its owner's success. Many of the episodes on the old TV series *The Twilight Zone* are of this sort. Often they are tricked out with O. Henry-type hooks. They seem to prosper best in short forms. Their conclusions often correlate with some sense of cosmic moral justice. But they need not. Such stories may involve horrific beings— e.g., the son risen from the dead in W.W. Jacobs's classic "The Monkey's Paw"; but in the main their energy is spent constructing a psychologically disturbing event of preternatural origins.[49]

One can neither deny that there are such stories nor that they are frequently grouped together with the type of fictions from which my theory has been derived. Nevertheless, I do think that there is an important distinction between this type of story—which I want to call *tales of dread*—and horror stories. Specifically, the emotional response they elicit seems to be quite different than that engendered by art-horror. The uncanny event which tops off such stories causes a sense of unease and awe, perhaps of momentary anxiety and foreboding. These events are constructed to move the audience rhetorically to the point that one entertains the idea that unavowed, unknown, and perhaps concealed and inexplicable forces rule the universe. Where art-horror involves disgust as a central feature, what might be called art-dread does not. Art-dread probably deserves a theory of its own, though I do not have one ready-to-hand. Presumably, art-dread will bear some affinities with art-horror since both traffic in the preternatural—with both supernatural and sci-fi variations. And, of course, some fictions may traffic in both art-horror and art-dread; the admixture may take a range of forms in different stories. However, the two emotions, though related, are still discriminable.

Fantastic Biologies and the Structures of Horrific Imagery

The objects of art-horror are essentially threatening and impure. The creator of horror presents creatures that are salient in respect to these attributes. In this, certain recurring strategies for designing monsters appear with striking regularity across the arts and media. The purpose of this section is to take note of some of the most characteristic ways in which monsters are produced for the reading and viewing public. This section could be subtitled: "How to make a monster."

Horrific monsters are threatening. This aspect of the design of horrific monsters is, I think, incontestable. They must be dangerous. This can be satisfied simply by making the monster lethal. That it kills and maims is enough. The monster may also be threatening psychologically, morally, or socially. It may destroy one's identity (William Blatty's *The Exorcist* or Guy de Maupassant's "The Horla"), seek to destroy the moral order (Ira Levin's *Rosemary's Baby* et al.), or advance an alternative society (Richard Matheson's *I am Legend*). Monsters may also trigger certain enduring infantile fears, such as those of being eaten or dismembered, or sexual fears, concerning rape and incest. However, in order to be threatening, it is sufficient that the monster be physically dangerous. If it produces further anxieties that is so much icing on the cake. So the creators of art-horror must be sure that the creatures in their fictions are threatening and this can be done by assuring that they are at least physically dangerous. Of course, if a monster is psychologically threatening but not physically threatening—i.e., if it's after your mind, not your body—it will still count as a horrific creature if it inspires revulsion.

Horrific creatures are also impure. Here, the means for presenting this aspect of horrific creatures are less obvious. So I will spend some time looking at the characteristic structures through which horrific impurity is portrayed.

As discussed in an earlier section concerning the definition of horror, many cases of impurity are generated by what, adapting Mary Douglas, I called interstitiality and categorical contradictoriness. Impurity involves a conflict between two or more standing cultural categories. Thus, it should come as no surprise that many of the most basic structures for representing horrific creatures are combinatory in nature.

One structure for the composition of horrific beings is *fusion*. On the simplest physical level, this often entails the construction of creatures that transgress categorical distinctions such as inside/outside, living/dead, insect/human, flesh/machine, and so on. Mummies, vampires, ghosts, zombies, and Freddie, Elm Street's premier nightmare, are fusion figures in this respect. Each, in different ways, blur the distinction between living and dead. Each, in some sense, is both living *and* dead. A fusion figure is a composite that unites attributes held to be categorically distinct and/or at odds in the cultural scheme of things in *unambiguously* one, spatio-temporally discrete entity.

The caterpillars in E.F. Benson's story of the same name are fusion figures insofar as they defy biology not only due to their extraordinary length but also because their legs are outfitted with crab pincers. Similarly, the blighted victim in John Metcalfe's "Mr. Meldrum's Mania" falls into this category since he is a combination of a man with the Egyptian god Thoth, already a fusion creature compounding an ibis head with a human body, not to mention his moon-disk and crescent accoutrements. Lovecraft's amalgams of octopi and crustaceans with humanoid forms are paradigmatic fusion figures, as are the pig-men in William Hope Hodgson's *The House on the Borderland*. Fusion examples from film would include figures such as the babies in the *It's Alive* series and the grotesqueries in *Alligator People* and *The Reptile*.

The central mark of a fusion figure is the compounding of ordinarily disjoint or conflicting categories in an integral, spatio-temporally unified individual. On this view, many of the characters in possession stories are fusion figures. They may be inhabited by many demons—"I am legion"— or one. But as long as they are composite beings, locatable in an unbroken spatio-temporal continuum with a single identity, we shall count them as fusion figures.

Also, I tend to see the Frankenstein monster, especially as he is represented in the Universal Pictures' movie cycle, as a fusion figure. For not only is it emphasized that he is made from distinct bodies, along with electrical attachments, but the series presents him as if he had different brains imposed upon him—first a criminal's and later Igor's. In this, the films appear to uphold the unlikely hypothesis that somehow the monster has a kind of continuing identity—one that is perhaps innocent and benign—in spite of the brain it has. Obviously, this is, to say the least, paradoxical, but if we allow the fiction of brain transplants, why quibble about whether the monster is in some sense the still the same monster it would have been had it not had a criminal's or Igor's brain foisted upon it?

The fusion aspect of the Frankenstein monster becomes quite hysterical in Hammer Films' *And Frankenstein Created Woman*. Dr. Frankenstein transfers the soul of his dead assistant Hans into the body of Hans's dead, beloved Christina, and Hans, in Christina's body, seduces and dispatches the hooligans who had driven Christina (i.e., Christina unified in mind and body) to her death.

The fusion figure may find its prototype in the sort of symbolic structure that Freud called the *collective figure* or *condensation* with respect to dreams. Freud writes that one way

> . . . in which a 'collective figure' can be produced for the purposes of dream-condensation [is] by uniting the actual features of two or more people into a single dream-image. It was in this way that Dr. M. of my dream was constructed. He bore the name of Dr. M., he spoke and acted like him; but his physical characteristics and his malady belonged to someone else, namely to my

eldest brother. One single feature, his pale appearance, was doubly determined, since it was common to both of them in real life.

Dr. R. in my dream about my uncle with the yellow beard was a similar composite figure. But in his case the dream-image was constructued in yet another way. I did not combine the features of one person with those of another and in the process omit from the memory-picture certain features of each of them. What I did was to adopt the procedure by means of which Galton produced family portraits: namely by projecting two images onto a single plate, so that certain features common to both are emphasized, while those which fail to fit in with one another cancel one another out and are indistinct in the picture. In my dream about my uncle the fair beard emerged prominently from a face which belonged to two people and which was consequently blurred. . . ."[50]

For Freud, the condensatory or collective figure superimposes, in the manner of a photograph, two or more entities in one individual. Similarly, the fusion figure of art-horror is a composite figure, conflating distinct *types* of beings. In his discussion of condensation, Freud stresses that the fused elements have something in common. However, in art-horror what the combined elements have in common need not be salient—in T.E.D. Klein's "Nadelman's God," the horrific entity has literally been constructed from a hodgepodge of garbage. As in the associationist writings of the British Empiricists, the fantastic fusion beings of horror are colligations of ontologi-cally or biologically separate orders.[51] They are single figures in whom distinct and often clashing types of elements are superimposed or condensed, resulting in entities that are impure and repulsive.

Freud notes that the collective structures we find in the dream-work are not unlike " . . . the composite animals invented by the folk imagination of the Orient."[52] Presumably, Freud has in mind here figures like the winged lions of ancient Assyria. Other examples of this type of condensation-figure would include the gargoyles on medieval cathedrals, the demon-priest (part rodent, part man) in the central panel of Hieronymus Bosch's *Temptation of St. Anthony* triptych, the chickens with the heads of human babies in Goya's "Ya van desplumadoes" in *Los Caprichos,* and characters like The Thing (a.k.a. Ben Grimm)—literally a man of stone—in the Marvel comic book series *The Fantastic Four.*

Of course, in these examples, the elements that go into the condensation or fusion are visually perceptible. However, this is not necessary. One might condense different ontological orders such as the animate and inanimate—e.g., a haunted house—and here nothing that meets the naked eye signals the fusion. And, furthermore, whether any of the preceding examples shall count as *horrific* fusion depends upon whether or not, in the representational context in which they appear, the beings so concocted match the criteria of art-horror.

As a means of composing horrific beings, fusion hinges upon conflating, combining, or condensing distinct and/or opposed categorical elements in a spatio-temporally continuous monster. In contrast, another popular means for creating interstitial beings is *fission*. In fusion, categorically contradictory elements are fused or condensed or superimposed in one unified spatio-temporal being whose identity is homogeneous. But with fission, the contradictory elements are, so to speak, distributed over *different,* though metaphysically related, identities. The type of creatures that I have in mind here include *doppelgangers,* alter-egos, and werewolves.

Werewolves, for example, violate the categorical distinction between humans and wolves. In this case, the animal and the human inhabit the same body (understood as spatially locatable protoplasm); however, they do so at *different times.* The animal and the wolf identities are not temporally continuous, though presumably their protoplasm is numerically the same; at a given point in time (the rise of the full moon), the body, inhabited by the human, is turned over to the wolf. The human identity and the wolf identity are not fused, but, so to speak, they are sequenced. The human and the wolf are spatially continuous, occupying the same body, but the identity changes or alternates over time; the two identities—and the opposed categories they represent—do not overlap temporally in the same body. That protoplasm is heterogeneous in terms of accommodating different, mutually exclusive identities at different times.

The werewolf figure embodies a categorical contradiction between man and animal which it distributes over time. Of course, what is being said of werewolves here applies to shape changers of every variety. In Kipling's "Mark of the Beast," the victim is on his way to becoming a leopard, while in Machen's "The Novel of the Black Seal," the boy-idiot seems to be transmutating into a sea lion. One form of fission, then, *divides* the fantastic being into two or more (categorically distinct) identities that alternatively possess the body in question. Call this temporal fission.[53] Temporal fission can be distinguished from fusion in that the categories combined in the figure of the fantastic being are not temporally simultaneous; rather, they are split or broken or distributed over time.

A second mode of fission distributes the categorical conflict over space through the creation of doubles. Examples here include the portrait in Oscar Wilde's *Picture of Dorian Gray,* the dwarf in the cavalier's body in Mary Shelley's "Transformation," and the doppelgangers in movies like *The Student of Prague* and *Warning Shadows.* Structurally, what is involved in spatial fission is a process of *multiplication,* i.e., a character or set of characters is multiplied into one or more new facets, each standing for another aspect of the self, generally one that is either hidden, ignored, repressed, or denied by the character who has been cloned. These new facets generally contradict cultural ideals (usually morally charged ones) of normality. The alter-ego represents a normatively alien aspect of the self. Most of my examples so far employ some mechanism of reflection—a portrait, a mirror, shadows—as the pretext for doubling. But this sort of fission figure can appear without such devices.

In the movie *I Married A Monster From Outer Space*, a young bride begins to suspect that her new husband is not quite himself. Somehow he's different from the man she used to date. And, she's quite right. Her boyfriend was kidnapped by invaders from another planet on his way back from a bachelor party and he was replaced by an alien. This double,[54] however, initially lacks feelings—the essential characteristic of being human in fifties sci-fi films of this sort—and his bride intuits this. Thus, the categorical distinction between humanity and inhumanity—marked in terms of the possession versus the lack of feelings—is projected symbolically by splitting the boyfriend in two, with each corresponding entity standing for a categorically distinct order of being.

The basic story of *I Married A Monster From Outer Space*—its sci-fi elements aside—resembles a very specific paranoid delusion called the Capgras syndrome. The delusion involves the patient's belief that his or her parents, lovers, etc. have become minatory *doppelgangers*. This enables the patient to deny his fear or hatred of a loved one by splitting the loved one in half, creating a bad version (the invader) and a good one (the victim). The new relation of marriage in *I Married A Monster From Outer Space* appears to engender a conflict, perhaps over sexuality, in the wife that is expressed through the fission figure.[55] Just as condensation suggests a model for fusion figuration, splitting as a psychic trope of denial may be the root prototype for spatial fission in art-horror, organzing conflicts, categorical and thematic, through the multiplication of characters.

Fission, then, in horror occurs in two major forms—spatial fission and temporal fission. Temporal fission— which the split between Dr. Jekyll and Mr. Hyde exemplifies—*divides characters in time*—while spatial fission—for instance, the case of doppelgangers—*multiplies characters in space*. Here characters become symbols for categorically distinct or opposed elements. In the case of fusion, on the other hand, categorically distinct or opposed elements are conflated or colligated or condensed into a single, spatio-temporally continuous entity whose identity is stable. Both fission and fusion are symbolic structures that facilitate—in different ways—the linkage of distinct and/or opposed categories, thereby providing vehicles for projecting the themes of interstitiality, categorical contradictoriness, and impurity. The fantastic biologies of horrific monsters are, to a surprising extent, reducible to the symbolic structures of fusion and fission.

In order to make a horrific monster—in terms of the impurity requirement—it is enough to link distinct and/or opposed categories by fission or fusion. In terms of fusion, one can put claws on Rosemary's baby, the devil in Regan, or a fly's head on Vincent Price's body. By fission, discrete and/or contradictory categories can be connected by having different biological or ontological orders take turns inhabiting one body, or by populating the fiction with numerically different but otherwise identical bodies, each representing one of the opposed categories. In the most fundamental sense of fusion and fission, these structures are meant to apply to the organization of opposed cultural categories, generally of a deep biological or ontological sort: human/reptile, living/dead, etc. But it is also true that in much horror, especially that which is considered to be classic, the opposition of such cultural categories in the biology of the horrific creatures portend further oppositions, oppositions that might be thought of in terms of thematic conflicts or antinomies which, in turn, are generally deep-seated in the culture in which the fiction has been produced.

For example, the horrific creatures in Blackwood's celebrated "Ancient Sorceries" are were-cats. An entire French town goes feline, at night indulging all manner of unmentionable (and unmentioned) debaucheries in the presence of Satan. In terms of my model, these creatures are the product of temporal fission. But this division—between cat and human—heralds other oppositions in the context of the story. An Englishman (perhaps the reincarnation of a cat man from bygone days) visits the town and is gradually tempted to join the coven. The opposition of cat versus human plays into further oppositions—sensual versus staid, nondirective activity versus conscientious, female versus male, and maybe even French versus British. That is, the salient opposition of different elements at the categorical level of biology might be thought of as prefiguring a series of further thematic oppositions.

Another example along the same lines would be Val Lewton's film *Cat People*. Irena is a shape-changer whose divided self is not only categorically fissured but also represents the opposition of chaste love versus violent sexuality. In terms of fusion, the vampire in Sheridan Le Fanu's *Carmilla* may be a case in point; for the opposition between living and dead in the monster's make-up portends a further thematic conflict concerning lesbianism.[56]

The notions of fission and fusion are meant to apply strictly to the biological and ontological categorical ingredients that go into making monsters. So it is sufficient for a being to be part man and part snake for it to qualify as a horrific fusion figure, or for a woman to be a lady by day and a troll or gorgon by night in order for her to qualify as a horrific fission figure. However, it is frequently the case that the oppositional biologies of fantastic beings correlate to an oppositional thematics. This is generally the case with what are thought to be the better specimens of horror. As a result, much of the work of the critic of horror, as opposed to the theoretician of horror, will be to trace the thematic conflicts that appear in her objects of study. That the creatures are fission or fusion figures may be less interesting than what this dimension of categorical interstitiality prefigures at the thematic level.[57] However, for purposes of theoretically identifying the symbolic structures through which myriad monsters are made, the notions of fission and fusion are crucial.

Along with fission and fusion, another recurring symbolic structure for generating horrific monsters is the *magnification of entities* or beings already typically adjudged impure or disgusting within the culture. In the concluding paragraphs of M.R. James's "The Ash-Tree," the gardener looks into the hollow of a tree trunk, his face contorts "with an incredulous terror and loathing," and he cries out with a "dreadful voice" before fainting. What he has seen is a poisonous spider—spawned from a witch's body for the purposes of revenge—that is as big as a man's head.[58] The spider, already a phobic object in our culture, exceeds in horribleness not only because of its supernatural provenance and unearthly abilities but especially because of its increase in size beyond the normal.

Things that creep and crawl—and that tend to make our flesh creep and crawl—are prime candidates for the objects of art-horror; such creatures already disgust, and augmenting their scale increases their physical dangerousness. In Stephen King's "Jerusalem's Lot," a hellish creature is summoned by means of an unholy book.

> Calvin pushed me and I tottered, the church whirling before me, and fell to the floor. My head crashed against the edge of an upturned pew, and red fire filled my head—yet seemed to clear it.
>
> I groped for the sulphur matches I had brought.
>
> Subterranean thunder filled the place. Plaster fell. The rusted bell in the steeple pealed a choked devil's clarion in sympathetic vibration.
>
> My match flared. I touched it to the book just as the pulpit exploded upward in a rending explosion of wood. A huge black maw was discovered beneath; Cal tottered on the edge, his hands held out, his face distended in a wordless scream that I shall hear forever.
>
> And then there was a huge surge of gray, vibrating flesh. The smell became a nightmare tide. It was a huge outpouring of a viscid, pustulant jelly, a huge and awful form that seemed to skyrocket from the very bowels of the ground. And yet, with a sudden horrible comprehension which no man can have known, I perceived *that it was but one ring, one segment, of a monster worm that had existed eyeless for years in the chambered darkness beneath that abominated church!*
>
> The book flared alight in my hands, and the Thing seemed to scream soundlessly above me. Calvin was struck glancingly and flung the length of the church like a doll with a broken neck.

Monsters of the magnified phobia variety were quite popular in fifties's movies (undoubtedly, they were suggested by the first radiation experiments on seeds). Some examples include: *Them!, Tarantula, Attack of the Crab*

Monsters, The Deadly Mantis, Giant Gila Monster, Monster From Green Hell, Attack of the Giant Leeches, The Spider, Black Scorpion, The Fly, The Monster That Challenged The World, The Giant Spider Invasion, Mothra, The Return of the Fly, the humungus octopus in *It Came From Beneath The Sea,* the big crawlers in *Rodan,* the giant grasshoppers in *The Beginning of the End,* and the proportionately towering black widow in *The Incredible Shrinking Man,* among others. Insofar as detached body parts can elicit revulsion, we encounter the *Crawling Eye* attempting to conquer the world. More recently, giant ants have eaten Joan Collins in *Empire of the Ants* and outsized rats have surrounded Marjoe Gortner in *Food of the Gods.* Of course, one cannot magnify just anything and hope for a horrific creature; few seem to have been convinced by the monster rabbits in *Night of the Lepus.* What needs to be magnified are things that are already potentially disturbing and disgusting.[59]

For the purposes of art-horror, one may exploit the repelling aspect of existing creatures not only by magnifying them, but also by *massing* them. In Richard Lewis's novel *Devil's Coach Horse* armies of bloodthirsty beetles are on the rampage, while the identity of the monstrous masses in Guy Smith's *Killer Crabs* and Peter Tremayne's *Ants* requires no further comment. These swarms of crawling things, grouped for an ultimate showdown with humanity, are, of course, really fantastical beings, invested with strategic abilities, virtual invulnerability, a hankering for human flesh, and often mutated powers unknown to present-day biological science. Carl Stephenson's "Leiningen versus the Ants"—surely the *Moby Dick* of the insect genre—is based on the scientifically correct observation that certain types of ants forage in large co-ordinated collectives, but he imbues these ants with qualities and powers that experts of the day would have found unprecedented.[60] They are hunting people and horses—rather than other insects like spiders, cockroaches, and grasshoppers—and the story strongly suggests that they knock out Leiningen's weir *in order to* cross the channel. Saul Bass's movie *Phase IV* presents the army of ants as a superior intelligence while in *Kingdom of the Spiders* the invading tarantulas enwrap an entire town in their web for purposes of food storage; in *Kiss of the Tarantulas,* the spiders become hit-men. As with the case of magnification, with massification it is not the case that any kind of entity can be grouped into horrific hordes. It must be the sort of thing we are already prone to find repellent—a point made comically by *The Attack of the Killer Tomatoes* (and its sequel, *The Return of. . . .*). Massing mountains of already disgusting creatures, unified and guided by unfriendly purposes, generates art-horror by augmenting the threat posed by these antecedently phobic objects.

Fantastic biologies, linking different and opposed cultural categories, can be constructed by means of fission and fusion, while the horrific potential of already disgusting and phobic entities can be accentuated by means of magnification and massification. These are primary structures for the construction of horrific creatures. These structures pertain primarily to what might be thought of as the biologies of horrific monsters. However, another structure, not essentially connected to the biology of these creatures, warrants discussion in a review of the presentation of horrific beings, for though not a matter of biology, it is an important recurring strategy in the staging of monsters. This strategy might be called horrific metonymy.

   Often the horror of horrific creatures is not something that can be perceived by the naked eye or that comes through a description of the look of the monster. Frequently, in such cases, the horrific being is *surrounded* by objects that we antecedently take to be objects of disgust and/or phobia. In "The Spectre Bride," The Wandering Jew, a fusion figure, does not initially appear disgusting; however, the wedding is associated by contiguity with disgust:

[The Wandering Jew] "Poor girl, I am leading thee indeed to our nuptials; but the priest will be death, thy parents the mouldering skeletons that rot in heaps around; and the witnesses [of] our union, the lazy worms that revel on the carious bones of the dead. Come, my young bride, the priest is impatient for his victim." As they proceeded, a dim blue light moved swiftly before them, and displayed at the extremity of the churchyard the portals of a vault. It was open, and they entered it in silence. The hollow wind came rushing through the gloomy abode of the dead; and on every side were the mouldering remnants of coffins, which dropped piece by piece upon the damp earth. Every step they took was on a dead body; and the bleached bones rattled horribly beneath their feet. In the centre of the vault rose a heap of unburied skeletons, whereon was seated a figure too awful even for the darkest imagination to conceive. As they approached it, the hollow vault rung with a hellish peal of laughter; and every mouldering corpse seemed endued with unearthly life.

Here, though the horrific bridegroom himself doesn't elicit disgust perceptually, everything that surrounds him and his hellish ministrations is impure by the lights of the culture. In a similar vein, Dracula, both in literature and on stage and screen, is associated with vermin; in the novel, he commands armies of rats. And undoubtedly, the association of horrific beings with disease and contamination is related to the tendency to surround horrific beings with further impurities.

In Clive Barker's *The Damnation Game*—a sort of update of *Melmoth the Wanderer*—the Mephistophelian character Mamoulian is ostensibly normal-looking but his associated minion, the Razor-Eater is a hulking zombie undergoing graphically described putrefaction throughout the novel, a feature made more unsettling by his always messy indulging of his sweet tooth. Likewise, the child possessed by the spirit of Beth in John Saul's *Suffer the Children,* though not outwardly disgusting herself, is surrounded by stomach-turning ceremonies such as a make-believe tea party attended by blood-splattered children, the skeleton of Beth, and a decapitated cat in a doll's outfit whose head keeps rolling off its shoulders. With Mamoulian and Beth the fantastic being is not perceptually repulsive but is linked by metonymy to perceptually disgusting things. Of course, even those creatures like Dracula though they may not, in the main, be portrayed as *perceptually* loathsome, are nevertheless still disgusting and impure; one doesn't require perceptually detectable grotesquerie in order to be reviling. Dracula strikes Harker as sickening though his appearance is not literally monstrous. In such cases, the association of such impure creatures with perceptually pronounced gore or other disgusting trappings is a means of underscoring the repulsive nature of the being.

In James Herbert's novel *The Magic Cottage,* the villainous magus Mycroft is a stately, altogether human figure who has at his disposal agencies marked by incredible noxiousness. In the final confrontation with the narrator, he summons them: the "carpet was ripping explosively all around me, and sluglike monsters oozed over the edges in shiny slimes. Hands that were scabbed and dripping pus clawed at the frayed carpet in an effort to drag the rest of their life forms out into the open. Those membranes, full of wriggling life, quivered their snouts in the air before curling over the edge. Wispy black smoke tendrils drifted up in lazy spirals, and these were full of diseased microorganisms, the corrupting evil that roamed the depths, subversives that searched for ways to surface, intent on finding exposure, definition—*actuality*. These were the infiltrating substances of evil."

Horrific metonymy need not be restricted to cases where the monsters do not look gruesome; an already misshapen creature can be associated with entities already antecedently thought of in terms of impurity and filth. Think of Murnau's *Nosferatu* and the remake by Werner Herzog, where the vampire is linked to unclean, crawling things. Similarly, zombies with great gobs of phlegm dangling from their lips exemplify horrific metonymy.

Fusion, fission, magnification, massification and horrific metonymy are the major tropes for presenting the monsters of art-horror.[61] Fusion and fission are means for constructing horrific biologies; magnification and massification are means for augmenting the powers of already disgusting and phobic creatures. Horrific metonymy is a means of emphasizing the impure and disgusting nature of the creature—from the outside, so to speak—by associating said being with objects and entities that are already reviled: body parts, vermin, skeletons, and all manner of filth. The horrific creature is essentially a compound of danger and disgust and each of these structures provides a means of developing these attributes in tandem.

Summary and Conclusion

Throughout the first part of this study, I have attempted to characterize the nature of the genre of horror. I have presumed that the genre of horror can be defined in terms of the emotion that such works are designed to elicit from audiences. That is, works of horror are those designed to function in such a way as to promote art-horror in audiences. Consequently, in order to fully identify the criteria for being a work of horror, one needs to characterize the emotion of art horror.

In this respect, I have noted that the emotional responses of the positive human characters to the monsters in their fictional worlds are particularly instructive. For, ideally, it would appear that the readers and viewers of horror fictions are supposed to parallel, roughly and in certain respects, the emotions of the human protagonists in the fiction, or, to say it slightly differently, we are supposed to share certain elements of the emotive responses to said monsters with the positive human characters in the relevant fictions. Specifically, we share with characters the emotive evaluations of monsters as fearsome and impure—as dangerous and repulsive—and this causes the relevant sensations in us. Unlike the characters in such fictions, we do not believe that the monsters exist; our fear and disgust is rather a response to the thought of such monsters. But our evaluative states do track those of the characters.

I hypothesized that the emotion of art-horror quintessentially involves a combination of fear and repulsion with respect to the thought of monsters like Dracula such that these cognitive states generate some sort of physical agitation, which might be as overt as tremblings and stomach churnings or as muted as tingling sensations or a heightened physical sense of apprehension, alertness, or foreboding. As will be argued in the next chapter, these can be elicited by the thought of such creatures and do not require beliefs in the existence of such creatures. The audience's psychological state, therefore, diverges from the psychological state of characters in respect of belief, but converges on that of characters with respect to the way in which the properties of said monsters are emotively assessed.

The argument for these results can be neatly summarized by recalling that virtually the same monster—in terms of its appearance—can figure in both a work of horror and a fairy tale. Gordon Browne's illustration of the Beast for Laura E. Richards's 1886 retelling of "Beauty and the Beast" could certainly work quite nicely as a graphic for Stephen King's *Cycle of the Werewolf,* just as Berni Wrightson's vision of the werewolf in that book would be a serviceable image of the Beast for most versions of the fairy tale.[62]

Indeed, one could conceive of the image of one monster type that could function both as both a fairy-tale beast and a horrific werewolf. In the language of Arthur Danto, we could imagine a fairy-tale beast that was indiscernible, to the naked eye, from a horrific werewolf.[63] And yet there is a difference between the reactions of the audience with respect to these two sorts of fiction. My project, then, is to derive the best explanation of the acknowledged difference between such a set of perceptually indiscernible and yet different creatures, which, in turn, will mark a distinction between the genres that they inhabit.

Here, it has often been observed that a crucial difference between fairy-tale monsters and horrific monsters concerns the ways in which the characters of these different respective genres react to them. Both Beauty and her father are scared by the Beast; but they do not react to him as if he were unnatural—that is, as if he were a violation of nature or an impure creature. He is, rather, a marvelous or fantastic entity in a world of the marvelous and the fantastic. He is not a cosmological or metaphysical category mistake. The universe of the fairy tale accommodates such creatures as the Beast as part and parcel of nature. He's frightening for being a largish, animal-type being with a foul temper. But he is not a violation of nature. And this is signaled by the way characters like Beauty and her father react to him.

Indeed, my claim in this case, that character response is generally decisive, is also supported by the fact that as Beauty's attitude to the Beast alters and becomes affectionate, the reader's fear with respect to the Beast diminishes proportionately. (This can also be observed in relation to Jean Cocteau's film *Beauty and the Beast* and in relation to the TV series of the same name[64].)

However, when one turns from a fairy tale like Madame de Beaumont's rendition of "Beauty and the Beast" to paradigmatic cases of horror, such as the Frankenstein monster, Dracula, Mr. Hyde, Lovecraft's Old Ones, and so on, the reaction of the human characters to such monsters changes. The monsters are regarded to be violations of nature, and abnormal, and this is made clear in the reactions of protagonists. They not only fear such monsters; they find them repellent, loathsome, disgusting, repulsive and impure. They are unnatural in the sense that they are metaphysical misfits, and, in consequence, they elicit disgust from fictional characters, and, in turn, they are supposed to elicit a congruent response from the audience.

I have tried to support my characterization of the reaction of characters to horrific monsters by developing this thesis through a consideration of many of the paradigmatic authors and stories of the horror genre. I have proceeded under the conviction that there is already a strong consensus about the central cases of horror, and we have shown, I think, that my characterization fits them. Many examples have also been chosen from less famous and perhaps even obscure entries in the field, in order to suggest the wide range across which this formula for horror recurs. In my own case, I found these examples and myriad others like them by reading and viewing broadly and randomly in the genre. The frequency with which the characterization based on the better-known works of horror was repeated in subaltern efforts was quite staggering. I wager that where other scholars randomly peruse the field, the confirming evidence will continue to mount.

In evolving the preceding characterization of the nature of the genre of horror, I have presupposed that the genre emerges around the middle of the eighteenth century. In this, I have I believe, accepted the prevailing view among literary historians of the matter, which sees the genre as a product of the English Gothic novel and the German *Schauer-roman* (shudder novel).[65] The issue of which novel is the first horror novel or the first Gothic novel can be argued and may well be undecidable. One candidate might be Horace Walpole's *The Castle of Otranto* (1764); however, it may be claimed that its tone, like that of William Beckford's *Vathek,* is not quite right. Nevertheless, there does at least seem to be consensus that the genre coalesced by the end of the eighteenth century.

If this is the case—and I will assume that it is on the basis of the authorities—the question naturally arises as to why the genre should emerge when it does. In this respect, it is useful to recall that the emergence of the horror genre—especially in the form of the Gothic novel—overlaps with the period that cultural historians call the "Enlightenment" or "The Age of Reason." This period is thought to span the eighteenth century and it is marked by the dissemination of the ideas of a narrow group of seventeenth-century thinkers—such as Descartes, Bacon, Locke, Hobbes, and Newton—to a relatively broad, reading public.

In general, it seems fair to presume that the reading public did not directly assimilate their knowledge of these seventeenth-century thinkers from original sources but learned of them through the work of people whom Crane Brinton describes as "what we should now call 'popularizers'—journalists, men of letters, the bright young talkers of the *salons.*"[66] Well-known figures of this sort include Voltaire, Diderot, Condorcet, Holbach, and Beccaria. The spirit of the Enlightenment rested on the immense achievements of natural science—with Newton standing out as an especial hero—and the philosophical attempts to create the framework of a unified science in the seventeenth century.

Reason was elevated as the major faculty and whatever hindered its flourishing was denounced. Religion was a special object of distrust because it valued faith and revelation over reason. The critical and skeptical attitude toward religion could escalate into atheism. Diderot has the figure of Nature address man in the following way:

> In vain, O slave of superstition, do you seek your happiness beyond the limits of the world in which I have placed you? Have the courage to free yourself from the yoke of religion, my haughty rival, which does not recognize my prerogatives. Cast out the Gods who have usurped my power, and return to my laws. Return to nature from which you have fled; she will console you and dispel all those fears which now oppress you. Submit to nature, to humanity, and to yourself again; and you will find flowers strewn all along the pathway of your life.[67]

Nature, here, of course, is the mechanical nature of the Newtonian system. And though a great deal of Enlightenment thought was not irreligious, a major tendency of the period was an opposition to superstition. The Enlightenment was inclined to view all aspects of the world as susceptible of scientific analysis; and, in this respect, the supernatural was regarded as a figment of the imagination.[68]

It is against this intellectual background that the horror novel emerges as a genre. Thus, it is tempting to speculate that there may be some relation between the horror genre and the pervasiveness of Enlightenment world view. Several hypotheses can be suggested about the historical correlation of these two phenomena. For example, it may be thought that the horror novel represents something like the underside of the Enlightenment. Where the Enlightenment valorizes reason, the horror novel explores emotions, indeed particularly violent ones from the point of view of fictional characters. This contrast, furthermore, might be amplified by associating the Enlightenment with objectivity and the horror novel with subjectivity.[69]

And where the Enlightenment convert strives for a naturalistic conception of the world, the horror novel presumes, for the purposes of fiction, the existence of the supernatural. Moreover, it might be said that in opposition to the Enlightenment's faith in progress, the horror novel indulges regression. Or, at the very least, the horror novel might be seen as a sphere in which superstitious beliefs are provided with a residual and ghettoized forum of expression. The horror novel, along with poems like Goethe's "The Erl King," that is, might be seen as the return of the Enlightenment's repressed.[70] Here, the horror novel can be thought of in several different ways: it might be construed as compensating for that which the Enlightenment suspects, operating like a kind of safety valve; or it might be conceived of as a kind of explosion of that which is denied.

However, provocative as these notions are, they may be very difficult to confirm. For if the relation of the horror novel to the Enlightenment is initially one of conflict, one wonders about whom the subjects who suffer this conflict are. Does the conflict rage in the soul of the readers of horror? But, then, do we know that the readers of horror were also converts to the Enlightenment world view? Indeed, isn't it more likely that most of the readers of horror were ordinary Christians rather than Enlightenment pundits? Or, perhaps we should think in terms of two groups of different and opposed readers such that the horror fans are driven to their novels by Enlightenment propaganda. But, again, the likelihood that horror readers were so persecuted by Enlightenment thinking is at least suspect, and, in any case, it would be exceedingly difficult to confirm. Of course, one might try to locate the conflict not in individuals but in the culture at large. Yet, this may be too anthropomorphic a view of society, while, at the same time, it needs quite a bit of spelling out. That is, how, except through the experience of individuals, would such a conflict be staged?

None of these worries conclusively defeats the preceding hypotheses about the relation of the horror genre to the Enlightenment. Instead, they represent requests for further research and conceptual clarification. I am not urging that these hypotheses be dismissed, but only that they be developed. They are tantalizing suggestions which are too conjectural to be endorsed at present.

However, there may be a connection between the horror novel and the Enlightenment that can be based on conceptual considerations rather than empirical ones. Throughout my discussion so far, I have stressed that the emotion of art-horror involves a notion of nature that the monster—upon whom the emotion is focussed—violates. Monsters are supernatural, or, if they are confected out of science fiction fancy, they at least defy nature as we know it. Horrific monsters, that is, embody the notion of a violation of nature. But to have a violation of nature, one needs a conception of nature—one that relegates the beings in question to the realm of the non-natural. And, in this respect, one might want to suggest that the Enlightenment supplied the horror novel with the norm of nature needed to produce the right kind of monster.

That is, where a reader operates with a cosmology in which witches, demons, werewolves, and spectral forces are part of reality, albeit a fearsome part, the sense of natural violation that attends art-horror is unavailable. The scientific world view of the Enlightenment, however, supplies a norm of nature that affords the conceptual space necessary for the supernatural, even if it also regards that space as one of superstition.

One would not wish to claim that the readers and writers of Gothics specifically and horror generally were uniformly believers in the Enlightenment. Nevertheless, the Enlightenment perspective on that which scientific reality encompasses and on what counts as superstitition was widely abroad. Readers and writers at the turn of the eighteenth century probably did not have a working view of science, nor did they necessarily accept everything that science proclaimed. However, like readers today, who are generally not on top of recent scientific breakthroughs, they probably had enough of a glimmering of that viewpoint to be able to identify, in the extremely broad way that art-horror assumes, that which science counts as a superstitious belief, especially in terms of a violation of nature.

One hypothesis, then, about the correlation of the Enlightenment and the emergence of the horror genre is that the genre presupposed something like an Enlightenment view of scientific reality in order to generate the requisite sense of a violation of nature. That is, the Enlightenment made available the kind of conception of nature or the kind of cosmology needed to create a sense of horror. It need not be supposed that the reading public accepted the totality of Enlightenment science, but only that they had an operational sense of what that conception regarded as outside the realm of nature. Nor is it presumed that readers agreed with this viewpoint, but only that for the purposes of entertaining a fiction, they could recognize and use its perspective on the boundaries of nature.[71]

Of course, this hypothesis might be susceptible to the kind of reservations discussed in terms of the return-of-the-Enlightenment's-repressed hypothesis. That is, it may be shown that the Enlightenment conception was not as broadly familiar to the reading public as we assume. My own hunch is that it is not problematic to believe that the view of nature proselytized by the Enlightenment was widely known, even if it was not embraced by the majority of the reading public. However, should this line of conjecture prove historically unsupportable, the upshot for this theory of the nature of art-horror is not devastating. It would only refute these thoughts about the origin of the genre of horror in the eighteenth century. It would not contest the characterization of the nature of that genre.

2

Metaphysics and Horror, or Relating to Fictions

In this chapter I will be concerned with exploring the relation between audiences and horror fictions. These relations require philosophical elucidation for, on the face of it, they involve what would appear to be curious interactions between actual readers/spectators, and nonexistent beings—that is, monsters as well as fictional protagonists. For example, we want to know how it is that we can be horrified by fictions—by beings and events that, in some sense, do not exist and which we must know do not exist, if we are to be art-horrified. In order to deal with these problems, we will finally have to say something about the ontological status of fictional beings which, I believe, will enable us to clarify the way in which nonexistent fictions can affect actual audiences—i.e., can move them to horror.

Most of this chapter will consider—under the subtitle of "Fearing Fictions"—a discussion of the way fictional monsters can excite real emotions in readers and spectators. The problem here is that many find such responses to fiction paradoxical. For if we know that there are no such things as monsters, many conclude that it follows that there is something mysterious about our being horrified by them. Indeed, this is but an instance of a putatively larger problem—call it the paradox of fiction—which causes us to wonder whether and how it is possible for us to respond with genuine emotion to that which we must know is not the case. I will attempt to dissolve the paradox of fiction by explaining why there is nothing amiss in responding with genuine emotion to fictional entities including monsters.

But, of course, in consuming horror fictions we are not only involved in relations with horrific beings; we are also in relations with fictional protagonists. In this context, one wonders whether there is something special about our relation to the protagonists in horror fictions. Do we, for example, *identify* with these characters—is our fear of monsters their fear of monsters?—or is the relation one other than identification? Thus, I will conclude this chapter with a discussion of the notion of character-identification. I will both criticize the notion of character-identification and attempt to offer alternative ways of thinking of our relations to the fictional protagonists in horror stories.

Fearing Fictions: On the Paradox Thereof and its Solution

Though in some sense the monsters of horrific fictions do not exist, they would appear to have causal consequences in the actual world—they art-horrify audiences. So one issue before us is to explain how it is that fictions can have impact on the actual world. This issue is further complicated by quandaries derived from the philosophy of mind. For the nonexistence of horrific creatures is, so to speak, not only a fact, but it would also appear to be a fact that is readily available to and acknowledged by the consumers of horrific fictions. However, audiences do appear to be frightened by horror fictions; indeed, they would seem to seek out such fictions, at least in part, either in order to be frightened by them or with the knowledge and assent that they are likely to be frightened by them. But how can one be frightened by what one knows does not exist?

For example, we think that the way to quiet an upset child is to reassure her that there are no such things as ghosts; that, it is believed, is the best way to remove the fear of specters. Yet horror audiences standardly start with this conviction. So how is it that they can be frightened by fictional monsters—monsters they know do not exist?

The problems here are at least twofold. There is the need for a metaphysical account of the way it is possible for fictions—i.e., in some sense *what is not*—to have an effect upon what is. Secondly, this relationship has to be solved in such a way that it deals with what, by consensus, appears to be paradoxical: that this causal relation, resulting in art-horror on the part of actual audiences, transpires in the face of the fact that actual audiences do not believe that monsters exist.

This second problem—which, after the example of Kendall Walton,[1] we can call *fearing fictions*—is, of course, really an instance of a broader philosophical problem, which may be dubbed the paradox of fiction. It can be encapsulated by the question: "How can we be moved by fictions?" For the purposes of this book, we need to explain how we can fear and be disgusted by fictional monsters. But the answer to this question is of a piece with the answers to questions such as "How can we grieve for King Lear?," "How does the plight of Oedipus move us to pity and fear?," "How does K., in the novel *The Trial*, elicit feelings of anguish and frustration from us?," and "Why does Eliot's Casaubon make us feel indignant?"

For starters, we might wonder whether there is really a problem here.

After all, it would seem to be a fact of human nature that we are emotionally moved by the personalities and situations of other people. All things being equal, we grieve for those on whom misfortune befalls, and we are indignant in the face of injustice. This is just a fact of life. So why is there anything mysterious about our reacting to fictional characters in the same way?

But consider a thought experiment. Imagine that a friend tells you that her sister, a brilliant scientist, has contracted an exotic disease that will kill her within the month. Also, her children, equally brilliant, not to mention well-behaved and full of promise, will be consigned to the care of a cruel and miserly uncle. Undoubtedly, he will put them on a diet of gruel, work the very heart out of them, and discontinue their ballet classes. As catastrophe compounds catastrophe, your consternation mounts. But now imagine that, as soon as you signal an emotional reaction, the friend tells you that she made the whole thing up. She has no sister, there are no children, and there is no gruel. Presumably, the emotion that had been building up dissipates, perhaps to be replaced by another—maybe anger about being gulled. Or, to take another example, what would happen to one's outrage about the circumstances of starving Ethiopians were one to learn that the entire coverage of the matter were a media fabrication? We might be vexed by the journalistic manipulation, but we could no longer be moved by the victims of starvation, were we to realize there are no such victims.[2]

What these thought experiments putatively indicate is that there is a necessary bond between our beliefs and our emotions. In order to have the relevant emotion—whether of grief or of indignation—we must have beliefs about the way circumstances lie, including beliefs that the agents entangled in those circumstances exist. Without the beliefs that there are Ethiopians and that they are starving, we cannot muster the emotion of outrage with respect to contemporary descriptions of them.

The necessity of such beliefs for such emotional responses is also supported by certain commonplace facts concerning what it takes to extinguish emotions. Where we learn that a story has been made up, our sympathies evaporate. Where we wish to persuade an acquaintance that his emotion is irrational, we try to show that the beliefs it is grounded upon are false, or at least misconceived (the latter perhaps being key to psychoanalytic therapy). That is, variations in beliefs seem to correlate with variations in the associated emotions. Moreover, this hypothesis would also seem to derive support from the sort of theory of the emotions I introduced in the last chapter. For, insofar as specifiable cognitive elements—most easily construed as beliefs—are essentially constitutive of the identity of a given emotion, then where the beliefs fail to obtain, the emotion fails to appear.

However, if beliefs of a certain sort are essential to emotional responses, then it becomes difficult to explain how we can have emotional responses to fiction. For it is a presupposition of the institution of fiction that the events and characters in such things as novels do not exist. There never was a Frankenstein monster, and every normal, informed reader knows (and therefore believes) that. Furthermore, in fictions that sport reference to the actual world—as *For Whom The Bell Tolls* does to the Spanish Civil War—the actual events and persons mentioned are subsidiary in the manner of their articulation to the story of the fictional characters and their adventures. To a degree, that is, they become "fictionalized" through their association with made-up characters and events. And this, too, is something of which normal, informed readers are aware.

But we have hit a snag or, at least, an apparent paradox. For on the one hand, our knowledge of the institution of fiction tells us that normal, informed readers do not believe that the characters and circumstances in fictions exist. Yet in order to have emotional responses to the characters in such stories, we would—on the model of our thought experiments—require beliefs that the victims over whose plights we exercise ourselves actually exist. One might, in the fashion of some theorists (to be discussed below), attempt to say that we do not, in fact, really respond emotionally to fictions and their inhabitants. But that, at least initially, doesn't seem to square with the facts. Prima facie, we do seem to respond emotionally to fiction. But how can this be rendered consistent with the preceding presuppositions: that emotional responses require our beliefs in the existence of the persons and events that comprise the objects of said emotions *and* that when it comes to fiction we know (and believe) that the characters and events involved do not exist?

Another way to approach this issue is to ask plainly how it is that our emotions dissipate when we learn that someone is telling us a cock-and-bull story, whereas our emotions don't seem to abate in the face of "official" fictions. What difference, in principle, is there between the sort of fabrications imagined earlier and a fiction? In both cases, the yarn is made up. So why should realizing that one sort of tale is concocted undercut our emotional responses, while, with the other sort of story, say *Crime and Punishment,* that it is a fiction in nowise deters an emotional response? In one case, we learn that the cock-and-bull story is a fiction after the fact, but why should that make a difference? Indeed, exactly the same story might be told as a fabrication or as marked as a fiction. And the former will, presumably, ill support emotional responses while the latter engenders them. How, it might be asked, is such variation in our apparent behavior or reaction consistent?

So, our emotional responses to fictions would appear to entail that we believe that fictional characters exist, while it is also simultaneously presupposed that normal, informed consumers of fiction do not believe fictional characters exist. Clearly, one way to attempt to explain this in a manner that removes the contradiction is to reject the premise that consumers of fiction do not believe in the existence of fictional characters. This might be called the illusion theory of fiction.

The Illusion Theory of Fiction

According to the illusion theory of fiction, when we are horrified by the manifestation of Mr. Hyde onstage, we believe that we are in the presence of a monster. Theatrical, or alternatively, cinematic techniques of verisimilitude so overwhelm us that we are deceived into believing that a monster really looms before us. Thus, in this view, it is not the case that normal, informed viewers do not believe that the relevant fictional entity does not exist. Via the illusions of the stage and screen, we are deceived into believing that Hyde confronts us. This maneuver will remove our contradiction, but at the cost of making us, if only for the course of the fiction, superstitious; that is, believers in vampires, alien invaders, or whatever other preternatural creatures are illusionistically contrived.

However, there are many well-known problems with illusion theories of this sort. First, such theories badly accord with what can be observed of the viewers of horror fictions. That is, if one really believed that the theater were beset by lethal shape changers, demons, intergalactic cannibals, or toxic zombies, one would hardly sit by for long. One would probably attempt to flee, to hide, to protect oneself, or to contact the proper authorities (the police, NASA, the bishop, the United Nations, the Department of Sanitation). People, that is, just don't behave as though they really believed there were monsters in the vicinity when they consume horror spectacles. Postulating this kind of belief may exonerate them from charges of inconsistency, but at the expense of making their behavior inexplicably complacent, if not downright self-destructive and dumb.

Moreover, though the illusion theory may seem to be applicable to visual fictions—plays and films, for example—it is less easy to apply it to literary fictions. What precisely is the illusion that overtakes us when we read that the child Regan is possessed in Georgetown? Do we think, as we read, that a little girl is swearing in backwards English at some D.C. priest? But that wouldn't be so scary if we're reading *The Exorcist* in Kansas City, would it? When the notion of an illusion is applied to drama and cinema, it affords a more reliable source of fear, for it proposes that we believe that the monster is actually within striking distance. But that kind of illusion, if it is to be the source of horror, does not mesh readily with the experience of reading. Indeed, illusion-talk probably is best applied to visual phenomena. Thus, in order to extend the illusion theory to literature, one would have to develop a model of literary illusion that would accommodate the experience and behavior of readers. To my knowledge no one has done that, nor does it seem an encouraging line of speculation.

Of course, an even deeper objection to illusion theories of audience response is that the kind of illusions postulated are such that they would wreck the very possibility of our appreciating fictions in general and horror fictions in particular. That is, if when reading or viewing fictions we came to be convinced, albeit by deception, that werewolves really existed in our vicinity, it would be difficult to continue to savor the story. One would want to take some practical measures to secure one's life and loved ones. A very condition of there being an institution of fiction from which we derive entertainment and pleasure is that we know that the persons and events are not actual. Obviously, in the case of horror, we could not be secure in our enjoyment of the spectacle if we believed in its reality. Were the illusion theory true, horror would be too unnerving for all save heroes, consummate masochists, and professional vampire killers. The illusion theory is simply at odds with the presuppositions of the institution of fiction (which some theorists might try to characterize by means of metaphors of distance) that make the appreciation of fiction possible.

One might attempt to save the illusion theory by replacing the notion that we are deceived by fictions with the notions that the techniques of fiction simply make us momentarily forgetful of our knowledge that neither Huck Finn nor Dracula exists. However, couching the theory in terms of forgetfulness rather than deception faces the same problems. A person forgetful of nonexistence of vampires should still behave more prudently than normal horror audiences do, while, at the same time, for however long we forget that Dracula isn't really in the theater, it is still true that we cannot really enjoy his deadly strategems.

At this point in the dialectic—if one is committed to removing that wing of our contradiction which says we disbelieve in the existence of fictional beings such as Dracula—we might attempt to come up with a psychological account of how our knowledge that Dracula does not exist is effectively neutralized while we watch fictions, thus allowing us to respond to him as though we believed him to be real. That is, we might try to argue that by virtue of some sort of psychological operation our knowledge that Dracula does not exist is somehow thrown out of gear in a way that enables or permits us to respond to depictions and descriptions of him with emotional conviction, i.e., as if we believed Dracula lived. A familiar term of art in this context is "the willing suspension of disbelief."

This notion is attributed to Coleridge who, in his *Biographia Literaria*, notes that it is an effect he aimed at in his projected portion of the "Lyrical Ballads,"

> . . . in which it was agreed, that my endeavors should be directed to persons and characters supernatural, or at least romantic; yet so as to transfer from our inward nature a human interest and semblance of truth sufficient to procure for

these shadows of imagination that willing suspension of disbelief for the moment, which constitutes poetic faith.[3]

Interestingly, for our purposes, Coleridge introduces the idea within the context of supernatural fictions. Moreover, it seems to be an expansion of an illusion theory of fictional response. For Coleridge notes that the planned "incidents and agents were to be, in part at least supernatural; and the excellence aimed at was to consist in the interesting of the affections by the dramatic truth of such emotions, as would naturally accompany such situations, supposing them to be real."[4] However, the state the reader is characterized as entering is somewhat different from those of illusion, deception, or mere forgetfulness. For states like illusion and forgetfulness suggest passivity and a lack of self-consciousness on the part of the audience.

The victim of an illusion has had something done to her; she has been caught unawares; she is deceived, which requires that she be not conscious of what is going on. On the other hand, forgetfulness is something that happens to one; I cannot be forgetful while simultaneously aware of what I have forgotten. But the idea of a "*willing* suspension of disbelief" has an active air about it. It sounds like something that one does to oneself and about which one is conscious. Putatively it has the net result that, for the duration of the suspension of disbelief, the reader takes the events and agents of the fiction to be real.

Coleridge is not particularly forthcoming about the way in which the suspension of disbelief is thought to work. It would seem that the disbelief to be suspended is, for our purposes, a belief such as "The Creature from the Black Lagoon does not exist." It is called a "disbelief" in the sense that it is a negative belief. By suspending such beliefs, whatever would stand in the way of our emotional response to—our horror at—the Creature is put on hold. This enables us to suppose the Creature to be real, thereby inviting emotional engagement. This process is under the direction of the will; we voluntarily opt to give up our conviction that the Creature does not exist, allowing an emotional response that presumes it, the Creature, does exist.

If this interpretation of the "willing suspension of disbelief," is accurate, then the idea has little to recommend it. At the very least, it seems to postulate an act of will on the reader's part that few, if any, can recall. Of course, if it is said that this activity is subconscious, then one wonders whether it should be identified as an act of will (a *willing* suspension) at all. Moreover, if it is said that we do not recall this action because it is repressed and/or unconscious, then it is even more unlikely that it is an act of volition.

Also, the idea of a willing suspension of disbelief—insofar as disbelief is just negative belief—seems to entail that it is possible for one to will what one believes. But, pace Descartes,[5] belief is not something that is under our control. We cannot will our beliefs. Just try. Take a proposition say—

"5+7=1492"; now try to will yourself into believing it. It can't be done. You might say that the problem here is that you know this proposition is false.[6] But try to will belief in a proposition—perhaps "There are lilacs in other galaxies"—of whose truth or falsity you hold no view. You can certainly entertain this proposition; you can understand it. But can you will yourself to believe it? Belief is not something that we add, by an act of will, to propositions we understand. Rather, belief is something that happens to us. Insofar as the notion of the willing suspension of disbelief implies we can directly control what we believe, the notion itself seems unbelievable.

But maybe it will be urged that this objection rides too much on the idea of willing a belief, whereas what is being willed is first and foremost a *suspension* of a belief. So when we are reading a horror fiction, we are not willing the belief that the Smog Monster is real, but only suspending the belief that the Smog monster is not real. Is this plausible?

In everyday life, on occasion, we come to suspend some of our beliefs. Many raised in the racist society of fifties' America believed that nonwhites were somehow inferior.[7] And, prior to the moment when we changed this belief, coming to recognize the equality of the races, the belief was already embattled. At a certain point in the evolution of our thinking, that is, many came to suspend the belief in white superiority as a stage prior to giving it up entirely. A condition, however, for suspending our belief in this matter was that the belief was being undermined. Our conviction had been shaken. Evidence and argument was piling up against it.

Moreover, the case is the same with philosophical issues. When Descartes encourages us to suspend our beliefs about the existence of the external world, he does so by undermining our certainty about such convictions by considerations such as that of the evil genius.[8] That is, before we can suspend a belief, we must have grounds to at least suspect that it is false.

But turning from these more or less straightforward cases of suspending beliefs to the case of the reception of fiction, one is struck by glaring disanalogies. Outside the context of fiction, beliefs must somehow be under fire before they are suspended. They are suspended because contesting considerations lead us to waver in regard to them. But our beliefs—that *Dracula* is a novel and that the Count does not exist—do not waver as we read. There is no evidence to undermine or contest these beliefs. They are not challenged such that we think we might have either to revise or reject them. The situation is radically unlike those in which garden-variety suspensions of belief occur. Therefore, there is little reason to assimilate our reception of fiction to the ordinary notion of suspending belief. And for those who maintain that there is some special or extraordinary, yet plausible, notion here to be explored, the burden of proof is on them to produce it.

With the issue of the suspension of belief, there may be a way in which it might be argued that it is, to a limited extent, under our control. We cannot simply will beliefs that would serve to contradict and thereby undermine the beliefs to be suspended. But we can put ourselves in certain situations in which we can predict that our standing beliefs will be challenged. A racist, perhaps one morally concerned to put his views to the test, can attend anthropology classes, a fundamentalist can attend lectures on evolution, and a believer that the earth is flat can visit observatories and talk to astronomers. That is, one can put oneself in contexts where evidence and argument that are likely to challenge and undermine one's beliefs abound, just as one can sedulously avoid such contexts if one wishes to sustain one's beliefs unscathed. However, this measured admission of the restricted degree to which the suspension of belief can be voluntarily guided offers no support to those who would wish to apply the notion to fictions. For we do not seek out the sort of contestations of our belief that Dracula does not exist in order to suspend it. Not only is there nothing to be found to undermine it; so there is nowhere to look for countervailing opinions. Moreover, even if there were countervailing opinions, we don't search for them while indulging our fictions. And, in any case, I submit we never actually give up our conviction that Dracula is a fiction.

Furthermore, in fact, it does not even seem that the notion of the willing suspension of disbelief really does the work that its proponent might intend for it. We began to consider it as a means of dispelling the contradiction that the reader—as an informed participant in the cultural practice of fiction—believes that the Golem does not exist, while the self-same reader—in being horrified by the Golem—shows, given the required conditions for emotional response, that she believes that the Golem exists. Supposedly, by suspending disbelief—i.e., the belief that the Golem does not exist—the contradiction is averted. But is it? For how will we know to suspend our disbelief unless we realize that the work before us is a fiction? That is, supposing that we can will to suspend disbelief in some special way that is appropriate to fiction, we will still have to know and to believe we are confronting a fiction—a concatenation of persons and events that do not exist—in order for us to correctly mobilize any processes of psychological suspension. So the notion of the suspension of disbelief does not get rid of the belief that the Golem does not exist; that belief is required in order to will the suspension of disbelief. The suspension of disbelief does not get rid of the problem. At best it relocates the contradiction by moving it back a step. It is not a solution to the problem but rather an obfuscatory redescription, at one remove, of the problem.

Moreover, as with less complicated variants of the illusion theory, the hypothesis of the willing suspension of disbelief would undercut the possibility of our responding appropriately to fictions. As emphasized earlier, in order to respond appropriately to something like a horror film—in order to stay in our seats rather than calling out the army—we must believe we are confronted with a fictional spectacle. Were we to suspend our belief that what we see is fictional and take it to be actual, the normal and appropriate pleasures of fiction would become impossible [9]

So far I have been reviewing theories that attempt to deal with the putative contradiction—that in responding to fictions emotionally we show we believe in the existence of those beings whose existence we also overtly deny—by challenging the assumption that we do, in some sense, deny the existence of the persons and objects of fictions. That is, by means of notions like illusion or the suspension of disbelief, the preceding theories contend that our beliefs that fictions are not actual is not as wholehearted as our animating paradox suggests. Fiction may promote the illusion of reality or the suspension of disbelief in such a way that it is possible for the audience to respond emotionally in a way that presumes the belief in the objects of their emotions. These theories have many detailed problems of the sort I have already reviewed, and, as stressed, they are uniformly unattractive because they systematically undercut the possibility our responding appropriately to fictions. Another way out of the contradiction needs to be found.

The Pretend Theory of Fictional Response

The strategy I have just examined for dissolving the paradox or contradiction of fiction is to deny that the audience—as a result of processes like illusion, forgetting, or suspension of disbelief—rejects the existence of fictional persons and events. However, another strategy agrees that the audience knows and believes it is consuming fictions—thereby averting the brunt of our arguments so far—but goes on to deny that the audience's emotional responses to fiction are genuine. The contradiction emerges because it is presumed that actual emotional responses require beliefs in the existence of the objects of said responses. So one way in which to resolve the inconsistency is to deny the premise that we are genuinely responding with emotion when we appear to emote with respect to fictions. For if our emotional response is not genuine, then there is no reason to postulate that it is subtended by our belief in the existence in the fictional persons and events we are responding to. That is, if our emotional response is itself, so to say, fictional, then we do not believe the Golem exists, and, consequently, there is no contradiction with the necessary requirement for consuming fiction, viz., that the audience believes they are being entertained by what, in the relevant sense, is not.

When, to take an example popular in the philosophical literature,[10] Charles cringes in his theater seat as the Green Slime advances toward the movie camera, we take him to be in the emotional state of fear. However, as we have seen, this would appear to generate a contradiction. For that would seem to indicate that Charles believes in the existence of the Green Slime, whereas normal movie-viewing is underwritten by the belief that such things as the fictional Green Slime do not exist. Faced with this problem, perhaps we should return to the data. Maybe our initial view was mistaken; maybe Charles was not really in terror of the Green Slime after all.

Of course, Charles may testify to being terrified. But, then, might it be that Charles was only under the illusion that he was terrified? Surely it is possible for one to misrecognize one's emotional state. Could we say that Charles is in some kind of a state, but that it is not terror? Rather, that Charles is in the grip of an illusion of terror?

Several considerations count against regarding Charles's terror as illusory. First, if Charles is somehow misapprehending his emotional state, we should want to know the identity of the state he is really in. We will only be convinced that he is not terrified if a plausible account can be provided of the actual emotional state he is in. But obviously the most plausible candidate for the emotional state that he is in is that of terror—certainly that's the state that makes the most sense in context.

But it might be suggested that Charles's illusion is not simply that of being terrified; it is also an illusion that he is in any emotional state whatsoever. The cinematic and narrative techniques of the spectacle before him have deceived Charles into believing that he is in an emotional state as well as into believing that it is a state of terror.

This theory, however, seems extremely implausible. One wants to know what the difference between being in the grips of an emotional state and being in the grips of an illusion of an emotional state amounts to. That is, even if I am under the illusion of being terrified, am I not still terrified?

But perhaps, there is a contrast here that can be elucidated by an example. One might find oneself breathing rapidly while one's muscles are contracting and then go on to suppose that one is frightened. Now, I am tempted to say that ordinarily if there is no object to this fear that I can identify, I am probably not in an emotional state of fear. Indeed, I might be better off going to a doctor than supposing I am in fear.

But even if one stipulates that when I suppose I am in fear I am under the illusion that I am terrified, this case does not appear to apply to Charles's case. For as the Green Slime advances, Charles is not just in a physiological state. His fear has an appropriate object, the Green Slime, even if it is fictional. And since Charles's state has an object, if we call it an illusion of fear, it will remain difficult to differentiate it from an actual state of fear. Thus, provisionally, it would seem that we cannot do away with the idea that Charles is in a genuine state of fear by resorting to illusory emotions.

Nevertheless, there is another theoretical option available with which to deny that Charles's fear is genuine. We need not say the fear is illusory. Rather, Charles's fear might be make-believe or pretend fear. That is, when Charles shrinks from the onslaught of the Green Slime, he neither believes that the Green Slime exists nor does he believe that he is really terrified. Instead, Charles pretends to be horrified by the Green Slime. He impersonates, so to speak, someone, in this case himself, who is in the state of fear. His fear is only pretend fear.[11] This idea that our emotional responses to fictions are themselves fictional—matters of pretend-play or make-believe—has been defended very ingeniously and skillfully by Kendall Walton.[12] And it is to his theory that we now turn.

Walton takes it to be an article of common sense that in order to fear something, Charles must believe that he is in danger. So if Charles is afraid of the Green Slime, by hypothesis, he must believe that he is in danger of the Green Slime's rampage, which, of course, also presupposes that he believes in the existence of the Green Slime. However, Walton also believes that in order for Charles to appreciate his film, he must believe that it is fictional and that the Green Slime does not exist. Hence, we face a familiar contradiction. Walton does not believe that we can give up Charles's belief that the film is a fiction. For how else will we explain Charles's failure to flee from the Green Slime? Nor does Walton think that we should relinquish the commonsense view that genuine fear requires a belief in real danger. Thus, he needs a reasonable account of Charles's behavior that will fit within these constraints. He conjectures, then, that Charles's fear is not genuine fear, and, therefore, that it does not involve a genuine emotion. It is fictional or pretend fear. In the context of the fiction, Charles accepts certain pretended beliefs—that the Green Slime is on the ooze—and these serve to generate pretend emotions—make-believe horror of the slime. The movie, so to speak, becomes a prop in Charles's game of make-believe in which Charles, enacting or impersonating himself, pretends to be horrified.

In order to get an inroad into this theory, let us consider a helpful example provided by Walton. Imagine a child playing a game of monster with her father. The father makes believe that he is a girl-eating troll, and every time he lurches toward his daughter, she screams and runs away from his touch. She feigns horror at his every advance and seeks safety behind a chair, peeling off blood-curdling shrieks with abandon. Similarly, Charles, for the sake of pleasure and entertainment, makes believe he is endangered by the Green Slime, and ventilates make-believe horror in whatever way he finds appropriate.

In criticizing illusion theories of fictional belief, I noted that were one really under the illusion that the Green Slime were advancing, one would not behave as one does in movie theaters; one would get out of there. Likewise, if the child were under the illusion that her father were a troll, she'd do more than hide behind a chair; nor would she spurn her mother's attempts to stop the roughhouse (since she would not believe that it was merely roughhouse). But she knows that father is only pretending to be a troll, and her horror, as well, is only make-believe. The fact that she knows the game is make-believe explains her behavior—explains the fact that she is not acting the way a truly horrified person would in the presence of a troll.

Similarly, Charles has entered a game of make-believe with the film. The fiction provides the basis for certain pretend beliefs which Charles then uses to play a game of make-believe fright. He doesn't rush from the theater; he is too busy playing his game of make-believe. He is not genuinely frightened of the Green Slime in such a way that presupposes its lethal existence. He is pretending to be horrified. And this explains the kind of actual, nondefensive behavior of normal movie viewers at horror films, which behavior, moreover, would remain mysterious under the illusion theory.

That Charles's emotion is a pretend emotion, engendered in the play of make-believe with the movie, does not preclude that it is intense. For one can be intensely engaged in make-believe, as one can be intensely engaged in games in general. According to Walton, the way this pretend emotional play begins is that Charles, making believe that he is beset by the Green Slime, develops a "quasi-fear," a state that comprises physiological aspects (e.g., the increase of adrenaline in the blood) and psychological aspects (e.g., the *feelings* or *sensations* of increased adrenaline).

That is, Charles, pretending, as it were, to be a character in a fiction in which the Green Slime is attacking him, has the belief that make-believedly the slime-beast endangers his life. Charles knows and believes (*de re*) that make-believedly (*de dicto*) the slime is after him. And this former belief causes a state of quasi-fear in Charles—he feels his heart pounding, his muscles bunching up, and so on. Charles's fear is make-believe fear because it rests upon what is make-believedly true in the fiction as that is supplemented by Charles's response to it.

Charles takes the state that he is in to be one of quasi-fear, rather than quasi-anger, quasi-embarassment, etc., because it is generated by the belief that make-believedly the slime is attacking him. Charles's quasi-fear is the result of realizing that make-believedly the slime threatens him. Thus, Charles realizes that he should respond with pretend fear to the film. What Charles experiences is not pretend fear; what he experiences is quasi-fear. And his recognition that the feeling generated in interplay with the fiction is quasi-fear leads him to go on to engage his game of make-believe in terms of pretend fear.

Of course, it may seem strange to say that Charles is playing a game of make-believe in which he pretends fear just because a game presupposes some rules or principles, and, if questioned, Charles might be hard put to come up with the rules of his game. But, Walton argues, it is very often the case that the rules of games of make-believe remain implicit or unstated. He maintains:

Principles of make-believe that are in force in a game need not have been formulated explicitly or deliberately adopted. When children agree to let globs of mud "be" pies they are in effect establishing a great many unstated principles linking make-believe properties of pies to properties of globs. It is implicitly understood that the size and shape of globs determine the make-believe size and shape of pies; it is understood, for example, that make-believedly a pie is one handspan across just in case that is the size of the appropriate glob. It is understood also that if Johnnie throws a glob at Mary then make-believedly Johnnie throws a pie at Mary. (It is *not* understood that if a glob is 40 per cent clay then make-believedly a pie is 40 per cent clay.)[13]

Thus, I think Walton supposes, the fact that Charles cannot articulate the rules of the game he is playing does not count against the fact that Charles is playing a game. Moreover, Charles's make-believe fear of the slime need not be a deliberate or reflective act. It is mobilized automatically by his realization of his quasi-fear sensations, whose identity and whose progress he has access to through introspection. The value of this emotional pretend play with fictions resides in the opportunities it provides us to make discoveries about our feelings, to accept them or to purge oneself of them, to vent repressed or socially unacceptable feelings, or to prepare oneself emotionally for the possibility of future situations by providing "practice" in responding to fictional crises.[14]

The strongest support for Walton's theory of pretend fear is that it provides ways to solve certain puzzles. Thus, any competing theory of fearing fictions will have to at least solve the same puzzles Walton's does while perhaps also showing the limitations of Walton's solutions. The most important puzzle that it resolves, of course, is how it is possible for us to fear what we believe does not exist. The pretend theory answers this by saying that we don't really fear fictions, we pretend to fear fictions, and this pretense does not logically presuppose that we believe that we are in danger or that the Green Slime exists. Walton averts contradiction by denying the "existence belief" flank of the puzzle.

Walton also adduces several other puzzles that he thinks his theory solves. For example, when we speak of fictions, we tend to say things like "Huck Finn and Jim lived on a raft" rather than "In the fiction, Huck Finn and Jim lived on a raft." In other words, we typically speak of the contents of fictions without adding the modal qualification "In the fiction." Walton maintains that we do not do this with respect to other intensional contexts: we say "O'Brien believes that the Pope is an Irishman" rather than "The Pope is an Irishman" when we are speaking within the context of O'Brien's beliefs. Moreover, Walton contends that this is not merely a matter of economy. On his theory, this deviation from the normal way in which we handle intensional operators is a function of the fact that when we are speaking about fictions, we are pretending that "Huck lived on a raft," so it is appropriate, in order to carry on the game of make-believe, that we do not say it is only make-believe. That is, for the purpose of sustaining our pretense, we do not say it is pretense; that would undercut the game.[15]

Some readers may be swayed in the direction of Walton's theory on the grounds that he does not endorse, viz., the way in which his theory might be co-ordinated with certain illocutionary theories of fiction. That is, on the face of it, Walton's theory of pretend emotions with respect to fiction may appear to have the advantage of fitting together neatly with an illocutionary theory of the nature of fiction.[16] This approach to fiction, which I am not attributing to Walton, employs speech act theory in order to define fiction.[17] One conclusion of this theory is that the author of a fiction is pretending to perform certain illocutionary acts, namely making a series of assertions. That is, the author is making-believe that she is recounting a sequence of events. The author does this intentionally. So what marks a novel, for example, as a piece of fiction is not a matter of any special semantic or syntactic features of the text, but rather the stance the author takes toward it. Specifically, the author writes *as if* she were narrating in the illocutionary mode of assertion. Of course, not only the author but also informed readers know that the text is a series of pretend assertions, not assertions outright.

The illocutionary theory of fiction is a powerful theory, so were it the case that Walton's theory of fictional emotions had some special connection with it, then, though Walton himself does not make such a move, many might count that as a strong consideration in favor of the pretend theory of fictional emotions. Of course, there is a striking similarity between the two theories, insofar as each depends on the notion of pretense. However, the theories do diverge in terms of what is pretended and who does the pretending. In the illocutionary theory of fictions, *the author* makes believe that she is *asserting* something, whereas in the pretend emotion theory, *the audience* makes believe that it is *emoting* something. Of course, there is no reason to suspect that these two theories are incompatible. But, on the other hand, the link between them does not appear necessary in any way. It may be the case that audiences respond to the pretend activity of authors with make-believe emotions. But it is also logically possible that audiences feel genuine emotion in response to fiction, even on the illocutionary view. That is, there do not seem to be any logical considerations that could stop one from endorsing a pretend theory of fictional assertion at the same time that one endorsed the view that audiences are genuinely moved by fictions. Thus, a proponent of Walton's theory cannot claim that it has some advantage vis-à-vis the illocutionary approach that recommends it over rival views.[18] Instead, it must be defended or criticized independently of the illocutionary theory. And, it is to such criticism that we now turn.

The key objection to Walton's theory, of course, is that it relegates our emotional responses to fiction to the realm of make-believe. Purportedly, when we recoil with apparent emotion to *The Exorcist,* we are only pretending to be horrified. But I, at least, recall being genuinely horrified by the film. I don't think I was pretending; and the degree to which I was shaken by the film was visibly apparent to the person with whom I saw the film. Walton's theory is a clever solution to the logical problem that art-horror raises. However, it does not seem to square with the phenomenology of art-horror. That is, Walton's theory appears to throw out the phenomenology of the state for the sake of logic.

One reason to be suspicious of the notion that art-horror is a pretend emotion rather than a genuine emotion is that if it were a pretend emotion, one would think that it could be engaged at will. I could elect to remain unmoved by *The Exorcist;* I could refuse to make believe I was horrified. But I don't think that that was really an option for those, like myself, who were overwhelmedly struck by it. Similarly, if the response were really a matter of whether we opt to play the game, one would think that we could work ourselves into a make-believe dither voluntarily. But there are examples, like the actual film *The Green Slime* (as opposed to Walton's version of it), which are pretty inept, and which do not seem to be recuperable by making believe that we are horrified. The monsters just aren't particularly horrifying, though they were intended to be. But that wouldn't seem to be a real problem in Walton's theory. For if I wanted my typically rousing afternoon of entertainment, I ought to have been able to make believe that I was horrified. That is, the fact that whether I am art-horrified or not seems to be beyond my control, makes the notion that it is a matter of my games of make-believe dubious. For playing a game of make-believe seems to me to be something that I decide to do.

And, of course, another reason to think that we are genuinely art-horrified rather than pretending to be in such a state is that we don't seem to be aware that we are playing a game of make-believe. Walton, as we have seen, has an answer for this objection. He holds that our games of make-believe are often underwritten by rules and principles that are tacitly accepted. That is, we abide by rules, perhaps even a great many of them, without being aware of them. So our putative lack of awareness has been explained away.

However, this won't work. For the argument is based on the very plausible observation that we are unaware of *some* of the rules of the game. However, the objection that we've just made is that it seems that we are altogether unaware of playing a game of make-believe. We are not merely unaware of tacitly respecting some of the details of the game; we are completely unaware of playing a game. It may be true, considering Walton's example of the mudpie game, that the players could not articulate all the rules of their game with any precision. However, it strains credulity to suppose that they could be playing a game of mudpies, and not be aware of it at all. I conjecture that when one child invites another into this game, they would say "let's play mudpies," on the model of "let's play cowboys and indians." But there are no such analogs with the case of consuming fictions, and, consequently, no sign of the awareness of playing a game.

It does not seem correct to say that we are playing a game, of make-believe or otherwise, if we do not know that we are. Surely, a game of make-believe requires the intention to pretend. But on the face of it, consumers of horror do not appear to have such an intention. Perhaps the theory might be saved by suggesting that the intention is repressed; but my guess is that Walton would be loath to invoke psychoanalysis. And, in any case, that would probably reduce the pretend theory to a version of some sort of illusion theory of fictional emotions, thereby, in all probability, conjuring up yet again the problems of that approach.[19]

In response to the request for some sign that we are playing the games of make-believe that Walton postulates, it might be said that the behavioral indications can be found in the very fact that we've opted to read a book or watch a film. That is, to put it another way, reading a book and watching a play or film is some kind of *sui generis* form of game-playing. But this does not seem persuasive. I read historical nonfiction and I watch documentary films, and I see no discernible difference in the way that I read and watch these from the way in which I read and watch fictions. If there is no game-playing connected to the nonfiction reading and watching, then I see no non-questioning begging reason to attach game-playing to the simple reading and watching of fictions. Moreover, one supposes that Walton's theory is meant to differentiate reading and watching nonfiction from reading and watching fiction. Thus, the possibility that his proposed differentia, make-believe games, could be rooted in reading and watching *simpliciter* would not seem available to proponents of his theory.

Perhaps the pertinent game-playing is a matter of reading or watching the fiction *knowingly*. But this does not seem adequate. For then, in the context of solving the paradox of fiction, the game of make-believe reduces to the reassertion of the flank of the contradiction that says that the audience knows it is attending to a fiction and says nothing at all about the putative nature of the emotional state it is in.

Another problem with Walton's version of the pretend theory is that it would appear to misdescribe the case. He repeatedly speaks as if Charles were afraid that the Green Slime is attacking him; when it moves at the camera, Charles is said to make believe that he, Charles, fears for his life. Moreover, this way of describing the case is not merely a *façon de parler;* it is connected with Walton's view that fear requires the subject's belief that she is in danger, and, by extension, that make-believe fear requires the pretense of danger. Moreover, insofar as pretend fear supplies a model for fictional emotions in general, I suppose that this theory would have it that if I am morally outraged by the Bronx D.A. in Tom Wolfe's *The Bonfire of the Vanities* I must be pretending that he is unjust to me.[20]

But what has happened to the literal characters of fictions? Aren't the emotions undergone while consuming fictions spent for them rather than for ourselves? Isn't the fear with respect to the Green Slime, however it is to be theorized, fear for what the slime will do to *them?* If some sort of danger needs to be recognized in this case, it is the danger the Green Slime presents to the protagonists.

At the very least, this observation calls into question the presupposition that fear requires the subject's belief that she, herself, is in danger. We can fear for others. This is a commonplace fact about everyday life. We can fear for the dog that runs into traffic just as we can fear for the fate of political prisoners in countries we will never visit. But if fear can be separated from the issue of our own security, and if we can fear for others while we believe we are safe, then might we not fear for the lives of fictional characters just as we fear for the lives of actual political prisoners? Moreover, as will be argued below, we may be moved emotionally not only in terms of fear for others, but by our recognition that something like the Green Slime is *fearsome* even if we do not believe it constitutes clear and present danger.

To block this objection, the pretend theorist may only need to retrench ever so slightly—maintaining that for fear a belief in really endangered persons, either oneself or others, is requisite. That is, fear requires belief in the existence of whomever is threatened. And this, of course, is a presupposition that we have encountered again and again; it is an instance of the general view that in order to respond emotionally we must believe in the existence of the objects of those emotions. And we do not have the required beliefs with respect to fiction.

However, one wonders whether the general view here is correct. In the first place, the general view seems to beg the question at issue. It maintains that a comprehensive examination of things reveals that we only respond emotionally where we have the appropriate existence beliefs. But, as a matter of fact, a great deal of what we would pretheoretically call emotional responses are to fictions. In seeking a general view of what emotional response requires, why have our responses to fiction been excluded from the data? Of course, if said responses are included in the data, then the general claim that emotional responses require existence beliefs will be false. Thus, the question is whether the view that emotional responses require existence beliefs begs the question against the view that we respond with genuine emotions to fictions.

As we have seen, philosophers other than Walton have invited us to subscribe to the view that emotional responses presuppose existence beliefs by considering the way our emotions appear to vanish when we learn that a given story of woe has been concocted out of whole cloth—for example, when we learn that a woman's story about the death of her anguished lover is a fabrication. And, if knowledge that the story is a fabrication is what dissipates emotion in this case, genuine emotion should also be impossible in the the analogous case of fiction, thereby opening the door to the postulation of something like pretend fear.

But perhaps the cases are not analogous. Perhaps it is not the fact that the cock-and-bull story is fabricated that dissipates its reigning emotion, but rather *learning that one has been gulled,* which replaces one emotion with another one, namely resentment or maybe embarrassment. Moreover, since one typically knows that a novel is a fictional fabrication, one does not feel resentful that one has been fooled. A fiction is not a lie and does not elicit the emotional response that a lie would. The same story that dissipated emotion as a cock-and-bull story, if sufficiently elaborated and marked as a fiction, could, all things being equal, sustain emotion. The relevant difference between the cases is that the cock-and-bull variation also involved the listener's rising emotion of anger.

It may be possible to offset the influence of the thought-experiment about the cock-and-bull story with a thought experiment of our own design. Imagine a psychological experiment where what is being tested is our emotional responses to the description of certain kinds of situations. We are told stories and asked how we feel about them. We aren't told whether the stories are true or false. We don't have any existence beliefs one way or another. It seems perfectly plausible that we might respond to one of the stories by saying that that it struck us as being very sad, and then go on to ask the psychologist whether it was true or made-up. Nor do I think that in these circumstances that we will demand to alter our report if we learn it was fabricated. My intuitions are that this is a perfectly plausible scenario and that it is nowise incoherent. If this example is acceptable, then we have some reason to believe that we can be moved by stories which we learn to be fictions. Moreover, if this thought-experiment is persuasive, it might be pointed out that a strong candidate for the reason that we are able to respond emotionally here, in contradistinction to the case of the cock-and-bull story, is that the issue of whether we have been taken in just doesn't arise.[21] The view that emotional response requires existence beliefs also faces the problem that even if it appears applicable to some kinds of emotional responses, like fear, it does not seem to apply to all kinds of emotional responses. Consider sexual arousal. If an attractive member of the sex of one's preference is described or depicted, desire will not be staunched by saying the description (or the depiction) is concocted. Or just daydream about the body in question; it may be make-believe, but the arousal is not.

With respect to art-horror, the observation that not every emotional response requires existence beliefs is particularly relevant. For disgust, a key component of my theory of art-horror, would not ordinarily demand existence beliefs. Imagine that, at a dinner party, someone starts telling a gruesome story about a senior citizen who is beheaded for purposes of suspended animation. As dessert is being served, we are told that the head accidentally fell into the cuisinart in the hospital cafeteria, unbeknownst to anyone. At that point, before our fabulator gets any further, we ask him to drop the anecdote. If he responds that he made the whole thing up, we are likely to continue to ask him to be quiet because the story is disgusting anyway. Thus, if art-horror is crucially comprised of disgust *and* disgust is an emotional response that does not require existence beliefs, then an emotional response (or perhaps part of an emotional response) to horror fictions can be coherently sustained even though we do not believe that horrific monsters exist.

Also, when one considers the issue of disgust with respect to horror films, it is doubtful that the art-horror in question can accommodate a theory of pretend emotion. For there are certain films and filmmakers, specializing in stomach churning spectacles. Here, I have in mind something like Dario D'Argento's *Creepers*. As the heroine thrashes about in the pool—full of decomposing bodies, sewerage, and insect larvae—and quaffs down viscous gobs of liquidy, brownish stuff, one's feeling of nausea surely is not quasi-nausea nor pretend disgust; it is indiscernible from real disgust. Indeed, I have expressly chosen some pretty noisome examples here. For if you have felt some tinge of revulsion reading my prose, then you have genuinely responded to what you know is fictitious.

Of course, granting that disgust may not require belief in the existence of the offending object, the million-dollar question remains as to whether the fear component in art-horror requires existence beliefs. And since not all emotional responses require existence beliefs, the possibility that fear does not remains at least an open question. Clearly one can be frightened by the prospect of something—like global nuclear war—which one knows has not and may never come to pass. Here, it may be countered that in order for our fear to be genuine, we must believe that the prospect is at least probable. But how probable? Isn't invasion by bug-eyed monsters probable, if only minimally? Is it enough for the prospect to be logically possible? But then any fiction that we do not believe to be self-contradictory should be satisfactory. Of course, it will be objected that we believe the probability should reach a more demanding level. But what exactly will it be?

Furthermore, I am not convinced that it is even necessary that the prospect in question be believed to be highly probable. One can imagine a piece of machinery of the sort one never encounters—gears meshing ominously—and one can imagine one's own hand or the hand of another passing through it and feel a shudder for one's thoughts. One may even experience a reflex, gripping at one's hand defensively. Surely the fact that our fear responses are on a hair-trigger—that they can be activated by imagined situations in such a way as to activate defensiveness—would be an evolutionary advantage. That shudder at the thought of the maw of the machine, moreover, is no less genuine than the arousal one experiences while imagining breathtaking beauties gamboling on one's mindscape.

I suspect that Walton would try to handle such cases by means of the notion of quasi-fear. When I get a feeling of arrest at the thought of my hand being crunched, the state I am in is that of quasi-fear. According to Walton, quasi-fear is generated by beliefs about what is make-believedly the case and it supplies the basis for my make-believe emotion.[22] One problem with this account is that Walton never explains why beliefs about what is make-believedly true only give rise to quasi-fears and pretend emotions rather than genuine fears and emotions. That is, it is never made clear why this must be the case. The claim would appear to rest solely on the presumption that this alone can make sense of the way in which we appear to respond with emotion to what we know is not the case. So one way in which to continue this debate with Walton—a way to be pursued below—is to show that this is not the only way to render our emotional responses to fiction intelligible and that a rival theory to the pretend theory—viz., the thought theory[23]—can do this while also preserving our conviction that we are really frightened by horror stories. Thus, to fully play out our rejection of Walton's view requires the elaboration of an alternative view.[24]

The Thought Theory of Emotional Responses to Fictions

The problem that we continue to deal with is this: emotional response is thought to require belief in the existence of its object; but with fictions we know that the Green Slime does not exist. So our fear in this case seems inconsistent with our knowledge. This inconsistency is at the root of the paradox of fiction. As we have seen, certain illusion theorists deal with this by denying that while consuming fictions we know them to be fictions. Rather, we are under the illusion that the Green Slime is advancing at us. Pretend theorists deny that this fits the data. To appreciate a fiction we must know the Green Slime is a fiction, and, knowing this, we do not flee from it. Instead, the pretend theorist denies the premise that we are genuinely afraid of the Green Slime; we are only making believe that we are afraid. Whereas the illusion theorist denies the premise that at the moment we are afraid we regard the Green Slime to be fictional, the pretend theorist denies the premise that our fear of the Green Slime is real fear.

Both the illusion theorist and the pretend theorist, however, accept the premise that genuine fear of the Green Slime requires a belief in the existence of the slime. The illusion theorist claims we have the requisite belief, if only for the duration of the fiction, whereas the pretend theorist claims that we do not have real emotions with regard to fictions. But perhaps the premise to be denied is the very one shared by the illusion theorists and the pretend theorists. That is, what we might wish to reject is the presumption that we are only moved emotionally where we believe that the object of our emotion exists. The possibility of denying this premise of the paradox opens a third avenue of theorizing, one that is based on the conjecture that it is the thought of the Green Slime that generates our state of art-horror, rather than our belief that the Green Slime exists. Moreover, art-horror here is a genuine emotion, not a pretend emotion, because actual emotion can be generated by entertaining the thought of something horrible.

(Thought here is a term of art that is meant to contrast to belief. To have a belief is to entertain a proposition assertively; to have a thought is to entertain it nonassertively. Both beliefs and thoughts have propositional content. But with thoughts the content is merely entertained without commitment to its being the case; to have a belief is to be committed the truth of the proposition.)

Standing on a precipice, though in no way precariously, one might fleetingly entertain the thought of falling over the edge. Commonly, this can be accompanied by a sudden chill or a tremor which is brought about, I submit, not by our belief that we are about to fall over the edge of the precipice, but by our thought of falling, which, of course, we regard as a particularly uninviting prospect. It need not be a prospect we believe is probable; our footing is secure, there is no one around to push us, and we have no intention of jumping. But we can scare ourselves by imagining a sequence of events that we know to be highly unlikely. Moreover, we are not frightened by the *event* of our thinking of falling, but by the *content* of our thought of falling—perhaps the mental image of plummeting through space.

Further evidence for the claim that we can be frightened by the content of our thoughts can be marshaled by reflecting on the ways in which one might attempt to deflect one's consternation during an especially unnerving horror film. One can avert one's eyes from the screen, or perhaps direct one's attention from the quadrant occupied by the object of our excitement. Or, one can attempt to preoccupy oneself with something else, defocusing one's view of the screen and worrying about how one intends to make the payments on the recently purchased Mercedes. In this case, one's attention need not be entirely diverted from the screen; one keeps track of what is going on peripherally in order to learn when it is safe to return there with attention fully focused.

Similar spectator strategies are also available when the viewer finds the proceedings unbearably suspenseful or unpalatably maudlin. And what one is doing in all these cases is distracting oneself from the thought of what is being portrayed on the screen. One is not attempting to extinguish the belief that the referent of the representation exists nor the belief that the representation itself exists. Rather, one is attempting not to think about the content of the representation—that is, not to entertain the content of the representation as the content of one's own thought.

There are obvious theoretical advantages in terms of the problem of art-horror to be derived by postulating that thought contents can generate genuine emotion. The thought of a fearsome and disgusting character like Dracula is something that can be entertained without believing that Dracula exists. That is, thought and belief are separable. Thus, if we grant that thought contents can frighten, then we shall have no problem saying that standard readers and viewers of fictions about the Count do not believe the Count exists. Moreover, our fear may be genuine fear, because thought contents we entertain without believing them can genuinely move us emotionally.

Walton's case for the pretend theory of emotions, it seems, rests primarily on his arguments that Charles does not believe that the Green Slime poses an actual danger to him. From this he surmises that Charles cannot really be in a genuine state of fear. So he hypothesizes that Charles's state is to be analyzed in terms of quasi-fears and pretend fears. But Walton's objections to the notion that Charles believes in the Green Slime, and the argument to the best explanation that produces the hypothesis of pretend emotions does not cut against the theory that it is the thought of the Green Slime that exercises Charles. For thoughts need not be beliefs and one can entertain the thought of the Green Slime without believing in the Green Slime. That is, the thought theory allows us to accept all of Walton's objections to any theories—such as illusion theories—that postulate Charles's belief in the Green Slime.

Walton, as well as the illusion theorists, takes it as an article of faith that genuine fear requires genuine belief in the dangerous being articulated in the fiction. Because it is such an article of faith, they have not foreclosed on the possibility that genuine fears can be generated by thought contents entertained as a result of the representational content of the fiction. But if it is reasonable to think that thought contents, as well as beliefs, can produce emotional states, then there is no reason to attribute either illusory beliefs or pretend emotions to audiences.

Earlier I noted that one problem with Walton's system was that he failed to explain why we should necessarily agree that beliefs about what is fictionally true (or, *fictionally* that p) should generate quasi-fears rather than genuine fears. Now, perhaps, my reservations concerning this matter can be made more explicit.

Reading Lovecraft's "The Call of Cthulhu," we learn that, in the fiction, the primal Great Ones have cuttlefish heads, scaly wings, dragonoid bodies, an intolerable odor, a sticky texture, and green skin. Fictionally, they are also very dangerous and could exterminate humankind effortlessly. We do not believe the Great Ones exist, but we believe that fictionally they have these properties. When we reflect upon these fictional beings, when we consider the sense or meaning of Lovecraft's descriptions of these fictional brutes, we recognize that the Great Ones combine a congeries of properties that are disgusting and frightening, and we are art-horrified.

We know that all this stuff about the Great Ones is fictional. However, the propositional content of Lovecraft's fiction constitutes the content of our thought about them, and we are horrified by the *idea* of them. If we can be horrified by thoughts, as earlier examples indicated we could, then we can be horrified by thoughts engendered in us by the horrifying descriptions of authors. Therefore, it does not seem to follow from the fact that we believe that fictionally the Great Ones are thus and so that our responses must necessarily be a matter of quasi-fears and pretend emotions. Walton has overlooked the possibility that in knowingly reading fictions we are led to reflect on the content of descriptions of monsters, which content becomes the basis of our thoughts and which content causes fear and loathing in us. That is, there is no reason to endorse the move from the fact that our beliefs only concern what is fictionally the case to the claim that our fears are quasi-fears and pretend emotions.

Since we know that the Great Ones are fictions and it is only the thought of them that is frightening and disgusting, we do not throw down our book and flee. Thus, the thought theory can explain the kind of anomalies that the pretend theory could and the illusion theory could not. At the same time, the thought theory also has the advantage of regarding our horror as genuine horror. It can accommodate the phenomenology of horror as well as dealing with the logical problems that art-horror in particular and fiction in general appear to pose. In this respect, it appears to be superior to pretend theories—theories which solve the puzzle by postulating a counterintuitive range of pretend activities, albeit mental ones.

One way to defeat the thought theory might go like this: what is really at stake here is to show that fear, grief, and so on with respect to fictions is not irrational. On the face of it, emotional responses to fiction looked like they had to be irrational because they seemed to involve a spectator in two contradictory states of belief—both believing the Green Slime exists and believing the Green Slime does not exist. And that's irrational. Now the thought theory gets rid of that particular species of irrationality, removing the contradiction by showing how we might be frightened by something we explicitly regard as fictional. However, it has gotten out of that contradiction by making us irrational in another way. Now what we're frightened by are thoughts or the contents of thoughts. But it is irrational to be frightened by mere thought contents. So if we want a theory that does not reduce us to this sort of irrationality, the pretend theory is still the strongest contender.

The question here, then, becomes whether it is irrational to be frightened or otherwise moved emotionally by thoughts. Clearly, it is irrational to be paralyzed by psychotic fantasies about being watched by Martians, but the thought contents we have in mind are not psychotic fantasies, for those involve the belief in the existence of Martians. The thought contents we have in mind are not be conceived on the model of psychotic, or even neurotic, fantasies. Likewise, the thought theory would render the reader irrational if it implied she embraced a contradiction. But there is no contradiction involved in being led to fear by reflection upon our thought contents.

Perhaps the idea is that being frightened by thought contents is just silly. However, "silly" might be the wrong way of putting it, if it is just a fact about humans that they can be frightened of the *idea* of such as the primal Great Ones. Since no contradiction is involved, this feature of humans may not be assessable in terms of irrationality. It is just the way we are built. It is a naturally endowed element of our cognitive and emotive structure, one upon which the institution of fiction has been erected.

Moreover, the idea that it is silly to be put in an emotional state by a thought content strikes me as being essentially moralistic—as making implicit appeal to some code of courage or manliness or practicality. But this kind of thinking could call the whole institution of fiction into question. Alternatively, I maintain that the practice of fiction—including our emotional responses, where appropriately motivated by the text—is actually built on our capacity to be moved by thought contents and to take pleasure in being so moved. Furthermore, it seems to me ill-advised to disparage our emotional responses to fictions as irrational if they accord with what is normatively appropriate within the institution of fiction. They are rational, in this sense, in that they are normal; they are not irrational in the sense of being abnormal.

Of course, we might say that responses to fiction were irrational if they somehow got in the way of practical pursuits. But then it would be a given person's indulgence of fiction that would be irrational and not the fact that he could be moved by thought contents. And the same person would be irrational in the same way if he spent too much time pretending to be frightened by fictions to the impediment of his practical interests.

By now the strategy behind the thought theory and certain considerations in its behalf should be clear enough. However, a more detailed account of these thought contents and their relation to fictional texts will be useful. The thought theory relies on making a distinction between thoughts and beliefs, on the one hand, and a connection between thoughts and emotions, on the other. I have tried to support the connection between thoughts and emotions by pointing to what I take to be interpersonally confirmable facts: e.g., our ability to frighten ourselves genuinely by conceiving that we are about to go over a precipice or to conceive our hand (or an acquaintance's) about to be crushed by a machine—where we actually believe the probability of such events is nil. So let us turn to the distinction between thoughts and beliefs.[25]

The purported quandary about responding emotionally to fiction is that an emotional response requires a belief that the object of the response exists. And this doesn't cohere with what we take the informed consumer of art-horror to believe. The particular object of art-horror is a monster. And readers of *Dracula* do not believe that the vampire Count exists. However, one can have the thought of Dracula or the thought of Dracula as an impure and dangerous being without believing that Dracula exists. In the last chapter, I noted Descartes's distinction between the formal reality of thought and the objective reality. One can have the thought of a unicorn, the thought of a horse with a narwhal horn, without believing that unicorns exist. The unicorn has objective reality (in the Cartesian sense, discussed earlier, rather than the contemporary sense) in thought as a congeries of properties. Similarly, we can think of Dracula as a collection of properties, namely the collection of properties specified in descriptions of Dracula in Stoker's novel. And it seems that there is no reason to deny that a thought—such as the thought of the collection of properties, labeled by the name "Dracula" in the novel—might move us emotionally; might, in fact, horrify us.

In the account that I have offered of art-horror, horror is an emotion directed at specific characters—specifically the monsters—in horror fictions. We are not horrified by the fiction as a whole, so to speak, but by the horrific characters described or, in the case of visual media, portrayed in the fiction, and bearing such names or labels as Dracula, the Green Slime, and so on. In horror fictions, these names do not refer to actual beings nor do we believe they refer to actual beings. Nor are we concerned with the truth value of sentences in which such names appear, as we are concerned with the truth value of the sentences in history books where names such as Alexander the Great, Lincoln, and Churchill appear.

In "On Sense and Reference," Gottlob Frege observes:

> In hearing an epic poem, for instance, apart from the euphony of the language we are interested only in the sense of the sentences and the images and feelings thereby aroused. The question of truth would cause us to abandon aesthetic delight for an attitude of scientific investigation. Hence it is a matter of no concern to us whether the name "Odysseus," for instance, has reference, so long as we accept the poem as a work of art. It is the striving for truth that drives us always to advance from the sense to the reference.[26]

For Frege, it is natural to think that every sign is connected with something to which it refers—its reference—and to its sense: the meaning of the sign, i.e., that which picks out its reference. With fiction, however, we are only concerned with the sense or meaning of the discourse in terms of the aesthetic consequences that reflection upon said meanings promotes.

Similarly, with horror fiction, we are concerned with the sense or meaning of the sentences in the text for the purpose of the emotions—particularly that of art-horror— they arouse in us. The names do not refer in their natural or customary fashion. They behave in a way that is far more analogous to the way Frege says the words of reported speech, i.e., the words in quotations, behave.

> In reported speech one talks about the sense, e.g., of another person's remarks. It is quite clear that in this way of speaking words do not have their customary reference but designate what is usually their sense. In order to have a short expression, we will say: In reported speech, words are used *indirectly* or have their *indirect* reference. We distinguish accordingly the *customary* from the *indirect* reference of a word; and its customary sense from its indirect sense. The indirect reference is accordingly its customary sense.[27]

Following Frege's suggestion that with epic poetry our preoccupation shifts from an interest in reference to an interest in sense, Peter Lamarque maintains that fictional names are used indirectly or have indirect reference to the sense of the sign.[28] The sign "Dracula" refers to its sense. But what is the sense of the name "Dracula?" It is the colligation of properties and attributes that Stoker imputes to the Count in the text of his novel. This assignment of attributes occurs through the descriptions of Dracula in the text, which descriptions are to be understood in their customary sense. "Dracula" is a label to which those descriptions attach, so to speak.

This approach involves regarding fictional names as having a sense. And though there are arguments in the philosophy of language against the notion that in ordinary usage proper names have a sense, it does seem at least plausible to think that fictional names have a sense, one constituted primarily by the descriptions of the character in the text. When one has in mind "Dracula," one is thinking about the collection of properties attributed to him. There is, of course, nothing else, strictly speaking, for one to think about. Moreover, that the attribution of sense to proper names has been challenged with respect to what might be called factual discourse, does not show that the view might not be applied to fiction. For there is no antecedent reason to presume that the theory of proper names for factual discourse and the appropriate theory for fictional discourse need be the same.

To see the relation between the descriptions of monsters in fictions and the thought content of audience members, it is helpful to recall John Searle's distinction between the illocutionary force of an utterance and its propositional content.[29] Two utterances—"I promise to come to church" and "Come to church!"—have the same propositional content, viz., "that I will come to church," though they differ in terms of their illocutionary force. If one analyzes fictional sentences in terms of the speech act approach, they too will have an illocutionary element, "it is fictional that," along with propositional content, for example, "that Dracula has fangs." The sense or propositional content of the description of the fictional Dracula provides the content of the reader's thought of Dracula; ideally, the reader's mental representation of Dracula is identified by and constituted from the propositional content of the descriptions in the text, though a great deal about how this is to be done with any precision in particular cases will be tricky to spell out.[30]

The name "Dracula" refers to its sense, the congeries of properties attributed to the vampire in the novel. As we reflect on what we read, we reflect on the attributed properties of the monster, which combination of properties is recognized to be impure and fearsome, resulting in the response of art-horror. Since we are horrified by thought contents, we do not believe that we are in danger, and do not take any measures to protect ourselves. We are not pretending to be horrified; we are genuinely horrified, but by the thought of Dracula rather than by our conviction that we are his next victim.

The thought theory solves the problem of how it is that we can be authentically horrified by fiction at the same time we do not believe in the existence of the monsters in the text. For we can think of the Green Slime without subscribing to its existence, and we can be horrified by the content of that thought. Whereas the illusion theory of response to fiction saddles the audience with false beliefs, and the pretend theory burdens us with make-believe emotions, the thought theory keeps our beliefs respectable and our emotions genuine.

In his defense of the pretend theory, Walton recommends it to us not only in terms of the way in which it dissolves the putative problem of our emotional response to fiction. He also maintains that the pretend theory explains why it is that when we speak of fictions, we do not preface our remarks with modal qualifications. That is, we say "Fyodor Karamazov is a buffoon," rather than "In the fiction *The Brothers Karamazov*, Fyodor is a buffoon." According to Walton, we can explain this as a continuation of our game of make-believe with respect to the fiction. Were we to qualify such statements modally, our play of pretense would be subverted.

But even if the pretend theory were correct in terms of our emotions, I find it strange to extend it to our talk about fictional works. On Walton's account, when we respond to fictions emotionally, we become a character in a fictional world—a character, for example, beset by the Green Slime. But when I tell someone about a novel, there is generally no reason to suppose that I am enacting a fiction—my pretend game of *The Brothers Karamazov*—for my interlocutor. One might perform such an enactment; but it strains credulity to think we are generally acting when we report on fictions.

My own suspicion is that we often forgo modal qualifications when we speak of fictions as a result of pragmatic considerations. That is, if we have reason to believe that our interlocutor knows we are speaking about a fiction, we delete the qualification "In the novel. . . ." On the other hand, we will add the qualification, at least as a preface to our remarks, when we are not sure that our audience knows we are discussing fictional characters. This is analogous to the case of discussing the beliefs of a philosopher with whom we disagree. If the context makes it clear that we are reporting Spinoza's theory, we need not preface each paraphrase by saying "Spinoza believes. . . ." If we are obviously reporting Spinoza's views, rather than our own, we will use many unqualified sentences such as "There is only one substance and that is God," instead of introducing each sentence with "Spinoza believes that. . . ."

Moreover, if these objections are sound, the pretend theory does not derive corollary support for its putative explanation of our deletion of modal qualifiers in reporting fiction. Its primary strength lies in its account of our emotional response to fiction, which account appears to me to be less persuasive than the thought theory, insofar as it denies the powerful intuition that our responses involve authentic emotion. Of course, the commitment to thoughts in the thought theory may raise fundamental philosophical quandaries for some; however, in the question of art-horror, the dependence on thoughts seems to me more palatable than the postulation of pretend emotions or audience beliefs in vampires.

Summary

At least since Samuel Johnson wrote his preface to *The Plays of Shakespeare,* the worry has been abroad that there is something peculiar about our responses to fiction. The question—which we call the paradox of fiction—concerns how it is possible for us to be moved emotionally by fictions since we know that what is portrayed in a fiction is not actual. Here, the often unstated cause of our perplexity is the presumption that we can only be moved by that which we believe exists. This paradox is very relevant to any discussion of art-horror, for we wonder how we be can be horrified by what we know does not exist.

The structure of this paradox revolves around the following three propositions, each of which seems true when considered in isolation, but which when combined with the other two yields a contradiction:

1) We are genuinely moved by fictions.
2) We know that that which is portrayed in fictions is not actual.
3) We are only genuinely moved by what we believe is actual.

There seem to be three options for removing the contradiction here. The illusion theory denies the second proposition, maintaining that for the course of the fiction we do not know that what is portrayed in the fiction is not actual. Instead, it is postulated that while attending to the fiction, we are under the illusion that what it reports is real. This theory confronts a series of problems which the pretend or make-believe theory seeks to avoid, by sustaining belief in the second proposition, but denying the first proposition. For the pretend theorist, the emotions we report when attending fictions are not genuine or authentic emotions but make-believe emotions. There are a number of liabilities with this theory. But the major liability is that it renders our emotional responses to fictions make-believe or pretend emotions. In order to avoid this consequence, while at the same time avoiding all the problems of the illusion theory, one may advance what I have called the thought theory. This theory denies the third proposition in the preceding triad. It maintains that we can be moved by the content of thoughts entertained; that emotional response does not require the belief that the things that move us be actual. We can be moved by prospects that we imagine. With respect to fictions, the author of such works presents us with conceptions of things to think about—e.g., Anna Karenina's suicide. And in entertaining and reflecting upon the contents of these representations, which supply us with the contents of our thoughts, we can be moved to pity, grief, joy, indignation, and so on. With respect to the genre of horror, the thoughts that we are led to entertain involve considering the fearsome and impure properties of monsters. And we are art-horrified.

In a very recent book, Bijoy Boruah has argued that reference to the imagination must be included in any account of our emotional responses to fiction.[31] If by "imagination" he means entertaining a thought non-assertively, then his view is compatible with ours. If, on the other hand, he means something more here—something to do with what the audience adds to the text—then the concept of the imagination seems misplaced. For in imagining, we are the creative and primarily voluntary source of the contents of our thoughts. But in reading fictions, the content of our thoughts comes, by and large, from the outside, from the determinate text we are reading or the already elaborated spectacle we are viewing. There is no reason to think that, standardly, we must add anything by way of imagery to what is already stated or implied by the fiction.

Character-Identification?

The previous section focused discussion on the relation of the audience to the fictional monsters that give rise to art-horror. In this section I want to take a brief look at the relation of the audience to the human protagonists in horror fictions.[32] Of course, insofar as these characters are fictional, the conceptual frameworks developed above apply to them. For example, our emotional responses to fictional protagonists, like our emotional responses to fictional monsters, are genuine, and these responses are directed at objects whose ontological status is that of thought contents. However, there is a question about fictional protagonists that rarely arises with fictional monsters of the horrific variety (lest they, like King Kong, become protagonists): namely, do we identify with fictional protagonists? That is, does following a fiction and becoming wrapped up in the fortunes of a character require some sort of curious metaphysical process, like Dr. Spock's Vulcan mind-meld, between the audience member and the protagonist, or, to put the matter differently, is our response to positive characters in fictions best explained by postulation of some process of character-identification between us and them.

Identification is a common notion in everyday talk about fictions. People say that they identify with this or that character in a soap opera. However, what is meant by "identification," in such cases, remains unclear. Indeed, whether the notion of character-identification is merely a metaphor or is meant to be a literal description of a mental state is generally not determinable in the context of daily conversation. Obviously, character-identification could mean a range of things and could be connected to a variety of different psychological theories. But the term is often used—even by professional critics—in a way that fails to specify exactly how we are to characterize the mental state to which speakers are referring.

Some candidates for what may be indicated by invoking the concept of character-identification might include: that we like the protagonist; that we recognize the circumstances of the protagonist to be significantly like those we have found or find ourselves in; that we sympathize with the protagonist; that we are one in interest, or feeling, or principle, or all of these with the protagonist; that we see the action unfolding in the fiction from the protagonist's point of view; that we share the protagonist's values; that, for the duration of our intercourse with the fiction, we are entranced (or otherwise manipulated and/or deceived) so that we fall under the illusion that each of us somehow regards herself to be the protagonist.

Some of these possibilities seem harmless enough. That is, certain of these states appear to be ones that raise no philosophical or psychological quandaries. One can like a character; can recognize similarities between the character and oneself; share values with a character; or, one can be concerned about or sympathetic toward a character. Doing these sorts of things with respect to fictional characters seems to be a legitimate expansion of responses we have toward living people—even if it might be very complicated to spell out the logic of these expansions. However, these usages do not seem to get to the very heart of what commentators have in mind when they invoke the notion of character-identification. Rather they seem to use the notion of character-identification to signal a more radical relation between the audience and the protagonist, one in which the audience comes to think of itself as identical to or one with the character—i.e., a state in which the audience member somehow merges or fuses with the character. Under this conception, when the audience member is given information about the ongoing story from the point of view of the character, we (mistakenly) accept (or confusedly take) the character's point of view to be our own. We are moved by the fiction in such a vivid way that we feel as though we are participants in it; specifically, we are thought to feel as though we were the protagonist.

Insofar as this conception of character-identification depends on a notion of illusion—the illusion that the audience member is the protagonist—it must confront problems that I have already discussed at some length. For in reading a novel or watching a play or a movie, the audience gives every indication that it knows that it is not the protagonist. One does not cower behind one's sofa sharpening stakes while watching reruns of *Dracula* on late night TV. Not only, as argued previously, is the viewer aware that she is watching a representation rather than the referent of the representation, but she is also aware that she is not the protagonist of the representation. As has been already argued, perhaps *ad nauseam,* the hypothesis of illusion—whether of the reality of the fiction or of one's identity with the protagonist—makes no sense in the face of the audience's behavior when consuming horror fictions.

Clearly, if the notion of character-identification is to make sense, it cannot be based on postulating an audience illusion of being identical with the protagonist. Some other account of character-identification is necessary. One possibility is to say that what is involved in character-identification is the exact duplication on the part of the audience of the protagonist's mental and emotional state. This, of course, can't be right because the character, presumably, believes that she is being assaulted by a werewolf, but the audience member does not. So perhaps the relevant duplication pertains only to emotional states. As Godzilla stomps Tokyo, the character fears for the fate of the human race, and so does the audience member.

If this is what is meant by character-identification, the concept confronts a number of deep problems. First, many of—probably most of—our responses to the protagonists in fictions, even on casual inspection, do not meet the requirement of emotional duplication. When the heroine is splashing about with abandon as, unbeknownst to her, a killer shark is zooming in for the kill, we feel concern for her. But that is not what she is feeling. She's feeling delighted. That is, very often we have different and, in fact, more information about what is going on in a fiction than do the protagonists, and consequently, what we feel is very different from what the character may be thought to feel.

Even in a case like the ending of Steve Rasnic Tem's short story "Worms," where Ella, to her horror and surprise, does realize that she is surrounded by hungry night crawlers, our emotional state does not duplicate hers because we are aware, as she is not, of the way in which her plight figures in an elaborate scheme of revenge.

Likewise, when a character is involved in a life and death struggle with a zombie, we feel suspense. But this is not an emotion that the character has the opportunity to indulge; she will be, one surmises, too involved in getting quit of the zombie to feel suspense about the situation. If we feel pity at Oedipus' recognition that he has killed his father and bedded his mother, that is not what Oedipus is feeling. He is feeling guilt, remorse, and self-recrimination. And, needless to say, we are feeling none of these.

The general point to be derived from these examples is that in a great many cases, the emotional state of the audience does not replicate the emotional state of the characters. With many of the best known types of relations between audiences and protagonists—such as pathos and suspense—there is an asymmetry between the emotional states of characters and those of audiences. However, one supposes that character-identification would require a symmetry between the emotional states of audiences and protagonists. At the very least, this implies that character-identification does not supply a comprehensive conceptualization of the relation of protagonists and audiences; there are too many cases that even upon superficial review do not correspond to a watered-down view of identification as the duplication of emotional states.[33]

Moreover, a less superficial probing of the relation of the audience's emotional states to the protagonists result in further disanalogies. For if the theory in the preceding sections is correct, then the audience's emotional response is rooted in entertaining thoughts, while the character's responses originate in beliefs. The character, it seems reasonable to suppose, is horrified, while the audience member is art-horrified. And, to compound matters, the audience's response to the protagonist will be involved with concern for another person (or person-type) while the protagonist beset by a monster is concerned for himself. That is, it is appropriate to describe the audience's emotional state as one of sympathy; but the character does not sympathize with himself. Speaking loosely, the character's emotions in such cases will always be self-regarding or egoistic, whereas the audience's emotions are other-regarding and altruistic. So, if these disanalogies are convincing, then it very well may be the case that character-identification never supplies an account of the audience's relation to the protagonist.

These objections ride on a conception of character-identification as the strict duplication of the emotional states of protagonists and audiences.

Construed this way, there can be no character-identification because the audience has emotions (suspense, concern, pity, etc.) that the characters do not, while protagonists have emotions and fears that the audience lacks (e.g., fear of extinction).

At this point, if one is to save the hypothesis of character-identification, perhaps the way to go is to drop the notion of a strict duplication of emotional states between the protagonist and the audience, and only require that there be a partial correspondence between the audience and the protagonist with respect to their emotional states.

Of course, one problem with this suggestion is that it remains unclear whether the self-direction of the character's emotion as well as its rootedness in beliefs will allow for even a partial correspondence between the emotional states of the characters and those of audience members. But, supposing these complications can somehow be dealt with, it seems to me that the notion of character-identification, grounded in partial correspondences between the emotive responses of protagonists and audience-members, is still dubious. For, among other things, if the correspondences are only partial, why call the phenomenon *identification* at all? If two people are rooting for the same athlete at a sporting event, it would not appear appropriate to say that they are identifying with each other. They may be unaware of each other's existence. And even if they are sitting next to each other, and are aware that they share a similar attitude toward the event, they need not be identifying. Nor is their emotional state literally the same as that of the athlete they are rooting for, since her concentration is probably of a different focus and intensity.

My objections to the notion of character-identification here may seem at odds with my earlier account of art-horror. For I have spoken of a parallel, in certain respects, between the emotional responses of characters in horror fictions and the emotional responses of the readers and viewers of these fictions. Indeed, I have claimed that it may often be the case that the characters' emotional responses to monsters in horror fictions cue the audience to the appropriate kind of response to the relevant monsters. Specifically, I maintain that the evaluative criteria—of fearsomeness and impurity—that the audience brings to bear in its response to horrific monsters echoes or matches the emotive evaluative responses of the characters to the monsters in the fiction. But sharing appraisals of the monster does not entail that I am identifying with the character or that I am in the same emotional state as the character. Having parallel emotive appraisals does not entail identification.[34]

Apart from the reasons already adduced for affirming crucial differences between my emotional state and the protagonist's at moments such as the monster's assault, we must also remember that in circumstances like these, the audience is not simply horrified but that that very horror is also a constituent in the audience's further emotional response to the larger situation, in which a horrifying monster is threatening a human protagonist. That larger situation is marked by the fact that the audience is outside it while the protagonist is inside it, which implies a substantially different affect. And, as well, that larger situation is also marked by the fact that the audience is probably caught up in some sort of altruistic concern whereas if the protagonist is feeling concern it is more-than-likely to be egoistic.[35] That is, the audience's overall emotional state is likely to differ from the emotional state of the character—even if we put aside the telling disanalogy that the character responds to a belief in a monster and the audience to entertaining a thought of a monster—because the audience's overall emotional response is to a situation which includes the character and the character's emotional response.

The object of the audience's overall emotional response, therefore, diverges from the object of the character's emotional response in ways that qualitatively differentiate the responses. That the two responses overlap in terms of certain elements—e.g., the emotive appraisal of the monster as something is threatening and repelling—does not indicate that the overall emotional states are the same, or that the audience member takes herself to be the protagonist. Sharing emotive responses cannot be a sufficient condition for identification. If it were, one audience member could be said to be identifying with every other audience member who regarded the monster with revulsion.

Again consider the example of tragedy. We respond to Oedipus' plight, which includes his own feelings of repulsion about incest, an evaluation which we may share. But this gives rise to an overall feeling in us which does not match up with Oedipus' emotional state. For example, if Aristotle is right, we come to fear that such calamities could befall us and, then, we undergo catharsis. But the time for fear has passed for Oedipus and he is wracked with guilt (and not relieved of anything as far as I can tell). Moreover, part of our response to Oedipus revolves around the fact that he is guilt ridden—that he is in an emotional state which we are not in.

Similarly, when a protagonist is cornered by a monster in a horror fiction, I may share his emotive appraisal of the creature. But this leads to a cluster of different feelings—directed to the situation as a whole—which are quite different from those plausibly attributed to the character: art-horror versus horror, sympathetic concern versus egoistic concern, suspense versus either concerted attention if the protagonist is to evade the monster or abject, paralytic terror if the protagonist is helpless prey. When a protagonist is attacked by a monster, we are not only horrified, but are concerned that such a person—the protagonist with all the virtues the plot has endowed him/her with—is in the clutches of a loathsome and threatening being. In general, our feelings of art-horror are constituent feelings in a more comprehensive response to a larger situation where we are concerned for the plight of the protagonist, whereas with respect to the protagonist's emotional state it seems plausible to see it as primarily directed to the monster without adding to it any explicit reflexive consideration, on the part of the protagonist, that a person like herself is in danger.

If these comments about the asymmetry of the emotional state of the audience and the protagonist are correct, then the notion of character-identification seems ill-advised. Clearly, there can be no character-identification if it requires perfect symmetry between the audience and the protagonist. Moreover, if all that is required is partial correspondence between the emotional states of the audience and the protagonist, then one wonders why the phenomenon is being called identification. For there can be partial correspondence without the respective emoters being usefully described as identical. With respect to horror, it may be the case, as I have argued, that we share emotive evaluations of the monster with the characters without our overall emotional states taking the same object or the respective subjects fusing.

One reason that commentators may be attracted to identification theories of the response to fictional protagonists may be that, without realizing it, they actually believe in a very radical sort of egoism—viz., that I can only be emotionally moved by situations that pertain to my own self-interests: indeed (and this is what makes it very radical egoism), they believe that I can only respond emotionally to what are literally taken to be my own interests. Thus, my emotional responses to fictional characters must be underwritten by my somehow identifying myself with the character, thereby, making her interests my own. However, if this is the motivation for the notion of character-identification, then it should be clear that the view should be abandoned, for there is abundant evidence that people actually do respond emotionally to situations where there is no plausible connection to their own interests.[36]

Earlier I noted that there might be some innocent uses of the concept of character-identification. For example, if I say I identify with a character that may merely mean that I like the character. Two things need to be said about these uses. First, they do not seem to be at the heart of the notion of character-identification; it is quite possible to like someone without feeling one with that person. The core meanings of character-identification really seem to require that I feel at one with or identical to another. And, of course, I have argued that with fictions there are reasons to resist the idea that we are *at one* with characters. This leads to my second point. If it is true that the fusion sense of identification is problematic and that it is this sense that really motivates most identification talk, then perhaps it will be profitable to regiment our use of language in such a way that we no longer employ—at least in our critical writing—innocent uses of the concept of identification, just because it opens the door to confusion by at least suggesting the dubious mind-meld notion of identification.

Character-identification is a concept that suffuses critical discourse about fictions. If it is jettisoned, one might fear that a cornerstone of critical discourse has been dislodged. If the edifice is not to collapse, what, one wonders, is to be put in its place? That is, if I don't identify with protagonists, what is it that I do when I respond to them? Here, I would like to stipulate that what we do is not identify with characters but, rather, we assimilate their situation.

When I read a description of a protagonist in a certain set of circumstances, I do not duplicate the mind of the character (as given in the fiction) in myself. I assimilate her situation. Part of this involves having a sense of the character's internal understanding of the situation, that is, having a sense of how the character assesses the situation. For example, with horror, when a character is beset by a monster, part of my response is grounded in the recognition that the protagonist regards herself as confronting something that is threatening and repellent. In order to do this, I must have a conception of how the protagonist sees the situation; and I must have access to what makes her assessment intelligible. In horror fictions, of course, this is easily come by. For since the consumer of the fictions and the protagonist share the same culture, we can readily discern the features of the situation that make it horrifying to the protagonist. To do this, we need not replicate the mental state of the protagonist, but only know reliably how she assesses it. And we can know how she feels without duplicating her feelings in ourselves. We can assimilate her internal evaluation of the situation without becoming, so to speak, possessed by her.

But in assimilating the situation, I also take an external view of it. That is, I assimilate features of the situation that for various reasons are not focused by the protagonist either because she does not know about them or because they are not plausible objects of her concern. Thus, I see the situation not only from the viewpoint of the protagonist, though I know that viewpoint, but rather, I see it as one who sees the situation from the outside as well— I see it as a situation involving a protagonist who has the viewpoint she has. With the onset of a monster, I see the situation, for example, as a situation in which someone—who is frightened and repulsed—is in danger. My response, that is, involves assimilating the internal point of view of the protagonist as part of generating another response, a response that takes account of the protagonist's response but which is also sensitive to the fact that the protagonist is assessing the situation in the way our internal understanding indicates.

In order to understand a situation internally, it is not necessary to identify with the protagonist. We need only have a sense of why the protagonist's response is appropriate or intelligible to the situation. With respect to horror, we do this readily when monsters appear since, insofar as we share the same culture as the protagonist, we can easily catch-on to why the character finds the monster unnatural. However, once we've assimilated the situation from the character's point of view, we respond not simply to the monster, as the character does, but to a situation in which someone, who is horrified, is under attack. His mental anguish is an ingredient in the sympathy and concern that we extend to the character whereas his mental anguish, however painful we infer it to be, is not an object of his concern. He is frightened by the monster, but he is not—or, at least, it is not plausible to suppose that he is—concerned that someone is in anguish. Or, to be more precise, no part of his concern is generated as the result of entertaining the thought that someone is in anguish, whereas that is, *ex hypothesi,* part of our concern.

In summary, the concept of character-identification does not appear to have the right logical structure for analyzing our emotional responses to protagonists in fiction in general and horror fiction in particular. "Identification" suggests that we fuse with characters or become one with them which would suggest, at least, that we duplicate their emotional states. But when we see the monster moving at his emotionally paralyzed victim, our emotional response takes into account the disabling paralysis of the victim.

Stated formally, a strong sense of character-identification would imply a symmetrical relation of identity between the emotions of spectators and characters. But generally, the relation is asymmetrical; the characters, in part through their emotions, cause different emotions in spectators. This logical asymmetry indicates that identification, a symmetrical relation, is not the correct model for describing the emotional responses of spectators. This is clearly the case with such characteristic audience responses as suspense and pathos. Moreover, if the intensity of our response to fictional characters can be adequately enough explained in those cases without reference to character-identification, why should we be forced to postulate character-identification to account for the same kind of intensity of response in other cases?[37]

3

Plotting Horror

Plotting Horror

Most of the artforms in which the genre of horror is practiced are narrative. The purpose of this section is to examine the narrative structures that are most often found in the horrific stories of literature, theater, cinema, radio and TV. First, I will look at some of the most characteristically recurring plots of the horror genre. This examination will be somewhat systematic, but it makes no claim to exhaustiveness. Next, the topic of narrative suspense will be explored; for though suspense is by no means an exclusive feature of horror—indeed, as I shall argue, it involves a discernibly different emotive object from art-horror—nevertheless, suspense is an extremely frequent effect of horror stories, and therefore needs to be addressed in any general discussion of horror narration. Lastly, the plot structure that Todorov christened "the fantastic" will be reviewed, both in terms of the way it functions in literature and in terms of what it reveals about the interest we take in horror; an attempt will also be made to expand Todorov's observations about the fantastic into an original explanation of certain cinematic devices that are often found in horror films.

Some Characteristic Horror Plots

Anyone familiar with the genre of horror knows that its plots are very repetitive. Though here and there one may encounter a plot of striking originality, in general, horror stories seem to differ more in surface variations than in their deep narrative structures. A horror adept has, typically, a very good sense of what is going to happen next in a story—or at least a very good sense of the range of things that can happen next. Part of the reason for this is that many horror stories—I suspect the majority—are generated from a very limited repertory of narrative strategies. Like many genres, the story lines in horror narratives are very predictable—but that predictability does not deter the horror audience's interest (indeed, audiences would appear to desire that the same stories be told again and again). My aim is to introduce some of the most important plot structures in the horror genre, in order not only to illuminate their fundamental organizing principles, but also to suggest, in part, something of the origin of the pleasure that horror aesthetes find in the genre. Again, I do not claim to be able to identify every horror plot, nor, perhaps, even all of the basic plots. My findings are provisional, though I hope that they are nonetheless instructive.

One way to itemize the recurring plots of horror would be to review each of its subgenres with an eye to isolating the stories it most frequently retells. For example, the most common ghost stories involve the return from the dead of someone who has left something unsaid or undone, who wishes something unacknowledged to be brought to light, or who wants revenge or reparation. Once the living discover this secret motive, they are generally on their way to sending the ghost back to where it came from.

Likewise, tales of malevolent houses—such as Stephen King's *The Shining,* Jay Anson's supposed nonfiction *The Amityville Horror,* and Robert Marasco's *Burnt Offerings*—characteristically recount the possession of the lives of new inhabitants of the home for the purpose of reenacting some past evil (haunted houses are generally haunted by the sins of the former inhabitants). That is, these stories involve a narrative of renewal, predicated upon restaging an altogether unsavory past.

However, though it appears to be the case that each of the subgenres of horror—vampire stories, zombie stories, werewolf stories, giant insect, giant reptile, and alien invasion stories—have particular tales (or, if you will, narrative themes) that they tend to rehearse again and again, it is also the case that, as well, these tales often share more abstract, deeper narrative structures with each other. Thus, while Stephen King's *Cycle of the Werewolf* replays the classic narrative themes of lycanthropy, and Jay Anson's *666* once again sets in motion Satan's schemes for world dominion, both plots share crucial formal structures that are also repeated in other subgenres which are as diverse as those of the toxic mutant, the defrosted prehistoric dinosaur, the mad scientist/necromancer, and so on.

Since my interest in this book is to speak of horror in a very general way, my focus, for the most part, will be on the abstract, narrative structures that cross and subtend the various subgenres of horror. Adopting this level of generality will also be useful when I come to suggest what it is about horror as a genre which entices people to indulge in it. This is not to deny that the study of the narrative themes of the subgenres of horror is worthwhile. Research along these lines is to be welcomed. Nevertheless, such research is likely to reveal the particular fascination exerted by each subgenre—and its compelling (repeated) myths—rather than something about the power of horror in general.

The Complex Discovery Plot

One way to approach the deep, abstract plot structures of the horror genre is to look at a fairly complicated generic plot structure in order to pinpoint some of its basic ingredients or functions, and then to see how these functions can be modified or recombined to form other generic plot structures. To that end, the first of the dozen or so structures of horror narration that I will discuss is what I call a *complex discovery plot*. This plot structure has four essential movements or functions. They are: onset, discovery, confirmation, and confrontation.[1]

The first function in the complex discovery plot is *onset*. Here the monster's presence is established for the audience. For example, in the film *Jaws*, we see the shark attack. We know a monster is abroad and about. The onset of the monster begins the horror tale proper, though, of course, the onset of the monster may be preceded in the narrative by some establishing scenes that introduce us to the human characters and their locales, and perhaps to their horror-relevant occupations, e.g., they're Arctic explorers or germ-warfare researchers.

Generally, the onset or arrival of a monster will be set out in one of two ways, which are analogous to the two ways in which a crime might be set out in a detective fiction. That is, we often distinguish between thrillers and mysteries when discussing detective stories. In a thriller, the audience knows who the culprit is from the start—even if the characters in the fiction do not—and this knowledge has the function of generating a great deal of suspense. Or, it may be the case that neither the audience nor the characters know "whodunit"; all that is known is that a crime—often a murder—has been committed, and the reader and the sleuth review the clues simultaneously in order to solve the mystery.

Similarly, a complex discovery horror story may begin in the manner of a thriller, by immediately revealing the identity of the monster to the audience (e.g., *Jaws* or Guy Smith's novel *Killer Crabs*); or in the manner of a mystery, by only showing us the dastardly effects of the monster—usually involving death and destruction, but also the strange behavior of the recently possessed. In the latter case, the audience, along with the characters, follows the accumulation of the evidence of monstrous, foul doings with an interest in learning what is behind all this carnage.

As well, the onset, in the sense of the manifestation, of the monster, may be either immediate or gradual. The horrific being, that is, may be identified for the audience immediately in an early or an opening scene (e.g., the movie *Night of the Demon*), or its presence and/or identity may be only gradually revealed. We may only learn what the monster is after encountering several of its murders or other effects, though, of course, we may learn this before any of the characters in the story does.

In this respect many horror stories employ what might be called phasing in the development of their onset movement. That is, the audience may put together what is going on in advance of the characters in the story; the identification of the monsters by the characters is phased in after the prior realizations of the audience. That the audience possesses this knowledge, of course, quickens its anticipation. Moreover, the audience often is placed in this position because it, like the narrator, frequently has access to many more scenes and incidents, as well as their implications, than are available to individual characters. For example, in Daniel Rhodes's novel *Next After Lucifer,* we realize that Courdeval, the hierophant of Belial, is taking possession of John McTell before he does—since we have learnt, among other things, that the crypt has been disturbed before McTell does—and we also figure out that Alysse is the virgin Courdeval's seeking before anyone else does since we, but not the characters, know the nature of the apparition that appears in her bath. This type of structure is quite common. The audience, then, often has a fuller picture of what is going down, or, to shift metaphors, the audience has more pieces of the puzzle than do the characters, which perspective results in the audience coming to its discovery in advance of the characters, and, thereby, elicits a keen sense of expectation from the reader or the viewer.

Also, onset, like many of the other functions in horror stories, can be iterated. There can, for example, be multiple onsets; in Richard Lewis's novel *Devil's Coach Horse,* the man-eating beetles appear in both Chicago and Cambridge, England. Also, there may be multiple temporal as well as multiple spatial onsets; the creature may arrive at different times as well as in different places, as in King's *It.*[2] The onset function, as well, can be quite sustained; nearly the whole of Don D'Ammassa's novel *Blood Beast* is preoccupied with the protracted process by which the gargoyle becomes manifest.

The onset of the creature, attended by mayhem or other disturbing effects, raises the question of whether the human characters in the story will be able to uncover the source, the identity and the nature of these untoward and perplexing happenings. This question is answered in the second movement or function in the kind of plot we are discussing; I call it *discovery.* That is, after the monster arrives, an individual or a group learns of its existence. The discovery of the monster may come as a surprise to the characters, or it may be part of an investigation; moreover, where the discovery is the outcome of an investigation, the investigation may progress either under the benighted assumption that human agency is responsible for the recent, nefarious happenings or under the hypothesis that some unnatural force (e.g., a werewolf rather than a rabid dog) is at large. Discovery proper occurs when one character or group of characters comes to the warranted conviction that a monster is at the bottom of the problem. Onset, loosely speaking, comprises the scenes and sequences involving the manifestations of the monster, prior to the discovery of the monster; the onset movement can become quite extended as evidence, often in the form of murders or other disturbing events pile up before anyone (living) has a glimmering of what is going on. Where an investigation into the cause of these manifestations is already underway, discovery movement in the plot emerges neatly out of the onset movement.[3]

In what I am calling the complex discovery plot, the discovery that a monster is at the root of recent evil is resisted, often by the powers that be. That is, though an individual or a group has discovered that some unnatural being is behind a rash of gruesome killings, this information is treated skeptically by certain third parties, often authority figures such as the police, eminent scientists, religious leaders, government officials, or the army. The monster's existence has been established, both to the audience and to a small stalwart band of discoverers, but for one reason or another the monster's existence or the nature of the threat it actually poses is not acknowledged. "There are no such things as vampires,." the police chief might say at this point in a horror plot. In the movie *Jaws,* the town council refuses to admit the presence of the shark because of the threat it poses to the tourist trade, just as Mayor Pearson rejects Chief Slaughter's proposals in David Morrell's novel *The Totem,* because it would endanger the sale of local livestock. The discovery of the monster, therefore, necessitates a further confirmation to the satisfaction of third parties of the monster's existence. The discovery of the monster by one person or group must be proven to yet another, initially skeptical person or group, often a person or group necessary to mount resistance to the monster.

In the complex discovery plot, then, discovery flows into the next plot movement, which is *confirmation*. As we will see later, it is the presence of the confirmation function in this particular type of story that makes it a *complex* discovery plot. The confirmation function involves the discoverers of or the believers in the existence of the monster convincing some other group of the existence of the creature and of the proportions of the mortal danger at hand (some of these monsters are often said to spell the end of human life as we know it).

The confirmation section of this sort of plot can be quite elaborate. As the U.N. refuses to accept the reality of the onslaught of killer bees or invaders from Mars, precious time is lost, during which the creature or creatures often gain power and advantage. This interlude also allows for a great deal of discussion about the encroaching monster, and this talk about its invulnerability, its scarcely imaginable strength, and its nasty habits endows the beast with qualities that prime the audience's fearful anticipation of its next manifestation. Much of the audience's reaction to fictional monsters often hinges on the features attributed to them prior to their being shown

nscreen or prior to their being described in a particular
ovel. Talking about the monster when it is not present
's reaction for those scenes where we see or read about the
And a great deal of this attribution of horrific properties to
place while the discoverers are proving their case about
the monster's existence and its awesome potentials.[4]

In both the discovery and the confirmation movements in horror stories,
a great deal of ratiocination may be exhibited. As a character develops the
hypothesis that a vampire is in the neighborhood, or strives to prove that
alien invaders are taking over, argument and explanation come to the fore.
In order to confirm her discovery of a monster, a character will have to
demonstrate that her claim more plausibly fits the facts than the rival theories
do. Much of the reasoning employed to this end will be of the sort philosophers call "hypotheses to the best explanation." For example, the vampire
hypothesis better comprehends such anomalies as wolves baying in the
middle of London, small bite marks on the victim's neck, and sustained
anemia despite countless blood transfusions than do any of the available
naturalistic accounts.[5]

Undoubtedly, as with the case of mystery stories, the play of reasoning
in many horrific tales contributes to the cognitive pleasure the stories afford.
Nor should we be surprised to find that the drama of proof plays such an
important role in horror stories, since, as I argued earlier, the object of art-
horror is that which is excluded from our conceptual schemes. Thus, the
plots make a point of proving that there are more things in heaven and earth
than are acknowledged to exist in our standing conceptual frameworks. One
thing that is particularly interesting about this plot structure is the tension
caused by the delay between discovery and confirmation. Thematically it
involves the audience not only in the drama of proof. But, additionally, as
the audience shares the knowledge of the existence of the monsters with the
discoverers, it places us in a delightfully superior position that is especially
pronounced when the gainsayers in question—generals, bishops, police
chiefs, scientists, heads of institutions, bureaucrats of all sorts, and so on—
are patent authority figures.

As with onset, the discovery and confirmation movements in a horror
narrative can be iterated. The monster can be discovered more than once by
different persons and groups, and its existence may have to be confirmed
to more than one group. Stephen King's recent *Tommyknockers* starts the
discovery/confirmation process several times, though for various reasons in
each case the effort aborts in the fiction.

After the hesitations of confirmation, the complex discovery plot culmi-
nates in *confrontation*. Humanity marches out to meet its monster and the
confrontation generally takes the form of a debacle. Often, there is more
than one confrontation. These may assume the shape of an escalation in

intensity or complexity or both. Furthermore, the confrontation movement may also adopt a problem/solution format. That is, initial confrontations with the monster prove it to be invulnerable to humankind in every way imaginable; but then humanity snatches victory from the jaws of death by concocting one "last chance" countermeasure that turns the tide. This countermeasure can be developed and theorized in a scene that occurs before its application, e.g., the scene where the mating serum is introduced in *Devil's Coach Horse;* or, it can be thought up during the heat of battle, at a moment of catastasis, e.g., when the police chief shoots at the explosive cylinder that the shark has in its mouth at the end of *Jaws.* In the majority of cases, humanity emerges victorious from its confrontation with the monster, though it *is* possible for us to lose—as we do in the conclusion of the remake of the movie *Invasion of the Body Snatchers.* Or, the monster may simply escape, as he does in the novel *Next After Lucifer.* Recent motion pictures, especially since Brian De Palma's *Carrie,* also frequently follow the victorious confrontation scene with an optional coda which suggests that the monster has not been completely annihilated and is preparing for its next onset (in a sequel, no doubt);[6] for example, the heroine sees a momentary reflection of Freddie Kruger at the end of *Nightmare On Elm Street (Part IV).*

In order to get a clear sense of the way the complex discovery plot works, it is helpful to consider how it functions in detail in a well-known work of horror. A very useful example in this respect is William Blatty's novel *The Exorcist,* a book that quite conceivably can lay claim to being the inaugural work of the present cycle of horror fiction. The book is rather complicated insofar as it aspires to more than mere horror—allegorically, it is an affirmation of the existence of inexplicable evil in the world (note the page of quotations that precedes the story), and it has a theory about the real purpose of demonic possession. However, despite these larger aims, the book shares with more modest horror stories the form of the complex discovery plot.

The book begins with a short prologue in Northern Iraq. This is not part of the complex discovery part proper, though it performs important functions with respect to the novel as a whole. It introduces us briefly to the exorcist, Lankester Merrin, who has a premonition of what is to come; the demon Pazuzu, whose realm is that of sickness and disease, is going to strike again. Also, we learn something about Merrin's spiritual crisis; he has difficulty *feeling* (as opposed to willing) love for other people, especially when they are deformed and diseased (Pazuzu's special province). This has led Merrin to worry about his faith.

This information about Merrin's spiritual state is relevant to Blatty's conception of demonical possession; for Blatty thinks that the demonic purpose of possession is not primarily to appropriate the soul of the possessed, but to undermine the faith of all those who surround and witness the spectacle: to make them doubt and despise themselves in such a way that they cannot believe that God could love them. Thus, when the exorcism eventuates, we find the demon taunting Merrin about his problems with loving others, just as it exploits Karras's (the younger exorcist's) guilt feelings about his mother.

The Exorcist moves into first gear with the section called "The Beginning." The primary function of this section is to stage very carefully the onset of the demon. The onset movement in *The Exorcist* is quite protracted. The first evidence of the arrival of the monster occurs on the second page of the first chapter; Chris MacNeil, a famous movie actress and the mother of Regan (the young girl about to be possessed), hears rappings in the attic, which she takes to be caused by rats. Other anomalies begin to accumulate: Regan hears strange noises issuing from her bedroom ceiling; her missing dress appears in an unexpected place; Regan's bureau appears to have been moved; Regan plays with an ouija board, talking to someone named Captain Howdy; one of Regan's stuffed toys is found in one of the rat traps in the attic; and Regan complains that her bed shakes at night.

The second chapter switches to Father Karras; he visits his mother in New York. This interlude establishes that Karras feels quite guilty about having left his mother in order to follow his priestly vocation. Later during the exorcism, the demon will use Karras's guilt about his mother to undermine his determination. Chapter Three, however, returns to the business of developing the onset of the demon. Evidence of the demon's presence intensifies in its frequency, its scale and its seriousness. Chris complains to a doctor that Regan is indulging in eccentric, attention-getting behavior: the rappings; losing things; complaints about furniture moving and about her bed shaking. After Chris takes Regan to a doctor, Chris learns that Regan is using extremely obscene language. By the end of the chapter, Regan's condition is rapidly deteriorating: she is uncharacteristically forgetful and untidy; she complains of nausea; there are more reports of Regan's use of unseemly language; and Regan insists that there is a foul, "burny" smell in her room, which no one can corroborate.

The signs of the demon's onset become more evident in the opening of the fourth chapter. Desecrations, recalling those of the Black Mass, have been discovered in a nearby church: human excrement has been placed on the altar, and a massive phallus has been attached to an effigy of Christ. Meanwhile, Regan's behavior is becoming increasingly stranger. She comes downstairs while Chris is giving a party, urinates on the living-room rug, and ominously predicts that one of the guests, an astronaut, will die in outer space. The conclusion of the chapter, which is also the conclusion of the first section of the book, goes out with a bang. Chris sees Regan's bed shaking violently—and inexplicably.

The second section of *The Exorcist,* entitled "The Edge," carries the onset of the demon forward to the point of its discovery. Regan is subjected to batteries of medical tests, while her symptoms become more and more lurid. She begins to undergo episodes in which her body is heaved about; in which she exhibits preternatural strength; in which her body becomes unaccountably elastic; and in which her voice changes. The doctors are mystified. Then Chris's director, Burke Dennings, is murdered in what appears to be a cult killing—his head has been rotated 180 degrees—and Regan is implicated. The doctors suggest the possibility of an exorcism as a means of countersuggestion. The section ends with the most vivid manifestation of the demon's presence so far. Chris finds Regan masturbating with a crucifix; she forces Chris's face into her bleeding crotch; and then Chris sees something completely supernatural—Regan rotates her head 180 degrees as if to admit that she has killed Burke.[7] By this point in the plot Chris has been convinced that Regan is possessed. Chris functions, that is, as the discoverer figure in the plot. At the opening of the third section, "The Abyss," she approaches Karras for the purpose of requesting an exorcism. Karras, however, resists the idea. At this point, the plot moves into the confirmation phase. Karras is the relevant authority figure, and it is he who must be convinced, against his skeptical reservations, that Regan is possessed. This process is quite elaborate. It takes over a hundred pages before Karras is finally swayed.

The complexity of confirming Regan's possession stems from several factors. Since Karras is a psychiatrist, he immediately searches for naturalistic explanations. Also, his investigation must follow Church procedure, so he must ascertain that the established criteria for possession have been unambiguously met. As readers, we learn a great deal about what it takes to count as a genuine possession; and as Karras tests to see that each criterion is met—and that rival explanations are not available—an extended drama of proof preoccupies the text.

What makes the confirmation of Regan's possession particularly intricate is that the demon inside her is playing with Karras. At certain points, it intentionally misleads Karras; it pretends to think that tap water is holy water and writhes when it is sprinkled over the bed. The demon wants Karras to hesitate in his conviction. It says, "We must give you some reason for doubt. Some. Just enough to assure the final outcome."

The demon teases Karras, speaking in languages Regan could not know, but refusing to carry on the conversations long enough for Karras to be utterly convinced that it is not mouthing catchphrases. Of course, by now the reader is convinced that Regan is possessed, in part because we are quite aware of the fact that the demon knows exactly what Karras wants confirmed and ingeniously frustates Karras's strategems. Finally, however, the signs become overwhelming. It is discovered that Regan is answering Karras's questions in backwards English—a diabolical way, shall we say, to meet the requirement that the possessed exhibit facility with alien tongues—and Regan, though strapped to her bed, has etched "help me" on her stomach (earlier Karras had predicted that this sort of manifestation would disappear once Regan's hands were secured—famous last words). So, "At 9:00 that morning, Damien Karras came to the president of Georgetown University and asked for permission to seek an exorcism."

The Church authorities are not as difficult to convince as Father Karras, and the plot begins to move from the confirmation phase to the confrontation phase as we turn from the third section of the book to the fourth, entitled "And let my cry come unto thee. . . ." This section begins by bringing us up to date on a plot complication that I have not yet mentioned in my paraphrase so far—there is a police investigation into Burke Dennings murder that has run parallel to the discovery and confirmation of Regan's possession. This is not an essential element of the complex discovery plot; however, it does enrich *The Exorcist* by adding yet another line of ratiocination to the text—this time displayed by Detective Kinderman—which ratiocination, with its surmises and hypotheses, ramifies the drama of proof.

The most important element of the fourth section of *The Exorcist* is the arrival of Father Merrin, accompanied by some background information about him, which is then followed by the exorcism itself. Depending on how you count them, the exorcism involves several confrontations with the demon. The demon renders the room icy cold; Regan levitates; but most importantly, the demon attacks the assembled—most notably the exorcists—where their psyches are most vulnerable. In the penultimate confrontation, Merrin dies, which vexes Pazuzu immensely since he/she/it thought he/she/it was on the verge of winning Merrin's soul; Pazuzu, one guesses, thinks this is a piece of cosmic dirty pool. Then Karras enters the room for the last confrontation, which heats up to the point where the priest calls the demon into his own body and, with his last ounce of willpower, hurls himself (and the demon) from Regan's bedroom window. Regan is cleansed and Karras lives just long enough to be absolved of his sins. At this point, the narrative is effectively over, though there is a brief epilogue that sketches the return to normalcy.

This sort of complex discovery plot—comprising onset, discovery, confirmation, and confrontation—is exemplified in innumerable horror stories of all sorts. Another very well-known example of it can be found in the widely used theatrical popularization of *Dracula,* adapted by Hamilton Deane and John Baldston. The onset of the vampire is signaled in the opening scene of the first act, where we learn that Lucy has been stricken by the same mysterious disease that has recently killed Mina. Medical science is stymied and Dr. Seward, Lucy's father, has called his old colleague, Professor Van Helsing, onto the case.

Van Helsing is the quintessential discoverer figure. Though it appears that he already comes to England suspecting that the problem is a vampire, he sets about piecing together the evidence to support his view and, of course, he has to identify the vampire. Initially, he thinks that it must be an Englishman (since vampires must sleep in their native soil), but eventually he discovers that it is Count Dracula. Dr. Seward resists the idea of vampires as unscientific, but Van Helsing and Harker, Lucy's lover, argue the case in a drama of proof that shows how the vampire hypothesis is irresistible. The process of confirmation is nowise as sustained as in *The Exorcist,* and by the second act Seward seems converted. The play then turns to a series of confrontations, culminating in the staking of Dracula in the secret passage between Seward's asylum and Carfax Abbey.[8]

A striking number of films have employed the complex discovery plot during the last decade and a half of the current horror cycle. One particularly successful example is *The Omen,* written by David Selzer and directed by Richard Donner. This film, like *Rosemary's Baby*—which as both a novel and a film prefigured the reigning horror cycle—concerns the advent of the Anti-Christ. A band of devil worshippers, mostly priests it appears, have substituted the son of Satan—called Damien—for the child of a wealthy American diplomat, Robert Thorn (played by Gregory Peck), who has presidential aspirations. Thus, it is implied that Satan is putting himself within reach of the White House.

Of course, neither Thorn nor his wife realizes that Damien is the Son of Satan. But all sorts of strange happenings begin to herald the onset of something unnatural. Some highlights: Damien's governess, seemingly in a trance, hangs herself at his birthday party; a bizarre new nanny, with a feral grin, shows up under dubious circumstances and soon after her a monstrous dog (with whom, the editing has suggested, Damien has telepathic communion) joins the household, against Ambassador Thorn's instructions; Damien has an inexplicable tantrum at the sight of a church; Damien scares away giraffes and enrages baboons at the zoo; and so on.

The role of the discoverer is distributed over two figures. The first is Father Brennan who—though he has learned who Damien really is—manages to inform Thorn of his son's nature in such a deranged and lunatic manner that Thorn discounts it (until, after Brennan's death, some of what the priest foretold comes to pass).[9] Then the discoverer role is taken up by a photographer named Jennings, whose snapshots of people around Thorn have a tricky habit of prophesizing their deaths. Jennings has also investigated Brennan and has, more or less, come to know most of what the priest knew.

Jennings lays his case before Thorn, who is becoming somewhat rattled by all the coincidences: his wife's pregnancy, as predicted by the crazy priest; the fact that Damien was born at 6 a.m. on June sixth (i.e., at 666), etc. But Thorn is nevertheless skeptical. For most of the rest of the film, he remains the figure for whom the existence of the Satanic plot must be confirmed. The drama of proof and the play of ratiocination become quite sustained: not only are we treated to glosses of the Book of Revelations that are then correlated to Damien's circumstances, but we learn that Damien's mother appears to have been a dog, and that Thorn's natural child had been murdered. The telltale evidence keeps piling up.

At certain moments—for example, after the attack at the cemetery and then after his wife's death—Thorn seems convinced. But he keeps backsliding. In Israel, he refuses to kill Damien; but when Jennings says he'll do it, Jennings is beheaded.[10] Understandably, this unnerves Thorn, so he picks up the ritual knives again and heads for London. But, even in London, he must perform one more test to confirm Damien's diabolism. As instructed by an Israeli exorcist, he cuts the child's hair and uncovers an incriminating birthmark (666). This is the last piece of evidence; the Anti-Christ hypothesis is finally confirmed to Thorn's satisfaction. And no sooner is it confirmed, then the first confrontation explodes: Thorn is assailed by the demonic governess with the feral grin, who seems to function rather as Damien's familiar. Thorn must also confront the household hound from hell. But despite his heroic efforts, he is gunned down before he can kill Damien on hallowed ground. Humankind loses this confrontation with Satan, and Damien seems to have become a ward of the President of the United States.

The complex discovery plot is one of the most frequent horror plots in use in recent literature and film, though it is also in evidence in earlier horror cycles. The giant insect films of the fifties, as well as alien invasion films, make quite wide use of this format as do earlier horror novels like *Carmilla*. However, it is not the only plot structure to be found in the genre,[11] and, at this juncture, it will be instructive to look at some other alternative plot structures.

Variations

One way to track down other operative horror plots is to note that many horror stories do not employ all of the functions or plot movements sketched in the account of the complex discovery plot. Often one observes that one can arrive at the characterization of the plot structure of a given horror story by *subtracting* various of the functions or plot movements from the complex discovery plot. For example, one quite common alternative plot structure is the *discovery plot* (as opposed to the *complex* discovery plot). This comprises three basic functions (though each may be iterated). These are: onset, discovery, and confrontation. That is, one very frequent horror plot is the complex discovery plot *sans* the confirmation function.

An example of what has just been called the discovery plot would be Charles Grant's novel *The Hour of the Oxrun Dead*. The novel begins with the savage murder of Ben. It is not the last murder, and it is supplemented by other strange doings. Natalie, eventually in concert with Marc, the newspaper reporter, performs the discovery function; and the discovery of the coven takes up most of the novel—in the manner of a mystery story's fitting together pieces of evidence—until the final confrontation, where Toal is defeated by means of the missing ring. There is no confirmation in the face of objections by third parties.

In terms of the internal structure of this novel, there is an obvious reason for this: all the powers that be—all those to whom one might wish to confirm the existence of the coven—belong to the coven. The discoverers, that is, must deal with the supernatural encroachments on their own. Clearly, any horror story that involves such conspiratorial take-overs of the everyday world will not have complete confirmation movements in them since the discoverers can only ultimately consult themselves. Of course, one variation here will be that the discoverers will approach someone who, unbeknownst to them, is complicit in the conspiracy; however, this will yield only further discovery of the nature of the enemy on their part, perhaps leading directly to confrontation.

Of course, the discovery plot can be found in horror stories where there is no overarching, supernatural conspiracy. After the onset of a horrific being, the hero or heroine may have no alternative—there's no time; there's no opportunity; there are no other living humans; the locale is too isolated; and so on—except to confront the monster on his/her/their own.

In M.R. James's "Casting the Runes," the onset of the demon and the necromancy of Karswell are established through the report of the death of John Harrington and the series of strange events befalling Edward Dunning, including the invasion of his household by some vaguely described monster. Dunning approaches Henry Harrington, and together they identify both Karswell as the source of their problem and the means by which his executions are brought about. Armed with this information, they inflict Karswell's spell upon Karswell without attempting to confirm their findings to a third party. Thus, the plot moves from the discovery phase to the confrontation phase with no stopover for confirmation.

King's novel *Cycle of the Werewolf* represents a fiction whose plot somewhat straddles the distinction between the complex discovery plot and the discovery plot. The reason for this is that the final confrontation scene has the moment of confirmation as a constitutive part. After the onset of the werewolf, Marty Coslaw, who has blinded the werewolf in one eye, infers that a local preacher is the monster; Marty lures him to his home, where he is armed with the requisite silver bullets, in order to destroy the creature. Prior to the confrontation, Marty does confide his suspicions to his Uncle Al because he needs Al to get him some silver bullets. Al is skeptical, but nevertheless helps Marty. Thus, when the werewolf is finally blasted, Marty's hypothesis is vindicated, to Al's (and everyone else's) astonishment. In this case, the confirmation function is piggybacked, so to speak, on the confrontation function.

My own inclination is to stipulate that this example falls in the category of the discovery plot. However, this case indicates that insofar as our various functions can be combined in single plot movements, there will be some irreducible vagueness in their application; things are not as neat, that is, as the present taxonomy may suggest, though the taxonomy may still be of use, especially at a moment like the present where so little has been written by way of the narratological analysis of horror.

Just as one can derive a serviceable horror plot by subtracting the confirmation function from the complex discovery plot, so one can also get an operational narrative by subtracting the confrontation function from the more complicated plot. This procedure yields the *confirmation plot,* which is composed of three movements or functions: onset, discovery, confirmation. An example of this would be the original film version of *Invasion of the Body Snatchers.* Inside the framing story, the onset of the pod invasion is developed until the doctor finally discovers its source; after aborted attempts at confirmation—aborted since all the authorities in the town are pod people—he escapes to tell his story to outsiders. Their disbelief, then, is dispelled when suddenly, at the end of the film, they learn that a truck has been discovered ferrying mysterious pods along the highway. We never see the confrontation between humanity and the pod people. The film ends with the resolution of the confirmation process.

Another possible triple movement plot would involve the sequence: onset, confirmation, confrontation. Since this formation lacks a discovery component, it will probably only be found in narrative contexts where the monster is already known to exist, so that the evidence of its presence, accumulated in the onset phase of the narrative, does not result in the original discovery of the creature, but in the confirmation of a monstrous being already known to exist in the world of the fiction. Perhaps sequels are good examples of this. That is, where it is already known by everyone in the fiction that Godzilla exists, the evidence of his return will confirm rather than originally indicate (i.e., discover) his presence.

One can also imagine a three-part plot structure comprising: discovery, confirmation, and confrontation. Here we have subtracted onset from the complex discovery plot. This sort of plot might occur where there is no available evidence of the onset of the monster until the moment of discovery. That is, the entire onset movement occurs when the creature is discovered. Sheri S. Tepper's novel *Blood Heritage* could be an example here. For over one hundred pages, we are involved in the mysterious disappearance of Badger's family. The presence of the demon Matuku-pago-pago is not directly manifested during this investigation. The demon explodes like a whirlwind out of its prison when Badger and his psychic company visit Baleford. The first appearance of the creature, then, affords the moment of its discovery—at least for Mahlia and the Professor. Moreover, it seems appropriate to call this sequence of events a discovery, insofar as it involves Mahlia and the Professor ratiocinating about the nature of the monster.

Since Badger resists the demon hypothesis, he supplies the sort of skepticism that requires confirmation. He is gradually convinced as confrontation is layered upon confrontation. An interesting feature of this particular novel, at least from the perspective of narrative structure, is that nested in the confrontation segment with respect to Matuku-pago-pago is a subplot involving the discovery of another monster, the succubus. So, embedded in the confrontation with Matuku is the onset and discovery of the succubus, which then dovetails with the confrontation with Matuku. This suggests that many of the structures I have identified so far can be recombined with each other to propose more and more intricate plots.

By subtracting functions from the complex discovery plot, I have sketched a series of tri-function horror stories. Further subtractions suggest a range of dual function narratives, including: onset/confrontation; onset/discovery; onset/confirmation; discovery/confrontation; discovery/confirmation; and confirmation/confrontation.

An example of the onset/confrontation plot would be Orson Welles's radio adaptation of *The War of the Worlds*. It opens with explosions on Mars, followed rather quickly by the landing of the alien cylinders. Very quickly, the cylinders open, and the war between humanity and the space invaders is on. There is very little to discover; everyone, all at once, knows that the Martians have arrived and that the confrontation has been joined. In the opening segment of the show, there is a residue of the confirmation theme; the scientist Pierson reassures us that there is no life on Mars—just before it takes up residence in New Jersey. However, the theme of confirmation cannot be sustained, since in short order the Martian presence is made apparent to the entire world. All that is left to do is to resist it. The rest of the story itemizes humanity's defeat in confrontation after confrontation until the *deus ex machina*.

Films such as Howard Hawks's *The Thing* and Ridley Scott's *Alien* would also appear modeled on the onset/confrontation structure. Again, this seems to be a function of the fact that there is really no distance between onset and discovery; they not only occur in the same instance, but there is no question about the existence and the nature of the present danger to all concerned. That is, there is no reason to establish that something monstrous, which defies our normal forms of conceptualization, is killing people, because its presence is there for all the characters to see. Some characters (often scientific researchers) might not think that the monster should be destroyed and may impede efforts to kill it. But there is no question that it is a monster that is at large.

Some play of ratiocination may occur in plots like this, where discoveries are made about the incredible properties of such monsters. But this ratiocination, like the skeptical residue in *The War of the Worlds,* is optional. These fictions can become war stories very quickly. These war stories can vary in scale from full-dress, tactical warfare, as in the case of *The War of the Worlds,* to platoon stories in which a handful of vulnerable warriors are cut off and effectively surrounded by a group of monsters or one monster who seems to have the ability to be everywhere, all at once. Films like *Alien, Creature,* and *The Thing* are good examples of the platoon monster film. Nor is this plot structure found only with reference to space invasion; the film *The Evil Dead* would also seem to be an example here.

Robert Bloch's short story "The Feast in the Abbey" illustrates the onset/ discovery plot. The onset involves the narrator's visit to the monastery and his increasing sense that there is something disturbingly wrong with the behavior of the monks. The moment of discovery occurs in the final paragraphs of the story, where the awakening visitor figures out that the monastery is an intermittently appearing, haunted coven, and that the meat that was served to him during the feast was from the body of his brother, a priest.

Perhaps Edith Wharton's "Afterward" can be construed as an instance of onset/confirmation. The story begins by telling the legend of a ghost who appears in a Dorsetshire household but whose presence, so local lore has it, can only be known long after the fact. An American couple—Ned and Mary Boyne—buy the house, and they seem very keen to meet the ghost. But as time wears on, there is no evidence of spectral manifestations, and they become skeptical about its existence—"their invisible housemate had finally dropped out of their references, which were numerous enough to make them soon unaware of the loss."

However, an exceeding strange event occurs; Ned Boyne disappears one day when an unidentified stranger calls, and Mary directs him to Ned's library. There is an extended search for Ned. But mysteriously, no trace of him can be found. There is no hint that anything of a supernatural order has transpired. But, in fact, the unaccountable disappearance of Ned, to which Mary finally adjusts, is the primary indication of onset that we have.

As the story unravels, Mary eventually comes to the conclusion that the strange, unidentified visitor, mentioned above, was the ghost of Robert Elwell whom Ned had done wrong in some sort of shady business deal. Apparently, the ghost had returned for its revenge. Mary only realizes this at the end of the story during an interview with a solicitor. And this inference on Mary's part functions to confirm the opening legend that one only becomes cognizant of the presence of the ghost in this haunted house long after its arrival.

One reason that I have assimilated Mary's recognition of the ghost's existence to the confirmation theme rather than to the discovery theme is that in its narrative setting, it does function to confirm the opening legend.

Moreover, this revelation does occur in a context of skepticism, as the young Americans have become somewhat disappointed in not having met the ghost.

Stories that deploy the onset/confirmation structure need somehow to presuppose the antecedent discovery of the unnatural being. For confirmation can only occur against the background of a previous discovery or hypothesis—one, indeed, that is generally subject to skepticism. One way to meet these conditions is to begin in a context where there is a local legend which may be disputed: perhaps some claim to the effect that either the Loch Ness Monster or the Abominable Snowman exists. The onset of the creature then confirms the disputed, local hypothesis. Such stories need not lead to confrontation. It may, as in the case of "Afterward," be too late for a confrontation; or, it may be that for one reason or another the humans in the story have neither reason nor means to confront the creature. Perhaps, they may even believe that it is best to let the monster continue its existence undisturbed. Such plots may be rare nowadays, since horror novels and movies put such a high premium on action and adventure that a rousing confrontation is hard to resist.

The classic movie *King Kong* exemplifies the discovery/confrontation plot. The film opens with the preparations for the journey to Skull Island and then the voyage itself. The impresario, Carl Denham, intends to make a movie there. He is motivated by rumors of a legendary being called Kong, but he doesn't know whether it exists or exactly what it is. There is no onset in the sense that Denham has any direct evidence of Kong's existence. The voyage is undertaken on the basis of a vague conjecture. Once the explorers reach the island—though it is clear that the natives believe in Kong—nothing happens that would straightforwardly indicate Kong's monstrous presence. Rather, his first manifestation—to collect his sacrificial bride—represents the moment of discovery. From then on, the film devotes itself to confrontation after confrontation, including abductions, chases, and behemoth battles.[12]

If it is correct to count it as a horror story, Sir Arthur Conan Doyle's *The Lost World* seems to have an overall plot structure that follows the rhythm of discovery/confirmation. In the opening sections of the book, Professor Challenger's discovery of the prehistoric life in South America is reviewed; but these discoveries are called into question by leading scientific authorities. In concluding segments of the text, however, Challenger's discoveries are corroborated when he exhibits an airborne, gargoylesque dinosaur to the scientific establishment.

Though this account of *The Lost World* is fine as far as it goes, it primarily applies to the overarching narrative structure of the text. It skips over the adventures in South America that engage the explorers as they secure their evidence. That segment of the book is full of confrontations. However, I am prone to regard these confrontations as functions nested within the confirmation process rather than initiating an independent plot movement insofar these confrontations do not have the sense of finality one finds in the confrontations that cap off the complex discovery plot. However, even if I am wrong in this matter, it does seem heuristically useful to think of *The Lost World* as an example of discovery/confirmation, for doing so at least indicates how this plot structure is likely to go. An initial, contested discovery calls forth a project or expedition for the purpose of corroborating it, and closure is secured when the confirmation can be made to stick.

The movie *Aliens,* the sequel to *Alien,* is an example of the confirmation/confrontation plot. The earlier film established that the planet was packed with the eggs of alien creatures; when communication with the mining outpost breaks down, it is presumed that those beings have overrun the industrial park, and a platoon of space-troopers is dispatched to confirm that surmise. After we are introduced to the "rainbow" platoon, the presence of alien nests is confirmed, and the plot settles into the kind of confrontations where human life, as we know it, is at risk.

Just as the ingredient functions of the complex discovery plot can be used to compose alternative horror plots of the two and three movement variety, so each of the functions on its own can comprise the stuff of a horror story. That is, in addition to the plots so far reviewed there are also pure onset plots, pure discovery plots, pure confirmation plots, and pure confrontation plots.

Stephen King's short story "The Raft" seems to be a pure onset plot. A group of adolescent swimmers sneaks out to a swimming pond off-season. They race out to a raft. Eventually, they notice what appears to be an oil slick. However, it is oddly self-propelled and it has a taste for human flesh. It would be peculiar to say that the "whatever-it-is" was discovered by the teenagers; rather, it seems to discover them. And as soon as it discovers them it starts to gobble them up one by one. They have no idea what it is, and no means to confront it. This is the kind of situation that could initiate a more complicated plot structure in which someone wonders what happened to the teenagers. But that never happens. The plot ends with Randy alone on the raft and destined to die. The story is all onset; it is what *Jaws* would be like if it ended with the first shark attack.

H.G. Wells's short story "The Empire of the Ants" is an example of a pure confirmation plot. The gunboat *Benjamin Constant* is dispatched in answer to reports about the onslaught of army ants on the Batemo arm of the Guaramadema River. Thus, the ants have already arrived and have been discovered before the story proper begins. The gunboat engages the ants in several ineffectual sallies and then returns to port for further instructions. The substance of the story, then, is to confirm the existence of the ants and to take note of their novel and rather extraordinary powers. The story closes by remarking that an English observer, Holroyd, is so shaken by the encounter that he undertakes to warn the world of the danger posed by this new species of ants; Holroyd is said to "believe that he has seen the beginning of one of the most stupendous dangers that have ever threatened our race." The story does not stage that confrontation; all its energies have been lavished on confirming the existence and the proportions of the threat.

Another Wells story, "The Valley of Spiders," may exemplify a pure confrontation plot. A band of riders, in pursuit of a woman and her friends, rides right into an area mysteriously festooned with cobwebs. Very quickly it becomes evident that these webworks are part of an unaccountably large lair of thousands of spiders. The riders have to fight their way out of the valley—and not all succeed. There is really no onset here for the riders invade the domain of the spiders; indeed, they career into it headlong and heedlessly. Nor is any time spent discovering or confirming the nature of their danger; they just see that they are surrounded by innumerable poison-ous spiders, and the life-and-death struggle begins. After one of the riders, the master, effectively escapes, he infers that the woman he has been chasing is still alive, and it is indicated that he is planning his revenge. But the central action of the story has been involved with the struggle to evade the spiders' clutches. The action revolves primarily around the simple, though horrify-ing, confrontation between the men and the spiders, which, among other things, highlights the ruthlessness of the master.

Many horror stories—especially, it seems to me, those of older vintage—appear to be what we can call pure discovery plots. The narrator simply recounts, step by step, how he or she became aware of the existence of a horrific being. An example of the pure discovery plot is H.P. Lovecraft's short story "Pickman's Model." As it opens, Thurber is ostensibly explain-ing to Eliot why he had broken off relations with the artist Robert Upton Pickman, a painter of morbid scenes—with titles like "Ghoul Feeding"—who has recently disappeared.

Thurber begins by noting that, unlike the middlebrow Boston art commu-nity, he was not put off by Pickman's daring canvases. That he defended Pickman in the face of his rejection by proper society earned him Pickman's confidence, and he was treated to a private interview at Pickman's secret studio.

Pickman tells him of all sorts of ancient, hidden tunnels under the city, and he shows Thurber paintings that unnerve even a steely-eyed connoisseur of the gruesome such as the narrator. These paintings seem to tell the story of a retrogression of the human to the animal. What particularly disturbs Thurber about these pictures is that they seem so realistic; they seem as though they were drawn from living models.

At one point, Thurber takes a photo off one of Pickman's works-in-progress. Thurber does not look at it immediately, and Pickman says he uses such photos as inspiration for backgrounds. Once, during their discussion,

Pickman excuses himself and goes into an adjoining room in order to shoot at what he says are rats in his own ancient tunnel-works. After their meeting, Thurber looks at the photograph. It is the spitting image of one of Pickman's monstrosities. Thurber realizes that "By God, Eliot, *it was a photograph from life.*" In other words, there are regressive ghoulies underneath Boston, and the unholy Pickman traffics with them in order to find his funest imagery. That is why his work is so realistic.

In this story, there is no onset; we have no reason to think that we are dealing with unnatural beings until the concluding revelation. Of course, there are Pickman's paintings, which, though repulsive and magnetically realistic, are represented as fictional. Retrospectively, we may conjecture that the rats Pickman shot at were really ghouls, but at that point in the story neither Thurber or the reader has grounds to suspect that monsters are afoot. The story does end by tying together a number of the anomalies it has presented— Pickman's realism, most notably. But it does so by discovering the existence of beings that have not saliently manifested their presence heretofore in the story except, perhaps, as creatures of folklore and fiction. The whole story leads up to and prepares for the discovery, from which no confrontation issues.

So far, then, I have identified the following fourteen, possible horror-story formats: onset; onset/discovery; onset/confirmation; onset/confrontation; onset/discovery/confrontation; onset/confirmation/confrontation; onset/discovery/confirmation/confrontation; discovery; discovery/confirmation; discovery/confrontation; discovery/confirmation/confrontation; confirmation; confirmation/confrontation; and confrontation.

These fourteen basic plot structures, of course, do not exhaust the full range of story schemes, even within this family of functions. For earlier it was noted that these plot functions can be iterated, and, as well, certain sequences of these plot functions can be nested—as subplots—within larger plot movements, as we saw in the case of *Blood Heritage*. Given these possibilities, the number of plots available in this family of functions becomes, in principle, mathematically astronomical.[13] And, of course, these complications can be even more various when one realizes that on occasion these plot functions can be piggybacked in such a way that more than one plot function is discharged by the self-same sequence of events in the narrative.

In outlining these plots, a certain linear ordering of functions has been respected. Where all the plot functions are present, onset is followed by discovery, which is followed by confirmation, which is followed by confrontation, and, where functions have been subtracted out, this linear ordering continues to operate in terms of what remains. This linear ordering follows a certain kind of logic: in order to be discovered, the monster must exist, and this is often established through onset; in order to be confirmed, a discovery has to have taken place; and in order to confront the monster, humanity or its representatives have to know of the nature and existence of the monster—which knowledge is generally secured by means of discovery and/or confirmation. There are, in other words, certain conceptual constraints on the order in which these plot structures can be combined.

In order to be discovered, confirmed, or confronted, the monster must exist. This can be established by staging an onset sequence. Of course, as we saw above, one can forego this phase of plot development; however, it remains the case that the existence of the monster must somehow be incorporated in the story, if it is to make sense. Likewise, to be confirmed, the existence of the monster has to have been discovered; if the discovery is not part of the action of the story, then it may be the case that the monster had been discovered at some time earlier than that being narrated—which earlier discovery must be referred to or presupposed (in the case of well-known sequels) within the story. Similarly, if a monster is to be confronted, it must be established that it exists, even if this is done in the heat of confrontation.

Obviously, these conceptual constraints apply first and foremost to what Russian Formalist critics and their followers call the *fabula* or story of a given narrative—i.e., the material about which the narrative concerns itself: a series of events that might be described with their chronological and causal order intact. However, the *sujet* or plot of a narrative may diverge compositionally from the chronology or causal order of the events it narrates. The plot—in terms of the order in which events are narrated—may rearrange the chronological or causal ordering of the basic story or *fabula* from which the plot is derived. The narrative may begin *in media res* and then backtrack, for example. Or, there may be flashforwards. Thus, though a horror plot (in the Formalist sense of *sujet*) may follow the linear order respected above, it need not.

For instance, the original plot structure of Robert Louis Stevenson's *The Strange Case of Dr. Jekyll and Mr. Hyde* (as opposed to a number of its adaptations for stage and screen) develops the onset and confrontation with Hyde before the reader and Utterson discover the what and the wherefore of the monster by means of the packet of letters Poole gives Utterson after Hyde's death. This indicates that horror narratives may be plotted at the level of the *sujet* in variance from the linear order respected above, and that, in consequence, there are even more available plot sequences in this family of functions than have been so far either mentioned or conjectured. That is, added to the combination of functions already countenanced are further permutations, involving the whole gamut of temporal plotting devices such as flashbacks, flashforwards and so on. In terms of the conceptual constraints already indicated, these temporally non-linear plots (with respect to their order of exposition) must abide by the constraints insofar as their underlying story or *fabula* is chronologically and causally intelligible. But if that condition is met, these plots may rearrange the functions in the order of telling in myriad ways. Moreover, the preceding constraint is not very difficult to accommodate. Therefore, added to all the linearly organized horror plots— that is, linear with respect to the order of exposition—and their expansions (by means of iteration, nesting, subplots, and so on), there are a multitude of further plots in this family whose innumerable variations I leave to the reader to work through and contemplate.

Overreacher Plots and Further Combinations

Thus far I have been exploring the range of horror plots that can be generated by means of the fourfold family of functions: onset, discovery, confirmation, and confrontation. These result in a wide range of very abstract plot structures that can be deployed across the many subgenres of horror—from the ghost story to the alien invasion saga to tales of vampires, werewolves, zombies, and demonic possession. However, in order to broaden our understanding of horror plotting, it is useful to consider at least one different recurring plot type of somewhat lower generality—one that is closely associated with one subgenre, specifically, that of the mad scientist, but which also subtends the plotting of other subgenres, where the blasphemous experiment may be replaced by the magical invocation of Satan, or, as in Lovecraft's "The Dunwich Horror," the Old Ones.

I call this structure the *overreacher plot* in honor of its main character: the mad scientist or the necromancer. Examples of it would include Curt Siodmak's novel *Donovan's Brain,* H.P. Lovecraft's short story "Herbert West, Reanimator," theatrical adaptations such as Leonard Caddy's *Jekyll and Hyde* and Victor Gialanella's *Frankenstein,* and movies such as *The Man with the X-Ray Eyes.* As these familiar titles indicate, the overreacher plot is concerned with forbidden knowledge—of either the scientific or the magical sort. This knowledge is put to the test in terms of either an experiment or an incantation of evil forces. Whereas the stories derived above from the complex discovery plot often stress the shortsightedness of science, the overreacher plot criticizes science's will to knowledge. That is, where the underlying theme of the complex discovery plot is often that there are more things in heaven and earth than are found in our philosophy (science, conceptual scheme, etc.), the recurring theme of the overreacher plot is that there is some knowledge better left to the gods (or whomever).

The basic, linear plot structure, or underlying *fabula* form of the overreacher plot, generally comprises four movements. The first involves the preparation for the experiment. The preparation movement has a variety of components. The first is practical: the overreacher must secure the materials requisite for the experiment. Thus, Gialanella's *Frankenstein* opens (Act 1,

Scene 1) in a graveyard where Victor Frankenstein is in the process of procuring dead bodies from the local grave-robbers, Hans Metz and Peter Schmidt.

However, the preparation for the experiment also characteristically has what might be called a philosophical side along with a practical side. For the overreacher will typically offer both an explanation and a justification for the experiment. That is, the overreacher often conveniently has an assistant or a friend or some other interlocutor to whom he can explain how the experiment is supposed to work and what its significance (moral, scientific, ideological, metaphysical, etc.) is supposed to be. The explanation is usually a mixture of popular mechanics and sci-fi mumbo-jumbo, while the justification can be quite megalomaniacal.[14]

In Gialanella's *Frankenstein*, Act 1, Scene 2 ends with Victor justifying his experiment to Henry Clerval: "Think, Henry, think! To have control of life and death. Perhaps to remove disease forever from the human frame. To insure eternally the existence of the greatest minds." In the opening of Act 1, Scene 3, Victor then goes on to explain how the experiment is going to work: "If a minor shock produces convulsive movement, might not a greater shock produce . . . continued animation?"

Often the explanation/justification component of the preparation movement of the overreacher plot takes place in the context of an argument or a debate. For example, in Caddy's *Jekyll and Hyde*, Jekyll's theory, which motivates his experiment, is outlined in Act 1, Scene 1, in which Dr. Lanyon and Jekyll continue their weekly dispute about whether the body is part of the brain. In Rouben Mamoulian's film *Dr. Jekyll and Mr. Hyde*, the explanation/justification opens the film in the form of a "daring" lecture.

The preparation movement may be preceded by or interspersed with certain establishing scenes that introduce us to the locale of the story as well as to characters other than the overreacher. Often these characters may be people who are especially close to the overreacher; establishing the overreacher's personal, family, and/or love relations can be very important in certain variations of this plot form. For not only do they often provide the resistance to the experiment that allows the overreacher to declaim his justification of it; but, as well, later in the plot (as we shall see) when the experiment goes haywire, it often endangers the experimenter's loved ones thereby supplying the motive for him to recant—as well as the stuff of suspense.

The preparation movement of the overreacher plot—as well as each of its more or less standard components—may be iterated, just as the functions of the complex discovery plot may be repeated. Moreover, the explanatory and justificatory elements of the preparation movement support the kind of play of ratiocination and the drama of proof found in the discovery and confirmation functions discussed above. Undoubtedly, the reasoning displayed by overreachers is, strictly speaking, nonsense; nevertheless, it has the shape of argumentation and demonstration and, however unsound it is in fact, it affords the formal pleasures of such exercises.

The preparation phase of the overreacher plot is followed by the experiment itself. On stage and screen, this can be an occasion for a great deal of pyrotechnics. Of course, the experiment may have to be performed more than once before it succeeds, or, at least, appears to succeed. The apparent success of the experiment may allow for some more megalomania on the part of the overreacher as well as for further debates about its justification; other characters may urge the experimenter to abort the venture. And, of course, it is also possible that the overreacher may immediately recant in the face of success, as he does in Mary Shelley's *Frankenstein*.

After the apparent or partial success of the experiment, it soon becomes clear that the experiment has gone awry. The monster that the experiment has created or otherwise brought into existence is dangerous. It kills and maims often innocent victims. In one standard variation of this plot, those most likely to be endangered by the monster are those who are near and dear to the experimenter. For example, in Mary Shelley's *Frankenstein,* the monster embarks on a conscious program dedicated to the destruction of Frankenstein's closest relations: William, Justine, Clerval, and Elizabeth. In movie adaptations of the Jekyll/Hyde story, in which Jekyll has a fiancee, she is likely to be a prime target. Of course, the monster's victims need not be friends and associates of the overreacher. The monster may be on a generic rampage. As well, this plot movement can be extended over quite a lot of murders.[15]

In many versions of the overreacher plot, it is the death and destruction unleashed by the monster—often with respect to the overreacher's loved ones—that brings the overreacher to his senses and commits him to destroying his creation. This leads to the last movement in the overreacher plot, viz., confrontation. Needless to say, it is not the case that all overreachers see the error of their ways. Some are prepared to defend their experiment and their creation to the death. These are mad scientists; often, in this variation, the confrontation phase of the plot will involve not only the destruction of the monstrous creation, but also that of the uncontrite overreacher who spawned it. As in the case of the complex discovery plot, the final confrontation phase of the plot can be iterated in a series of seemingly all-or-nothing battles.

A basic sketch of the overreacher plot includes four movements: preparation for the experiment; the experiment itself; the accumulation of evidence that the experiment has boomeranged;[16] and the confrontation with the monster. In order to get a concrete feel for this plot scheme, let us consider a brief paraphrase of Curt Siodmak's novel *Donovan's Brain*.

The story is set in the southwest in the early forties. The narrator, Patrick

Corey, is the overreacher. His particular ambition is to keep brains, detached from their bodies, alive in what he calls "an artificial respiratory." As the story opens, he is preparing for an experiment: he purchases a monkey. Once he wins the monkey's confidence, he kills it, and attaches its brain to his machines. He shows his successful experiment to a local physician, Dr. Schratt, who is horrified by his research, and they argue about the propriety of "invading God's own hemisphere." Schratt accuses Patrick of lacking human emotion, fetishizing mathematical precision, and being heedless of the consequences of his research. This argument continues on numerous other occasions. We also learn, early on, that Patrick lives with his wife Janice, who loves him, but from whom he is estranged; predictably enough, when the crucial experiment gets completely out of hand, she will be in deep trouble.

The day after Patrick's discussion with Schratt, the monkey brain dies. But no sooner does it expire, than Patrick gets an emergency telephone call asking him to provide medical assistance at the scene of an airplane crash. Patrick agrees. Two of the victims have been decapitated, while the third, the eponymous Donovan, is dying. Patrick decides he has a use for Donovan's brain. The operation of removing the brain and installing it in an appropriate vat is described in detail—as well as the necessary cover-up.

Once the brain has been successfully relocated, Patrick devotes himself to attempting to communicate with it. It is at this point that Patrick confides his justification of the experiment to the reader:

> Without a doubt a precise thought process was going on in this eyeless, earless matter. It might, like a blind man, feel the light or, like a deaf one, perceive sound. It might, in its dark mute existence, produce thoughts of immense clarity and inspiration. It might, just because it was cut off from the distractions of the senses, be able to concentrate all its brain-power on important thoughts. I wanted to know those thoughts! But how could I get in touch with the brain? It could not talk or move, yet if I could study its thinking, I might learn about the great unsolved riddles of nature. The brain might, in its complete solitude have created answers to eternal questions.

As various modes of communicating with the brain are explored, the brain is growing into what may be a new species of formless creature. Schratt has warned: "Patrick! You're creating a mechanical soul that will destroy the world." At the same time, it is apparent to the reader that the brain is coming to exert more and more control over Patrick, though he continues, for quite some time, to believe that he is in control of the experiment. The brain soon has power over Patrick at a distance, and can turn him into an instrument of its will.

Effectively, the brain dispatches Patrick to Los Angeles to carry on its affairs. It is the brain of W.H. Donovan, an extremely wealthy man who was both willful and unscrupulous. Patrick acquits its eccentric errands, which turn out to be the brain's way of seeking a rather primitive form of justice. Eventually, as might be expected, these escalate to attempted murder. Finally, even Patrick has to admit that he is no longer in control and that the experiment has run amuck. He instructs Schratt by telephone to stop feeding the brain, but Schratt, unpredictably, refuses. Patrick now says "Donovan's brain dwelt vampire-like in my body. . . ."

Janice realizes that Donovan's brain has complete control of Patrick; and Donovan, a paranoid type (as it turns out), uses Patrick's body to attack Janice. But just at the moment when the Donovan-creature is about to do Janice in, Patrick, suddenly and inexplicably, regains control of his body. Most of the remainder of the novel explains how it was that while Donovan's brain was taking Patrick over, Schratt was preparing to destroy the brain. So at the very instant that the Donovan-creature lowered over Janice, Schratt noticed the angry, neurotic deflections on the encephalogram, and, surmising that the brain was about to kill, Schratt hurled himself on the vat, killing the brain while, simultaneously, the brain killed Schratt with some kind of mind wave. Thus, the confrontation movement of the plot is told to us in what might be thought of as a flashback.

Of course, the classic source for overreacher stories like *Donovan's Brain* is Mary Shelley's *Frankenstein*. And in that novel, one finds clear evidence of the four-function structure of preparation/experiment/boomerang/confrontation. One reason that I have not chosen to illustrate this plot structure by means of Shelley's *Frankenstein* is that, although it evinces the overreacher plot, it also has other ambitions which make its expositional ordering somewhat more complex than lesser literary examples of the subgenre. These ambitions center around the theme of the absence of love.

One element of this theme, which affects the superstructure of the exposition, is the conflict that Shelley draws between the claims of family and love versus the pursuit of knowledge. This theme is introduced in Robert Walton's introductory letters to his sister, Mrs. Saville. Walton has chosen to leave home for the sake of scientific exploration. This framing device is obviously posited as an analogue to Victor Frankenstein's story, for Frankenstein, as well, sacrifices, in more ways than one, family, friendship, and love for knowledge. One way of reading Frankenstein's story is as cautionary advice to Walton.

Once Frankenstein's story begins, it takes the basic structure of the overreacher plot. However, here too there is a complication, since another element of the theme of the absence of love focuses on the alienation of the monster. So embedded in the overreacher plot is the subplot about the monster's (at times seemingly unjustified) isolation from and deprivation of fellow feeling, and its psychological repercussions. Thus, though *Franken-*

stein contains an overreacher plot, and may even have some claim to being the most popular progenitor of many overreacher stories, it is more complex in both theme and exposition than many of the tales it prefigures.

My initial characterization of the overreacher plot takes a temporally linear, forwardly moving form. However, the functions may be rearranged, as was the case with the functions in the family of the complex discovery plot. In the classic German film *The Cabinet of Dr. Caligari,* as it was originally scripted, we learn about the experiment and its preparations *after* the final confrontation with Cesare. As well, the functions in the overreacher plot can be iterated and nested in many different ways, thereby providing an ample range of variations.

Also of interest is the fact that the overreacher plot can be combined with the functions in the family of the complex discovery plot to produce ever more complicated stories. One way to do this is to make either the overreacher or his/her experiment or the result of his/her experiment the object of discovery and/or confirmation. For example, bodies might start disappearing, which leads to an investigation, which leads to the discovery and confirmation that Dr. So-and-so is preparing an experiment; however, the discoverers are too late to stop the experiment. They enter the laboratory just before the mad scientist throws the switch (but leaving enough time for the mad scientist to explain and justify the experiment). The untoward and dire consequences of the experiment ensue and continue until the final confrontation with the newly created monster.

Or again, the onset of a newly created monster is discovered, after which the experiment and its preparation are told in flashback up to the dire consequences that comprise the onset, and then perhaps the existence of the monster is confirmed and the final confrontation staged. One sketch of this combination plot would yield seven movements—onset; discovery; confirmation; preparation for the experiment; experimentation; untoward results; and confrontation, where confirmation as well as discovery may come after or between the next three movements in the structure. Clearly, this structure, in terms of the order of exposition, could be modified by means of flashbacks, flashforwards, iterations, nestings, and the like. As well, serviceable combination plots could also be derived by way of subtracting functions.

Though I shall refrain from exploring in detail the range of permutations of available combination plots of this sort, it should be incontestable that such stories are quite common. I have already referred to *The Cabinet of Dr. Caligari,* which in the story inside the framing story, involves the discovery and confirmation of the experiment. Likewise, H.G. Wells's *The Island of Dr. Moreau* combines elements of the discovery plot with the overreacher plot, insofar as the narrator, Edward Prendick, is involved in a sustained process of discovery concerning what is happening in Moreau's lab. It is not until the fourteenth chapter that we get Moreau's account which fills us in on the background—on both the means and the justification of his experimentation. Nor is this sort of plot restricted to unholy, scientific experiments. Lovecraft's "The Dunwich Horror" combines overreacher and discovery elements where the results of Wilbur Whateley's "experiment"—which is discovered and then confronted by Dr. Armitage—owes more to mysticism than to mechanics.

The budget of plots characterized in the preceding discussion gives, I hope, a reliable picture of the basic story structures of a large number of horror narratives. It also suggests many of the ways in which further horror stories can be constructed. I would not, however, wish to claim that this taxonomy exhausts the compass of horror narratives. I am well aware of stories that do not fit this schematization neatly.

One recent example is the bestseller *Watchers,* by Dean R. Koontz. The story involves two experimental animals: a super-intelligent golden retriever called Einstein and his nemesis, a simian-like monstrosity called the Outsider. Both escape from the Banodyne laboratories. The plot is organized essentially in terms of three pursuits: the government is after both the animals, especially the Outsider, who leaves a swath of carnage wherever he goes; a Mafia hit-man is after the golden retriever, whom he thinks he can sell to someone for lots of money; and the Outsider is after Einstein, whom he loathes, since everyone seems to love the dog at his expense.

The story opens as Travis Cornell finds the golden retriever in a forest and, unbeknownst to Travis, the retriever, in effect, warns him of the onset of the Outsider. Gradually a friendship develops between Travis and the dog, and gradually Travis discovers what a genius the dog is. Travis and the dog befriend Nora, and she also learns how smart the dog is. These discoveries are developed in parallel tandem with the plot events that initiate the three chases alluded to above. The dog alerts Travis to the twin dangers of pursuit by the Outsider and the government, and Travis and Nora, people individually afraid of risking friendship, become as a family—with the dog as a kind of child—in the process of evading their pursuers.

The plot involves discovery and confirmation elements. However, these pertain primarily to the discovery and confirmation of the intelligence of the dog, who is anything but a horrific monster. The Outsider—the monster in the piece—is not really a major subject for discovery, except for a subplot about a lawman named Johnson. Thus, though *Watchers* is similar in extended ways to some of the plots discussed, it is not a clear-cut example of any of them. And, as well, its emphasis on chase and evasion sets the primary tone of the work. It is rather like an action thriller with a monster in it. This is not said in order to dismiss it as a horror novel, but only to acknowledge that there are more horror plots, and perhaps even more basic horror plots, than my review of the characteristically recurring stories in the genre indicates.

However, even if my inventory of plots is incomplete, I think that it is fair to say that it does succeed in canvasing quite a lot of the characteristically recurring plot structures in the genre. Moreover, this taxonomy of plots also exhibits certain patterns that may be instructive about the pleasure that horror stories afford their audiences.

On the Impact of Characteristic Horror Narratives

I began by noting that many of the artforms that practice horror are narrative. Horror, it seems, flourishes most notably in narrative artforms. This is not to say that horror cannot exist in non-narrative forms—such as non-narrative painting—but only that when we think of horror what come to mind paradigmatically are narratives as those are embodied in novels, short stories, plays, movies, radio shows, TV programs, and so on. Thus, it seems reasonable to hypothesize that a major source of pleasure with respect to the horror genre is related to narrative. Perhaps Stephen King would appear to subscribe to some such view when he writes in the preface to his collection of short stories, *Night Shift,* that "All my life as a writer, I have been committed to the idea that in fiction the story value holds dominance over every other facet of the writer's craft. . . ." But, in any case, narrative would seem to be crucial to most of the essential works of horror. Consequently, if horror narratives have some saliently recurring features, they may help to explain the appeal of the genre.

Looking at the field of plot structures recounted so far, one is struck by one theme that cuts across the majority of these examples. That theme is discovery. In the overreacher plot, the overreacher discovers some secret of the universe, often to the dismay of the rest of humanity. And, in most of the plot structures derived from the complex discovery story, the discovery of that which heretofore was denied existence is foregrounded.

Admittedly, these two plot families make different points about our relation to the unknown. The overreacher plot warns against wanting to know too much while many of the plots in the complex discovery family chide humanity for being too complacent about the unknown. One family of plots chastens the desire to know everything while the other is an attack on rigid, commonplace, myopic thinking—that is, one plot constellation says there are things better left unknown, while the other implies that to refuse to admit the existence of the hitherto unknown is a deep flaw. However, though the themes, here, at one level of analysis, appear incompatible, they nevertheless share a basic subject matter—viz., knowing the unknown—which subject matter serves to motivate not only basic plot movements but also those interludes, beloved to the genre, which I have referred to as the play of ratiocination and the drama of proof.

Even in those plots that do not involve fully developed discovery and/or confirmation functions, in the vast majority of cases we nevertheless still tend to find some play of ratiocination. There is usually some conjecture about the nature and origin of the monster, if only to discuss the best way to destroy it. Plots comprising confrontation completely unalloyed with ratiocination about the nature of the monster are rare, as are completely unexplained onsets. This is not to say that there are no examples of such plots; but only that they are the exception rather than the rule. Moreover, the most frequently recurring horror plots, it seems to me, tend to involve either discovery, confirmation, or both, while plots lacking these functions nevertheless contain residues of these functions that abet some play of ratiocination. Often, this play of ratiocination concerns the nature or pertinent aspects of the monster in order to figure out how it is best opposed.[17]

Likewise, turning to the overreacher family, experiments or incantations without explanations and/or justifications, no matter how silly, are hard to come by, indicating again that some sort of imitation of reasoning, proof, and demonstration is generally important to the narrative engine that drives the horror story.

Undoubtedly there can be horror stories that simply stage the struggle between humanity and some monster. One would not refuse to categorize a story as horrific simply because it had no element of discovery or ratiocination. The conflict between humanity and the inhuman, or between the normal and the abnormal, is fundamental to horror. Nor is much theoretical advantage to be gained by saying that simple, unadorned conflicts between humanity and the inhuman are likely to be rather impoverished examples of the genre, though that may be empirically accurate. Nevertheless, admitting that there can be such horror stories should not preclude the insight that most horror stories, including the most distinguished ones, tend to be elaborated in such a way that the discovery of the unknown (voluntarily or otherwise), the play of ratiocination, and the drama of proof are sustaining sources of narrative pleasure in the horror genre.

There are, of course, crime stories that involve no discovery or ratiocination—that propose nothing more than extended fisticuffs and shoot-outs with bad guys. But this would not lead us to deny that being engaged in or caught up by the play of reasoning by the detective or private-eye is not one of the major narratological calling cards of the crime genre. Similarly, though the drama of discovery may sometimes be absent in horror stories, it remains a central, characteristic source of pleasure in the genre.

Moreover, there is a certain fit between our findings about horror narration and about the nature of horror. The emotion of art-horror is generated in part by the apprehension of something that defies categorization in virtue of our standing or commonplace ways of conceptualizing the order of things. That this subject matter should be wedded to narrative structures that enact and expatiate upon the discovery of the unknown seems perfectly appropriate. The point of the horror genre, if the first part of this book is correct, is to exhibit, disclose, and manifest that which is, putatively in principle, unknown and unknowable. It can be no accident that the plots that are characteristically mobilized to motivate this moment of unavoidable recognition are concerned to show that, within the fiction, what is unknown is *known* or has become, as the plotting would have it, undeniable. Rendering the unknown known is, in fact, the point of such plots, as well as the source of their seductiveness.

That is, horror stories are predominantly concerned with knowledge as a theme. The two most frequent families of plot structures are those of the complex discovery cluster and the overreacher cluster. In one variant of the complex discovery example, the monster arrives, unbeknownst to anyone, and sets about its gruesome work. Gradually the protagonist, or a group of protagonists, discovers that a monster is responsible for all those unexplained deaths. However, when the protagonists approach the authorities with this information, the authorities dismiss the very possibility of the monster. The energies of the narrative are then devoted to *proving* the monster's existence. Such a plot celebrates the existence of things beyond the boundaries of common knowledge.

Plots in this family, concerned with discovery and confirmation, are concerned at the level of narrative with the process of disclosure and revelation—specifically the disclosure and revelation of that which is excluded from our standing conceptual categories. Given that the object of emotional focus in horror stories is that which is unknown, that many of the plot structures revolve around disclosure, revelation, discovery, and confirmation seems quite appropriate. That revelation should be accompanied by the play of ratiocination about the unknown and horrific monster also appears eminently natural, since the presentation of the unknown calls forth the desire to know more about it.

In a variation of the theme of the unknown, the overreacher plot proposes a central figure embarked on the pursuit of hidden, unholy, or forbidden knowledge. Once the scientist, alchemist, priest, or magus acts on this forbidden knowledge—e.g., brings a golem to life—inestimable, maleficent power is released and the consequent destruction becomes the stuff of the story. Whereas the protagonists in the complex discovery family of plots generally must go beyond the bounds of common knowledge, overreachers are warned not to exceed them. But both major plot families characteristically take the compass of common knowledge as their basic *donnee* and explore it, albeit for different thematic effects. This, of course, fits very nicely with a theory that regards cognitive threat as a major factor in the generation of art-horror.

At the level of narrative effect, the introduction of processes of proof and discovery are ways of securing and holding the audience's attention. This is not to deny that, in the fiction, these discoveries are not celebrations of the exercise of pure thought, since these discoveries are usually connected to the question of the survival of the human race, an issue to be resolved or at least frequently alluded to in the confrontation movements of the subtending *fabulae*. Nevertheless, a great deal of the sustaining interest in horror stories concerns the discovery of the unknown. The majority of horror stories are, to a significant extent, representations of processes of discovery, as well as often occasions for hypothesis formation on the part of the audience, and, as such, these stories engage us in the drama of proof.

Horror and Suspense

A key narrative element in most horror stories is suspense. Narrative suspense can occur within most, if not all, of the plot movements discussed in the previous section. An incident in the onset movement, for instance, might involve an innocent victim being suspensefully stalked. Or, our discoverers might be pursued by the monster, resulting in a suspenseful chase scene. Confirmation might take place as the monsters stealthily surround those debating its existence, while confrontations, of course, can be occasions for suspenseful battles upon which hang the fate of human life. Similarly, suspense can attend the preparations for the overreacher's experiment or the experiment itself.

At the same time, suspense may result not only within discrete plot movements—and the subscenes and sequences that they comprise; suspense may also eventuate from the way in which various plot functions are woven together. The confirmation of the existence of the monster may be protracted; the authorities just won't listen to, what in the fiction, counts as reason. Their stubbornness, however, allows for precious time, in which the monster builds its forces, to slip away, and, thereby, provokes suspense over the question of whether humanity will be able to prevail. Likewise, once the overreacher's creation goes beserk, suspense arises concerning the issue of whether it can be effectively confronted and subdued.

Suspense, then, can figure in horror stories at every level of narrative articulation. However, suspense is not unique to horror. For suspense cuts across genres. It can be found in comedy, melodrama, crime stories, spy novels, westerns, and so on. Though not a feature that differentiates horror stories from other sorts, and though a feature that may not appear in every horror plot (recall "Pickman's Model"), suspense, nevertheless, is integral to much, even if not all, horror. That is, the relation between horror and suspense is contingent, but also unavoidably pervasive. Thus, in order to illuminate thoroughly the way horror stories function, one must show how horror and suspense can work together—albeit contingently—in concert.

Suspense, as I shall show, is a different emotion from art-horror, for it takes a different object; though, at the same time, the objects of horror can come to play a crucial role in generating suspense. But before this can be explained, the nature of suspense must be elucidated. And once the nature of suspense is unpacked, we can begin to illustrate how suspense and horror may be combined in co-ordinated narrative structures.

Characterizing suspense, however, will prove a complicated project. For though it is a concept that we constantly use to discuss narrative art, it has not been subject to precise enough theorizing. That is, though frequently employed, suspense is a pretty amorphous concept in narratology. In his book *Narrative Suspense,* for example, Eric Rabkin counts anything that draws a reader through a story as a suspense element.[18] But this is too broad. For instance, it includes under the label of suspense the continuation of a repeating motif of images.

In discussing artworks, critics seem prone to regard any structure that involves anticipation as suspense. But this is to mistake the species for the genus. Outside art, anticipation and suspense are discriminable. As Husserl points out, every experience involves anticipation to some degree. But experiences of suspense are much less frequent.[19] Likewise, when it comes to narrative art, it is advisable to keep the concept of suspense more narrowly defined than that of anticipation *simpliciter.*

Certain contemporary students of the narrative may feel my claim—that we lack an adequate account of suspense—is exaggerated. In their opinion, Roland Barthes is thought to have provided us with a rigorous characterization of suspense in his "Structural Analysis of Narrative."[20] There Barthes states:

> Suspense is clearly only a privileged—or "exacerbated" form of distortion: on the one hand, by keeping a sequence open (through emphatic procedures of delay and renewal), it reinforces the contact with the reader (the listener), has a manifestly phatic function; while on the other, it offers the threat of an uncompleted sequence, of an open paradigm (if, as we believe, every sequence has two poles), that is to say, of a logical disturbance, it being this disturbance which is consumed with anxiety and pleasure (all the more so because it is always made right in the end). "Suspense," therefore, is a game with structure, designed to endanger and glorify it, constituting a veritable "thrilling" of intelligibility: by representing order (and no longer series) in its fragility, "suspense" accomplishes the very idea of language. . . .

This immensely, though typically, turgid passage has many problems, some of which I will take up later. For the moment, however, let it suffice to note that in his concern to situate "suspense" on a continuum with (at least his own very dubious idea of) narrative in general and with language ("the very idea of language"!), Barthes has failed to distinguish suspense from his own vague concept of narrative except to say that the former is an intense or privileged extension of the latter. This seems neither true—some narrative forms neither engender suspense nor do they resemble the structure of suspense—nor informative. What accounts for the occurrence of privileged moments of suspense over and above the mere experience of ordinary narrative linkages? At times, Barthes's supposed concept of suspense blends into ideas of tension, structural tension, and closure. Such a concept of suspense is too abstract and ill-formed to be useful. Thus, before turning to the issue of suspense and horror, I will have to set forth a more perspicuous conception of suspense.

But to speak of narrative suspense, I must perforce backtrack at least one step further. I must speak a bit about narrative, especially narrative as it occurs in popular fictions. For suspense, or at least suspense of the sort I am concerned to elucidate, is a functional variation of the basic forms of popular narration.

Erotetic Narration

One hypothesis, which has proved to be very powerful in studying the logic of popular narratives, is the idea that scenes, situations, and events that appear earlier in the order of exposition in a story are related to later scenes, situations, and events in the story, as questions are related to answers. Call this erotetic narration. Such narration, which is at the core of popular narration, proceeds by generating a series of questions that the plot then goes on to answer.

In a mystery story, for example, a murder early on generates a question—whodunit?—to which later scenes contribute towards answering in the form of clues and which the final or penultimate scene—the summing up by the detective—conclusively answers. Or, in V.C. Andrews's novel *Flowers in the Attic,* the harsh treatment and imprisonment of the children, after they arrive at their grandparents' home, evokes the question for what wrong they are being punished, which is answered (it's incest) by the end of the story.

Likewise, the hijacking of some nuclear devices at the beginning of a spy thriller posits questions about who stole the bombs and for what purposes. A great deal of the plot will be preoccupied with answering these questions. And once the generally appalling and unscrupulous use planned for the weaponry is identified, the further, altogether pressing question arises as to whether it can be thwarted.

The internal structures of the multi-function horror plots reviewed in the preceding section can be analyzed readily on the model of the question/

answer model. The onset of the monster raises the question of whether it will be discovered. Its discovery leads either directly to the question of whether it can be destroyed, or, if the discoverers need outside support, it leads to the question of whether they will be able to convince the authorities of the existence of the monster and of the danger it poses.

Similarly, the preparation for the overreacher's experiment prompts the audience to anticipate whether or not it will succeed. The experiment phase of the plot first answers that question positively, but then goes on to note complications—usually in the form of innocent victims or other mishaps. These untoward consequences, then, lead to the question of whether and how the monster can be defeated and the experiment ultimately laid to rest. Thus, the basic narrative connective—the rhetorical bond between plot movements—in the horror story (as in other popular narratives) is the question/answer format.

Moreover, the erotetic linkage in popular fictions not only connects the large plot movements, but also tends to provide the rhetorical bond for smaller units of narration. One scene may give rise to the next on the question/answer model. In Chapter Twenty of Stephen King's (non-horror novel) *Misery,* the captive writer, Paul, secretly wheels himself into the kitchen, where he steals a knife. This raises the question of whether his captor, Annie, will realize that he's gotten out of his room and whether he will be able to kill her. In short order, it is revealed that she's on to him, and has retrieved her kitchen knife. This, in turn, raises the question of whether and how this particular psychotic intends to retaliate—which question is answered when she takes an axe to his legs.

Of course, actions and events within scenes can also be rendered intelligible by these erotetic structures. All the dialogue and action in Chapter Eighteen of Richard Matheson's novel *I Am Legend* contribute to answering, often misleadingly, the presiding question of whether Ruth can be trusted.

Since most popular narratives involve a series of actions, it may seem natural to think that causation (i.e., the causal entailment of later scenes by earlier scenes) is the major connective between scenes and/or events in popular fictions. However, it is implausible to suggest that scenes follow each other in most popular narratives by a chain of causal entailments. In fact, most succeeding narrative scenes are causally underdetermined by what precedes them in the story.

In the example just cited from *Misery,* it would be impossible to infer from earlier stages of the plot that Annie knows what Paul is doing. Rather, the connection between his actions and her knowledge, in terms of what is narrated, is weaker than a causal one; indeed, the reader only comes to learn that Annie does know what Paul is doing when she says she does.

But claiming that the relation between the narration of Paul's actions and the later scenes is weaker than that of causal entailment does not deny that the reader finds the connection between these narrative events quite intelligible. For the earlier scenes, quite explicitly, raised the question of whether Annie knows Paul has found a way to leave his room. Thus, the scene where Annie confronts Paul with her knowledge flows quite coherently, though not by causal entailment, from earlier scenes in the story. The basis of that coherence is not causal; rather it is erotetic.

That is, the later scene fits as a coherent and connected expansion of the story because it delivers an answer to a question that earlier scenes and events had already posed saliently in the text for the reader. In this case, our sense that the narrative is proceeding intelligibly results from the fact that earlier scenes in the story brought two well-structured possibilities to the forefront of our attention: Annie knows/Annie doesn't know. Which of these possibilities is to be actualized in the story is not implied causally by earlier scenes. The question is, rather, answered directly in Chapter Twenty-Two. Chapter Twenty-Two is not strictly entailed by the earlier section of the novel. Yet it seems to make sense; the rhetorical smoothness here is a function of the fact that it is maximally relevant to what precedes; it answers the vital, well-structured question of the events that lead up to it.

In the example above, the relevant narrative possibilities were structured in terms of binary alternatives. This need not always be the case; before the detective in a mystery story sums up his findings, there are as many available alternative answers to the ruling question—whodunit?—as there are available suspects. The detective's display of ratiocination finalizes one of these alternatives. The logical connection between this finalization of alternatives and what went before is that of the relation between a question and a relevant answer.

In the *Misery* case, using the idea of a question to capture the idea of raising narrative possibilities seems appropriate since the most convenient way in ordinary language to state such possibilities is "Will x happen or not?—e.g., will Annie find out or not?" The concept of the question, as well, enables us to explain one of the most apparent audience responses to popular narratives: expectation. That is, the audience expects answers to the questions that the narrative saliently poses about its fictional world.

Popular novels are often called "page-turners" in honor of the way they keep their readers obsessively entranced. As well, it is commonly thought that this is a function of the heavy emphasis that they place on narrative. The erotetic model of narration, applied to popular fictions, suggests what the nature of the connection between the page-turning phenomenon and the kind of narration employed in popular fictions: viz., the reader is turning pages to find out the answers to the questions that have been saliently posed to her.

At the same time, the questions a story poses delimit the range of what can happen next, since narrative questions will generally have a delimited range of answers. The constraints the narrative questions place on what will happen next are the source of the story's coherence. Audience expectations, then, are not a matter of the audience knowing what will happen next—in the sense of my expecting to go to work tomorrow—but expectations about the likely range of what can happen next. The reader, or the film viewer, is able to follow a popular narrative because it proceeds intelligibly by answering those questions it has saliently posed and which the audience has taken up.

Some may balk at this account of the way in which popular narratives are followed by readers; they will find it implausible to characterize readers of popular fictions as in a constant process of question-formation. Such spectators, it might be argued, are not introspectively aware of framing questions internally, nor are they subvocalizing these questions as they furiously turn their pages. So the challenge is to say in what respect such readers (and film spectators) are possessed of the kinds of questions hypothesized above.

Clearly, I must argue that the audiences of popular fictions *often* frame their questions tacitly and that their expectation of answers to these questions *often* remains implicit in their following the story. I say *often* here just because in some cases we are aware of our questions. But in other cases we may not be so aware and the idea of a tacit question must be introduced to handle those particular cases.

The notion of a tacit or implicit expectation—one of which we are unaware until it is, perhaps, subverted—should not strain credulity. After all, we often reach for a glass, without reflection, only to be surprised that it is no longer there; obviously, we tacitly thought it was there, and our expectation is manifested by being implicit in our behavior.

When following a popular narrative, a movie for example, I want to claim that the spectator internalizes the whole structure of interests depicted in the drama, and this structure includes alternative outcomes to various lines of action, which the spectator must keep track of in some sense before one alternative is actualized, in order for the movie to be received as intelligible. I postulate that the spectator does this by tacitly projecting the range of outcomes as tacit questions or implicit expectations, which the narratologist can represent as questions.

The tacit question model explains then how spectators are able to regard popular movies as intelligible in terms of the ways in which the questions logically constrain the range of answers the audience expects. Intelligibility, that is, is a function of the narrative proceeding according to a constrained itinerary, delimited by questions saliently posed by earlier plotting.

One reason to accept the tacit question model is supplied by the results of subverting postulated expectations. If we stop a film like *Dawn of the Dead* midway, the tacit questions soon surface: "Were they turned into zombies;

did they escape the shopping center; or did they live there happily ever after?" Similarly, tacit questions will emerge, I predict, if we wrench a popular novel like Tom Clancy's *Patriotic Games* from a reader (that is, if we don't just get punched in the nose).

At first glance, it may appear that the question/answer model is ill-conceived to handle non-linear narrative manipulations like flashbacks. However, the purpose of most flashbacks in popular narratives is to answer questions (or to offer information in the direction of an answer) about why characters are behaving as they do in the present or how the situation got to be this way. For example, the flashback that composes the bulk of Shelley's *Frankenstein* comes in answer to the implicit question about why it was that Walton found Victor hanging out on an iceberg.

In using the question/answer model as the core concept in characterizing popular narratives, I am not suggesting that it is a competitor with organizational taxonomies based on temporal relations such as parallel development, flashbacks, and so on. For the interrogative—will x be executed or not?—can be articulated by alternating two scenes of parallel action, as it is in D. W. Griffith's film *Intolerance*. The idea of parallel narration describes a temporal relation in a fiction, as does the idea of a flashback, while the question/answer model describes the rhetorical-logical relation of scenes in the narrative.

My central hypothesis, then, which will be crucial to my analysis of suspense, is that the major connective or logical relations in most popular narratives is erotetic. The best way to attempt to confirm this hypothesis is to start reading popular fictions and/or start watching movies and narrative TV programs and to note the way in which their plotting can be almost completely explained on the interrogatory model.

Of course, some qualifications are necessary here. Though the question/answer structure is fundamental to popular narration, such narratives are not composed solely of simple questions and answers. Not every scene or event in a popular narrative can be described as posing a simple question or answer. Most narratives have scenes and describe events with more complicated functions than merely instilling a simple question or answer.

Many scenes in popular narratives function to introduce characters, locales, states of affairs, events, or important attributes of characters, locales, etc., without necessarily raising a question. Establishing scenes often initiate popular narratives but one can come at any point when the story involves the addition of new characters, locales, and so forth.

Scenes or events in popular narratives may simply pose a question, or answer a question that was made salient earlier in the story. However, a scene may also merely sustain an ongoing question posited earlier in the tale. For example, as the body count keeps mounting in *Jaws* in scene after scene, the question of what is killing them is intensified or sustained, rather than posing a new question or answering the presiding one.

Moreover, a given scene may only incompletely answer a reigning question; in the stage adaptation of *Dracula* cited earlier, Van Helsing at one point concludes that a vampire is at large, but he doesn't know who it is; that question remains to be answered in an later development. And finally, some scenes or events in popular fictions answer one question, only to introduce one or more other questions; e.g., we know that there is a ravening alien in our outpost, but this leads us to ask what it is, and whether and how we can kill it. Answering such questions could dominate the rest of the plot.

These basic erotetic plot functions yield a picture of the narrative skeleton of a great many popular fictions. Whether a scene or an event in a popular narrative is part of the core of the plot depends upon whether it is part of the circuit of questions and answers—including sustaining questions, incomplete answers, simple questions, and simple answers, or combined questions and answers—that unify the action in the plot. A scene or event that is not involved in establishing characters, locales, etc., and which lies outside this network of questions and answers is a digression. A digression, of course, need not necessarily be something bad; digressions may enrich the fiction as a whole, as do the essays on the history of symbols in Victor Hugo's *The Hunchback of Notre Dame*.

Digressions of certain sorts, such as the periodic copulations in William Johnstone's porno-occult trilogy (*The Devil's Kiss, The Devil's Heart, The Devil's Touch*), may be *de rigeur* in certain genres and subgenres. So it makes no sense to suggest that digressions are anomalous in popular fiction. But the page-turning effect, which is particularly relevant to the issue of suspense, is primarily a function of the kind of erotetic narration that is the most generic means for unifying action in popular fiction.

Before turning, finally, to the topic of suspense, a crucial distinction between two types of narrative questions needs to be drawn. So far I have been primarily emphasizing the question/answer model as a means of linking scenes. But questions are also a means for organizing whole narratives. Thus, it pays to stress a distinction between macro-questions and micro-questions in popular narration. The entirety of King's *Misery,* save some establishing flashbacks and the text of *Misery's Return* is organized around Paul's plight, which raises the question of whether or not Paul will escape or die. In essence, *Misery* is organized around one overarching macro-question.

Moreover, a popular fiction may have more than one macro-question. In James Whale's film *Bride of Frankenstein,* two major questions, which ultimately dovetail, structure the plot. The first question is will Baron Frankenstein be persuaded by Dr. Petorius to perform a re-animation experiment (finally, he will), while the second question is will the monster finally have a friend (finally, he won't; the bride can't stand him). These two questions, alternatively, supply the basic problematic of the majority of the scenes in the film. The monster keeps searching for a friend in scene after abortive scene (e.g., the interlude with the blind man)—thereby reasserting that question—while Petorius tempts Frankenstein in alternating scenes. Then the two macro-questions converge when the object of the experiment becomes the creation of a female being, specifically a potential friend for the monster.

Bride of Frankenstein has two ruling macro-questions, but it also has a large number of micro-questions that connect scene to scene and fictional event to fictional event. For example, the rescue of the drowning girl by the monster raises questions about how she will respond to her savior; this question narratively unifies the subsequent rejection of the creature. Thus micro-questions organize the small-scale events in the plot, even as they carry forward the macro-questions in the story.

In this example from *Bride of Frankenstein,* the micro-question is an instantiation, so to speak, of one of the major, iterated macro-questions. However, the micro-questions that unify action sequences in a story need not only iterate a presiding macro-question. In James Herbert's novel *The Fog,* an organic cloud is rendering people insane. John Holman, an operative of the Department of the Environment, has discovered the source of all the recent destructive behavior, but the police department is taking a long time to confirm his hypothesis. During this interlude the Fog is growing in size as well as garnering more and more victims.

In the second half of Chapter Eight, we meet an initially mild-mannered character named Edward Smallwood. We also learn that he really dislikes his boss, Norman Symes, that he has been in the presence of the Fog, and that he has a headache—the telltale symptom of Fog contamination. This, given the way the story has been developed, sets up the micro-question of whether or not Smallwood will kill Symes. A positive answer to the question is at first deflected by comedy; Smallwood's madness immediately manifests itself—innocently enough—as he walks through town kicking people in the ass. We think there's no murder in this man, even when he's crazy. However, when we move to the next scene, Smallwood locks Symes in a bank vault, answering the animating question that opens the subplot and giving it closure. The micro-question of whether or not Smallwood will kill Symes unifies the brief episode, while forwarding the general movement of the plot by sustaining the macro-question of whether the Fog's existence will be acknowledged by the authorities in time.

I have spent some time distinguishing micro-questions and macro-questions since suspense can be generated by either level of erotetic narration. And now that some of these rudimentary tools for characterizing narrative have been set out,[21] we can turn to an analysis of fictional suspense in general, and of suspense in horror fiction in particular.

The Structure of Suspense

Suspense in fictional narratives is generated as an emotional concomitant of a narrative question that has been raised by earlier scenes and events in a story. To take a shopworn example, the heroine is tied to the railroad tracks; the locomotive is steaming at her. Will she be crushed or saved? Suspense arises when a well-structured question—with neatly opposed alternatives— emerges from the narrative and calls forth what was earlier referred to as a simple answering scene (or event). Suspense is an emotional state that accompanies such a scene up to the point when one of the competing alternative outcomes is actualized.

But saying that suspense arises as a narrative question is not enough to isolate suspense because, as I argued earlier, the question/answer nexus is a characteristic linkage of most popular narratives, whereas most narrative linkages need not involve suspense. They may involve anticipation, but suspense is a subcategory of anticipation, not the whole of it.

Anticipation may be a necessary condition for suspense, and a question/ answer relationship is a necessary condition for narrative suspense. However, more must be added to the concepts of anticipation and questioning before we can arrive at a manageable notion of suspense.

Suspense in life, as opposed to fiction, is not just anticipation, but anticipation where something desired is at stake—a job, admission to a school, securement of a loan, passing an exam, escaping a nasty situation. Moreover, whatever is at stake has some psychological urgency partly because the outcome is somehow uncertain. Turning from life to fiction, we can see that in the largest number of the relevant cases in popular fiction, the elements of everyday suspense—desirability and uncertainty—are still in operation; however, in the largest number of cases of suspense in popular fiction, the range of each of these central elements has been narrowed, so that the objects of fictional suspense are the morally right (as the pertinent subclass of desirability) and improbability (as the pertinent subclass of uncertainty). In popular fiction, suspense generally obtains when the question that arises from earlier scenes and/or events has two possible, opposed answers which have specific ratings in terms of morality and probability.

The actual outcome—one of the alternative answers which is eventually posited in the fiction—is irrelevant to the question of whether a scene or an event or a series of scenes and events involves suspense. That is, whether the heroine on the tracks is saved or crushed is irrelevant to the issue of whether the moments leading up to that outcome are suspenseful. Suspense, rather, is a function of the structure of the narrative question as it is raised by factors earlier in the story.

Specifically, suspense in fiction generally results when the possible out-comes of the situation set down by the story are such that the outcome that is morally correct, in terms of the values inherent in the fiction, is the less likely outcome (or, at least, only as likely as the evil outcome). That is, suspense in fiction, in general, is generated by combining elements of morality and probability in such a way that the questions that issue in the plot have logically opposed answers—x will happen/x will not happen—and, furthermore, that opposition is also characterized by an opposition of morality and probability ratings.[22]

The possible outcomes in terms of combinations of morality/probability ratings are as follows:.

   I.   moral/likely outcome

  II.   evil/likely outcome

 III.   moral/unlikely outcome

 IV.   evil/unlikely outcome

My thesis is that, in general, suspense in popular fiction occurs when the alternative outcomes—the alternative denouements of an answering scene— have the characteristics of II and III above. When our heroine is tied to the tracks, the moral outcome—her rescue—is unlikely, while the evil outcome—her destruction—is probable. I claim that, as an empirical matter, most suspense in horror fiction accords with this pattern. To summarize these hypotheses, I am suggesting that, in the main, suspense in popular fiction is a) an affective or emotional concomitant of a narrative answering scene or event which b) has two logically opposed outcomes such that c) one is morally correct but unlikely and the other is evil and likely.[23]

It is to be hoped that this formulation will ring true for at least simple examples. In Richard Connell's classic suspense story "The Most Dangerous Game," Sanger Rainsford, the accidental visitor to General Zaroff's "Ship-Trap Island," is to be set loose in the jungle with a knife and a modicum of food and to be hunted by Zaroff for three days. Rainsford seems to have little chance for survival. Zaroff is an erudite and experienced hunter both of animals and men; he has an assistant; he has hunting dogs; he knows the island intimately; he has firearms; and he has no scruples about killing humans. Zaroff has, in other words, all the advantages. At the same time, his sport—hunting humans—is morally loathsome, as the narrative makes abundantly clear. Suspense takes us in its emotional grip as we excitedly turn the pages of this tale—precisely because the story has the structure indicated above. "Will Rainsford live or will he die?" is the animating macro-question, whose outcomes are either morally correct but unlikely (that Rainsford will survive) or evil but likely (that Rainsford will become yet another one of Zaroff's trophies).[24]

Or, to consider another famous case, in D.W. Griffith's film *Way Down*

East, it is most likely that the heroine will go over the waterfalls; that is, as the scene unfolds, the boy's rescue attempt—hopping from one block of ice to the next—seems futile. Of course, after the scene is over, the probability of the rescue is one. But prior to that, the prospects of saving the heroine are extremely low. Moreover, there is evil in this scene, a natural evil in theological jargon, since innocent human life and suffering are threatened by implacable natural forces. The moral effort—the rescue—is unlikely, while an evil outcome—a natural evil in this case—appears inevitable.

Chases, races, escapes, rescues, and battles (from fist fights to interstellar invasions)—the very staple of popular movies—become suspenseful just in case the outcomes of these events are such that two logically opposed conclusions are in the forefront of the spectator's attention, and, moreover, in such a way that the likely outcome is patently evil while the moral outcome appears to be a long shot. Suspense does not seem to take hold in fiction—whether cinematic, theatrical, or literary—where the moral outcome appears likely or the evil outcome doomed.[25] If Superman's enemies are equipped with nothing more than Saturday Night Specials, the audience will not feel suspense (unless, of course, there is the danger that the bad guys can use them on an innocent hostage before Superman can do anything about it).

Given this characterization of suspense in popular fiction, it is easy to see how suspense can be generated by horror narratives. Monsters and their projects in horror fictions are irredeemably evil. They are generally immensely powerful, or, at least, have some obvious advantage over humans, and, furthermore, they often benefit from operating in secrecy. That they are frequently not believed to exist further enhances their edge over poor, benighted humanity. Monsters, that is, generally have the upper hand in horror fictions; in most cases, there would be no point to the fiction if they did not. Consequently, when monsters are encountered by humans, the situation is ripe for suspense, for the monster's minatory motives have the best chances of success.[26]

Suspense can be generated in horror stories at virtually every level of narrative development, from that of incident and episode to the overarching plot structure. In early onset scenes, suspense accrues as the audience is made aware that the monster is stalking an innocent, oblivious victim. Or, if the monster's prey is apprised of looming dangers, suspense may be provoked as the monster begins to chase its fleeing victim. Similarly, as humans struggle against the monster, suspense may attend the confrontation. Moreover, suspense can be built into large-scale plot movements: the unholy experiment may appear to be unstoppable; the discoverers must elude pursuit in order to spread the word; or humanity must hazard an untested gambit in its final confrontation with the beast. Indeed, the very processes of discovery and confirmation in horror stories often become the object of suspense, for the discovery and confirmation of the existence of the monster is generally unlikely or at risk, and if those discoveries and confirmations do not succeed, humanity or a part of it will be doomed (a fate that we, perhaps anthropocentrically, regard to be morally evil).

As well, the major plot functions or plot movements in the characteristic horror narratives can be interrelated suspensefully. As noted above, Herbert's *The Fog* is a very pure example of the complex discovery plot. In it, the police take quite a long time before they are convinced of the hero Holman's hypothesis about the Fog. They have good reason for this: Holman, due to the Fog, has recently suffered a mental breakdown and he has been associated with a couple of extremely compromising situations. The result of this is that the confirmation of his discovery is protracted. Thus, interwoven with the development of the confirmation movement are further episodes of onset as the Fog increases its power, besets more victims, and heads, ominously, toward larger population centers. In other words, as the confirmation of the Fog's existence becomes more dilatory, the likelihood that the Fog will become invincible increases. The very prudence of the police comes to function as a causal factor in making the ultimate evil in the novel more probable.

In terms of the vocabulary employed above, suspense in horror fictions, as in other types of popular narrative, can accompany both micro-questions and macro-questions. In Matheson's *I Am Legend,* there is an excellent example of suspense generated by a micro-question. It begins when Robert Neville, the last (and, therefore, legendary) human on earth (everyone else is a vampire) loses track of the time and suddenly realizes that the sun is about to set and that hundreds of the thirsty undead will begin to prowl. Most of the fifth chapter is preoccupied with Neville's attempt to reach his fortified home—which, to make matters worse, he's left open.

Since there are so many vampires, since they are everywhere, and since they tend to congregate around Neville's home, things do not look rosy for the last man. Even if he gets home, it is possible that he will lock himself in with some uninvited, bloodthirsty visitors. Most of the chapter is devoted to his action-packed attempts to return home. He is endangered at every turn, and his escapes are consistently hair's breath. Even when he finally reaches his own driveway, he leaves his keys in his car, which makes it even more improbable that he will be able to reach his house.[27]

Obviously, suspense can operate thoughout an entire horror fiction. In the film *Night of the Living Dead,* the overarching macro-question becomes, early on, whether or not the small company of the living, who are sequestered in the house, can survive and avoid zombification. Their chances are not good, and they only get worse. They are vastly outnumbered; they are cut off and surrounded in the manner of an entrapped platoon. No one knows they are there. Two of the group—Barbara and Judith—are prone to hysterics, and, as a result, are liabilities.

Another key factor working against the probability that humanity will triumph is that the group is divided amongst themselves: Ben, the black hero, is for staying upstairs and trying to hold off the zombie attack, while the acrimonious Harry Cooper argues for staying in the cellar. This argument is not simply a matter of tactics; it is a battle of wills pitched over who is to be "boss." Thus it is significant, because it signals that the humans are in danger of fighting among themselves when they can least afford to. As well, Karen, Harry's daughter, is dying, which effectively means that they have a potential zombie, or ghoul (since these creatures eat dead flesh) in their very midst.

All these factors, which define the surrounded group's plight, make it less and less probable that the humans can survive. The film, of course, is narrated from the point of view of humanity and, therefore, it is to be presumed that human survival is unarguably the morally correct outcome. Thus, the group's situation is structured in a way to generate suspense, and this underlying structure makes the group's every confrontation with the zombies suspenseful in addition to probability factors that are added in each particular scene—that is, the scene in which Ben, Tom, and Judith try to refuel the truck is already suspenseful, given the number of encircling zombies, and then the scene becomes even more suspenseful when the truck starts to burn. The micro-question of the scene—will they refuel the truck or not?—in other words, not only hinges on incidents in the scene (the accidental fire) but also is related to the overarching macro-question of the film and the probability factors that already motivate it.[28]

Since the audience's appreciation of relative probabilities is at the heart of suspense, it is necessary that the countervailing probabilities be posed saliently. In *Night of the Living Dead,* the debates about whether to stay upstairs or downstairs do this quite effectively, since, no matter which side seems stronger, in outlining each alternative the very precariousness of the situation is stated. In the stage adaptation of *Dracula,* discussed previously, even more suspense is generated by the overt statement that if Dracula is not staked immediately, he can put himself to sleep for one hundred years and thereby elude his pursuers forever.

Obviously in most horror fictions the effectiveness of the monster is clearly demonstrated in the earliest lethal or demoralizing encounters with humans. But this quite evident indication of the improbability of human effort in the face of the monster is also reiterated and underlined by those scenes in which the discoverers talk about its powers and properties and try to ascertain what, if any, vulnerabilities the creature has. The general, often stated, unlikelihood of most attempts to deal with the monster make most encounters with monsters in horror fictions suspenseful. Much of the energy of a horror fiction will be devoted to establishing the improbability of success and the downright chanciness of any attempt to confront the monster.

For the most part, horror fictions spend more time establishing the improbability of the success of humanity's efficacy vis à vis the monster than they do establishing the monster's evilness. For in most cases, it is just presumed that the monster, insofar as it is an inhuman challenge to human life, is evil. This is not to say that time may not be spent stressing that this or that vampire, demon, witch, wizard, etc. is unspeakably evil, but only that its evil and the immorality of its enterprises can be put in place rather quickly. More attention must be spent, in general, establishing that its progress is unstoppable.

This can be developed through the narration of scenes and events in which the monster shows itself to be immensely powerful or invulnerable: it flicks humans aside with glancing blows and nothing can stop it, neither rifles, cannons, nor electricity. Talk about the monster's indomitability also enhances the audience's perception of the improbability of besting the beast.

Of course, in most cases, the monster finally has to show some weakness: it must fear fire or crucifixes, or be susceptible to stakes through the heart or atomic harpoons. However, even here, if the final confrontation is to be suspenseful, there must be some doubt about whether the countermeasure can be successfully applied and/or whether it will, in the last instance, be genuinely effective. Again, if the human effort against the monster could not but succeed—if it were probable, especially highly probable—the confrontation would not be suspenseful.[29]

One ostensible deviation in horror fictions from the formula for suspense advanced above occurs when, in the confrontation with the monster, the audience begins to feel what might be called sympathy for the devil. A famous example of this might be the penultimate scene of *King Kong*. At a certain point, as the battle atop the Empire State Building rages and it appears that Kong is doomed, the audience begins to think that there is something both sad and wrong about his destruction. Yet there is still suspense. But this seems to fly in the face of our theory of suspense. For if one identifies Kong's abduction of Anne as the wrong in the scene, then suspense is occurring where the evil outcome—the successful abduction of Ann—is unlikely (since Kong just can't stand up against machine gun fire).

However, this apparent counterexample is more complicated than it may initially appear. For as the final scene unfolds, it becomes clear that Kong, who, understandably, comprehends little about life in the big city, is attempting to protect his beloved Anne from the planes, just as he defended her from the beasts of the jungle on Skull Island. As well, once he is not crushing subways, we realize that Kong is also a victim, one thoughtlessly displaced from his natural abode. That is, during the last scene our moral assessments of the situation are shifted, due to factors manipulated by the film itself. So it is the case that suspense is generated over Kong's death. But this is not a counterexample because, due to the emphasis on Kong's evident virtue and unfair displacement, his death begins to be perceived to be morally wrong. As he tetters on the parapet of the tower, a wrong is perceived to be probable.

Sympathy for the devil is a recurring theme in horror fiction, from Shelley's creature and Varney the Vampire to Koontz's Outsider and the spider-like thing in Raymond Feist's recent novel *Faerie Tale*. Where suspense appears to be generated from the demise of a monster, I suspect that attention to the fiction will reveal that this is generally due to the fact that the moral assessments of the monster in the story, or the grounds for the audience's moral evaluation of the monster, have been shifted in the monster's favor.

If this theory of suspense is persuasive, then it should be equally convincing that the art-emotion of suspense and that of horror are different. The object of suspense is a situation or an event; the object of horror is an entity, a monster. Moreover, the evaluative criteria brought to bear in these alternative art-emotions also differ. Of course, the type of situation which generates suspense in horror fictions will typically include a monster by whom the audience is art-horrified. But suspense can occur in other than horror contexts, where the evil at issue is not a monster.

The situation toward which the emotion of suspense is directed in horror fictions will also contain a protagonist. In general, the protagonist is someone beset by a monster. However, it is important to emphasize that the emotion—suspense—with which the audience regards this situation is not a simple duplication of the emotional state of the human protagonist, as some identification theories of audience response might have it. This can be readily seen by recalling that very often the reader or viewer of a horror fiction has access to more information about the situation than does the character. For example, the monster may be stalking a character who is unaware of the monster's presence or even its existence. In such cases, there can be no question of the audience's identifying with the emotional state of the character, since the character has no cause for consternation.

Moreover, these situations, in terms of audience suspense, seem no different in kind from cases where the character is aware of the presence or existence of the monster. So if there is no need to postulate audience identification in the former cases, there would appear to be no pressure to postulate it in the latter cases. As well, when a character is confronted by a monster, one would like to hypothesize that she really has no time to indulge suspense; she should undertake some evasive action in which she has utter faith. If she does not, it is likely that she is just abjectly terrified in a way that renders her utterly immobilized, leaving little room for any other affect.

But even if this bit of armchair psychology on my part is overly speculative, it still remains that the emotional states of characters and audiences must be different, insofar as the audience's feeling of suspense is rooted in the *thought* of the situation—which is why the audience does not feel personally endangered—whereas whatever emotion the character feels grows out of her *belief* that she is endangered, which belief accounts for her discernibly different behavior from that evinced by the audience.

Though the art-emotions of horror and suspense are discrete, they can be combined quite easily. And, as even a casual acquaintance with the genre of horror indicates, they are often found in tandem. These two affects can coexist and function to bring about a concerted effect at every level of narrative articulation in horror fictions. Furthermore, suspense can also come to play a crucial role in what was previously identified as one of the most characteristic themes of horror narration, viz., that of discovery (and of confirmation as a form of secondary discovery). For the very process of the discovery of the monster in a horror fiction can become an object of high suspense.

In the preceding section, I argued that the drama of disclosure is an abiding, though not necessarily absolutely essential, attraction in the horror genre. Typically, the disclosure or discovery of the monster is served up with a special fermata in horror fictions. Impediments often block full disclosure: either the characters are initially kept in the dark about the existence and the nature of the monster, or both the characters and the audience are. Whether or not the monster will be discovered often becomes a source of suspense; for as long as the monster remains undiscovered, the audience perceives that it is likely that evil will continue to persist, if not flourish. And even in cases, where the audience does not yet know for certain that a monster or a demon is the source of prevailing altercations, nevertheless suspense may obtain, because the fiction itself makes it likely that the trouble is some horrific evil, and tension builds to the point where this probable, evil alternative is finally revealed. Thus, though suspense and horror are distinct—there may be suspense stories without horror and horror stories without suspense—they also have a natural, though contingent, affinity.[30]

The Fantastic

"The fantastic" is the label of a literary genre defined by Tzvetan Todorov in his book of the same name.[31] Because its central effect—"fantastic hesitation"—is primarily a matter of plotting, I have included my discussion of it in this chapter. However, for reasons that will become evident, the pure fantastic plot is not an example of horror as I have defined it. Thomas Mann's "The Wardrobe," for instance, exemplifies the fantastic rather than the horror story, as does a recent pulp novel like Richard O'Brien's *Evil*.

The fantastic is a genre unto itself, albeit one that is a near neighbor to the horror genre, and one that bears intimate relations to certain forms of horror plotting. Thus, though the pure fantastic plot is not an example of the horror narrative, thinking about the fantastic reveals important features of many of the horror stories of literature and film.

A well-known and paradigmatic example of Todorov's fantastic is Henry James's "The Turn of the Screw." As is generally agreed, this tale is narrated in such a way that the reader cannot tell at the end of the tale whether the house is genuinely haunted or whether the apparent haunting is the product of the hysterical imaginings of a disturbed governess. That is, the book supports two alternative readings: a supernatural one and a naturalistic one— the latter explaining the anomalous events in the story psychologically; the former accepting those events as real. The astute reader realizes that neither of these interpretations is conclusive, and, therefore, vacillates or hesitates between them. For Todorov, this vacillation or hesitation between supernatural and naturalistic explanations is the hallmark of the fantastic.

In this respect, the fantastic is not a subgenre of horror as I have conceptualized it. For on my account, horror is signaled by the presence of monsters who *cannot* be accommodated naturalistically by science. That is, sooner or later, in what I am calling horror stories, the readers/viewers and/or the characters admit that some supernatural (or sci-fi) entity, which defies the compass of science as we know it, exists, and that it is causing all our troubles.[32] Thus, whereas the fantastic is defined by an oscillation between naturalistic and supernatural explanations, horror requires that at some point attempts at ordinary scientific explanations be abandoned in favor of a supernatural (or a sci-fi) explanation.

Though the fantastic is distinct from horror, it is not completely alien to it. For the play between supernatural and naturalistic explanation has a crucial role in many horror plots. In the complex discovery plot, for example, the characters, as well as the reader, may be caught between opting for supernatural and naturalistic explanations through the discovery and confirmation movements of that plot. Often, horror plots unfold as if they were exercises in the fantastic, witholding—from characters and audiences—until the moment of discovery the information that the agency behind all the recent disturbances *is* a supernatural being. That is, many horror stories begin, so to speak, as fantastic narratives, but become horror as soon as the fact of the monster's existence is revealed to and acknowledged by the reader. Thus, because of this obvious relation between horror and the fantastic, it is useful to explore the extent to which Todorov's discoveries about the fantastic correlate with certain features of horror narratives.

Todorov formally defines the fantastic in terms of three features:

First, the text must oblige the reader to consider the world of the characters as a world of living persons and to hesitate between a natural and a supernatural explanation of the events described. Second, this hesitation may also be experienced by a character, and at the same time the hesitation is represented, it becomes one of the themes of the work—in the case of naive reading, the actual reader identifies himself with the character. Third, the reader must adopt a certain attitude toward the text: he will reject allegorical as well as "poetic" interpretations. These three requirements do not have equal value. The first and the third actually constitute this genre; the second may not be fulfilled.[33]

Since the second condition is optional and the third condition is negative, the first attribute cited above supplies us with the positive essence of the genre: that the events in the story be susceptible of two interpretations—one naturalistic and one supernatural—and that neither of these interpretations decisively outweighs the other. That is, the events in the story must remain ambiguous with respect to these competing explanations for the reader. For example, though the events in the story be of a startling kind, we may refuse to consign them to the realm of the supernatural either because, given the narrative itself; it may turn out that reports of these events are really dreams; or that there is the possibility of chicanery of some sort (the house seems haunted but the bumps in the night have been staged by relatives who wish to drive the beneficiary of a will mad); or because it is possible that the informants in the story are deranged. And, because these possibilities are left open in the story, the reader cannot settle for the supernatural interpretation. Rather, the reader suspends judgment between the naturalistic and the supernatural explanation.

Shirley Jackson's novel *The Haunting of Hill House* strikes me as an example of the pure fantastic plot as Todorov theorizes it. Dr. John Montague assembles a group for the purpose of investigating Hill House, a place with a longstanding reputation for being haunted. Throughout the story strange events occur that raise the possibility that there are supernatural doings afoot. However, the text does not really ever preclude the possibility that these events might not be naturalistically explained, in part because the researchers never really sit down and review the incidents in such a way that a case is decisively made concerning the probable origins of these anomalies.

The events that bring the story to its close revolve around Eleanor Vance. She is a sheltered spinster who has had little experience of the world beyond her family, whom she hates; she also shows a tendency toward feelings of persecution. She can become quite jealous and resentful of what she may only be imagining are slights and implicit promises reneged. By the ninth chapter, she is quite withdrawn and she apparently hears voices that are heard by no one else.

The house seems to beckon her to climb a stairway whose supports are rotted away. The reader wonders whether the house is causing Eleanor to relive past, sordid events, notably a suicide that had occurred in this vicinity of the house decades before. Eleanor is finally saved by the other psychic researchers, who think it best to send her home. They are obviously shaken by Eleanor's behavior, and they clearly think it is dangerous. But they do not corroborate outright our suspicion that Eleanor is possessed, and their behavior is equally compatible with the belief that she is merely unhinged in a way that she might cause her to harm herself.

As Eleanor drives off, she crashes into a great tree, which also recalls an earlier death at Hill House. With this, the research team quits Hill House and the book ends.

There is, of course, a strong suggestion that the house has taken possession of Eleanor and has forced her to relive its terrible past—and this, indeed, is one of the donnees of the haunted house genre. However, the possibility also looms that Eleanor is mentally unstable. Even before the issue of the supernatural becomes a live one, she has an overwhelming desire to "belong" and to be loved. When she feels thwarted in this regard, she appears to assuage what she takes for rejection by feeling that she belongs (to?) in Hill House. Since a great deal of Eleanor's situation is narrated from her point of view, we don't know whether the inexperienced Eleanor's assessments of her co-researchers is accurate or imagined. But there is something emotionally wrong with Eleanor, so the possibility that she is projecting her own attitudes and desires onto others, such as Theodora, has to be kept open while we read.

When the most dramatic candidates for supernatural foul play occur at the end of the novel, the situation again is narrated from Eleanor's point of view. Her thoughts are obsessive, and detached in a way that could indicate either possession or madness. We cannot tell whether she's gone batty, or whether the house has taken control of her. What's really lacking in the narrative—and I take this to be part of Jackson's strategy—is an analysis of either of the two "possession" scenes by the rest of the group. That is, though we may be predisposed to a supernatural account of what has happened, we would like it corroborated by some sort of ratiocinative discussion by "outside" eyewitness observers who might be in a position to detect some heretofore unmentioned bit of behavior or some other circumstance that would tip the balance in terms of a supernatural account. We never get this, however, and that makes it difficult to adopt the supernatural hypothesis without qualms. Like many stories in the fantastic mode, *The Haunting of Hill House* makes the supernatural explanation tempting, and perhaps might even be said to give it a slight edge. However, just enough is left ambiguous that we cannot in good conscience accept it with thorough conviction.

Le Fanu's short story "Green Tea" represents an interesting deviation from this norm. It records the suicide of a minister named Reverand Jennings who believes that he is being tormented by a small, black, malignant monkey. The story is assembled out of the notes and letters of Dr. Hesselius, who specializes in what he calls metaphysical medicine. In the course of the tale, a supernatural account of the monkey is at least insinuated; as Dr. Hesselius peruses the works of Swedenborg in Jennings's library, we learn of the doctrine of associate spirits, i.e., the supposition of creatures, taking animal forms representative of direful and atrocious lusts, who are attached to the human soul and who, if they (the associate spirits) knew of "their being thus conjoint with a man," would speak to him with the intent to destroy him. This description, of course, fits the monkey who later besets Jennings and whom only Jennings can see.

The story, however, does not ultimately endorse this explanation. Rather, Hesselius argues in a letter that Jennings suffered from hallucinations due to drinking green tea. This is connected to Hesselius's rather bizarre conviction that the brain controls the body by means of a kind of nerve fluid, and that habitual use of green tea, which Hesselius calls an abuse, somehow pollutes this nerve fluid which, in turn, upsets the interior eye of the brain. This situation can be cured by the simple application of iced eau-de-cologne. Unfortunately, Hesselius protests, he was unable to apply this treatment to Jennings before his suicide, but he is sure he could have cured the minister had he had the opportunity.

However, though the story ends with a naturalistic interpretation, one tends to distrust it. The talk of nerve fluids and iced eau-de-cologne seems pretty crack-brained. But, even more to the point, Le Fanu seems to be setting Hesselius up. Hesselius admits that he has not treated Jennings, and it is not clear that he has even examined him medically. At best he has listened to Jennings's story, and, it seems, he even doubts that he has heard the whole of it. In this context, Hesselius seems to be extremely overconfident. Add to this the exceedingly recherche nature of his hypothesis, and one feels uneasy accepting the naturalistic explanation with which the fiction concludes. We keep wondering about the possibility, in the fiction, that the vile monkey may be an "associate spirit."

Whereas many tales of the fantastic advance an initially strong case for a supernatural explanation while also leaving a nagging loophole for a naturalistic comeback, in "Green Tea," Le Fanu gives the naturalistic explanation a lot of fanfare, indeed perhaps too much, leaving a daunting supernatural loophole.[34]

Though he does not use Todorov's vocabulary, Douglas Gifford interprets James Hogg's *The Private Memoirs and Confessions of a Justified Sinner* in a way that situates it in the category of the fantastic. Gifford writes:

The *parts* of the novel (three of them: Editor's narrative, Memoirs and Confessions of the sinner, and Editor's comments at the end) and the arrangement of characters and incidents within the parts are designed so that they fit an overall pattern of rational/objective experience set against supernatural/subjective experience. This is not a total separation—but broadly one can argue that in part one the rational mind of the reader *and* writer struggle to impose a logical explanation for the events therein; while in part two the reader tends, temporarily at least, to allow himself to be carried by the subjective account of supernatural events. Part three is a weighing-up of the two claims with new evidence on both sides, which significantly comes to no final resolution of both or either decision.[35]

Hogg's novel recounts the experiences of a man, Robert Wringhim, who reportedly kills, among others, his brother, his mother, a girl he seduced, and finally himself—while also hastening his (presumed) father to a premature death. His actions can be understood either in terms of his falling under the sway of a diabolical *doppleganger*, or in terms of his religious fanaticism and festering resentments which cause him to fantasize the very existence of the malicious demon whom he can then identify as the actual source of all this wrongdoing.

The narration keeps these two interpretations in balance by telling the story twice. First, the fictional editor supplies us with an account of the career of the justified sinner which, though it records some strange events, nevertheless supplies what reads like a roughly plausible, naturalistic story (once some allowance is made for the likelihood that at certain points some of the characters may be suffering perceptual illusions).[36]

The next part of the book is narrated from the point of view of the justified sinner; it is at variance with the previous account in ways that strongly indicate that it has been distorted by the psychological needs of the clearly self-deluded narrator. For example, Wringhim renders his role in twice-told events more heroically than did the earlier account. Moreover, since it is in this section that the supernatural interpretation is advanced in its fullest detail, the fact that the narrator gives the appearance of being increasingly unstable implies that we cannot accept his account unreservedly, for it may be nothing more than the projection of a self-serving, lunatic fantasy, a means by which Robert Wringhim denies his crimes.[37]

In the last section, more evidence is added on both sides of the scales, but without forcing them one way or the other. The fictional editor of these papers concludes of Robert Wringhim: "In short, we must either conceive him not only the greatest fool, but the greatest wretch, on whom was ever stamped the form of humanity; or, that he was a religious maniac, who wrote and wrote about a deluded creature, till he arrived at that height of madness that he believed himself the very object whom he had been all along describing." That is, the justified sinner is the greatest fool and wretch under the supernatural interpretation; for if the alter-ego figure is real, then only an idiot could fail to see it as a demon and fall for its transparent machinations. Or, alternatively, Robert is mad, and his confession a tormented fabrication. The text refuses to say which alternative is most compelling, and the reader is left in a state of suspended judgment.

The fantastic proper comprises stories where the hesitation between naturalistic and supernatural explanations is sustained throughout the narrative and where, by the end of the story, the reader can judge neither of the rival interpretations to be indisputably authoritative. Of course, many stories may not exemplify the pure fantastic proper, but only sustain the hesitation between the naturalistic and the supernatural to a point, often near the end of the narrative, when finally one interpretation outstrips its competitor. This, of course, generates the possibility of two more, alternative sorts of stories: ones which start in the fantastic vein but which opt for a naturalistic explanation of the anomalous events recounted, and those which start in a fantastic vein and ultimately go with the supernatural explanation of their provenance. Todorov calls the former sort of plot the "fantastic-uncanny" and the latter the "fantastic-marvelous."[38] These plots represent genres that border, so to say, the genre of the pure fantastic.

Conan Doyle's mystery novel *The Hound of the Baskervilles* is a specimen of the fantastic-uncanny plot. Murders occurring in the context of an ancient curse are shown, by the inimitable Sherlock Holmes, to be the product of a human conspiracy. That is, Holmes solves the case in the end with an authoritative naturalistic explanation. On the other hand, many of the horror plots discussed in this chapter fall into the category of the fantastic-marvelous: the reader, often along with the characters, vacillates between naturalistic and supernatural explanations—say between wild dogs and werewolves—until the naturalistic explanations are exhausted, and the existence of the monster is discovered and confirmed.

Of course, such horror stories are, in fact, a subcategory of the fantastic-marvelous. But it is not the case that all stories in the fantastic-marvelous mode are horror stories. For, on my view of horror, the supernatural or sci-fi monster whose existence is finally acknowledged must be fearsome and disgusting. But the fantastic-marvelous is equally satisfied whether the marvelous being is horrifying or not. For example, the marvelous being whose existence is finally acknowledged might be a benevolent angel.

The trick to generating the fantastic—whether throughout the story as a whole (the pure fantastic) or only in some subsegment of it (e.g., the fantastic-marvelous)—is to keep the evidence as indecisive as possible. This indecisiveness must be woven into the fabric of the story. The narration, that is, must modulate the flow of information in such a way that the alternative hypotheses are advanced and sustained, or, at least, in such a way that both are advanced and neither is irretrievably undermined until the moment of discovery. Of course, in the pure fantastic neither alternative is ever satisfactorily defeated.

One way this can be done is by channeling the evidence for a supernatural hypothesis through characters whose sanity is in question (or, who are in some other way unreliable). Thus, part of the narration will include incidents or observations, whether from "inside" or "outside" the character, that render the character's reports equivocal.

It can also be done, as Todorov stresses, by narrating the evidence, at the sentential level, in terms of propositional attitudes that are epistemically weak. Todorov offers this example from a randomly chosen excerpt from Gerard de Nerval's *Aurelia:*.

> *It seemed to me that* I was returning to a familiar house. . . . An old servant whom I called Marguerite and whom I *seemed to have known* since childhood told me. . . . *I believed* I was falling into an abyss which split the globe. *I felt* painlessly swept away by a flood of molten metal. . . . *I had the sense* that these currents were constituted of living souls, in a molecular state.[39]

That is, the language of seeming, believing, feeling, and sensing here does not allow us to take the states of affairs putatively reported above to be decisively veridical. Thus, in using this type of language to advance the plot, the author is able to introduce the possibility of naturalistically inexplicable incidents. At the same time, these apparent reports cannot be endorsed unqualifiedly, since they are offered in the contexts of psychological states that do not logically warrant the inference that the alleged states of affairs obtain.[40]

This choice of language, then, will be especially strategic not only in exercises in the pure fantastic but also in horror narratives of the fantastic-marvelous subcategory in which the author wishes the reader to hesitate, perhaps in the early onset movement of a plot, over whether the monster is naturalistically explicable or supernatural. The use of weak modals and other qualifiers—like "maybe" and "perhaps," along with hypothetical constructions—enables the author to intimate the existence of the supernatural without fully corroborating it.

So far, following Todorov, my discussion has pertained to literature. However, some of his observations can also be extended to the discussion of cinema in several ways. At first, this claim may seem dubious. For there are not very many examples of the pure fantastic in cinema. Perhaps Jack Clayton's 1961 *The Innocents*—an adaptation of James's "The Turn of the Screw"—is one; but such films are rare. However, there are many cases of the fantastic-uncanny and the fantastic-marvelous modes in film; indeed, in terms of our interests, the largest number of examples of the fantastic-marvelous genre in cinema are probably horror films.

It might appear that the reason that cinema affords so few examples of the pure fantastic has to do with the photographic basis of the medium. That is, once the supernatural agent is shown, that's it; there is no further question of its existence. For the normal viewer will take the cinematographic image to imply that the monster exists in the fiction. However, this overlooks the fact that there are numerous cinematic devices and conventions available to the filmmaker that can render the information presented in the film ambiguous in ways that are at least functionally equivalent to some of the linguistic means sketched above.

The plot of a movie can, of course, represent a character as unstable, thereby introducing the possibility that his point of view shots may be unreliable. And this can be compounded by rendering the shots visually obscure in such a way that the viewer cannot be sure of what she (or the character) is seeing. In *The Innocents,* some of the shots of the "ghosts," rendered through the governess's point of view, are long shots that are also somewhat overexposed in a manner that undercuts our certainty about what we are seeing and that opens a space for interpretation—especially given the governess' already psychologically suspect behavior.

Indeed, much of what we are shown on screen in a horror film may be shaped in such a way that, even if it is not channeled through the point of view of an unreliable character, it nevertheless gives us pause about whether we should accept it as conclusive evidence of supernatural machinations. For example, often the putative monster is kept offscreen. We suspect that it exists, but our epistemic basis here remains solely inferential.

For instance, when Irena stalks Alice alongside the park in *Cat People*—a complex discovery plot that induces the hesitation of the fantastic-marvelous mode—the scene is laid out by cutting from Irena, in her human form, to Alice in alternating shots. When we see shots of Alice, initially, we hear the sound of Irena's high heels against the pavement. However, at a certain point, the high heels stop clattering, which alerts us to the possibility that Irena has just turned into a panther. We don't know that she has turned into a panther; we haven't seen the transformation; we infer it. However, we realize at the same time that our inference could easily be contravened by later evidence. Here the very means of cinematic narration—editing and asynchronous sound—are deployed in such a way that we are invited, even prompted to buy into a supernatural account, but the "fragmentary" structure of the devices also lend an inkling of cautious skepticism.

Similarly, when we see what look like paw prints lead into what look like the impressions of high heels, we infer that this is evidence of Irena's metamorphosis, but, simultaneously, we realize that this is not as compelling as would be a scene where we saw her transformation with our own eyes. Indeed, I suspect that most viewers, here, realize that we are being teased; that we are being induced to favor the interpretation that Irena is a shape-changer on a contestable epistemic warrant, one far weaker than seeing the metamorphosis directly. And, as well, I conjecture that this ideally leads viewers to recognize that the issue between the supernatural and the naturalistic explanation will be settled in terms of whether or not the expectation of finally, literally seeing the cat creature onscreen is fulfilled.

A film like *Cat People* is a repertory of cinematic devices and conventions for undermining our *certainty* that the supernatural is at large, at the same time that evidence for existence is being advanced. Everything in the film points to the likelihood that Irena is a shape-changer, but, until the end of the film, one hesitates to embrace this view without question. After Irena stalks Alice, the camera cuts to dead sheep, and we infer that Irena gutted them. But this, again, is an inference; we are not eyewitnesses. Rather, the potential to narrate visually in cinema by means of editing's capacity to engage the audience inferentially is further exploited, in films like *Cat People*, to render the audience uncertain about what the editing, strictly speaking, warrants. Or, to put the matter more simply, a film like *Cat People* uses editing, ideally, to call to the audience's attention that it is inferring the existence of the cat creature which also, again ideally, makes us sensitive to the fact that our surmises are based on something less than eyewitness certainty.[41]

To consider another example, when we hear what we think is Irena growling, a bus pulls onscreen so as to introduce the possibility that what we thought was a growl might have been the sound of the bus's door opening. We are pretty sure that it was a growl; but we realize that were we, for instance, testifying in a courtroom, our perception here could be challenged.

Likewise, when Alice is beset in the swimming pool, we never see Irena in her animal form. We hear growls, but this might be explained away in terms of the kind of echoes one hears in indoor pools. As well, the scene is dark and full of shimmering shadows; it is the kind of place where one might easily suffer visual confusion. Of course, throughout *Cat People*, most of the scenes where Irena is in her cat persona are exceedingly dark; the cat, if there is a cat, is black and easily camouflaged; and its supposed presence is only suggested by obscuring shadows and offscreen growls. Moreover, this evidence occurs in the context where a naturalistic explanation of Irena's anxiety is being advanced by the somewhat slimy psychiatrist. In order to defeat his hypothesis decisively, the audience, I think, feels that it needs an unambiguous, eyewitness look at the cat creature.

The audience does get a brief glimpse of the panther after Irena has killed the psychiatrist;[42] and by the end of the film, the case for the supernatural interpretation is secure. However, the drama of the film has been built around prolonging the moment when the spectator feels confident that the supernatural case is incontestable. Moreover, the supernatural case is really primarily incontestable for the spectator. Since Irena releases an actual panther from the zoo just before she dies of wounds inflicted in the struggle with the psychiatrist, one suspects that the police in the world of the fiction would explain away the psychiatrist's death by way of the escaped panther.

That is, Alice and Irena's husband would have a hard time confirming the existence of supernatural agency to the authorities.

In *Cat People*, the use of darkness, shadows, offscreen sound, and editing function for the audience like linguistic qualifiers such as "It seems that. . . ." They advance the supernatural hypothesis, but they leave the possibility of a naturalistic loophole. The way that this loophole operates, however, is a bit complicated. It relies upon an implicit distinction between irrefutable eyewitness evidence and conjecture.[43]

When the audience hears an offscreen growl, or sees that Alice's robe is torn to shreds, or sees the shadow of a large cat locked in struggle with the psychiatrist, the spectator surmises that Irena is a cat creature. However, at the same time, we are aware that the knowledge is inferential and that it could be subject to interpersonal contestation. Because of this, the audience hesitates to decide unquestionably to side with the supernatural interpretation, though that interpretation is the most seductive one.

The audience behaves in this way, I suspect, because we ask ourselves whether if we were trying to make the supernatural case to a third party, the reported evidence of our senses would be accepted without resistance as certain. And, of course, it is clear that it would not, due to the admitted darkness of the scenes and to the fact that about ninety-nine percent of what we claim to be the case is based on inference. We realize that we are not ideal eyewitnesses, and we take it, I think, that the supernatural hypothesis cannot be accepted until we can eyeball the monster to our own satisfaction, and to the satisfaction of something like the police department or a court of law.

What films like *Cat People* exploit in order to generate hesitation over embracing a supernatural explanation is the criteria, used in our culture by such practices as the law, for knowledge by observation. That is, by means of narrating via such devices as offscreen sound, dark lighting (or, as in *The Innocents*, other forms of visual interference like overexposure or forms of visual obscurity like long camera-to-subject distances), shadows, and so on, the spectator becomes aware that her sense of what is going on is really a matter of impressions and inferences, rather than eyewitness certainty. Without this eyewitness certainty, the evidence of our senses is not beyond a reasonable doubt. And until the film of the fantastic-marvelous variety delivers that sort of eyewitness certainty, the supernatural hypothesis cannot be embraced unwholeheartedly. Or, at least, this seems to me to be a major presupposition of this sort of genre film.

Horror cinema, in other words, can engender the kind of uncertainty requisite for "fantastic hesitation" by playing off the standards of our culture for knowledge from observation, especially as those standards are embodied in such activities as legal testimony. Within our culture we have certain criteria for evaluating claims to knowledge derived from the senses. These include that the object of perception be seen clearly and distinctly, at a distance at which identification is reasonable; that it be apprehended for a period of time sufficient for recognition; that it be apprehended directly and without intervening obstacles; and so on. Cinema—by means of editing, camera angulation, camera positioning, lighting, pacing (both inside and between shots), object placement, set design, and so on, can problematize any or all these conditions for knowledge by observation for the spectator, thereby forcing the viewer to the position of saying (of Irena for example) that we *thought* or *believed* that she stalked Alice in her panther form rather than that we *knew*—during the scene with the bus for instance—that she had metamorphosed. Thus, at the level of cinematic narration (comprising both its visual and aural devices), film can provoke the kind of hestitation requisite for the fantastic or the fantastic-marvelous.

Another device that cinema has for engendering the suspicion of the supernatural while refraining to corroborate it is what I call unassigned camera movement. In *The Changeling,* for instance, the camera begins to move around George C. Scott in his study. It is not supplying new narrative information nor is its movement explicitly correlated within the scene to the movement of any specific character. It has no assignment either in terms of narrative or characterological function. But it does call attention to itself. The audience sees it. And the audience cannot help postulating that the camera movement *might* represent the presence of some unseen, supernatural force that is observing Scott for devilish purposes. The audience cannot know this for sure; but the point of the camera movement is to prompt the spectator into a state of uncertainty in which she is tempted toward a supernatural account, which can nevertheless not be embraced outright because she lacks the kind of eyewitness certainty discussed above.

The filmmaker can also exploit the ambiguity of certain Hollywood codes in order to elicit "fantastic hesitation." In *Curse of the Cat People*—a film of the pure fantastic category which is not a horror film—the character of Irena from *Cat People* appears to a lonely child. In *Curse,* however, Irena is an angelic rather than a horrific figure. She befriends the child and her intercessions are beneficial. Nevertheless, there is an ambiguity in the film as to whether Irena is something like a fairy godmother or, rather, an imaginary friend confected out of the child's psychological needs. This ambiguity, moreover, carries over to the scenes of Irena's visitations. These scenes are lit differently from other scenes in the film, and they exploit the Hollywood codes of "the apparition." However, since these codes are the same for intense psychological states as they are for numinous, supernatural events, they abet, rather than solve, the question of whether Irena's origin is psychological or metaphyiscal. Thus, insofar as psychological states, including dream states, can mobilize the same levers of cinematic stylization, "fantastic hesitation" can be exacerbated by introducing images coded in this way in narrative contexts that have already advanced a contest between naturalistic and supernatural interpretations. Initially, *Nightmare on Elm Street* may have benefited from this type of ambiguity, though by now informed viewers know that Freddie is "for real."[44]

Also, this use of ambiguous coding in film may be somewhat analogous to the literary use of strained, vague or highly metaphorical language in inner monologues, where such writing is ambiguous between a psychological or a supernatural interpretation. For example, in *The Haunting of Hill House,* when Eleanor turns her car suicidally, we read:

> I am really doing it, she thought, turning the wheel to send the car directly at the great tree at the curve of the driveway, I am really doing it, I am doing this all by myself, now, at last; this is me, I am really really really doing it by myself.
>
> In the unending, crashing second before the car hurled into the tree she thought clearly, *Why* am I doing this? Why am I doing this? Why don't they stop me?

Here, it seems to me, the obsessive repetition could indicate psychological disturbance as well as violent possession; and her final questions are ambiguous between being understood either as indicating that she is not really doing it (the house is), or as "what am I doing, am I crazy?"

Both literature and cinema have comparable resources for generating "fantastic hesitation." Just as cinema can problematize the indications of putative, supernatural phenomena in terms of their eyewitness reliability, the writer can do likewise by means of syntactically disjunctive reportage, obscure descriptions, citation of the poor visibility or atmospheric interference that attends the supposed monster's onset, and so on. Both literature and cinema can rely on implication rather than manifestation in order to induce positively inclining audience expectation about a supernatural hypothesis, while simultaneously prompting a desire that this be corroborated by some eyewitness information of the following sorts: in cinema, a straightforward depiction of the monster; in literature, a straightforward description of the monster; in literature or cinema, a sighting of the monster by a reliable character, channeled through the appropriate, point-of-view structure of the relevant medium. In the pure fantastic, of course, that corroboration will never be delivered. In the fantastic-marvelous mode, which is the mode most pertinent to the study of horror, such forms of corroboration will be mandatory.

As I noted above, the pure fantastic, as characterized by Todorov, is a separate genre from horror as conceptualized in this book. But the fantastic has clear links to horror which can be informative about a great many horror plots. For many horror plots, notably those involving what, in the first part of this section, were called discovery and confirmation, enjoin "fantastic hesitation" on the part of the readers and/or characters. Indeed, many horror plots fall, quite obviously, into the category of the fantastic-marvelous. Horror is not equivalent to the fantastic-marvelous, however, since there are plots of this sort—those whose marvelous beings are not fearsome and disgusting—that are not samples of horror, while there are horror plots which may provide no interlude of "fantastic hesitation" for the reader.

Nevertheless, a large number of horror plots do afford some element of "fantastic hesitation," and are outright examples of the fantastic-marvelous, while a great many more that lack this component, vis à vis the reader's experience, represent fantastic-hesitation at the level of the characters. Though the latter examples are not examples of the fantastic-marvelous, they do still retain important elements of the play of conflicting interpretations, even if these are proffered to an audience that has the luxury of knowing what and who is right.

The theme of "fantastic hesitation," then,—whether in a pure form, or in a bastardized form where it has been delegated exclusively to characters—pervades much horror plotting. And this is interesting in terms of what I have noted, on several earlier occasions, about recurring horror-plot elements such as ratiocination, the drama of proof, and the play of rival hypotheses. For undoubtedly "fantastic hesitation" calls forth these kinds of responses on the part of the audience, the characters, or both. That is, where there is "fantastic hesitation," there is likely to be not only a conflict of interpretations, but a deliberation about this conflict in terms of ratiocination, the drama of proof, and the play of competing hypotheses. These may be either represented by characters or evoked in the audience or both, when it comes to horror. Nevertheless, either way they ensnare the audience in an aesthetic counterfeit of argumentation and engage it by means of a process of discovery, albeit a fanciful one, in something like an intellectual adventure.

Of course, by "intellectual adventure," I am in nowise suggesting that a horror fiction educes its audience to participate in the recondite rigors of something like Grand Unification Theory. The arguments and discoveries available in horror plots are not only false—there are no werewolves, and electrifying a corpse will only get you roasted flesh—but they are also relatively simple. Nevertheless, one does get drawn into them, for though they are but fanciful representations of even more fanciful discoveries, they tend to have the structure of arguments with moves and countermoves that command attention, and, where hypotheses are involved, they carry the kind of gratification that any successful prediction does. They are exercises in very low level ratiocination, but they nevertheless afford the pleasure that attends any discovery and confirmation, or any puzzle and its solution. All proof has a certain drama about it; horror plots exploit the drama of proof in a way that is, moreover, particularly appropriate thematically, since the subject of the horror story is that whose existence is denied or is unthinkable and that, in consequence, demands proof.

4

Why Horror?

Why Horror?

There is a theoretical question about horror which, although not unique to horror, nevertheless is not one that readily arises with respect to other popular genres, such as mystery, romance, comedy, the thriller, adventure stories, and the western. The question is: why would anyone be interested in the genre to begin with? Why does the genre persist? I have written a lot about the internal elements of the genre; but many readers may feel that in doing that their attention has been deflected away from the central issue concerning horror—viz., how can we explain its very existence, for why would anyone *want* to be horrified, or even art-horrified?

This question, moreover, becomes especially pressing if my analysis of the nature of horror is accepted. For we have seen that a key element in the emotion of art-horror is repulsion or disgust. But—and this is the question of "Why horror?" in its primary form—if horror necessarily has something repulsive about it, how can audiences be attracted to it? Indeed, even if horror only caused fear, we might feel justified in demanding an explanation of what could motivate people to seek out the genre. But where fear is compounded with repulsion, the ante is, in a manner of speaking, raised.

In the ordinary course of affairs, people shun what disgusts them. Being repulsed by something that one finds to be loathsome and impure is an unpleasant experience. We do not, for example, attempt to add some pleasure to a boring afternoon by opening the lid of a steamy trash can in order to savor its unwholesome stew of broken bits of meat, moldering fruits and vegetables, and noxious, unrecognizable clumps, riven thoroughly by all manner of crawling things. And, ordinarily, checking out hospital waste bags is not our idea of a good time. But, on the other hand, many people— so many, in fact, that we must concede that they are normal, at least in the statistical sense—do seek out horror fictions for the purpose of deriving pleasure from sights and descriptions that customarily repulse them.

In short, there appears to be something paradoxical about the horror genre. It obviously attracts consumers; but it seems to do so by means of the expressly repulsive. Furthermore, the horror genre gives every evidence of being pleasurable to its audience, but it does so by means of trafficking in the very sorts of things that cause disquiet, distress, and displeasure. So different ways of clarifying the question "Why horror?" are to ask: "Why are horror audiences attracted by what, typically (in everyday life), should (and would) repell them?,," or "How can horror audiences find pleasure in what by nature is distressful and unpleasant?"

In what follows, I will attempt to find a comprehensive or general answer to the question of what attracts audiences to the horror genre. That is, I shall try to frame a set of hypthoses that will supply a plausible explanation of the attracting power of horror in its many manifestations across the different centuries and decades, and across the different subgenres and media in which horror is practiced. However, in this regard it is important to emphasize that, though a general account of horror may be advanced, this does not preclude the possibility that it can be supplemented by additional accounts of why a particular horror novel or film, a particular horror subgenre, or a particular cycle within the history of horror also has some special levers of attraction over and above those that are generic to the mode of horror. That is, an explanation of basic pleasures or attractions of the horror mode is compatible with *additional* explanations of why, for example, *Rosemary's Baby* exercises its own particular fascination; of how werewolf stories, while sharing the allures of ghost stories and other horrific tales, have allures of their own; and of why horror cycles, like the Hollywood movie cycle of the thirties, gain attractive power by thematically developing concerns of especial appropriateness for the period in which they were made.

A general theory of horror will say something about the probable roots of attraction and pleasure throughout the genus of horror, but this does not deny that various of the species and specimens of the genre will have further sources of attraction and pleasure that will require, correspondingly, *added* explanations. In most cases, such (added) explanations will be developed by critics of the genre. However I would like to address one particular case here which is especially relevant to readers of this book. In concluding, I will attempt an account of why at present horror is so compelling, that is, an account of why the horror cycle within which we find ourselves exerts such a commanding impression on its continuing, avid audiences: that is to say on us (or at least many of us).

The Paradox of Horror

In an earlier section, I explored, with relation to horror, what might be called the paradox of fiction—the question of how people can be moved (e.g., be horrified) by that which they know does not exist. In this section, I shall take a look at another apparent paradox that pertains to the genre: what might be called the paradox of horror. This paradox amounts to the question of how people can be attracted by what is repulsive. That is, the imagery of horror fiction seems to be necessarily repulsive and, yet, the genre has no lack of consumers. Moreover, it does not seem plausible to regard these consumers—given the vast number of them—as abnormal or perverse in any way that does not beg the question. Nevertheless, they appear to seek that which, under certain descriptions, it would seem natural for them to avoid. How is this ostensible conundrum to be resolved?

That the works of horror are in some sense both attractive and repulsive is essential to an understanding of the genre. Too often, writing about horror only emphasizes one side of this opposition. Many journalists, reviewing a horror novel or movie, will underscore only the repellent aspects of the work—rejecting it as disgusting, indecent, and foul. Yet this tack fails to offer any account of why people are interested in partaking of such exercises. Indeed, it renders the popularity of the genre inexplicable.

On the other hand, defenders of the horror genre or of a specific example of it will often indulge in allegorical readings that make their subjects appear wholly appealing and that do not acknowledge their repellent aspects. Thus, we are told that the Frankenstein myth is really an existential parable about man thrown-into-the-world, an "isolated sufferer."[1] But where in this allegorical formulation can we find an explanation for the purpose of the unsettling effect of the charnel house imagery? That is, if *Frankenstein* is part *Nausea,* it is also part nauseating.

The dangers of this allegorizing/valorizing tendency can be seen in some of the work of Robin Wood, the most vigorous champion of the contemporary horror film. About *Sisters,* he writes:

> *Sisters* analyzes the ways in which women are oppressed within patriarchal society which one can define as the professional (Grace) and the psychosexual (Danielle/Dominique).[2]

One wants to say "perhaps, but. . . ." Specifically, what about the unnerving, gory murders and the brackish, fecal bond that links the Siamese twins? In general, Wood's strategy is to characterize monsters as heroic because, for him, they represent what society, in the name of normality (and, often, the nuclear family) unconsciously represses. However, in elucidating what he takes to be the emancipatory and uplifting aspects of monsters, sight is lost of their essentially repulsive nature. Wood, of course, does not say that his movie monsters are not repulsive; however, in his explications of their galvanizing fascination in the recurring saga of the return of the repressed, their more loathsome—though essential—horrific features are all but forgotten.

Nevertheless, works of horror cannot be construed as either completely repelling or completely attractive. Either outlook overlooks something of the quiddity of the form. The apparent paradox cannot simply be ignored by treating the genre as if it were not involved in a curious admixture of attraction and repulsion.

The need to account for the peculiar nature of horror had already begun to strike writers in the eighteenth century. John and Anna Laetitia Aikin, in their essay "On the Pleasure Derived From Objects of Terror," write that " . . . the apparent delight with which we dwell upon objects of pure terror, where our moral feelings are not in the least concerned and no passion seems to be excited but the depressing one of fear, is a paradox of the heart . . . difficult of solution."[3] This question, of course, was not unique to tales of terror and horror. At roughly the same time, Hume published his "Of Tragedy," wherein he seeks to explain how the audiences of such dramas are "pleased in proportion as they are afflicted."[4] Hume, in turn, cites Jean-Baptiste Dubos and Bernard Le Bovier Fontenelle as earlier theoreticians concerned with the problem of how pleasure is to be derived from that which is distressful, while the Aikins themselves tackle this general problem in their "An Enquiry into those Kinds of Distress which excite agreeable Sensations."[5] And with reference to the sublime and objects of terror, Edmund Burke attempts to account for the way in which pain can give rise to delight in Part IV, Section V of his *A Philosophical Enquiry into the Origin of our ideas of the Sublime and Beautiful.*[6] Thus, the paradox of horror is an instance of a larger problem, viz., that of explaining the way in which the artistic presentation of normally aversive events and objects can give rise to pleasure or can compel our interests.

However, before turning to some of the eighteenth century solutions that are given to this puzzle—some of which, I believe, may still suggest useful generic answers to the problem of horror—it is instructive to recall several of the more recent, better-known answers to the problem, if only to gain some appreciation of the contours and constraints of arriving at a general account of the attractiveness of the horror genre.

Cosmic Awe, Religious Experience, and Horror

One authority often cited in attempted explanations of horror is H.P. Lovecraft, an esteemed practitioner of the genre who also wrote an influential treatise entitled *Supernatural Horror in Literature.*[7] In Lovecraft's view, supernatural horror evokes awe and what he calls "cosmic fear." Whether a work of horror evokes cosmic fear is, in fact, the identifying mark of the genre for Lovecraft. He writes:

> The one test of the really weird is simply this—whether or not there be excited in the reader a profound sense of dread, and of contact with unknown spheres and powers; a subtle attitude of awed listening, as if for the beating of black wings or the scratching of outside shapes on the known universe's utmost rim.[8]

Cosmic fear for Lovecraft is an exhilarating mixture of fear, moral revulsion, and wonder. He says of it: "When to this sense of fear and evil the inevitable fascination of wonder and curiosity is superadded, there is born a composite of keen emotion and imaginative provocation whose vitality must of necessity endure as long as the human race itself."[9] The capacity for this sensation of fear, which Lovecraft believes is coeval with religious feeling, is instinctual. Humans, it appears, are born with a kind of fear of the unknown which verges on awe. Thus, the attraction of supernatural horror is that it provokes a sense of awe which confirms a deep-seated human conviction about the world, viz., that it contains vast unknown forces.[10]

This capacity for awe, presumably to the detriment of our culture, is demeaned by what is called "materialistic sophistication." Nevertheless, sensitive people, imbued with imagination and the ability to detach themselves from the everyday, can be brought to an awareness of it—which awareness amounts to the apprehension of "a malign and particular suspension or defeat of those fixed laws of Nature which are our only safeguard against the assaults of chaos and the daemons of unplumbed space."[11]

Though it is difficult to put all this together, the gist of Lovecraft's theory seems to be that the literature of cosmic fear attracts because it confirms some instinctual intuition about reality, which intuition is denied by the culture of materialistic sophistication. This is something akin to the religious feeling of awe, an apprehension of the unknown charged with wonder.

Personally, I find it hard to tell whether this is supposed to be important from a primarily objective or a primarily subjective viewpoint. The objective interpretation would be that the literature of supernatural horror emotionally enlivens our sense that there *really* are things in heaven and earth not countenanced by materialistic sophisticates; whereas the subjective interpretation would remain neutral on what is really the case, but would maintain that the literature of supernatural horror keeps alive the *instinctual feeling* of awe about the unknown. If the latter interpretation is what Lovecraft has in mind, it must be admitted that he does not say why it is important for this feeling of awe or cosmic fear to be sustained. Perhaps he believes that it is an essential part of what it is to be human (i.e., to respond humanly to the world), or, in a related vein, because it is an indispensable corrective to the dehumanizing encroachment of materialistic sophistication.

But, in any case, it is clear that literary supernatural horror—which, by means of the morbidly unnatural (the repulsive), evokes cosmic fear—is attractive because this kind of awe responds to or restores some sort of primordial or instinctual human intuition about the world. The fact that Lovecraft is answering the question of how a distressful thing, like fear, can be positively compelling in terms of cosmic fear may not be as circular as it sounds. Fear itself is distasteful and would naturally be avoided; but cosmic fear is not simply fear, but awe, fear compounded with some sort of visionary dimension which is said to be keenly felt and vital. Thus, cosmic fear or awe, if there is such a thing, could be desirable in a way that fear *simpliciter* is not.

The relation of the repulsive in horror to this sense of awe is that the morbidly unnatural is what it takes to trigger it. So, we seek the morbidly unnatural in horror literature in order to experience awe, a cosmic fear with a visionary dimension that corresponds to instinctual, human views of the universe. The morbidly unnatural is a means to awe, and is sought not for its own sake but for that state which it induces in the audience. Stated less abstractly, Lovecraft appears to think that supernatural literature affords something like religious experience as well as a corresponding reaction against some kind of dessicating, positivist world view. It is for such reasons that the "sensitive" seek it out.[12]

In the few pages in which Lovecraft treats the origin and compelling force of supernatural horror, he manages to suggest an amazing number of assumptions of all sorts—some psychological, some sociological, some metaphysical—while also making a great many, albeit rather vague, assertions. It would undoubtedly take a great deal of space to dismantle these views, in part because it would take a long time to work them up interpretively to the point where they could be profitably engaged by argument. However, one point may be briefly made against Lovecraft's procedure that not only reveals its shortcomings, but also a recurring problem about answering the paradox of horror.

Earlier it was noted that Lovecraft not only locates what is positively compelling in the genre in virtue of provoking cosmic fear; he also takes cosmic fear to be definitory of the genre of supernatural horror. In other words, he both classifies and *commends* works of horror by means of the same standard. Thus, any candidate for the class of supernatural horror will not be included in that class if it fails to perform the commendable service of engendering cosmic fear.

But surely there are many horror stories that fall short of raising cosmic fear—a feeling that is bound up with a world view and that borders on a religious experience. Indeed, many horror stories seem oblivious to the grand (philosophical?) project of engendering cosmic awe. Perusing my bookshelf, I come upon *Crabs on the Rampage* by Guy N. Smith (author of

The Origin of the Crabs, Crabs' Moon and so on). It is, I submit, undeniably an example of horror, but it neither evokes cosmic fear nor awe. The crabs themselves provoke what we call art-horror, but art-horror need not be the emotional confirmation of one world view (one that is that coeval with religion) nor the denial of another (that of materialistic sophistication).[13]

As a result, Lovecraft, undoubtedly, would be tempted to reject *Crabs on the Rampage* as a member of the class of supernatural horror literature. But this is arbitrary. Awe is one effect of (perhaps) relatively high achievement within the horror genre, not the very sign of the genre. That is, a horror story that provokes awe would (probably) be a very good horror story; it would be commendable; but goodness, as anyone who knows the genre admits, is not one of its invariant calling cards. Lovecraft's classificatory standard for inclusion into the genre is too narrow; it really tracks one form of goodness or commendability or high achievement in the genre.

Indeed, my own suspicion is that awe, cosmic fear, and quasi-religious experiences are rare concomitants of supernatural horror fiction. They may occur in some of the work of Charles Williams, where they are good-making features. But they are not evoked nor does there appear to be an attempt to evoke them in much horror literature. Lovecraft's commitment to cosmic fear as the defining characteristic of horror literature in effect seems to be a matter of installing his preference for one type of good-making feature as the criterion for membership in the genre; that is, Lovecraft confuses what he regards as a level of high achievement in the genre with what identifies the genre.

Lovecraft's emphasis on cosmic fear and awe fits candidates like Algernon Blackwood's "Willows" quite well, since in that story the feelings of awe and cosmic intuition are directly stated. It is no wonder that Lovecraft finds it to be one of the greatest tales of supernatural horror. And it is, partly for the reasons Lovecraft gives. However, what makes that a particularly commendable tale of horror should not be set forth as a necessary expectation of any work in the genre.

Moreover, if this is correct, then it has immediate ramifications for what Lovecraft says with respect to the compelling attraction that the genre affords its audience. For if awe is not the common effect of the genre, then the attractiveness of the genre as a whole—apart from those specimens of it that deal in cosmic fear—cannot be explained by reference to it. The notions of cosmic fear, awe, and quasi-religious feeling, that is, are not comprehensive or general enough to capture what is compelling about the ordinary run of the genre. They do not resolve the paradox of horror for the typical case.

Cosmic fear may be relevant to explaining why some works of horror attract their audiences (though, I suspect, not as many works as Lovecraft has in mind); but it is not fundamental enough to explain the attractiveness of horror across the board. This point may be obscured while reading

Lovecraft since, given his putative classificatory scheme of things, the genre is identified in terms of cosmic fear; but once we see that Lovecraft's classificatory scheme really represents a covert preference for one sort of (possibly) especially commendatory, horrific effect, we note that cosmic fear is a special source of interest, occurring only in some works of horror, and that it is not pervasive enough to account for generic fascination with the genre.

The analogy between our response to horror and religious feeling as well as reference to some sort of instinctual feelings—especially in terms of what is lacking or denied in a materialist or positivist culture—occur not only in Lovecraft but are often cited in other accounts of horror. Space does not permit a discussion of all the ways in which these factors are worked into explanations of horror. But, at this point, some remarks about the limitations of adverting to these notions may be helpful.

First, the experience of supernatural horror in the arts is frequently analogized to religious experience. One supposes that if this analogy were convincing, then seeking after art-horror is no more unintelligible than seeking after religious experience, with all that that costs. Perhaps both satisfy an instinctual conviction in something beyond our ordinary concepts; perhaps stimulating that conviction is worth all the unpleasantness and anxieties it may entail—particularly, one might add, in materialist and/or positivist times.

There are many substantive claims here, the discussion of which would take us way beyond the compass of this book. However, we may be able to dodge many of them quite legitimately by simply asking whether the analogy between the experience of art-horror and the religious experience is apt. For if it is not, then the explanations falter, no matter what the truth is about our instinctual yearnings (if we have any).

The analogy between horror and religious experience is often framed, explicitly or implicitly, in terms of the analysis of religious or *numinous* experience developed by Rudolf Otto in his extremely influential, widely read, proto-phenomenological classic *The Idea of the Holy*.[14] I do not know whether this analysis of religious experience is correct; however, it is the one that commentators generally deploy, knowingly or unknowingly, when they contrive a correlation between horror and religious experience. Thus it seems pertinent to ask whether the experience of horror in literature parallels the religious or numinous experience as Otto conceptualizes it.

For Otto, religion has a nonrational element, an ineffable object which he refers to as the *numen*. This is the object of religious experience, or *numinous* experience. The terms in which this experience is characterized, as is well known, are *mysterium tremendum fascinans et augustum*. That is, the object of religious experience—and here it helps to have something like God in mind—is tremendous, causing fear in the subject, a paralyzing sense of being overpowered, of being dependent, of being nothing, of being worthless.

The numen is awe-ful, resulting in a sense of awe.[15] The numen is also mysterious; it is wholly other, beyond the sphere of the usual, the intelligible, and the familiar in such a way that it induces a stupor, a blank feeling of wonderment, an astonishment that strikes one dumb, a kind of amazement absolute.[16] This encounter with the wholly other does not simply terrify the subject; it also *fascinates* her. Indeed, its tremendous energy and urgency (*tremendum*) excites also our homage (hence, *augustum*).

Now if one reads this formula in a vague and decontextualized way, it is easy to draw correlations between most (though not all) of it and what one might wish to say of the objects of art-horror. The objects of art-horror have power, i.e., they are fearsome, and they engender a paralyzing sense of being overwhelmed; they are mysterious in a way that stuns, rendering one dumb and astonished by the onset of otherness, if the fiction is artful. And, as well, this fascinates the audience—perhaps it even fascinates the fictional characters,[17] and this may account for their frequent paralysis.

But these are only extremely glancing correlations. Otto's numen is wholly other. It defies the application of predicates and even the manifold of predicability itself.[18] But this is not the case with the monsters of horror. For even if they cannot be named outright in terms of the standing concepts of the culture, they can be situated in terms of those concepts as combinations, magnifications, etc. of what already is. That is, monsters are not wholly other, but derive their repulsive aspect from being, so to speak, contortions performed upon the known. They do not defy predication, but mix properties in nonstandard ways. They are not wholly unknown, and this is probably what accounts for their characteristic effect—disgust. Nor does one feel worthless before (or dependent upon) the monsters of horror as one might before a deity.

Because it is *tremendum,* the numen commands not only fascination, but it is also august, objectively valuable, commanding homage. This does not really fit the horror case at all. Most often we do not feel compelled to pay homage to the monster. Certainly there are some horror plots where paying homage to the monster—Satan, Rawhead Rex, Dracula, the primal Old Ones, and so on—may be part of the story. But this is true only in some cases—and, therefore, is not a general mark of horror—and, even in those cases, it pertains only to some of the characters in the story and not to the audience. That is, reading about the coven in Blackwood's "Secret Worship," does not prompt us to become hierophants of Lucifer. Moreover, Otto himself, one suspects, would not approve of his characterization of numinous experience being extrapolated to horror; in his opinion dread of daemons and fear of ghosts represents a lower stage of development than does religious experience.[19] Thus, it would appear hazardous to attempt to explain the attractive power of horror on the basis of an analogy with the attractive power of religious experience, because it is not clear that the analogy between the religious experience and the experience of art-horror is reliable.[20]

Similarly, there is something strained in the hypothesis that horror functions somewhat like a haven for religious feeling in materialist or positivist times. For religion, even ecstastic religion, is easily available in ungodly cultures like the United States where the horror genre presently thrives (even as presidents dabble in astrology). If religious experience is what people really want, they can get it directly—without searching for surrogates like horror fiction.

Nor does it seem helpful to connect horror with some sort of atavistic instincts. Admittedly, the imagery of horror may spring from ancient intimations of animism and from residues of a kind of literal totemic thinking that compounds species. However, this is probably explicable culturally without resorting to notions of a racial memory. Moreover, if the instinct here is some sort of instinctual fear, then invoking it will not solve the paradox of horror, for one is still left supposing that instinctual fear, like plain old fear, is something we ordinarily want to avoid.

Of course, phrases like "instinctual fear" may really be a kind of shorthand for the complicated notion that in the positivist, materialist, bourgeois culture in which we find ourselves, certain thrills and fears that were commonplace to our cave-dwelling ancestors are rare; and these thrills can be retrieved somewhat by consuming horror fictions. Being thrilled, even frightened (albeit aesthetically), it might be said, relieves the emotional blandness of something called modern life. [21]

The underlying presumption here is that being in an emotional state is invigorating and, if we don't have to pay the price of the emotional state (in the way, for example, that fear customarily requires danger), then we will view being in that state as worthwhile.[22] Now it may be true that emotional states are often invigorating in this way (i.e. they provide an adrenaline surge), and that we will pursue them for this very reason if no risk is involved. And it may also be true that this supplies part of the reason that horror fiction appeals. But, it may be equally true that this is why adventure fiction, romance fiction, melodrama, and so on, appeal. That is, if the point is that being in a detached (whatever that means) emotional state—instinctual or otherwise—is part of what explains our attraction to the horror genre, this is not a very specific explanation, for it will probably play a role (if it *does* play any explanatory role anywhere) in the explanation of the audience's attraction to every popular genre.[23]

Another way of explaining the attraction of horror—one that may be connected with elements of the religious account—is to say that horrific beings—like deities and daemons—attract us because of their power. They induce awe. In one mode of speaking, it might be said that we identify with monsters because of the power they possesss—perhaps monsters are wish-fulfillment figures. In earlier sections of this book, I have been chary about the notion of identification. However, the view may be stated neutrally in terms of admiration. It might be argued that we so admire the power monsters have that the disgust they engender is outweighed.

This explanation fits some cases very nicely. With figures like Melmoth the Wanderer, Dracula, and Lord Ruthven (in John Polidori's *The Vampyre*) the monstrous entity is seductive, and part of that seductiveness has to do with its force. But, then again, the zombies in *Night of the Living Dead,* are not seductive, nor is their unavoidable power—only the numbers are on their side—a source of admiration. Thus, the—let us call it—*admiration for the devil* explanation of horror does not account for the genre as a whole. Though useful for explaining aspects of the attraction of some of the sub-genres of horror, it is not comprehensive of horror in general.[24]

The Psychoanalysis of Horror

So far in my review of well-known attempts at explaining the attraction of horror, I have not mentioned psychoanalysis. This is undoubtedly the most popular avenue for explaining horror nowadays. Moreover, even if it turns out—as I will argue—that psychoanalysis does not offer a *comprehensive* account of horror, psychoanalysis nevertheless may still have much to say about particular works, subgenres, and cycles within horror, if only because various psychoanalytic myths, images, and self-understandings[25] have been continually and increasingly appropriated by the genre throughout the twentieth century. That is, if psychoanalysis does not afford a comprehensive theory of horror, it remains the case that psychoanalytic imagery often reflexively informs works within the genre which, of course, makes psychoanalysis germane to interpretations of specific instances of the genre. Psychoanalysis, in other words, may still be unavoidable in discussing the genre—or, more accurately, certain instances of the genre—whether or not it offers an adequate general theory of the genre and its attractive powers.

Needless to say, there are many ways in which psychoanalysis has been or could be enlisted in explanations of horror. Space, and perhaps patience, does not allow a detailed examination of them all, or even of a substantial number of them. In what follows, I shall review some of what I take to be the more powerful claims of psychoanalysis regarding what I have called the paradox of horror. And though I suspect that these do not deliver a comprehensive answer to the questions posed here, I do not deny that for certain cases—of specific fictions, subgenres, or cycles—that the psychoanalytic framework may add to our understanding of the material at hand. This will be the case most noncontroversially where specific examples of horror are inflected by psychoanalytic myths or where psychoanalytic imagery itself converges on significant cultural myths (and therefore matches, so to speak, the analogous myths in given horror fictions).

When I first began to study horror seriously, I was attracted to a psychoanalytic model of explanation,[26] specifically to the one developed by Ernest Jones in his *On the Nightmare*.[27] This approach seemed to me especially fruitful because it was sensitive to the essential ambivalence that horror seemed to enjoin: the pull of both attraction and repulsion. Thus, the psychoanalytic model developed by Jones appeared particularly fitted for the task of analyzing horror, since it met what I have called the paradox of horror head-on.

In *On the Nightmare*, Jones uses a Freudian-derived—i.e., wish-fulfillment style—analysis of the nightmare in order to unravel the symbolic meaning and structure of such figures of medieval superstition as the incubus, vampire, werewolf, devil, and witch. A central concept in Jones's treatment of the imagery of nightmare is conflict or ambivalence. The products of the dream-work are said to be often simultaneously attractive and repellent, insofar as they function to enunciate both a wish and its inhibition. Jones writes:

> The reason why the object seen in a nightmare is frightful or hideous is simply that the representation of the underlying wish is not permitted in its naked form so that the dream is a compromise of the wish on the one hand and on the other of the intense fear belonging to the inhibition.[28]

For example, according to Jones, the vampires of superstition have two fundamental constituent attributes: revenance and bloodsucking. The mythic vampire, as opposed to the contemporary vampire of movies and pulp fiction, first visits its relatives. For Jones, this stands for the relatives' longing for the loved one to return from the dead. But the figure is charged with terror. What is fearful is bloodsucking, which Jones associates with seduction. In short, the desire for an incestuous encounter with the dead relative is transformed, through a form of denial, into an assault—attraction and love metamorphose into repulsion and sadism. At the same time, via projection, the living portray themselves as passive victims, imbuing the dead with a dimension of active agency that permits pleasure without blame. That is, the dead are proposed as the sinful aggressors while the living are putatively hapless (and, therefore, "innocent") victims. Lastly, Jones not only connects bloodsucking with the exhausting embrace of the incubus but with a regressive mixture of sucking and biting characteristic of the oral stage of psychosexual development. By negation—the transformation of love to hate—by projection—through which the desired dead become active, and the desiring living passive—and by regression—from genital to oral sexuality—the vampire legend gratifies incestuous and necrophiliac desires by amalgamating them in a fearsome iconography.

That is, for Jones the nightmare and figures of the nightmare like the vampire—i.e., the very stuff of horror fiction—attract because they manifest wishes, notably sexual wishes. However, these wishes are forbidden or repressed. They cannot be acknowledged outright. This is where the horrific, repulsive imagery comes in. It disguises or masks the unacknowledgeable wish. It functions as camouflage; the dreamer cannot be blamed for these images by her internal censor because they beset her; she finds them fearsome and repulsive, so she cannot be thought to enjoy them (though she really does savor them insofar as they express deep, psychosexual wishes, albeit in mufti). The revulsion and disgust the horrific imagery provokes is the price the dreamer pays for having her wish fulfilled.

Jones developed this hypothesis to analyze a certain class of dreams, viz., nightmares, and he applied it to what he regarded as recurring figures of nightmare. However, it is not difficult to extend this style of analysis to horror fictions, especially, if, like Freud, one is willing to regard popular fiction as a species of wish-fulfillment.[29] On this extension, the horrific images of this genre represent compromise formations. Their repulsive aspects mask and make possible various sorts of wish-fulfilment, notably those of a sexual sort. The apparent seductiveness of Dracula is no misperception; Dracula is enacting a wish, indeed an incestuous one. The audience can deny this to her censor, by pleading, in her own defense, that she is horrified by the vampire. But this is really a dodge. The repulsion is the ticket that allows the pleasurable wish-fulfillment to be enacted.

So the paradox of horror can be explained by someone extrapolating from Jones by saying that the ambivalence felt toward the objects of horror derives from a deeper ambivalence about our most enduring psychosexual desires. The repulsive dimensions of horrific beings function to satisfy the censor; but, in fact, they are really a deceptive device which make the deeper pleasure of the satisfaction of presiding psychosexual wishes possible. We are attracted to horror imagery because, appearances notwithstanding, such imagery permits the satisfaction of deep psychosexual wishes. Nor could these wishes be tolerably satisfied unless the censor were paid its due. That is, the revulsion at the creatures of horror in fact is the means through which—given a Freudian view of the way in which the economy of the individual is set out—pleasure can be secured.

Consequently, there is no really deep paradox of horror, for the repulsiveness of its monsters is what makes them attractive for the scheming, circuitous psyche. What appears to be displeasure, and, figuratively speaking, pain, in horror fictions is really the road to pleasure, given the structure of repression.

With its stress on ambivalence, a Jones-like, psychoanalytic theory of horror has the right structure for our purposes. It explains how audiences can be attracted to horror despite the ostensible disgust it enjoins. This disgust, of course, is not illusory; the audience is repulsed. But this disgust is, more importantly, functional. It exacts a little discomfort in exchange for greater pleasure. Nor could pleasure be secured unless this discomfort were exacted.

Obvious liabilities of this theory, however, are that it requires 1) an animating wish which, in turn, 2) must be understood as sexual, if only in the extended sense of the concept of sexuality that Freudian psychology licenses. With respect to the second of these requirements, it is at least not easy to discern a latent *sexual* wish behind each and every one of the monsters in the gallery of horror fiction.

Certain horrific beings, of course, do seem to fit this characterization rather nicely. Vampires are perhaps the best examples: they seduce, but both characters and audiences behave as if they find these creatures unbearably disgusting and fearsome. And one can see with a film like Val Lewton's *Cat People* (which, of course, is influenced by Freudian ideas) how both Irena and the audience regard her ostensibly unholy, shape-changing self as the cost of her sexuality. Nor would one wish to deny that certain stories, like M.R. James's "Oh Whistle and I'll Come to You My Lad," might be cogently interpreted as the presentation of repressed homosexual desire, in this particular case via the agency of the spirit in the bed.[30] However, it is far more difficult to see the way in which humans trampled by big gorillas or emulsified by Godzilla's death-dealing halitosis can gratify a *sexual* wish.

At this point, the ingenious psychoanalytic interpreter may attempt to evolve a chain of associations that gets us from such things as men being possessed by vegetables to a sexual desire. Nevertheless, we will have every right to suspect the strained associations and ad hoc hypotheses that are likely to ensue as little more than an attempt to make the data fit the sexual wish-fulfillment theory.

As a hard-line Freudian, then, Jones suffers from his overemphasis on the degree to which incestuous desires shape the conflicts in the nightmare (and, by extension, in the formation of the monstrous beings of horror fictions). For he claims that these always relate to the sexual act.[31] And this, I submit, will not be a comprehensive enough perspective to accommodate a great many of the creatures of the horror genre.

However, if one is prone to this form of analysis, one might attempt to recoup the situation by easing the requirements that such figures embody wish-fulfillments that are sexual in nature. One might claim, in a gesture of catholicity, that these figures can also manifest repressed anxieties (rather than irreducible wishes) which, in turn, may not be only sexual in nature. With respect to the nightmare, John Mack has argued that the hard-line Freudian position is too narrow and that "the analysis of nightmare regularly leads us to the earliest, most profound, and inescapable anxieties and conflicts to which human beings are subject: those involving destructive aggression, castration, separation and abandonment, devouring and being devoured, and fear regarding loss of identity and fusion with the mother."[32]

Widening the ambit of what can be expressed of that which is repressed in this way obviously enhances the reach of the psychoanalytic model. Horrific creatures and their doings need not be traced back to their manifestation simply of sexual wishes, but can be linked with a whole panoply of repression: to anxieties and infantile fantasies as well as sexual wishes. Thus, the recent popularity of telekinetic nastiness in films and novels like *The Exorcist, Carrie, The Fury,* and *Patrick* might be explained as gratifying the infantile conviction in the unlimited power of repressed rage—the belief in the omnipotence of thought—while at the same time costuming this repressed fantasy in the drapery of horror.

That is, the reader treats Carrie in all her unstoppable fury as a monster at the same time that Carrie realizes or enacts an infantile fantasy of revenge in which, conveniently, looks *can* kill. As a monster, Carrie is horrifying; but at the same time, she provides an opportunity for a guilty fantasy—one tinged with anxiety—to surface. Thus, Carrie's horrific aspect enables the fruition of a deeper pleasure, viz., the manifestation of the infantile delusion of the omnipotence of the will.[33]

Clearly, the more suppressed psychic sources—above and beyond repressed sexual desires—that the analyst takes as prospects for covert (and presumably gratificatory) manifestation, the more figures of horror she will be able to explain in this way. If this hypothesis is successful, every figure of horror will be connected to some infantile anxiety, fantasy, wish (sexual or otherwise), trauma, and so on. Further, it will be presumed that the manifestation of any form of repressed material affords pleasure and that the horrifying aspect of monsters is the cost for lifting or releasing this repression.

Still, I wonder whether every monster in horror fiction will be traceable to repressed subject matter in this way. As we saw in the discussion of the ways monsters are constructed, there are certain routine manipulations that can be performed on cultural categories that result in what I earlier called horrific beings. Horrific beings, that is, seem to be producible by what might be thought of as almost formal operations on cultural categories.

Take an insect's head and put it on a human torso and add webbed feet and you've got a monster; it can horrify, when placed in a suitable dramatic structure, even if it does not attempt to eat or to abduct anyone. It is not clear to me that monsters confected this way must necessarily touch any infantile traumas or repressed wishes or anxieties.

Or, for instance, mass any type of insect—save perhaps butterflies and ladybugs—give them intelligence, a taste for "big game," and put them on the march, and you've probably just cast the antagonists for a horror fiction. But, again, in opposition to the expanded, psychoanalytic hypothesis introduced in the paragraph before the preceding one, it is not obvious that the symbolism of these monsters will be of any psychoanalytic significance within the context of the fiction under discussion. Nor am I just imagining counterexamples; monsters that tax psychoanalytic analysis—even of the expanded sort we are now considering—are rampant in horror fictions.

A pertinent counterexample can be found in the man- and woman-eating cephalopods—called *Haploteuthis*—in H.G. Wells's short story "The Sea Raiders." The discovery of these horrific beings quickly turns into confrontation, followed by subsequent information about further appearances of these voracious deep-sea-beings. The story is primarily concerned with action, and, secondarily, with a bit of ratiocination about the cause of the onslaught of the cephalopods. But this is never connected within the story with the type of associative chains that might lead back to early traumas or conflicts. No characters are developed in a way that would enable us to consider the cephalopods as objective correlatives for their repressed psychic conflicts, nor are the cephalopods described in a manner that would lead one to invoke standard forms of psychoanalytic symbolism.

It is true that the cephalopods come from the deep, but it is hard to gloss this as repression of psychic material, since one cannot specify the content of whatever repressed material they might be supposed to represent. One might say that since the cephalopods devour people, they represent repressed, infantile anxieties about being devoured. But, on the other hand, since some deep-sea creatures do devour humans, and since being literally devoured is a legitimate adult fear, and since there is nothing in this story to suggest a connection with the child's putative fear of being eaten by a parent or parental surrogate, there is no real force to claiming that the cephalopods are some sort of parent figure and that the story manifests a deep-seated, *infantile* fear of being gobbled up by Mom and Dad.

This case should serve as a counterexample both to the narrow psychoanalytic attempt to reduce horrific figures to repressed, *sexual* wish-fulfillments, and to the broader approach which reduces said figures to anxieties and wishes which may be sexual or which may mobilize other, latent, archaic material.

Moreover, if this counterexample is persuasive, then it is easy to see that there are many more where it came from (and not just from beneath the sea). Like the cephalopods, innumerable dinosaurs frozen in icebergs or found on lost continents, giant insects in jungles, and octopii from outer space *need not* figure as emblems of psychic conflict. Therefore, the psychoanalytic reduction of horrific creatures to the objects of repression is not comprehensive for the genre; not all horrific creatures portend psychic conflict or desire. Therefore, the psychoanalytic dissolution of the paradox of horror—in terms of the wages of the return of the repressed—is not perfectly general.[34]

In order to advance the argument above, I have not challenged the viability of psychoanalysis as a mode of interpretation or explanation. Nor would such a challenge be appropriate in a book like this—it would require a book unto itself. However, for my purposes, it is possible to remain neutral on the question of the overall epistemic standing of psychoanalysis as either science or hermeneutics. For we have seen that even if it were well-founded, it nevertheless still fails to provide a comprehensive account of the figures of horror, and, consequently, of the paradox of horror.

There may be horror fictions that accord with psychoanalytic models; obviously, this is most likely where the fictions have been influenced perceptibly by psychoanalysis. But there may also be horror fictions that, *sans* authorial intent, touch the kinds of traumas, wishes, and conflicts that concern psychoanalysis. And with such stories, if psychoanalysis or some form of it is true (which admittedly may be a big *if*), then the psychoanalytic attractions in the cases in question may provide added force to the as yet unidentified source of the genre's attraction in general. That the force they supply is supplemental in the relevant cases, of course, follows from the acknowledgment that the psychoanalytic account is not comprehensive for the genre—that is, does not cover all the obvious kinds of cases.

Before leaving the topic of psychoanalysis and horror, further comment on the relevance of the notion of repression may be useful. Most psychoanalytic theories of horror will employ some notion of repression in the discussion of horror and related genres of fantasy. The objects of such genres will be taken as figures of repressed material and their appearance in the fiction will be thought to release repression in a way that is pleasurable. Thus, most psychoanalytic approaches will presume, virtually axiomatically, that if a horrific creature can be designated as a figure of repressed psychic material that will, in turn, support an explanation of the way in which the figure yields pleasure through manifesting what is repressed. A further step would be to regard such manifestations of the repressed as transgressive or subversive, concepts that also, in current usage, seem to have a connection with pleasure, i.e., with a sense of liberation.

The psychoanalytic correlation of repression with such things as monsters and ghosts finds influential precedence in Freud's essay "The 'Uncanny.' " Though I suspect that the objects Freud thinks are captured under the rubric of the *uncanny* are more numerous and diverse than what I take to be the objects of art-horror, it does seem fair to surmise that Freud thinks that these latter objects will all fall into the class of uncanny things (along with a lot of other stuff).

Concerning the experience of the uncanny, Freud writes that it "occurs either when repressed infantile complexes have been revived by some impression, or when the primitive beliefs we have surmounted seem once more to be confirmed."[35] To experience the uncanny, then, is to experience something that is known, but something the knowledge of which has been hidden or repressed. Freud takes this to be a necessary, though not a sufficient condition, of the experience of the uncanny: " . . . the uncanny is nothing else than a hidden, familiar thing that has undergone repression and then emerged from it, and that everything that is uncanny fulfills this condition."[36]

Now many contemporary theorists, such as Rosemary Jackson, think of cultural categories as repressive schematizations of what is.[37] And, in this light, the creatures of art-horror are manifestations of what is repressed by the culture's schematizations. She writes:

> . . . fantastic literature points to or suggests the basis upon which the cultural order rests, for it opens up, for a brief moment, on disorder, on to illegality, on to that which is outside dominant value systems. The fantastic traces the unsaid and the unseen of culture: that which has been silenced, made invisible, covered over and made absent."[38]

and

> Themes of the fantastic in literature revolve around this problem of making visible the un-seen articulating the un-said. Fantasy establishes or dis-covers, an absence of separating distinction, violating a 'normal', or commonsense perspective which represents reality as constituted by discrete but connected units. Fantasy is preoccupied with limits, with limiting categories, and with their projected dissolution. It subverts dominant philosophical assumptions which uphold as 'reality', a coherent, single-viewed entity. . . . [I]t is possible to see its [fantasy's] thematic elements as deriving from the same source: a dissolution of separating categories, a foregrounding of those spaces which are hidden and cast into/as darkness, by the placing and naming of the 'real' through the chronological temporal structures and three dimensional spatial organization.[39]

For Jackson, fantasy and, one assumes, horror (as a subcategory of fantasy), exposes the limits of a culture's definitional scheme of what is; fantasy problematizes categories in a way that shows that which the culture represses. In this respect, it is possible to see a subversive function to the genre; by reversing or inverting the culture's conceptual categories, fantastic literature subverts repressive cultural schemes of categorization. One supposedly repressive category, of central importance, which is subverted in this way is the idea of a person: "Fantasies of deconstructed, demolished or divided identities and of disintegrated bodies, oppose traditional categories of unitary selves."

Though Jackson does not address the problem of the paradox of horror directly, it is easy to see what her implicit answer to it would be. The objects of art-horror violate the culture's standing concepts and categories; they present figures that cannot be (cannot exist) according to the culture's scheme of things. Insofar as the culture's scheme of things is repressive, the presentation of things that defy that schematization lifts or releases repression, if only momentarily. This, one presumes, is pleasurable; moreover, Jackson suggests that this also has some vague political value, i.e., that it is "subversive" in the arena of cultural politics.

To a certain extent, Jackson's view of the nature of horrific beings corresponds to the characterizations advanced earlier in this book. The objects of horror, in my account, are impure, and this impurity is to be understood in terms of the ways in which horrific beings problematize standing cultural categories in terms of interstitiality, recombinative fusions of discrete categorical types, and so on. Thus, I can concur with Jackson's notion that such objects are the unseen and the unsaid of culture. However, unlike Jackson, I see no reason to think that these categorical permutations are necessarily, in all cases, repressed. Insofar as these categorical permutations are not part of the standing categories of the culture, they may be unthought (until the fiction maker does so); and since they are outside our standard repertoire of concepts, they represent possibilities that are generally unnoticed, ignored, unacknowledged, and so forth. But repression involves more than lack of awareness. It involves the suppression of awareness for the sake of some specific dimension of psychic functionality.

But a large number of horrific beings are not repressive figures of this sort. We are not prepared with a ready cultural category for the large insect-slaves in the film *This Island Earth*. They are part insect and part man while, at the same time, they confound normal expectations about inside and outside since their brains are clearly exposed. The possibility of such a recombinative being is not something our cultural categories lead us to expect; many perhaps never dreamed of the possibility of such a creature until they saw *This Island Earth* or a poster thereof. But this is not because we have been repressing the possibility of these monsters.

I think that the reasons that support this claim are twofold: first, with many of the monsters of horror fiction, we have no antecedent awareness of them which we are repressing—they are merely unthought; second, with examples like this one, which might be thought to be derived from almost formal operations on our cultural categories, it is difficult to specify the psychic value that repressing them would promote. That is, horrific fictional creatures may be concocted by means of routine deformations, recombinations, subtractions, etc., performed on the paradigms of our cultural categories. But there are no grounds for predicting that these formal operations will, in every case, link up with repressed material. In fact, I have proposed cases—such as Wells's cephalopods and the slave creatures in *This Island*

Earth—where the notion of repression appears out of place. Thus, if this argument is convincing, the repression hypothesis championed by Jackson and others does not provide a comprehensive account of the horror genre.[40]

Jackson's statement of the repression hypothesis is sometimes disconcerting. One way of reading her claim is that what she calls the culture's unseen and un-said—that which the culture's categorization renders invisible, hidden, and so on—involves some denial, perhaps for ideological purposes, of reality. Undoubtedly, a culture's concepts makes thinking about some possibilities less likely than thinking about other possibilities. However, this need not entail any denial of reality. Our culture's categories may make it unlikely (*unlikely* rather than impossible) that we think about jellyfish as big as houses coming from Mars to conquer the world. However, that's no offense against reality; there are no such jellyfish. Nor am I being enthnocentric, anthropocentric, or naughty in any other way when I say so.

Moreover, Jackson's extreme suspicion of a culture's categorical schemes is virtually paranoid; culture is portrayed as something that stands in the way of our interaction with reality. But one should, in contrast, regard culture—especially in terms of the way in which its concepts organize our negotiations with the world—as a means by which we come to know reality.

I should also say that I find Jackson's notion that fantasy is, by nature, inherently subversive politically or culturally to be strained. The idea seems to be that since the genre affirms that to which the culture denies existence it is oppositional and perhaps utopian—celebrating as possible states of affairs that are off-limits to the culture's imagination.

This line of argument bears a number of formal similarities with the radical arguments that maintain that fiction—because it represents what is not the case—and art in general—because it is autonomous from the realm of the practical and the instrumental—are emancipatory as such. For fiction and art (according to Herbert Marcuse, for example) celebrate the possibilities of either reality being other than the way it is or other than the way the culture says it is, thereby promoting a sense that reality (notably social reality) can be changed. Fantasy, fiction, and art, given their very nature, are, according to such views, said to be automatically emancipatory by virtue of their ontological preconditions. The content of a particular fantasy story, fiction or artwork does not cancel the inherent utopian dimension of the form in question.

But I think that these arguments are highly suspect. They hypostasize fiction, art, and fantasy in such a way that they are seen as emancipatory as a function of their very essence. Fiction, art, and fantasy are treated as morally good in virtue of their ontological status. Not only does this seem overly sentimental, but I think it flies in the face of the facts. Surely there can be and have been morally and, more to the point, politically obnoxious fictions, artworks, and fantasies.

And that fictions represent what is not the case does not automatically entail or encourage anything about socially relevant reconstruction. That Robinson Crusoe never was says nothing about whether capitalism can be overthrown. Similarly the mere representation of werewolves is not a political act, nor even a cultural/political act. Reading *fictions* about creatures that do not accord with a culture's conception of what there is does not challenge the cognitive status quo, and, most assuredly, it does not challenge the status quo.

One may describe the creatures of horror and fantasy as subverting cultural categories in the sense of not fitting them; but to regard this sense of *subversion* as politically significant is a species of equivocation. This is not to say that a particular horror or fantasy fiction might not be politically motivated; the original plan of *The Cabinet of Dr. Caligari,* as is well known, was to make a politically pointed allegory. However, whether a fantasy fiction is politically subversive depends upon its internal structure and the context in which it is made, not on its ontological status.

One cultural conception which Jackson thinks comes under especial subversive fire in the fantasy genre is that of the person as a unitary self. The genre, for example, is populated by beings comprised of multiple selves or creatures that are undergoing disintegration. Jackson reads this as an assault on the dominant culture's conception of the self. However, this characterization hardly withstands scrutiny. Many of the divided, disintegrating selves of fantasy fiction—Dr. Jekyll, Dorian Gray, werewolves, and so on—in fact literalize popular religious and philosophical views of the person (as divided between good and evil, between reason and appetite, between human and beast). Thus, these creatures do not subvert the culture's conceptions of personhood, but rather articulate them, or, at least, certain of them. Jackson's mistake, like that of so many other contemporary theoreticians, is to suppose that our culture has only one concept of the person *and* that is always of a unitary self. Such views are tragic in the sense in which it was said that Herbert Spencer felt that tragedy was a theory killed by a fact.

The General and the Universal
Theories of Horrific Appeal

So far this chapter has been littered with failed attempts to provide a comprehensive way of coming to terms with the paradox of horror. Religious analogies and psychoanalytic theories alike have been rejected as insufficiently general. Pace the religious hypothesis, not all the objects of art-horror instill awe, while in the case of psychoanalysis, not all are necessarily objects of repression. Having discarded these more familiar approaches to the paradox of horror, the burden is now upon me to propose a theory of my own.

Earlier it was mentioned that an awareness of the paradox of horror had already dawned on eighteenth-century theorists. The question they asked about tales of terror, as cited, was in fact part of the more general aesthetic question of how it is possible for audiences to derive pleasure from any genre—including not only horror but tragedy as well—whose objects were things that ordinarily cause distress and discomfiture. That is, encountering things such as ghosts or Desdemona's massacre in "real life" would be upsetting rather than entertaining. And, of course, what is disgusting on-screen or on the page is genuinely disgusting. It is something that we would ordinarily seek to avert. So why do we seek it in art and fiction? How does it give us pleasure and/or why does it interest us?

In order to answer these questions, I think that it is quite helpful to return to some of the very authors who first asked them—specifically, Hume and the Aikins—to see what they have to say. I will undoubtedly have to modify and amplify their accounts. However, a review of their thoughts will serve to orient us toward what I believe is at least part of a comprehensive answer to the paradox of horror.

In order to appreciate the way Hume's observations on tragedy can contribute to answering the paradox of horror, it is important to keep in mind that the horror genre, like that of tragedy, most generally takes a narrative form. Indeed, I spent a Chapter Three attempting to review a large number of the narrative elements in the horror genre. That horror is often narrative suggests that with much horror, the interest we have and the pleasure we take may not primarily be in the object of art-horror as such—i.e., in the monster for its own sake. Rather, the narrative may be the crucial locus of our interest and pleasure. For what is attractive—what holds our interest and yields pleasure—in the horror genre need not be, first and foremost, the simple manifestation of the object of art-horror, but the way that manifestation or disclosure is situated as a functional element in an overall narrative structure.

That is, in order to give an account of what is compelling about the horror genre, it may be wrong to ask only what it is about the monster that gives us pleasure; for the interest and pleasure we take in the monster and its disclosure may rather be a function of the way it figures in a larger narrative structure.

Speaking of the presentation of melancholy events by orators, Hume notes that the pleasure derived is not a response to the event as such, but to its rhetorical framing. When we turn to tragedy, plotting performs this function. The interest that we take in the deaths of Hamlet, Gertrude, Claudius, et al. is not sadistic, but is an interest that the plot has engendered in how certain forces, once put in motion, will work themselves out. Pleasure derives from having our interest in the outcome of such questions satisfied. Hume writes:

ⅼ any intention to move a person extremely by the narration of any event,
⁚ method of increasing its effect would be artfully to delay informing him
nd first to excite his curiosity and impatience before you let him into the
secret. This is the artifice practiced by Iago in the famous scene of Shakespeare;
and every spectator is sensible, that Othello's jealousy acquires additional force
from his preceding impatience, and that the subordinate passion is here readily
transformed into the predominant one.[41]

Hume's idea is that once a tragic, unsettling event is housed in an aesthetic
context, with a momentum of its own, the predominant feeling response,
in terms of pleasure and interest, attaches to the presentation as a function
of the overall, narrative structure. That is, the ostensibly "subordinate passion," but the one keyed to the structure, becomes predominant. Hume
notes:

> These instances (and many more might be collected) are sufficient to afford us
> some insight into the analogy of nature, and to show us, that the pleasure which
> poets, orators, and musicians give us, by exciting grief, sorrow, indignation,
> compassion, is not so extraordinary or paradoxical as it may at first sight appear.
> The force of imagination, the energy of expression, the power of numbers, the
> charms of imitation; all these are naturally, of themselves delightful to the mind:
> and when the object presented lays also hold of some affection, the pleasure
> rises upon us by the conversion of this subordinate movement into that which
> is predominant. The passion, though perhaps naturally, and when excited by
> the simple appearance of a real object, it may be painful; yet is so smoothed and
> softened, and mollified, when realised by the finer arts that it affords the highest
> entertainment.[42]

With tragedy, the "affection" Hume thinks takes hold is narrative expectation, which certainly harkens back to Aristotle's observations about the
audience's anticipation of recognition and reversal in plays of that sort. Thus,
it is not the tragic event in itself that imparts pleasure, but rather, the way
it is worked into the plot.

Similarly, the Aikins look to the plot, in large measure, to account for the
interest and pleasure taken in the objects of terror.[43] They think the question
may be stated badly if we attempt to account for the pleasure derived from
terror fictions solely in terms of saying how the objects—monsters, for our
purposes—are attractive or pleasurable for their own sake. They write (in
the first person, singular):

> How are we then to account for the pleasure derived from such objects? I have
> often been led to imagine that there is a deception in these cases; and that the
> avidity with which we attend is not a proof of our receiving real pleasure. The
> pain of suspense, and the irresistible desire of satisfying our curiosity, when
> once raised, will account for our eagerness to go quite through an adventure,

though we suffer actual pain during the whole course of it. We rather chuse to suffer the smart pang of a violent emotion than the uneasy craving of an unsatisfied desire. That this principle, in many instances, may involuntarily carry us through what we dislike, I am convinced from experience.[44]

One need not buy everything that Hume and the Aikins assert wholesale. I, personally, doubt that suspense is aptly described as painful, while the mechanics of Hume's transition of a subordinate passion to a predominant one are somewhat unfathomable, if not wrong (since the tragedy of the event and our predictably distressed reaction to it seems to me to be an inseparable element of the narration). However, their shared notion, that the aesthetic contrivance of normally upsetting events depends upon their contextualization in structures like narrative, is particularly suggestive with respect to the paradox of horror.

For, as noted, a great deal of the horror genre is narrative. Indeed, I think it is fair to say that in our culture, horror thrives above all as a narrative form. Thus, in order to account for the interest we take in and the pleasure we take from horror, we may hypothesize that, in the main, the locus of our gratification is not the monster as such but the whole narrative structure in which the presentation of the monster is staged. This, of course, is not to say that the monster is in any way irrelevant to the genre, nor that the interest and pleasure in the genre could be satisfied through and/or substituted by any old narrative. For, as I have argued earlier, the monster is a functional ingredient in the type of narratives found in horror stories, and not all narratives function exactly like horror narratives.

As we saw in my analysis of horror narratives, these stories, with great frequency, revolve around proving, disclosing, discovering, and confirming the existence of something that is impossible, something that defies standing conceptual schemes. It is part of such stories—contrary to our everyday beliefs about the nature of things—that such monsters exist. And as a result, audiences' expectations revolve around whether this existence will be confirmed in the story.

Often this is achieved, as Hume says of narrative "secrets" in general, by putting off the conclusive information that the monster exists for quite a while. Sometimes this information may be deferred till the very end of the fiction. And even where this information is given to the audience right off the bat, it is still generally the case that the human characters in the tale must undergo a process of discovering that the monster exists, which, in turn, may lead to a further process of confirming that discovery in an ensuing scene or series of scenes. That is, the question of whether or not the monster exists may be transformed into the question of whether and when the human characters in the tale will establish the existence of the monster. Horror stories are often protracted series of discoveries: first the reader learns of the monster's existence, then some characters do, then some more characters do, and so on; the drama of iterated disclosure—albeit to different parties— underwrites much horror fiction.[45]

Even in overreacher plots, there is a question of whether the monsters exist—i.e., of whether they can be summoned, in the case of demons, or of whether they can be created by mad scientists and necromancers. Further-more, even after the existence of the monster is disclosed, the audience continues to crave further information about its nature, its identity, its origin, its purposes, and its astounding powers and properties, including, ultimately, those of its weaknesses that *may* enable humanity to do it in.

Thus, to a large extent, the horror story is driven explicitly by curiosity. It engages its audience by being involved in processes of disclosure, discovery, proof, explanation, hypothesis, and confirmation. Doubt, skepticism, and the fear that belief in the existence of the monster is a form of insanity are predictable foils to the revelation (to the audience or to the characters or both) of the existence of the monster.

Horror stories, in a significant number of cases, are dramas of proving the existence of the monster and disclosing (most often gradually) the origin, identity, purposes and powers of the monster. Monsters, as well, are obvi-ously a perfect vehicle for engendering this kind of curiosity and for support-ing the drama of proof, because monsters are (physically, though generally not logically) impossible beings. They arouse interest and attention through being putatively inexplicable or highly unusual vis-à-vis our standing cul-tural categories, thereby instilling a desire to learn and to know about them. And since they are also outside of (justifiably) prevailing definitions of what is, they understandably prompt a need for proof (or the fiction of a proof) in the face of skepticism. Monsters are, then, natural subjects for curiosity, and they straightforwardly warrant the ratiocinative energies the plot lavishes upon them.

All narratives might be thought to involve the desire to know—the desire to know at least the outcome of the interaction of the forces made salient in the plot. However, the horror fiction is a special variation on this general narrative motivation, because it has at the center of it something which is given as in principle *unknowable*—something which, *ex hypothesi,* cannot, given the structure of our conceptual scheme, exist and that cannot have the properties it has. This is why, so often, the real drama in a horror story resides in establishing the existence of the monster and in disclosing its horrific properties. Once this is established, the monster, generally, has to be confronted, and the narrative is driven by the question of whether the creature can be destroyed. However, even at this point, the drama of ratioci-nation can continue as further discoveries—accompanied by arguments, explanations, and hypotheses—reveal features of the monster that will facili-tate or impede the destruction of the creature.

To illustrate this briefly, let us consider Colin Wilson's novel *The Mind Parasites*. The story is presented as a compilation of the chronicle of humanity's confrontation with the mind parasites. This chronicle has been drawn from a number of sources. So, from the perspective of the order of the presentation of the fiction, it begins with the presupposition that the mind parasites—called Tsathogguans—exist. But the exposition proceeds by laying end to end successive discoveries of the existence of these creatures, among other things (such as the discovery of the ruins of an ancient city— a red herring, as it turns out). The major character, Gilbert Austin, first discovers his friend's—Karel Weissman's—discovery of the Tsathogguans, which itself comprises a narrative of discovery. Austin then goes through his own process of discovery. In the course of both discoveries the possibility that the discoverer is insane has to be disposed. Austin then proceeds to convince his colleague Reich of the existence of the mind parasites; this is not difficult, but it allows for more ratiocination and the compiling of a little more evidence.

Austin and Reich then impart their discoveries to a select group of other scientists, many of whom are killed by the mind parasites. But enough survive to share their discoveries eventually with the President of the United States. The plot, in other words, proceeds by means of the revelation of the existence of the Tsathogguans to increasingly larger groups of people. But even when Austin has secured sufficient government aid to confront the mind parasites, further discoveries are mandated by the story. Austin says:

> It was maddeningly frustrating. We possessed the great secret; we had warned the world. And yet, in a fundamental sense, we were as ignorant as ever. Who were these creatures? Where did they come from? What was their ultimate aim? Were they really intelligent, or were they as unintelligent as the maggots in a piece of cheese?

Of course, the reader wants to know the answers to these questions as well, and we stay on board to get them till the end of the plot. Moreover, it is not until then that we learn of the properties of the Tsathogguans (and their relations to the Moon) that make possible their final destruction.

The Mind Parasites contains a great deal more "philosophizing" than many horror fictions, employing a somewhat mystical brand of phenomenology as a weapon against the Tsathogguans in a way that ought to provoke Husserl's return from the dead. But by virtue of being what might be called a narrative of continuous revelation or disclosure, it is representative of a large body of horror fictions.

What is revealed and disclosed, of course, are monsters and their properties. These are appropriate objects of discovery and revelation, just because they are unknown—not only in the sense that the murderer in a detective

ιknown, but also because they are outside the bounds of knowl-
outside our standing conceptual schemes. This, as well, accounts
their revelation and the disclosure of their properties is so often
ιp in processes of proof, hypothesis, argument, explanation (includ-
ι-fi flights of fancy and magical lore about mythological realms, po-
tions, and incantations), and confirmation. That is, because horror fictions
are predicated on the revelation of unknown and unknowable— unbelievable
and incredible—impossible beings, they often take the form of narratives of
discovery and proof. For things unknown in the way of monsters obviously
are natural subjects for proof.

Applied to the paradox of horror, these observations suggest that the
pleasure derived from the horror fiction and the source of our interest in
it resides, first and foremost, in the processes of discovery, proof, and
confirmation that horror fictions often employ. The disclosure of the existence of the horrific being and of its properties is the central source of pleasure
in the genre; once that process of revelation is consummated, we remain
inquisitive about whether such a creature can be successfully confronted,
and that narrative question sees us through to the end of the story. Here,
the pleasure involved is, broadly speaking, cognitive. Hobbes, interestingly,
thought of curiosity as an appetite of the mind; with the horror fiction, that
appetite is whetted by the prospect of knowing the putatively unknowable,
and then satisfied through a continuous process of revelation, enhanced
by imitations of (admittedly simplistic) proofs, hypotheses, counterfeits of
causal reasoning, and explanations whose details and movement intrigue the
mind in ways analogous to genuine ones.[46]

Moreover, it should be clear that these particular cognitive pleasures,
insofar as they are set in motion by the relevant kind of unknowable beings,
are especially well served by horrific monsters. Thus, there is a special
functional relationship between the beings that mark off the horror genre
and the pleasure and interest that many horror fictions sustain. That interest
and that pleasure derive from the disclosure of unknown and impossible
beings, just the sorts of things that seem to call for proof, discovery, and
confirmation. Therefore, the disgust that such beings evince might be seen
as part of the price to be paid for the pleasure of their disclosure. That is,
the narrative expectations that the horror genre puts in place is that the being
whose existence is in question be something that defies standing cultural
categories; thus, disgust, so to say, is itself more or less mandated by the
kind of curiosity that the horror narrative puts in place. The horror narrative
could not deliver a successful, affirmative answer to its presiding question
unless the disclosure of the monster indeed elicited disgust, or was of the
sort that was a highly probable object of disgust.

That is, there is a strong relation of consilience between the objects of art-
horror, on the one hand, and the revelatory plotting on the other. The kind

of plots and the subjects of horrific revelation are not merely compatible, but fit together or agree in a way that is highly appropriate. That the audience is naturally inquisitive about that which is unknown meshes with plotting that is concerned to render the unknown known by processes of discovery, explanation, proof, hypothesis, confirmation, and so on.

Of course, what it means to say that the horrific being is "unknown" here is that it is not accommodated by standing conceptual schemes. Moreover, if Mary Douglas's account of impurity is correct, things that violate our conceptual scheme, by (for example) being interstitial, are things that we are prone to find disturbing. Thus, that horrific beings are predictably objects of loathing and revulsion is a function of the ways they violate our classificatory scheme.

If what is of primary importance about horrific creatures is that their very impossibility vis à vis our conceptual categories is what makes them function so compellingly in dramas of discovery and confirmation, then their disclosure, insofar as they are categorical violations, will be attached to some sense of disturbance, distress, and disgust. Consequently, the role of the horrific creature in such narratives—where their disclosure captures our interest and delivers pleasure—will simultaneously mandate some probable revulsion. That is, in order to reward our interest by the disclosure of the putatively impossible beings of the plot, said beings ought to be disturbing, distressing, and repulsive in the way that theorists like Douglas predict phenomena that ill fit cultural classifications will be.

So, as a first approximation of resolving the paradox of horror, we may conjecture that we are attracted to the majority of horror fictions because of the way that the plots of discovery and the dramas of proof pique our curiosity, and abet our interest, ideally satisfying them in a way that is pleasurable.[47] But if narrative curiosity about impossible beings is to be satisfied through disclosure, that process must require some element of probable disgust since such impossible beings are, *ex hypothesi,* disturbing, distressful, and repulsive.

One way of making the point is to say that the monsters in such tales of disclosure have to be disturbing, distressful, and repulsive, if the process of their discovery is to be rewarding in a pleasurable way. Another way to get at this is to say that the primary pleasure that narratives of disclosure afford—i.e., the interest we take in them, and the source of their attraction—resides in the processes of discovery, the play of proof, and the dramas of ratiocination that comprise them. It is not that we crave disgust, but that disgust is a predictable concomitant of disclosing the unknown, whose disclosure is a desire the narrative instills in the audience and then goes on to gladden. Nor will that desire be satisfied unless the monster defies our conception of nature which demands that it probably engender some measure of repulsion.

In this interpretation of horror narratives, the majority of which would appear to exploit the cognitive attractions of the drama of disclosure, experiencing the emotion of art-horror is not our absolutely primary aim in consuming horror fictions, even though it is a determining feature for identifying membership in the genre. Rather, art-horror is the price we are willing to pay for the revelation of that which is impossible and unknown, of that which violates our conceptual schema. The impossible being does disgust; but that disgust is part of an overall narrative address which is not only pleasurable, but whose potential pleasure depends on the confirmation of the existence of the monster as a being that violates, defies, or problematizes standing cultural classifications. Thus, we are attracted to, and many of us seek out, horror fictions of this sort despite the fact that they provoke disgust, because that disgust is required for the pleasure involved in engaging our curiosity in the unknown and drawing it into the processes of revelation, ratiocination, etc.

One objection to this line of conjecture is to point out that many of the kinds of plot structures found in horror fiction can be found in other genres. The play of discovery and confirmation, supported by ratiocination, can be found in detective thrillers. And the plots of the disaster movies of the first half of the seventies often also look like horror plots; but instead of ghouls and vampires calling for discovery and confirmation, potential earthquakes, avalanches, floods, and simmering electrical systems are the culprits.

Of course, with detective stories and disaster films, the evil that is disclosed is not impossible nor, in principle, unknown. This not only means that these narratives do not characteristically cause disgust, but that there is a qualitative difference in the kind of curiosity they invite and reward. My point here is not that one kind of curiosity is higher or lower than another kind; but only that there can be different kinds of curiosity engaged by plot structures that at a certain level of abstract description look formally equivalent, in terms of their major movements. However, it is one thing to be curious about the unknown but natural, and another thing to be curious about the impossible. And it is the latter form of curiosity in which horror fictions typically traffic.

Two other, I think, deeper objections to the preceding hypotheses about the paradox of horror are:

1) So far the conjecture only deals with horror narratives, indeed, only with horror narratives of a certain sort—namely those involving such elements as discovery, confirmation, disclosure, revelation, explanation, hypothesis, ratiocination, etc. *But* there are instances of the horror genre, e.g., paintings, that need not involve narrative; *and* there are, according to my review of characteristic horror plots, horror narratives that don't involve these elements. There may be, for example, pure onset or pure confrontation plots. Moreover, earlier hypotheses about the paradox of horror were rejected because they were not sufficiently comprehensive. But since there are instances of horror that are not narrative and since there may be horror

narratives that do not deploy the elements of disclosure so far identified as the central source of attraction to horror, this conjecture must be rejected as failing its own standards of generality.

2) This conjecture seems to make the experience of being horrified too remote from the experience of the genre. The revulsion we feel at the horrific being is too detached from the source of attraction we find in the genre. This is peculiar, since it is the emotion of art-horror that differentiates the genre. Indeed, it is very often the expectation that a given fiction is defined by this emotion that leads us to select it over candidates from other genres. So one seems justified in supposing that what makes the genre special must have some intimate connection with what draws audiences to seek it out especially. But the account, thus far, falters in this respect.

The first criticism is absolutely on target about the limitations of my hypothesis *in its present state*. My view is not yet sufficiently comprehensive. The horror genre includes examples, like photographs and paintings, that do not involve sustained narration, especially sustained narration of the particular sort I have emphasized; and, there are horror narratives of the pure onset or pure confrontation variety that do not offer audiences the refined and sometimes intricately articulated strategems of disclosure referred to above. However, I do not regard these observations as decisive counterexamples to my approach, but rather as an opportunity to deepen and expand it, indeed in ways that will also enable me to handle the second of the objections in the course of adjusting my position in order to accommodate the first objection.

I do think that the best account that can be given of the paradox of horror for the *majority* of works of horrific art will be very much like the one that I have already offered. However, it is true that it fails to cover non-narrative horror and horror fictions little concerned with the drama of disclosure. To deal with these cases more needs to be said; but the more-that-needs-to-be-said fits with what has already been said in a way that enriches while also extending the theory developed so far.

Central to my approach has been the idea that the objects of horror are fundamentally linked with cognitive interests, most notably with curiosity. The plotting gambits of disclosure/discovery narratives play with, expand, sustain, and develop this initial cognitive appetite in many directions. And as well, this is the way in which horror fictions usually go.

But it would be a mistake to think that this curiosity is *solely* a function of plotting, even if the plotting of certain types of fictions—namely those concerned with disclosure—brings it to its highest pitch. For the objects of art-horror in and of themselves engender curiosity as well. This is why they can support the kind of disclosure plots referred to above. Consequently, even if it is true that horrific curiosity is best expatiated upon within disclosure plots, and that, in its most frequent and compelling cases, it does mobilize such plots, it is also true that it can be abetted and rewarded without the narrative contextualization of disclosure/discovery plotting. Thus, it can be the case that while horror is most often, and perhaps most powerfully and most primarily, developed within narrative contexts of disclosure, it may also obtain in non-narrative and non-disclosure contexts for the same reason, viz., the power of the objects of art-horror to command curiosity.

Recall again that the objects of art-horror are, by definition, impure. This is to be understood in terms of their being anomalous. Obviously, the anomalous nature of these beings is what makes them disturbing, distressing, and disgusting. They are violations of our ways of classifying things and such frustrations of a world-picture are bound to be disturbing.

However, anomalies are also interesting. The very fact that they are anomalies fascinates us. Their deviation from the paradigms of our classificatory scheme captures our attention immediately. It holds us spellbound. It commands and retains our attention. It is an attracting force; it attracts curiosity, i.e., it makes us curious; it invites inquisitiveness about its surprising properties. One wants to gaze upon the unusual, even when it is simultaneously repelling.

Monsters, the anomalous beings who star in this book, are repelling because they violate standing categories. But for the self-same reason, they are also compelling of our attention. They are attractive, in the sense that they elicit interest, and they are the cause of, for many, irresistible attention, again, just because they violate standing categories. They are curiosities. They can rivet attention and thrill for the self-same reason that they disturb, distress, and disgust.

If these confessedly pedestrian remarks are convincing, three interesting conclusions are suggested. First, the attraction of non-narrative- and non-disclosure-type narration in horror is explicable, as is disclosure-type narrative, fundamentally by virtue of curiosity, a feature of horrific beings that follows from their anomalous status as violations of standing cultural schemes. Second, horrific creatures are able to contribute so well to sustaining interest in disclosure plots to an important degree just because in being anomalous, they can be irresistibly interesting. And lastly, with special reference to the paradox of horror, monsters, the objects of art-horror, are themselves sources of ambivalent responses, for as violations of standing cultural categories, they are disturbing and disgusting, but, at the same time, they are also objects of fascination — again, just because they transgress standing categories of thought. That is, the ambivalence that bespeaks the paradox of horror is already to be found in the very objects of art-horror which are disgusting and fascinating, repelling and attractive due to their anomalous nature.[48]

I have identified impurity as an essential feature of art-horror; specifically, the objects of art-horror are, in part, impure beings, monsters recognized as outside the natural order of things as set down by our conceptual schema. This claim may be tested by noting the truly impressive frequency with which the apparition of such monsters in horror fictions correlates explicitly in such texts with mention of revulsion, disgust, repulsion, nausea, abhorrence, and so on. The source of this attitude, moreover, seems traceable to the fact that they, as David Pole puts it, "might in a way be called messy; they defy or mess up existing categories . . . . [W]hat initially disturbs us is most often merely a jumbling [or obfuscation] of kinds."[49] But at the same time that the breakdown of our conceptual categories disturbs, it also fixes our attention. It stimulates our cognitive appetite with the prospect of something previously inconceivable.

The fascination of the horrific being comes in tandem with disturbance. And, in fact, I would submit that for those who are attracted to the genre, the fascination at least compensates for the disturbance. This may be explained to a certain extent by reference to the thought theory of fictional emotion discussed earlier in this book. According to that view, the audience knows that the object of art-horror does not exist before them. The audience is only reacting to the thought that such and such an impure being might exist. This mutes, without eliminating, the disturbing aspect of the object of art-horror, and allows more opportunity for fascination with the monster to take hold.[50]

One supposes that fascination would be too great a luxury to endure, if one, against all odds, were to encounter a horrific monster in "real life." We, like the characters in horror fictions, would feel distressingly helpless; for such creatures, insofar as they defy our conceptual scheme, would leave us at a loss to think of how to deal with them—they would baffle our practical response, paralyzing us in terror (as they generally do to characters in horror fictions for the same reason). However, with art-horror, it is only the thought of the creature that is at issue; we know that it does not exist; we are not taxed literally by practical questions about what is to be done. So the fearsome and loathsome aspects of the monsters do not impinge upon us with the same practical urgency, allowing a space for fascination to take root. So, as a second approximation for resolving the paradox of horror, we can explain how it is that what would, by hypothesis, ordinarily distress, disturb, and disgust us, can also be the source of pleasure, interest, and attraction. With reference to art-horror the answer is that the monster—as a categorical violation—fascinates for the self-same reasons it disgusts and, since we know the monster is but a fictional confection, our curiosity is affordable.

This position enables us to give an answer to the justified objection to our first response to the paradox of horror, which response was so wedded to disclosure type narratives, to wit: non-narrative examples of art-horror, such as those found in the fine arts and narrative horror fictions that do not deploy disclosure devices, attract their audiences insofar as the objects of art-horror promote fascination at the same time they distress; indeed, both responses emanate from the same aspects of the horrific beings. The two responses are, as a matter of (contingent) fact, inseparable in horror. Moreover, this fascination can be savored, because the distress in question is not behaviorally pressing; it is a response to the thought of a monster, not to the actual presence of a disgusting or fearsome thing.

If it is true that fascination is the key to our attraction to the art-horror in general, then it is also the case that the curiosity and fascination that is basic to the genre also receive especial amplification in what I have referred to as narratives of disclosure and discovery. There curiosity, fascination, and our cognitive inquisitiveness are engaged, addressed, and sustained in a highly articulated way through what I have called the drama of proof and such processes of continuous revelation as ratiocination, discovery, hypothesis formation, confirmation, and so on.

At this point, then, I am in a position to summarize my approach to the paradox of horror. It is a twofold theory, whose elements I refer to respectively as the universal theory and the general theory. The universal theory of our attraction to art-horror—which covers non-narrative horror, non-disclosure horror narratives, *and* disclosure narratives—is that what leads people to seek out horror is fascination as characterized in the analyses above. This is the basic, generic calling card of the form.

At the same time, I should also like to advance what I call a general—rather than a universal theory—of the appeal of art-horror. The most commonly recurring—that is to say the most generally found—exercises in the horror genre appear to be horror narratives of the disclosure sort. The attraction of these instances, like all other examples of the genre, are to be explained in terms of curiosity and fascination. However, with these cases, the initial curiosity and fascination found in the genre are developed to an especially high degree through devices that enhance and sustain curiosity. If the genre begins, so to speak, in curiosity, it is enhanced by the consilient structures of disclosure plotting. In such cases, then, what attracts us to this sort of horror—which seems to me the most pervasive[51]—is the whole structure and staging of curiosity in the narrative, in virtue of the experience of the extended play of fascination it affords. That is, as Hume noted of tragedy, the source of our aesthetic pleasure in such examples of horror is primarily the whole structure of the narrative in which, of course, the apparition of the horrific being is an essential, and, as the universal theory shows, a facilitating part.

An earlier objection that I posed to my first approximation of the appeal of art-horror said it made the source of attraction in the genre too remote from the identifying emotion in the genre; it seemed to defer our pleasure into an exclusive concern with plot, which, of course, would also make it seem that similar plots without horrific beings—such as detective thrillers and disaster movies—could act as substitutes for art-horror. But I am now in a position to explain why it is not the case that explaining the appeal of the genre in terms of curiosity and facination must detach that appeal from the central emotion of art-horror.

For I have argued that the objects of art-horror are such that they are both disgusting and fascinating, both disturbing and interesting, because they are classificatory misfits. The relation between fascination and horror here is contingent rather than necessary. That is, the objects of art-horror are essentially categorical violations and, as a matter of fact, categorical violations will quite regularly be the sorts of things that will command attention. Fascination and horror are not related by definition. Not everything that fascinates horrifies and not everything that horrifies fascinates. However, given the specific context of horror fiction, there is a strong correlation between fascination and horror due to the fact that horrific monsters are anomalous beings. That is, both fascination and art-horror converge on the same type of objects just because they are categorical violations. Where there is art-horror, there is likely to be at least the prospect of fascination. Fascination is not remote from art-horror, but is related to it as a probable recurring concomitant. Moreover, it is a recurring concomitant because the genre specializes in impossible, and, in principle, unknowable beings. This is the attraction of the genre. Detection thrillers and disaster films that mobilize analogous plot structures do not afford the same type of fascination, and, therefore, are not exact substitutes for horror fictions. We seek out horror fictions because the specific fascination they afford is bound up with the fact that it is animated by the same type of object that gives rise to art-horror.

A question raised by this account of the paradox of horror—in terms of the contingent relation of art-horror and fascination—is how, precisely, these two states are thought to relate to each other. Following Gary Iseminger, we may consider two possible relations between the distressful emotions provoked by a fiction (e.g., art-horror), on the one hand, and the pleasure derived from the fiction (e.g., fascination) on the other: namely, the integrationist view and the co-existentialist view.[52] According to the integrationist, when one derives pleasure from a melodrama, one is saddened by the events depicted and the very sadness contributes to the pleasure we take in the fiction. On the co-existentialist view, the feeling of pleasure with reference to distressful fictions is a case of one feeling being strong enough to overcome the other, as in the case of "laughter through tears." In the case of a melodrama, the co-existentialist account says that sadness and pleasure exist simultaneously, with the pleasure compensating for the sadness.

It may not be the case that one can settle the issue between the co-existentialist and the integrationist hypotheses in a way that applies to all genres. One genre may be more susceptible to an integrationist account and another to a co-existentialist account. And, indeed, even within one genre, there may be co-existentialist and integrationist accounts depending upon the segment of the audience to which one refers. With respect to art-horror, the preceding explanation in terms of the contingent relation of fascination to fear and disgust leans more in the direction of the co-existentialist view.[53] This account is aimed at the average consumer of horror (in contradistinction to certain *specialized* consumers to be discussed below). In the case of the average consumer of art-horror, the claim is that the art-horror we feel is finally outweighed by the fascination of the monster, as well as, in the majority of cases, by the fascination engendered by the plot in the process of staging the manifestation and disclosure of the monster.

However, a critic of this solution would probably respond by saying that if we agree with the co-existentialist line of thought here, then it would seem to follow that if readers can have their quest for fascination satisfied by descriptions of monsters that are not horrifying, then they are likely to be satisfied by stories—like fairy tales and myths—in which the monsters are not horrifying. Moreover, if this is the case, then the pleasure to be had from horror fictions is not perfectly unique and does not individuate the genre. And, furthermore, if one could have the fascination without being horrified, i.e., by opting for a genre that delivered the same pleasure *sans,* for example, disgust, wouldn't it always make sense to choose the fairy tale?

To a qualified degree, I am willing to go along with part of this. But at the same time, I do not find it totally damning. It seems to me that consumers of horror are most often consumers of other sorts of monster fantasies as well.[54] The audience for the non-horror movie *Jason and the Argonauts* and the horror film *An American Werewolf in London* is probably roughly the same, and the pleasure it takes from the manifestation of monsters in each example is comparable. To a certain extent, such audiences may feel that with respect to pleasure, one movie might be as good as another on any given evening. However, it is also compatible with this that the pleasures to be had from many horror films, especially ones involving certain distinctive plot structures, may still equal or exceed the pleasure to be had from comparable fairy tales and myths, even subtracting the price being horrified exacts. So even though the pleasures to be had from these alternatives are of the same kind, there is no guarantee that an example of one genre provides a greater degree of it than another. Consequently, it would not make sense always to choose fairy tales and odysseys over horror fictions. Moreover, it does not seem to me to be a problem for the theory advanced in this book that certain genres that *obviously* belong to the same family—such as supernatural or monster fantasies—all deliver comparable pleasures; for example, this admission does not indicate that we cannot still differentiate these genres along other dimensions.

In general, I think that we can account for the pleasure that average consumers take in horror fiction by reference to the ways in which the imagery and, in most cases, the plot structures engage fascination. Whatever distress horror causes, as a probable price for our fascination, is outweighed for the average consumer by the pleasure we derive in having our curiosity stimulated and rewarded. However, even if this is the case for most consumers of horror, one could not deny that there may be certain audiences who seek horror fictions simply to be horrified. One suspects that some members of the audience for the *Friday the 13th* series may be like this; they attend simply for the gross-out. Horror films that have fascinating monsters but ones that are not very, very disgusting or revolting might be regarded as inferior by such connoisseurs of gore.

If this is an accurate description of some horror consumers, it would not seem captured by the co-existentialist account. For here the disgust engendered by the fiction appears to be essentially, rather than contingently, connected to the relevant audience's pleasure. So some kind of integrationist account of horror may be called for. One way of developing an integrationist account for these cases would be to extrapolate, following Marcia Eaton, from Susan Feagin's account of what she calls our *metaresponse* to tragedy.[55] According to Feagin, the pleasurable response to tragedy is really a response to a response. That is, in a move reminiscent of the Aikins, Feagin thinks that the pleasure we take from responding with sympathy to tragic events in a fiction is a pleasurable response to finding ourselves the types of people who are morally and humanly concerned in this way. Analogously, it may be the case that those who savor the revulsion in art-horror—but not for the sake of fascination—are metaresponding to their own revulsion.

What could this response possibly be? Perhaps it involves a kind of satisfaction in the fact that one is capable of withstanding heavy doses of disgust and shock. Here, of course, it pays to recall that audiences for horror fictions are often adolescent males, some of whom may be using the fictions as macho rites of passage. For them, horror fictions may be endurance tests. Undoubtedly, this is not the brightest aspect of the horror genre, nor are horror fictions that are made exclusively to serve this purpose salutary. However, one must admit that the phenomenon exists, and that, in this particular case, an integrationist account, outfitted with the idea of metaresponses, may be necessary.

However, for most horror consumers, and judging by their construction, for most horror fictions, the co-existentialist hypothesis seems most accurate. It maintains that the pleasures derived from art-horror are a function of fascination, which fascination compensates for the negative emotions engendered by the fiction. This thesis can be applied to the manifestation of the monster pure and simple (the universal theory of horrific appeal); or it can be applied to the manifestation of the monster where this is embedded within a narrative context that orchestrates the manifestation of the monster in such a way that the whole process of narrative staging becomes the primary source of pleasure (the general theory of horrific appeal). As indicated earlier, the latter application seems to me to be the one that is most relevant and most closely suited to the largest number of cases, as well as to the most compelling cases, of art-horror that have so far been produced.

One advantage of this theoretical approach over some of the rival theories, like psychoanalysis, is that it can accommodate our interest in horrific beings whose imagery does not seem straightforwardly, or even circuitously, rooted in such things as repression. That is, the religious awe explanation and psychoanalytic explanations of horror confront counterexamples in those cases of horror where the monsters seem to be produced by what might be thought of as virtually formal processes of "categorical-jamming." Wells's cephalopods engender neither cosmic awe nor are they worked up pointedly enough in the text to be linked with some identifiably repressed material. Thus, these attempted explanations are not sufficiently comprehensive, because they cannot assimilate that which we can call formalistically (or formulaically) constructed horrific beings.

My approach, on the other hand, has no such problems with horrific beings generated solely by classificatory obfuscation, since I trace their fascination (as well as their distressfulness) to their category-jamming. Thus, the comprehensiveness of my theory in the face of such counterexamples counts as a strong consideration in favor of my theory.

At this point, it may be helpful to remind the reader that I have been concerned to find a comprehensive account of the appeal of horror—that is, an account of horror that pertains to its attraction across periods of time, across subgenres and across particular works of horror, whether they be masterpieces or not. In this respect, I am, in part, regarding horror as what Fredric Jameson has called a mode. He writes:

> when we speak of a mode, what can we mean but that this particular type of literary discourse is not bound to the conventions of a given age, nor indissolubly linked to a given type of verbal artifact, but rather persists as a temptation and a mode of expression across a whole range of historical periods, seeming to offer itself, if only intermittently, as a formal possibility which can be revived and renewed.[56]

To ask what is compelling about horror as a mode is to ask for the most basic, recurring "temptations" afforded by the genre for what one supposes to be the average audience. My answer is the detailed account of fascination and curiosity found above. This answer seems more comprehensive than psychoanalytic and religious explanations of horror as a mode—more encompassing of the widest number of recurring cases.[57]

However, having said this, I do not necessarily preclude that psychoanalytic and religious explanations may not offer supplemental insight into why particular works of horror, particular periodic cycles, or why specified subgenres may exert their own special attractions over and above the generic attraction of the mode. Whether and to what extent such explanations are convincing depends on the critical and interpretive analysis of individual subgenres, cycles, and works. I have no theoretical reason to announce ahead of time that such critical work may not inform us about the levers of attraction that certain cycles, subgenres, and individual works deploy over and above the generic attractions of the mode. The persuasiveness of such critical work will have to be judged on a case by case basis. I have only been concerned to advance a view of the generic power of the horror mode and I will not here and now express any principled reservation to the possibility of the application of religious criticism, myth criticism, psychoanalytic criticism, cosmic-awe criticism, etc. to isolated cycles, subgenres and works in the horror mode.

It is my impression that the curiosity/fascination resolution that I have offered to the paradox of horror—despite its reliance on somewhat technical notions like categorical violations, and co-existentialism—is pretty obvious. It is certainly not as jazzy as many reductivist psychoanalytic theories. In fact, it may strike many as not being theoretical at all, but as nothing but a long-winded exercise in common sense.

I do think that the approach—especially in the way it works out the interplay of the forces of attraction and repulsion—is elucidating; though I can see why when stated in abbreviated form—horror attracts because anomalies command attention and elicit curiosity—it may sound platitudinous. Three remarks seem appropriate here: first, the very comprehensiveness of the explanation of the phenomena that we are seeking might tend to make the solution appear truistic and trivially broad, even if it is not; second, that the theory seems commonsensical need not count against it—there is no reason to think that common sense cannot contribute insight; and last, as perhaps a corollary to the latter observation, that competing explanations resort to arcane sources is not of necessity a virtue in their favor.

Horror and Ideology

I began my discussion with the question of why the horror genre persists, which question I transformed into one about what possible cause people could have to seek out that which is ostensibly distressing. The problem of the continued existence of the horror genre was reduced to the issue of why we do not simply avoid the horror genre altogether, since, in my account, it promotes genuine fear and disgust. I have attempted to explain this by means of the universal and general theories of horror, in terms of the way in which the horrific beings that define the genre command our interest, fascination, and curiosity, which pleasures outweigh whatever negative feelings such anomalous creatures make probable. These features of the genre—interest, fascination, and curiosity—especially as amplified in the genre's major narrative formations, explain why horror fictions continue to be consumed and produced, often cyclically.

A politically minded critic, however, might balk at this way of dealing with the persistence of the horror genre. He might complain that its bias is too individualistic, whereas a truly effective explanation of the existence of the horror genre should highlight the pertinent socio-political factors that give rise to it. In this case, emphasis would, nowadays, be likely to be placed on the ideological role that horror fictions play. The argument would be that horror exists because it is always in the service of the status quo; that is, horror is invariably an agent of the established order. It continues to be produced because horror is in the interest of the established order. This supposes that the creations of the horror genre are always politically repressive, thereby directly contradicting the (equally incorrect) view, discussed earlier, that horror fictions are always emancipatory (i.e., politically subversive).

One way to attempt to connect the horror genre with the purposes of politically repressive social orders would be thematic. That is, one would attempt to show that there are certain politically repressive themes found comprehensively across the genre which the genre tends to reinforce. For example, it might be argued that the horror genre is essentially xenophobic: monsters, given their inherently hostile attitude toward humanity, represent a predatory Other, and mobilize, in a way that interactively reinforces, negative imagery of those political/social entities which threaten the established social order at the level of nation, class, race, or gender.

Clearly there is some undeniable evidence in favor of at least entertaining this hypothesis: H.P. Lovecraft's racism; fifties science fiction films that depict alien invaders as transparent icons for communism; the syphilitic depiction of aggressive, female sexuality in such Cronenberg films as *They Came From Within* and *Rabid*.

Or, in a related thematic vein, horror fictions might be thought to have the function of scaring people into submissively accepting their social roles. Again, there is some suggestive evidence for this. Feminists have pointed out that, in many recent horror fictions, often the victims of the monster's grisly onslaught are sexually active adolescent women. One interpretation of this is that they are being taught a lesson: "Fool around and this is what you can expect/deserve." Moreover, the female victim has been a staple of the horror genre since the days of the Gothic. The abduction of women—often as a thinly veiled euphemism for rape—might be seen as the articulation of an enduring sexist warning that women should keep in line because they always are and ought to be at the mercy of males in patriarchal society.

Undoubtedly, thematic interpretations of this sort can be made to fit *certain* horror fictions within certain social contexts. That is, there is no reason to think that horror fictions cannot be vehicles for ideologically repressive themes. Fifties horror films probably did significantly interact with the way many Americans came to think of communists. However, two initial problems vex the attempt to explain the persistence of horror by means of the propagation of ideological themes.

First, none of the ideological themes adduced by commentators seems to be sufficiently general. There are sexist, racist, anti-communist, and xenophobic horror fictions, but not every horror fiction falls into one of these categories nor even into the disjunction of these categories. That there are horror fictions that do not fall into some of these specific categories can be indicated by the example that there are horror fictions that will elude charges of sexism insofar as they have neither women characters, nor are the monsters characterized by means of (culturally derived) feminine imagery nor is their lack of women characters worked into any detectable derogation of women. And, of course, most horror fiction has nothing to do with anti-communism, while many British ghost stories concern British ghosts, thereby problematizing accusations of racism and xenophobia. Indeed, many horror fictions seem too indeterminate from a political point of view to be correlated with any specific ideological theme.[58]

One cannot reject the possibility that someone someday will discover an ideological theme that runs through all of horror fiction. But until it is articulated, it is fair to presume that the thematic ideological accounts offered so far are not comprehensive enough to cover the genre as a whole (however useful they may be for analyzing individual fictions, subgenres, and cycles).[59]

A second reason to doubt the claim that all horror fictions are, from a thematic point of view, repressive is simply that there seem to be examples of thematically progressive horror fictions. One thing that Mary Shelley's *Frankenstein* is about is illustrating the notion that a person is not innately evil but rather is driven to what we now call anti-social behavior as a result of the way he or she is treated by society. The creature keeps making this point throughout the novel, and nothing in the writing indicates that he hasn't got a point. This was, and, I take it, still is, an enlightened view politically.

There are also a large number of horror novels that celebrate the revolt against (often aristocratic) tyranny, such as Edgar Rice Burroughs's Caspak and Pellucidar series. A great many horror fictions oppose slavery and racial oppression; domination of one group of beings in the horror genre by a putatively superior species almost always heralds a revolt in which the master-species (master-race) receive their just deserts.

George Romero's *Night of the Living Dead* cycle is explicitly anti-racist as well as critical of the consumerism and viciousness of American society,[60] while certain Hammer films, like *The Revenge of Frankenstein,* stigmatize classism by showing that the villain is really the discernibly upper-class Baron himself, who harvests the organs and limbs he needs for his experiment from the underclass (who, predictably, revolt).

There were anti-war horror fictions during the Vietnam debacle, made, for example, by filmmakers such as Bob Clark; and many horror fictions oppose the damage done to our ecology by business and government, while others oppose the "medicalization" of everyday life; and so on. Examples can be multiplied endlessly; but the point is general. Just as Karl Marx called capitalists vampires and werewolves, utilizing horror iconography for progressive purposes, so the creators of horror fiction can apply the imagery of fear and disgust against the forces of political or social repression.

I don't suppose that everyone will agree with all of these counterexamples. However, I think that the general point is unavoidable: horrific imagery can be, and has been, used in the service of politically progressive themes within given social contexts. If one rejects my specific examples, there are enough problem cases so that I can comfortably leave it to the reader to choose her own.

So, the notion that the horror genre persists because it provides the useful service of projecting ideologically repressive themes can be questioned in the first instance by noting that horror fictions do not always, and, therefore, do not reliably, perform this function because 1) many may not project any ideological theme, repressive or otherwise, and 2) because they may often project significantly progressive themes.

If the response to this is that horror fictions always inevitably project repressive themes, then we should want an explanation of this inevitability. If the basis for the inevitability is that all symbolic activity in modern capitalist society inevitably projects repressive themes, we may a) wonder whether this is so, but, in any case, b) point out that this renders the idea that political repression supplies an explanation of the persistence of horror inoperable, since repression will attach to all symbolic activity in this account and much symbolic activity does not continue to persist.

Thus far we have contested the notion that horror persists because it always disseminates politically repressive themes. The rejection of this hypothesis was a matter of pointing to places where it seems daunting to specify the ideologically tainted theme of various horror fictions and to other places where the politically significant theme in the horror fiction appears progressive. At this point, the proponent of the repression view of the persistence of horror might wish to shift gears, in order to argue that the ideological work that horror fiction does for the status quo is not at the level of overt themes—thought of as propagandistic messages—but at the level of the basic form of the genre. That is, there is something about the deep structure of the horror fiction that places it in the service of the established order so that said order, in consequence, guarantees its persistence (presumably by continuing to produce horror entertainments rather than emancipatory entertainments).

Stephen King has colorfully articulated the correlation between the structure of horror fiction and the established order on several occasions:

> . . . horror fiction is really as Republican as a banker in a three-piece suit. The story is always the same in terms of its development. There's an incursion into taboo lands, there's a place where you shouldn't go, but you do, the same way that your mother would tell you that the freak tent is a place you shouldn't go, but you do. And the same thing happens inside: you look at the guy with three eyes, or you look at the fat lady or you look at the skeleton man or Mr. Electrical or whoever it happens to be. And when you come out, well, you say, "Hey, I'm not so bad. I'm all right. A lot better than I thought." It has that effect of reconfirming values, of reconfirming self-image and our good feelings about ourselves.[61]

And:

> Monstrosity fascinates us because it appeals to the conservative Republican in a three-piece suit who resides within all of us. We love and need the concept of monstrosity because it is a reaffirmation of the order we all crave as human beings . . . and let me further suggest that it is not the physical or mental aberration in itself which horrifies us, but rather the lack of order which these situations seem to imply.[62]

And

> . . . the creator of horror fiction is above all else an agent of the norm.[63]

What King may have in mind here—which has been developed in a less colloquial idiom by contemporary theorists[64]—is that the horror narrative appears to proceed by introducing something abnormal—a monster—into the normal world for the express purpose of expunging it. That is, the horror story is always a contest between the normal and the abnormal such that the normal is reinstated and, therefore, affirmed. The horror story can be conceptualized as a symbolic defense of a culture's standards of normality; the genre employs the abnormal, only for the purpose of showing it vanquished by the forces of the normal. The abnormal is allowed center stage solely as a foil to the cultural order, which will ultimately be vindicated by the end of the fiction.

In my own account of horror, I have urged that monsters be understood as violations of standing cultural categories. In this light, the confrontation and defeat of the monster in horror fictions might be systematically read as a restoration and defense of the established world view found in existing cultural schemas. Moreover, the world view at stake here is not only epistemic, but is linked or invested with value. What is outside a culture's cognitive map is not simply inconceivable but unnatural in a value-laden as well as an ontological sense.

That is, the anomalous beings that I have been discussing are not only ontologically transgressive. Most often they also do morally transgressive things. There is a fit, within the genre, between their being the unknown and their performance of the forbidden: sucking blood; kidnapping babies for Black Masses; abducting maidens; destroying skyscrapers; and so on. Indeed, the fit would seem to be often even more intimate than mere constant conjunction, because, without special scientific or philosophical training, people are wont to imbue the categorical structures of their society with evaluative urgency. What lies outside their classificatory system is taboo, abnormal, or, more generically, bad. Thus, when the monstrous disruption of the everyday is confronted and destroyed in a horror fiction, the rectitude of a morally charged, culturally rooted, classificatory order may be thought to be simultaneously reaffirmed.

In this view, the deep structure of the horror fiction is a three-part movement: 1) from normality (a state of affairs in which our ontologico-value schema rests intact); 2) to its disruption (a monster appears, shaking the very foundations of the culture's cognitive map—which affront itself may be perceived as immoral/abnormal—and, predictably, the monster also does forbidden things like eating people);[65] 3) to the final confrontation and defeat of the abnormal, disruptive being (thereby restoring the culture's scheme of things by eliminating the anomaly and punishing its violations of the moral order). Within this associative constellation, order is restored not only in the sense that there's no more carnage; but, putatively, the established cultural order that reigned prior to the perturbations introduced in the fiction is functioning once again.

In order to get a feeling for this type of account it may be helpful to draw a brief analogy between it and once popular anthropological accounts of "rituals of rebellion," i.e., rituals, like the ancient saturnalia or the present day Carnival, that provide a circumscribed "space," so to speak, in which customary decorum, morality, and taboos may be relaxed; and conceptual schematizations—of, for example, the relations between species—may be turned upside down, backwards, and inside out. Such rituals, of course, typically end with the reinstatement of social order; and they are sometimes interpreted as providing a social safety valve for release of tension engendered in the cultural organization of experience. Though such rituals obviously include some criticism of the social order, they contain that protest in a way that preserves and strengthens it.[66]

Applied to the horror genre, the analogous interpretation might run as follows: with the onset of the monster in a horror fiction, a cultural space is opened in which the values and the concepts of the culture can be inverted, reversed, and turned inside out. This is presumably cathartic for the audience; it allows the opportunity for thoughts and desires outside the culture's notions of acceptability to take shape. But the condition that permits this transgression of the norm is that, when all is said and done, and the narrative achieves closure, the norm has been reconstituted—the ontologically offensive monster has been removed and its ghastly deeds punished. So the norm emerges stronger than before; it has been, so to say, tested; its superiority to the abnormal is vindicated; and supposedly wayward, maybe brooding, thoughts and desires—from the perspective of the dominant cultural viewpoint—have been, figuratively speaking, lanced.

Modern horror fictions, in this light, might be thought of as rituals of inversion for mass society. And the function of such rituals—as literally acted-out in their plot structure—is to celebrate the dominant cultural viewpoint and its conception of the norm. The norms that are relevant here are taken to be political, and their valorization ideologically charged. Thus, the constant rehearsal of the underlying scenario of horror fictions inevitably bolsters the status quo.

If this account is successful, it might provide us with the grounds for thinking that the horror genre inevitably serves ideology—which, in turn, might appear to yield an explanation of why horror is perennially with us. However, it does not seem to me that the theory is persuasive. First, it does not offer a comprehensive view of the horror genre; it really applies to narrative horror which though, as I have stressed, is the most central manifestation of the genre, is nevertheless not the whole of it. Horror in the fine arts may be non-narrative and, therefore, not involved in instantiating the normal/abnormal/normal scenario. This view of horror has nothing to say about those cases.[67]

So it remains undemonstrated that non-narrative horror—and, consequently, that horror as a whole—subserves ideology due to the sort of underlying structural feature to which the theory draws attention.

Second, it is a standard variation of the horror genre that sometimes the horrific being is not expelled or eliminated at the end of the story. Sometimes the house does take possession of its victim (Marasco's novel *Burnt Offerings*); sometimes Satan is birthed (Levin's novel *Rosemary's Baby*); sometimes the invaders from outer space do take over (Philip Kaufman's film remake of *Invasion of the Body Snatchers*) or are, at least, undefeated (Tobe Hooper's *Lifeforce*). Moreover, the audience may be left at the end of a horror fiction wondering whether the monstrous disruption has been scourged from the earth (John Carpenter's remake of *The Thing;* Wes Craven's first film in the *Nightmare On Elm Street* series). And the severed arm is still at large at the end of Gary Brender's short story "Julian's Hand," as are the undead in King's *Pet Sematary* and the possessed medievalist in Daniel Rhodes *Next, After Lucifer.*

Nor is this only the case in what might be thought of as contemporary horror fiction. The town of the cat people still stands at the conclusion of Blackwood's "Ancient Sorceries"; Mr. Meldrum has been transformed into Thoth at the end of John Metcalfe's "Mr. Meldrum's Mania"; the beckoning fair one, in Oliver Onions's story of the same name, does take possession of Oleron; it is unclear whether the hand in Harvey's "The Beast with Five Fingers" has been destroyed; Lovecraft's beings from ancient, alien races generally survive discovery; etc., etc.

Thus, if we are to read the normal/abnormal/normal plot structure as an allegory of the reinstatement of the status quo, what are we to say of the standard deviation from this triad that moves from the normal to the abnormal and leaves it at that? Are these rather familiar plot gambits anti-establishment? Do they contest the status quo? One doubts this conclusion, but how will the theory under examination avoid it? Furthermore, how will catharsis (a perhaps dubious notion to begin with) work in these cases? For if the reinstatement of the normal is a key element for closing the safety valve, what turns the screw back when the abnormal is not expelled?[68]

In response to these counter-instances, one might attempt to rebuild the theory by claiming that it is only meant to characterize those cases of horror where the normal/abnormal/normal model of narration is in operation. That would not be a comprehensive theory of horror; but it would cover a lot of ground nevertheless. However, I doubt that even this scaled-down theory of the persistence of horror will succeed.

For this theory piggybacks or associates a great many concepts that I think it would be better to keep separate. For example, the theory more or less equates the normal—in the sense of classificatory and moral categories—with the status quo of a given political order. When these norms are contested, the political order is contested; when they are reaffirmed, the political order is reaffirmed.

But should these norms be so readily segued with elements of a political order? Remember the kinds of norms that are being violated: on the conceptual side, they are distinctions like those drawn between animal and vegetable and between humans and flies; on the moral side, they are prohibitions against eating human flesh, wanton killing, abduction, and so forth. If there is a dominant political order that regards these norms as fixed, it is equally true that nondominant, oppositional, emancipatory movements within society will also abide by these norms.

Horrific beings, that is, do not contravene cultural norms at any level that marks a political difference between the dominant status quo and those it putatively represses. Neither eating human flesh nor denying the difference between insects and humans is on the political agenda of any liberation movement that I know of. Challenging cultural norms, then, at this level of abstraction, does not touch the political foundations of a social order, and, consequently, reasserting these norms[69] would have no significance with respect to reconfirming the political status quo.

Another way to get at this point is to notice that there may be a slide in the account between two notions of the "normal." On the one hand, "normal" may be seen to refer to the norms of our classificatory and moral schemes. On the other hand, "normal" may refer to the ethos and behavior of those who unquestioningly conform to some vision of (culturally, morally, politically) complacent middle-class life—the organization man, the moral majority, the silent majority, etc. The ideological account of horror under examination seems to move from the observation that horrific beings are abnormal in the first sense of the term, to the view that their defeat reasserts normality in the second sense of the term, which, of course, is a sense that would be relevant to certain aspects of contemporary cultural politics. But this surely rests on simply equivocating over certain meanings of *normality*.

Yes, trolls are likely to have bad table manners and not vote Republican; if they cared about international politics, they might be communist. But this is not the level of *normality* that is typically being breached in horror fictions; and it is not the kind of normality that is at stake in confrontations with monsters, save in those texts where such associations are evidently mobilized in the presentation.

Another concept which is equivocated in the structural account of the ideological address of the horror genre is *order*. Conceptual and moral order—and the cultural schemes thereof—are treated as equivalent to repressive social orders. But again, distinctions between insects and humans and prohibitions against ravaging villages are not necessarily tied to repressive social forces. They are more generally embraced cultural principles, and they are most likely to be shared by contesting socio-political groups in any given community. Thus, reaffirming them does not correlate with reaffirming the dominance of any social group, except within fictions where the threat of disorder is explicitly tied to the perseverance of a dominant social group.

But, at the same time, the use of the imagery of restored order can also be appropriated within the context of a given horror fiction to valorize oppositional sentiments. That is, since the kind of order that is restored in horror fictions (where it is restored) is recognized as desirable by every socio-political alignment in the culture, if an oppositional horror fiction were to use it to stigmatize the dominant social class as abnormal, the reassertion of the norm at the end of the fiction would count as an assertion of the normative superiority of the oppositional group. That is, the sequenced pattern—normal/abnormal/normal—can be homologously expanded upon starting with either the status quo or its antithesis in its opening position.

However, if we admit that the sense of order which attends the destruction of the monster in certain horror fictions can be used associatively, in the contexts of specific fictions, to either uphold or contest (indeed it may be deployed to do neither) the existing status quo, then we have given up the structural account that says horror fiction always serves the interests of the dominant social class.

The sense of order built into such narratives is not inherently repressive or conservative; in specific instances, it may be put in service against the status quo. Or, it may not. Moreover, determining the way that the sense of order is deployed in a given fiction would have to be done on a case by case basis. Thus, the structural account of the generically reactionary nature of horror, when put under pressure, turns into a matter not of structure per se, but of the way specific works may employ certain structural possibilities—like the sense of order—to project certain themes.

However, as I have argued, these thematic commitments might go either way with respect to the status quo. Indeed, I would want to say that a horrific fiction could employ the sense of order under discussion and have no detectable political or ideological commitments regarding the status quo. My point here, of course, is theoretical. I do not deny that a given work of horror fiction could be used rhetorically to support a dominant, repressive social order in given circumstances. And with such cases, I do not doubt that an ideologically minded critic could show how a given work or a group of works promote an ideologically pernicious viewpoint. What I do deny is that horror fiction either always or necessarily operates in this way. I also question whether its service to the dominant ideology is utterly pervasive, not because I think the majority of horror fictions are emancipatory but because my hunch is that many of them may be politically vague or trivial.[70] But, in any case, the question of which and how many or what proportion of horror fictions are reactionary cannot be settled a priori—as proponents of the structural hypothesis suggest—but requires empirical research.

That research may, of course, show that a great many horror fictions are reactionary; I can certainly think of a lot of examples that are. However, that will not show that the ideological account of the persistence of the horror genre is superior to the account we have offered. The reason for this is that even if it were true that horror fictions serve the dominant ideology, that would not explain why they persist. For in order to serve the dominant ideology, there would have to be something about such fictions that attracted audiences to them. At best, the ideology thesis would explain why a dominant social order would permit the existence of horror fictions, and, *possibly,* in part, why it (in the form of capitalist enterprises) would produce them. It would not explain why audiences are receptive to them; it would not explain why people go to them, indeed, why many seek them out.

That is, people do not read horror fictions nor do they attend horror spectacles at gunpoint. Nor (as I have learnt the hard way) does one receive tax deductions or government support for consuming horror. The genre has a certain appeal, and that appeal requires a theory even from those who want to hypothesize that it serves the status quo. For in order to serve the status quo, it would have to be capable of attracting audiences in the first place. And the universal and general theories of horrific attraction, developed previously, give us an account of that generic appeal.

The ideological theory of the persistence of horror—either stated in terms of themes or structure—in fact is not really even a competitor to the theory I have propounded, since such theories would require an account at the level of analysis of my theory in order to explain why even if all horror fictions are complicit with the status quo, they are able to command attention. There must be something over and above their ideological allegiance that makes such fictions attractive, since ideological allegiance to the status quo is no guarantee that a form of art or entertainment will have any audience appeal, and, therefore, no guarantee that the form will persist.

So, even if it were true that the status quo had an interest in horror, the question of why horror can be a viable vehicle for implementing that interest remains. That is, if horror fictions always do perform some service for the status quo, we still must learn why they are attractive to their audiences, since without an answer to that question we wouldn't understand how they could be exploited for ideological purposes.

Again, I have no doubts that a given work of horror could serve the interests of the status quo, nor that a critic might be able to show how a given work or group of works does this. What I do not think can be shown is that horrific fiction is necessarily complicit ideologically; I even doubt that it could be shown that all existing works of horror are irredeemably repressive politically. And, in any case, showing that horror is ideologically useful to the forces of political and/or cultural repression would not really account for the persistence of the appeal of the genre. For the genre would have to have some appeal of its own already in order to be enlisted in the service of the status quo. And it is an account of that antecedent appeal which I have attempted to formulate.

Earlier I rejected another politicized view of the attracting power of horror fiction, viz., that it is always emancipatory. This view, of course, is the contrary of the view that horror is always reactionary, though each, interestingly, may attempt to advance their claims on the basis of what might be thought of as an allegorical reading of certain deep structures of the genre. I have tried to show in detail what is wrong with each of these views respectively. Let their dual failure serve as an admonition against such "a prioristic" allegorizing of fictional structures.

Horror Today

I have been preoccupied with providing a comprehensive theory of why the horror genre persists across the years, i.e., across decades and generations. I have posed this problem as the question of why people would find entertaining and seek out that which, at a cursory glance, we might expect them to regard as distressful and as something to be avoided. A comprehensive solution has been proposed, one which attempts to make use of findings from earlier chapters about the nature of horror and about the characteristic plots in the genre.

The argument has been that if horror is, in large measure, identified with the manifestation of categorically impossible beings, works of horror, all things being equal, will command our attention, curiosity, and fascination, and that that curiosity, as well, can be further stimulated and orchestrated by the kind of narrative structures that appear so frequently in the genre. Moreover, that fascination with the impossible being outweighs the distress it engenders can be rendered intelligible by what I call the thought theory of our emotional response to fiction, which maintains that audiences know horrific beings are not in their presence, and, indeed, that they do not exist, and, therefore, their description or depiction in horror fictions may be a cause for interest rather than either flight or any other prophylactic enterprise.

This theory affords an account of the basic appeal of the horror genre—an account of the fundamental feature of the genre that is potentially attractive across the wide variety of its members. That is, I have tried to isolate the most common denominator of average audience appreciation with respect to horror. This does not preclude the possibility that individual works of horror, subgenres, and cycles may not have resources of attraction above and beyond the fundamental or generic appeal of the genre in general. A given work of horror can possess literary merit, may make acute social observations, be darkly humorous, tightly plotted, and so on. And these attributes, *ceteris paribus,* will enhance their appeal over and above the attractions of the genre as such. And, for some audiences, concerned with endurance tests as rites of passage, horror may also perform a very special service.

Furthermore, many of the views that I rejected as comprehensive accounts of the most common denominator of the genre's address may, in fact, track the power of particular works of horror, particular subgenres and cycles. That is, some works of horror, due to the interplay between their internal structure and their context of production and reception, may, in addition to stimulating the kind of fascination I have examined, also attract audiences because they promote "cosmic awe," because they lift psychosexual repressions, because they transgress oppressive cultural orders, or because they confirm the status quo for conservatively minded audiences, and so forth. That these sources of attraction do not seem available comprehensively across the genre does not show that they may not be relevant to the explanation of the appeal of individual works of horror, specific subgenres, or particular cycles. Whether and to what extent these notions contribute to our knowledge of segments of the horror genre are matters for further research, probably best undertaken by those (unlike me) who already have some faith in these hypotheses.

Among the many things that a comprehensive theory of horror leaves unexplained is why horror seems to have especial popularity in one period of time and not another. A comprehensive theory, as I have used that concept, tells us what sources of appeal the genre has across the disparate times and places where the genre has some appreciators. But in telling us about the generic power of horror, it does not say why exactly horror sometimes commands large followings but, at other times its audience is loyal but small. That is, my theory does not explain why at certain historical junctures, like our own, horror suddenly becomes a reigning popular genre, though it does seem clear that horror tends to thrive cyclically.

I will not attempt here to construct a theory of horror cycles. However, since this very book is probably a response to finding ourselves somewhere amidst such a cycle, it may seem appropriate, in the present context, to supplement this account of the generic appeal of horror with some speculation about the causes of the current popularity and appeal of horror.

I began this book by noting that for over a decade and a half, horror has been a reigning popular genre. At one point in 1987, it was rumored in the publishing world that one out of every four books being printed had Stephen King's name on the title page.[71] And this book probably could not have found a publisher except for the fact that horror commands an unprecedented following nowadays. So in concluding this treatise on horror, some thoughts on the appeal of horror today—that is, on the appeal of the present cycle— may be in order. This, of course, is a highly speculative venture—even more speculative than what has preceded it—as is any attempt at writing historical explanations of one's own times and circumstances. So read these conjectures of an armchair sociologist with a bucket of salt (not blood) ready to hand.

It is frequently remarked that horror cycles emerge in times of social stress, and that the genre is a means through which the anxieties of an era can be expressed. That the horror genre should be serviceable in this regard comes as no surprise, since its specialty is fear and anxiety. What presumably happens in certain historical circumstances is that the horror genre is capable of incorporating or assimilating general social anxieties into its iconography of fear and distress.

Film history provides several well-known examples of this. The horror films in the style of what is called German Expressionism were produced in the crisis milieu of the Weimar Republic; the Universal cycle of horror classics, in the United States, occurred during the Great Depression; the science fiction/horror cycle of the early fifties, in America, corresponds to the early phase of the Cold War. Moreover, these different cycles tended to use their horrific imagery to express certain anxieties that correlate with the uneasy temper of their times.

In the early thirties movie cycle, one finds a certain recurring sympathy for the monster. Frankenstein's creation, King Kong, the Werewolf of London, and even Dracula, who at one point yearns, in a moment of disconsolateness, to be truly dead, engender a kind of concern and pathos, even though this alternates with feelings of horror toward them. This concern seems to be a response to a recognition that these beings are alienated; often they are victims of circumstances beyond their control. Frankenstein's creature and King Kong, especially, appear, at moments, to be persecuted outsiders.[72] Moreover, the fear of being outside civil society through no fault of one's own is understandably poignant in times such as the Great Depression, when so many were threatened by the prospect of unemployment. This is not to say that these films either subverted or confirmed the existing social order, but only that they expressed recognizable anxieties—which were by no means repressed—and provided images for thinking about (or, at least, dwelling on) them.

Sympathy for the monster, on the other hand, is not a possibility exploited in fifties' monster films. Giant insects, carnivorous vegetables, and bug-eyed aliens do not engender pathos; it is hard to imagine extending a succoring hand to a tarantula the size of a tractor. These monsters are outsiders, and, without question, that's where they belong. The only way they can get inside, so to speak, is by forcible invasion. And, of course, invasion is the leading preoccupation of film of the fifties' sci-fi cycle. Furthermore, it is pretty clear that these invaders are really stand-ins for the INTERNATIONAL COMMUNIST MENACE.[73]

At the end of one of the inaugural films in this cycle, *The Thing,* the audience is sent out of the theater with the warning to be vigilant and to look to the skies; ostensibly to be ready for flying saucers, but one suspects, in the era of air raid drills, for Soviet bombers as well. Also, the monstrous villains of these films were often insects or vegetables, bereft of ordinary human emotions (just like those dirty reds), and they were out to conquer the world (ditto).

In this cycle, pure intelligence (marxist intellectualism and scientificity) was often pitted against feeling in the contest of inhumanity versus humanity; and the invaders often tended to be collectivist and anti-individualist. Infiltration by extraterrestrial fifth columnists, posing as Mom and Dad, was one of their most loathsome tricks. Certainly, in contrast to the more politically amorphous horror films of the thirties, the vocabulary of ideologically motivated suspicion, whipped up by the forces of anti-communism, helped shape the language of fear employed in these films, at the same time that the narrative structures of the horror genre provided more than ample pretexts for accommodating paranoia.

The anxiety model has also been applied to literature. Writing of the outpouring of horror fiction between 1872 and 1919, Jack Sullivan claims:

> . . . the dark, apocalyptic quality of early modern horror fiction is absolutely contiguous with a spirit of restlessness and malaise that some historians, citing the works of Freud, Huysmans, Schoenberg, and others, view as an emotional key to the age and as a premonition of World War I.
>
> Stephen Spender, T.S. Eliot, and many others have written eloquently about the atmosphere of trauma that darkened this period and manifested itself in increasingly bizarre and subjective modes of expression. This was a transitional age characterized by convulsive social changes, ugly repercussions from an unpopular war, economic instability, a sneering cynicism about government and the established order, and a fascination with counter-cultures and occult societies. Since this is the cataclysmic climate in which the tale of terror seems to flourish, it is perhaps no accident that the Vietnam and Watergate periods also witnessed a spectacular revival of the genre.[74]

Similarly, in theorizing the current thriving literary subgenre of what she calls "family horror," Ann Douglas contends:

> The genre of "family horror" records the strange forms and transformations into which the contemporary middle-class family falls: its subject is the splitting of the atom of the nuclear family. This fictional family is twice nuclear. It consists of the now-classic small nucleus of parents and one or two children. It represents the first American families parented by young adults who were themselves born just before and after the official inauguration of the nuclear age at Hiroshima on August 6, 1945, and who are consciously bringing children into an atomic world. In these thrillers, parental characters, like many of the authors who create them, are baby-boomers, creatures of the sixties, dramatized and imagined as they begin families in the seventies and eighties: in other words they are protagonists of pressing, intricate and culturally telling contradictions.[75]

Thus Douglas correlates the appearance of demonic babies with the rocky coming of age of the demographically staggering and institutionally disruptive, post-war generation as it attempted to negotiate the pressures of an increasingly precarious market society without the resources of an extended family.

As these examples indicate, it is at least plausible to hypothesize that horror cycles are likely to occur in periods of pronounced social stress in which horror fictions serve to dramatize or to express the prevailing malaise. Here one need not go on to say that they vent or release these anxieties by means of some such contested process as catharsis; it is enough to say that they are prone in such periods to command special interest, insofar as they project representations that match such anxieties and, therefore, address, if only by means of galvanizing imagery, pressing concerns. So, if at present we find ourselves in a horror cycle, by hypothesis, we could attempt to explain its provenance and tenacity by isolating the sources of social stress and the anxieties with which the cycle correlates.[76]

Ann Douglas suggests that some of the anxieties or feelings that are articulated in the subgenre of family horror, a subgenre which, in terms of literature kicked off the cycle with entries such as Tryon's *The Other*, Levin's *Rosemary's Baby*, and, of greatest significance, Blatty's *The Exorcist*, the movie version of which also inaugurated the film cycle which has itself generated such epicycles as the *Omen* series, and the *It's Alive* series. Other contemporary subgenres also exploit the culture's prevailing fears, often medical ones: the iconography of cancer, via graphic physical deterioration; the fear of communicable sexual disease; the fear of medical technology; fears of toxification; etc. But the issue before us now is not that of matching contemporary subgenres with contemporary anxieties *ad seriatum*, but of attempting to suggest a cluster of anxieties and feelings, evinced by the cycle as a whole, which, in turn, might explain the current obsession with horror.

In organizing my thoughts about the pertinacity of contemporary horror, I find it useful to draw an analogy between this genre and yet another contemporary obsession, whose cultural lifespan (beginning in the mid-seventies) corresponds roughly to that of the present horror cycle. What I have in mind here is postmodernism. What I would like to suggest is that the contemporary horror genre is the exoteric expression of the same feelings that are expressed in the esoteric discussions of the intelligentsia with respect to postmodernism.

I have argued that, in general, works of horror represent transgressions of the standing conceptual categories of the culture. Within horror fictions, standing classificatory norms are dislodged; the culture's criteria for *what is* is problematized. Correspondingly, postmodernism is marked by a strong attraction to conceptual relativism. That is, across the various articulations of postmodernism is the recurring theme not only of moral relativism but of conceptual relativism—a conviction that our standing ways of carving up the world are in some sense arbitrary. They can be deconstructed. They do not really refer to the world. Such views are often accompanied by the suspicion that failure to see this putative fact about our concepts is itself a problem, sometimes called logocentrism.

Personally, I am not convinced by the philosophical arguments advanced by the postmodernists. But at the same time, one cannot ignore their capacity to fascinate a generation of intellectuals. Insofar as that fascination rests in suspecting the inadequacy of our conceptual schemes, it reflects a feeling on the part of intellectuals that is enacted by the contemporary horror fictions consumed by mass audiences.

Shifting gears, one notes that the contemporary horror genre also differs from previous cycles in certain respects that also bear comparison with the themes of postmodernism. First, works of contemporary horror often refer to the history of the genre quite explicitly. King's *It* reanimates a gallery of classic monsters; the movie *Creepshow* by King and Romero is a homage to *EC* horror comics of the fifties; horror movies nowadays frequently make allusions to other horror films while *Fright Night* includes a fictional horror show host as a character; horror writers freely refer to other writers and to other examples of the genre; they especially make reference to classic horror movies and characters.

The genre is particularly reflexive and self-conscious at present, though not in a brooding manner. Specifically, it is highly intertextual in an overtly self-declaiming way.[77] The creators and the consumers of horror fictions are aware that they are operating within a shared tradition, and this is acknowledged openly, with great frequency and gusto. This, of course, is also a feature of the postmodernist artists of high culture. Whether for purposes of political criticism or for nostalgia, postmodern art lives off its inheritance, so to speak. It proceeds by recombining acknowledged elements of the past in a way that suggests that the root of creativity is to be found in looking backwards. The horror fiction of the present, though not lacking in energy, also refers back to earlier times, to *classic* monsters and myths, as if in a gesture of nostalgia.

Another way in which the contemporary horror genre differs from preceding cycles is in its degree of graphic violence. Horror fictions perennially gravitate toward violence; but the contemporary variations regularly offer descriptions and depictions of gore that go far beyond what one finds in the tradition. With certain horror artists, like Clive Barker, this is a point of especial pride. Contemporary horror violence may not differ in kind with that of the past; but it differs nevertheless in vast degree.

One particular dimension of this violence is the extreme gross fury visited upon the human body as it is burst, blown up, broken, and ripped apart; as it disintegrates or metamorphoses; as it is dismembered and dissected; as it is devoured from the inside out. And, of course, the last decade has seen the perfection of what is called the *splatter film,* and, in literature, what Peter Haining, the most prolific living horror anthologist, calls (disapprovingly and perhaps, in some cases, uncharitably) "butcher shop horror." [78]

In the contemporary horror genre, the person is so often literally reduced to mere meat; indeed, the "person-as-meat" could serve as the label for this tendency. And, in turn, this reduction of the person correlates in certain respects with what postmoderns herald as the "death of man." Within the horror fiction of the present, a person is not a member of some privileged ontological category but rather always potential grist for the genre's satanic mills.[79] Even those we identify as heroes and heroines can readily wind up under the chopper.

The present horror cycle and postmodernism correlate insofar as both articulate an anxiety about cultural categories; both look to the past, in many cases with pronounced nostalgia; both portray the person in less than sacrosanct terms. Moreover, this cluster of themes becomes intelligible when one realizes that both the horror genre and the flap about postmodernism have emerged on the heels of the evident collapse of Pax Americana. That is, the horror genre with its anxiety over the instability of cultural norms and postmodernist relativisms of every shade, along with their mutual penchants for nostalgia, arise at just that point in history when the international order set in place at the end of the second world war seems to have fallen into unnerving disarray.

That disarray includes not only the demotion of the global power of the United States—illustrated by the loss of the Vietnam War, the oil crises, the ascendency of Japanese industry and commerce (not to mention West Germany, Korea, Taiwan, etc.), the inability of the United States to secure its ends abroad at will—but, also internal tensions which, with reference to the U.S. at least, encompass unending spectacles of political scandals, widely publicized business scams, economic altercations of all sorts including the oil crises and recessions, the debt crisis, the claims for enfranchisement of heretofore disempowered groups such as women and minorities. Predictably as the verities of the American Imperium falter, an overwhelming sense of instability seizes the imagination in such a way that everything appears at risk or up for grabs, even that which on sober reflection is still intact. Relativism, both conceptual and moral, is a probable response at the level of thought to such social instability, while horror fiction, with its structural commitments to the fragility or instability of standing cultural norms, becomes a ready pop-artistic symbol for feelings that "the center cannot hold."

The nostalgia that is apparent in the intertextuality of much horror fiction, and which at least appears to underwrite much of what is called postmodern (i.e., "after-the-modern"), again, looks back to a time that seemed, probably mistakenly, more settled in its convictions than is possible in the present. As well, the world view of Pax Americana, which made a kind of extravagant individualism its ideological centerpiece, was a fantasy which was easier to sustain in the context of the rising productivity and international hegemony which reassured the well-being of a majority middle class, as well as their faith in the nostrums of personal efficacy and a secular morality of prosperity and conformism. The undermining of that sense of security may well be symbolized in the extreme iconography of personal vulnerability, rooted in bodily degradation, in the horror genre, on the one hand, and the excessive denial (the defensive lowering of expectations?) of the category of person-hood by postmoderns, on the other hand.

As the shocks of the late sixties and seventies battered (and continue to batter) the American order as a whole, the tenuousness of the individualist creed becomes more and more apparent; confidence is replaced by a sense of the vulnerability, impotence, and contingency of individual lives. Nor can the sense that one is part of a larger national project, manifestly destined, be sustained. And it is this sense of loss which I think the demotion of the person in the contemporary horror fiction emblematizes and to which I think postmodernist slogans, stateside, about "the death of man" refer. What is passing, attended by feelings of anxiety, is the social myth of the "American"[80] individualist which, in the case of horror, is enacted in spectacles of indignity, directed at the body, and which, in another register, is articulated in manifestos by postmodernist nihilists, most often those of a literary persuasion.

In characterizing the destruction of the body in contemporary horror fiction in this way, I do not mean to deny that it also is often connected with mobilizing many of the medical anxieties and phobias of the day, but projecting those anxieties, as well, dovetails into expressing an overall sense of vulnerability that itself seems to be a function of the collapse of the American Empire and the culture of the indomitable individual that it was supposed to guarantee.

Contemporary horror fiction, then, articulates the anxieties attending the transition from the American Century to the "we know not what" for mass audiences, in a manner analogous to the way postmodernism articulates intimations of instability for intellectuals. In both cases, the reactions may seem extreme. The deep norms of the culture need not be thought to be at risk, even if American hegemony is. However, over-reaction in times of social stress is surely comprehensible. And, I submit, that the undeniable popularity of horror fiction and postmodernism is a response to feelings of instability prompted by the recognition that the post-World War II order and its subtending culture is in turmoil.

Of course, even if my extended analogy here with postmodernism is inaccurate, it may still be the case that we are onto something of contemporary relevance with respect to horror fiction. For even if postmodernism is not a kind of nihilistic response to the demise of *Pax Americana,* it may still be the case that contemporary horror fiction embodies such cultural anxieties. Its expatiation on the instability of norms—both classificatory and moral—its nostalgic allusions, the sense of helplessness and paralysis it engenders in its characters, the theme of the person-as-meat, the paranoia of its narrative structures, all seem to address an uncertainty about living in the contemporary world which is made more urgent since within memory—

or the illusions of memory—there is the belief that there was a time, not so long ago, when things seemed stable and a sense of certainty prevailed.

Since the horror genre is, in a manner of speaking, founded upon the disturbance of cultural norms, both conceptual and moral, it provides a repertory of symbolism for those times in which the cultural order—albeit at a lower level of generality—has collapsed or is perceived to be in a state of dissolution. Thus, horror, a genre which may typically only command a limited following—due to its basic powers of attraction—can command mass attention when its iconography and structures are deployed in such a way that they articulate the widespread anxiety of times of stress.

As a consequence of the Vietnam War and the parade of disillusionments that followed in its trail, Americans have recently and continuously—often for good reason—been disabused of their Dream. Understandably, commentators have traded on the suggestive verbal substitutability of the *American Dream* with the *American Nightmare*. The sense of paralysis, engendered not only by massive historical shocks, but by an unrelenting inability to come to terms practically with situations, which persistently seem inconceivable and unbelievable, finds a ready, though not a total, analogue in the recurrent psychic demoralization of the fictional victims left dumbfounded by horrific monsters. For better or for worse, Americans have been irreparably shaken by "incredible" events and changes for nearly two decades.[81] And horror has been their genre.

Notes

Introduction

1 Stephen King, "On Becoming a Brand Name," in *Fear Itself*, ed. Tim Underwood and Chuck Miller (New York: New American Library, 1982), pp. 15–16.

2 According to the theory that will be developed in this book, *The Other* is not really a straightforward case of pure horror. I include it here, however, because it is usually mentioned as important to the emergence of the genre.

3 It is interesting to flip through a book of interviews like *Faces of Fear* and to note the number of horror writers who cite horror films as their enduring and endearing initiation into the genre. This is true even of a eminent forefather like Robert Bloch. See Douglas E. Winter, *Faces of Fear: Encounters with the Creators of Modern Horror* (New York: Berkley Books, 1985).

4 For example, editor Marshall B. Tymm's extremely useful *Horror Literature: A Core Collection and Reference Guide* (New York: R.R. Bowker Company, 1981) begins entries for the genre in 1762.

5 Frederick S. Frank, "The Gothic Romance: 1762–1820," in *Horror Literature*, p. 11.

6 Montague Summers, *The Gothic Quest: A History of the Gothic Novel* (London: Fortune, 1938).

7 J.M.S. Tompkins, *The Popular Novel in England* (London: Methuen, 1969), p. 245.

8 See Donald Glut, "Frankenstein Haunts the Theater," in his *The Frankenstein Legend* (Metuchen, New Jersey: The Scarecrow Press, 1973).

9 *Varney the Vampire* is sometimes attributed to James Malcolm Rymer.

10 In terms of the theory to be propounded in this book, most of Poe's work does not fit into the genre of horror. I would prefer to regard Poe as a master of terror, not horror. However, I include mention of him in this introduction not only because he is, pretheoretically, associated with the genre, but also because in his conception of the importance of depicting the psychological sensations of characters he exerted a crucial and direct influence on many major horror writers like H.P. Lovecraft and his followers.

11 Benjamin Franklin Fisher, "The Residual Gothic Impulse: 1824–1873," in *Horror Literature*, p. 177.

12 Gary William Crawford, "The Modern Masters: 1920–1980," in *Horror Literature*, p. 279.

13 One could, for example, read the sixties novel *Dagon* as, in part, an avant-garde *hommage* to Lovecraft.

14 Another source of horrific entertainment for baby-boomers was, of course, the comic book.

15 Aristotle, *Poetics*, trans. Benjamin Jowett and Thomas Twining (New York: The Viking Press, 1957), p. 223.

1 The Nature of Horror

1 Henceforth, art-horror will in almost all cases be simply rendered as horror.

2 For an overview of the tradition from which the horror genre emerges see Elizabeth MacAndrew, *The Gothic Tradition* (New York: Columbia University Press, 1979).

3 I am at pains to stress the historicity of the phenomenon in question in order to avoid the fashionable charge of ahistoricism so frequently leveled at philosophers of art nowadays. The theory of horror offered in this book is not a transhistorical account, but a theory of a historical genre and its affects.

4 See, for example, Isaac Asimov's introduction to *I Robot*.

5 For information on this genre development see Robert Kenneth Jones, *The Shudder Pulps* (New York: New American Library, 1978). Jones maintains that most of the work in this prolific area of publishing suggests supernatural machinations only to dispel them with a rational explanation at the end of the story. There are, of course, exceptions to this, such as Arthur Burks's "Devils in the Dust," which would count as horror. Jones discusses this minor variation of the genre in his chapter "Weird Fantasy."

6 See *The Drama Review*, vol. 18, no. 1 (T–61) (March, 1974). For generalizations about the genre, see Frantisek Deak, "The Grand Guignol," in the same issue.

7 Indeed, there is a creature that looks rather like Chewbacca in *Return of the Vampire*.

8 Tzvetan Todorov, *The Fantastic* (Ithaca: Cornell University Press, 1975).

9 Such as Terry Heller, *The Delights of Terror: An Aesthetics of the Tale of Terror* (Urbana: University of Illinois Press, 1987).

10 See my "Back to Basics," in *The Wilson Quarterly*, vol X, no. 3 (Summer, 1986) for a discussion of the beatific genre.

11 This is not to say that the audience response to monsters is the same as the response of the characters. Audience members do not believe that they are being attacked by monsters or that the monster in the fiction exists, though the fictional characters do. Also, the fictional characters do not take pleasure from the manifestation of the monsters in the story, though the audience does. So the audience's responses and the characters' are not strictly equivalent. This is why I have said that the audience's emotional response runs parallel to the emotions of the fictional characters *and not that* the audience's emotions and those of the characters are identical. For a discussion of the audience's emotional response to the monster, see the next chapter. For a discussion of the pleasure the audience takes in being horrified, see the last chapter in this book.

　　For the purposes of this book, when it is said that the audience's emotional responses *parallel* those of characters, that is a term of art that means that the audience's *evaluative thoughts* about the kind of creature the monster represents correspond to the evaluative beliefs that fictional characters have about the monster. Here, the idea of an *evaluative thought*—both in terms of the way emotions are evaluative, and in terms of the way that audience's emotions are connected to thoughts—are technical notions to be taken up later in this chapter and the next. That the audience's evaluative thoughts about the fictional monster correspond to the emotional evaluations and beliefs of fictional characters in no way implies that the audience accepts the existence of the fictional monster, though, of course, the characters do.

12 Though in the vast majority of cases the audience's emotional response to the monster is cued, in certain pertinent respects, by a character's response, this is not absolutely necessary. The audience, for example, may be offered a glimpse of the monster before any character is and, if the monster is a sufficiently disgusting aberration of nature and/or the audience knows that the work in question is horror, then they could be horrified without a fictional exemplar. In the standard case, however, there are fictional exemplars, and it is on this general sort of case that I am attempting to build my distinction between horror fictions and mere stories with monsters in them

13 The pertinent respects here comprise the evaluative criteria and some of the behavioral activity of the audience which parallel the response of fictional characters. These notions will be clarified when I come to speak of the structure of emotional response.

14 Every country should have one.

15 In Sheridan Le Fanu's *Carmilla,* for example, the victim of the vampire says: "I experienced a strange and tumultuous excitement that was pleasureable, even and anon, mingled with *a vague sense of fear and disgust."* (Emphasis added)

The degree to which explicit mention is made of feelings like disgust, revulsion, and their cognates in horror literature is statistically overwhelming. And it is on the strength of this empirical finding that the case to be developed above is based. However, it should be noted that one may have a work of art-horror where the revulsive character of the monster is not stated outright in the text. But, in those cases, I conjecture the text will imply, in a pretty straightforward manner, either through language (e.g., reference to odors or bodily deformation and disintegration, or through a description that otherwise disgusts the reader) or through character behavior that the monster is disgusting.

16 The account of the emotions adopted here closely follows that of William Lyons in his *Emotion* (New York: Cambridge University Press, 1980). Also relevant are Irving Thalberg, "Emotions and Thought," in *Philosophy of Mind,* ed. by S. Hampshire (New York: Harper and Row, 1966); Thalberg, "Constituents and Causes of Emotion and Action," *Philosophical Quarterly,* no. 23 (1973); and Thalberg, *Perception, Emotion and Action* (New Haven: Yale University Press, 1977) especially chap. 2.

17 Since I will not be talking about dispositional emotions, henceforth the word "emotion" refers only to occurrent emotions.

18 This is not an exhaustive list nor is it supposed that an exhaustive list is possible.

19 A view something like this appears to be advanced by Bertrand Russell. He writes "An emotion—rage, for example,—(is) a certain kind of process. The ingredients of an emotion are only sensations and images and bodily movements succeeding each other according to a certain pattern" from *The Analysis of Mind* (London: Unwin, 1921), p. 265. Here an emotion is identifed in terms of a unique pattern of feeling. In the analytic tradition of philosophy, this approach was attacked in an important early paper by Errol Bedford entitled "Emotions," *Proceedings of the Aristotelian Society,* vol. 57 (1956–57). In terms of this book, however, I wish to emphasize that I want to part company from Bedford's tendencies in the direction of Rylean behaviorism.

20 Likewise, Mary's states of fear are accompanied by a "rush of adrenaline." But if we drug Mary with adrenaline and put her in a room where there are no objects that she believes are dangerous, we will not, I think, be prone to say that she is afraid. See Robert M. Gordon, *The Structure of Emotions* (New York: Cambridge University Press, 1987), p. 86. In this book, Gordon classifies horror as what he calls a factive emotion. However, he is

dealing with what I earlier categorized as a natural emotion. I suspect that in order to handle art-emotions like art-horror Gordon's system will need to be amplified.

21 Here someone may charge that I am using the word "feeling" too narrowly. I am reserving it for physical states. Feelings, on the contrary, it might be argued, are comprised of more than physical sensations. That move, however, is to exit the argument and to redefine *feelings*, perhaps as equivalent to *emotions*. Certainly ordinary usage allows for these terms to be employed interchangeably. However, such a use of "feelings" cannot be seriously advanced in the argument above without begging the question. Moreover, as will soon become apparent, if one construes feelings to be emotions and believes that, in this sense, feelings are more than a matter of physical states, then that person has no quarrel with me.

22 Throughout this account of the structure of the emotions, the cognitive component of the emotions will include beliefs and *thoughts*. The purpose of emphasizing thoughts here will become quite evident in the next chapter where it is argued that the objects of art-horror concern our thought contents with respect to the monster and not our belief in an *existing* monster. In the exposition of the structure of the emotions above, the discussion of cognitive component should be understood as ranging over both beliefs and thoughts. For expositional purposes, sometimes the inclusion of thoughts is not made explicit; however, in most cases, what is said of the role of beliefs in this account should also be understood to pertain to thoughts.

23 Moreover, it is this sort of thought experiment that inclines me to maintain that the relation between the cognitive states and the agitation is a causal one.

24 Actually, this account needs a bit more expansion since we may be emotionally moved by someone else's situation and since it should be made explicit that our construals and evaluations may be a matter of either beliefs or thoughts. That is, rather than believing that the Green Slime exists and that it is dangerous, I may be frightened by thinking of a kind of (nonexistent) creature like the Green Slime whose properties would be thought to be threatening if there were such a being.

25 In the matter of the horrific touch, H.P. Lovecraft makes an interesting observation in his *Supernatural Horror in Literature* (New York: Dover Publications, 1973), p. 102. Speaking of M.R. James's ghosts, he writes: "In inventing a new type of ghost, he has departed considerably from the conventional Gothic tradition; for where the older stock ghosts were pale and stately, and apprehended chiefly through the sense of sight, the average James ghost is lean, dwarfish, and hairy—a sluggish, hellish night-abomination midway betwixt beast and man—usually *touched* before it is *seen*."

26 Since this theory is of art-horror, which is itself connected to an imaginative genre, I have not felt it to be necessary in my definition to underscore that the monsters in question are fictional.

27 In his *Danse Macabre* (New York: Berkley Books, 1987), Stephen King isolates three different emotional levels of horror (pp. 22–23): terror, horror, and revulsion. He says "I recognize terror as the finest emotion and so I will try to terrorize the reader. But if I find that I cannot terrify, I will try to horrify, and if I find that I cannot horrify, I'll go for the gross-out." Terror, for King, is a kind of apprehension of the unknown; no monster is manifested but our imagination of what might be is nerve wrenching. In horror, the monster is shown or described; its physical wrongness causes a physical reaction. With revulsion, the monster is so gross that the physical reaction is one of extreme disgust. So, for King, terror is fear + imagination; horror is fear + graphic portrayal; and revulsion is fear + gross, graphic portrayal. The emotional affects available in the genre, then, are a continuum of levels of response.

    Though these distinctions make a certain operational sense, I don't think that they

.provide an adequate map of art-horror, for I would want to argue that some element of revulsion must be present in what King calls terror and horror, as well as in "the gross-out." Of course, King and I may be talking at cross-purposes since he thinks of revulsion in terms of something that causes a spectator to literally gag with disgust whereas I am using revulsion not only to cover that case but also cases where we are unsettled, perhaps only mildly, by the apprehension of impurity.

King's category of terror reminds one that there is a certain school of thought with regard to horror that is nicely characterized by Lovecraft's formula "Just enough is suggested, and just little enough is told" (*Supernatural Horror in Literature*, p. 42). The notion here is that the best horror works by suggestion, by getting the reader to imagine what is the case. The presumption is that the reader can scare himself—can imagine what horrifies herself most—better than any author.

Lovecraft, himself, works this aesthetics of suggestion into a definition of horror in terms of cosmic fear, a kind of secular awe. But I don't think that this line of thought is useful in thinking about the definition of horror. For it really indicates an aesthetic preference for one type of horror. It does not manage to classify horror; by this approach "horror" becomes an honorific or evaluative term, signaling achievement against a certain aesthetic standard. Moreover, this standard is explicitly rejected by a number of horror authors. Clive Barker says: "There is a very strong lobby that says you can show too much. Wrong. Not for me. You can never show too much," and "Now everything that I know about *my* stories, I put on the page. So when something appalling happens, everything I can conceive of about the scene goes down in print. I want it to be imagined, in the reader's mind, as completely as *I* can imagine it. For me, the joy of horror fiction is pushing the boundaries of the imagination and saying, 'Let's confront the reader with something totally off the wall.'" (an interview in *Faces of Fear*, by Douglas Winter [New York: Berkley Books, 1985], pp. 213–214). One cannot, therefore, use suggested or imagined fear to define horror without begging the issue between a Lovecraft and a Barker.

28 An example of a novella where the issue of the touch of the horrific creature is pervasive is the novella *The Black Spider* by Jeremias Gotthelf; even when the fearsome Spider is lodged in a containing post, the narrator says: "But I will confess, never in my life have I prayed as I prayed when I held that dreadful post in my hands. My whole body was on fire, and I couldn't help looking to see if there were any black spots coming out on my hands or anywhere else on me, and a load fell from my heart when at last everything was in its place." In this tale the Spider is a identified as a contagious scourge, a veritable rampaging plague. This, of course, suggests that there is a certain sense to the correlation between contamination imagery in works of horror and the tendency of characters to shrink from the touch of horrific creatures. That is, insofar as such creatures are identified or associated with contamination, one fears any contact with their vile bodies. Perhaps, as well, the recurring descriptions of such monsters as unclean connects with the notion that they are contaminated and infectious and that even brushing against them is risky.

29 See O.H. Green, "The Expression of Emotion," *Mind,* vol. 79 (1970); and Lyons, *Emotion,* chap. 5. In *Action, Emotion and Will* (London: Routledge and Kegan Paul, 1963), Anthony Kenny calls this the appropriate object of them emotion (p. 183).

30 More needs to be said of the sense of possibility here. For the most part, logical possibility is what we have in mind. But there are complications. For in certain horror stories, especially ones involving time-travel, we may meet up with creatures that are not only physically impossible, but logically impossible as well. In order to handle these, we may have to talk about *ostensibly*, logically possible beings—beings whose logical impossibility is not foregrounded by the text; beings whose logical impossibility may even be obscured by the text. The prospect that we can mentally entertain impossibilities is explored,

though inconclusively, by Roman Ingarden, *The Literary Work of Art*, trans. G. Grabowicz (Evantson: Northwestern University Press, 1973), pp. 123–24.

31 The notion that literature clarifies and teaches us the criteria of emotions has been argued by Alex Neil in his "Emotion, Learning and Literature," a paper delivered at the meetings of the American Society for Aesthetics in Kansas City, Missouri on Oct. 30, 1987. Neil's argument figures in his claim that literature can give us knowledge about the world, specifically knowledge about how to apply the language of everyday emotions. Literature does this by exemplifying the criteria of application of emotive terms in descriptions of characters. Likewise, I want to claim that the criteria for art-horror is to be found in character reactions in the works in the genre. Audiences ideally model their responses on them. But, I do not wish to argue that art-horror teaches us about the world; for I doubt that art-horror as described is an everyday emotion. Perhaps it is an emotion that we only encounter when attending to examples of the horror genre. This is not to say that Neil's general theory is wrong; but only that art-horror is not a robust example of it.

(One place where something like art-horror can be found in everyday life, it should be noted, is in the language of racism. Racist rhetoric often portrays its victims as interstitial and impure. Black people have been treated as though fusions of ape and human as have the Irish—see *Apes and Angels* by L. Perry Curtis (Washinton D.C.: Smithsonian Press, 1971).

From another direction, my notion that works in the horror genre instruct the audience about how they are to respond might correlate with recent research in literary studies— sometimes slotted under the rubric of reception studies—to the effect that there is some sort of contract between the reader and the work. Part of the substance of that contract, in my account, is that the audience model its response to monsters in terms of the evaluative categories exemplified by characters. Of course, the audience may refuse the contract. A particularly inept monster may raise laughter rather than horror. The character's response is not the whole story. The monster must be appropriately fearsome and disgusting. If it is not, the audience may just reject the contract.

32 Mary Douglas, *Purity and Danger* (London: Routledge and Kegan Paul, 1966).

33 Here one recalls the particular disgust that Roquentin feels toward viscosity in Sartre's novel *Nausea*.

34 "Object" and "entity" are stressed here in order to block certain counterexamples. Category errors and logical paradoxes, though they may horrify philosophers, are not normally regarded as impure. But neither do they belong to the domain of "objects and entities." For the purpose of analyzing art-horror, the domain of objects that are to be assessed in terms of impurity are *beings*. Indeed, they are a special sort of beings, viz., monsters.

35 In terms of fine art, Sibylle Ruppert mixes different species in her horrific charcoal drawing, such as *The Third Sex*. Also see Lucas Samaras's *Photo-transformation* in this respect. H.R. Giger's work not only compounds the categorical opposites of the organic and the mechanical but also those of inside and outside.

36 Consider the movie titles: *It Came From Outer Space, It Came From Beneath the Sea, It! The Terror From Beyond Space, It Conquered The World, It's Alive, It Lives Again, Them!*, and *They*. Titles like *The Thing, The Swamp Thing, The Creature from the Black Lagoon, Terror Out of the Sky, Monster, Monster from Green Hell, Monster from a Prehistoric Planet, Monster on the Campus, Monster from the Surf, Monster of Piedras Blancas, The Monster That Challenged the World* each in its own way bespeaks the theme of the lack of convenient linguistic categories with which to precisely label horrific beings. In a number of the preceding cases, the best we can do is to locate the monster in space (e.g., in Piedras Blancas).

37 In John Barrymore's 1920 version of *Dr. Jekyll and Mr. Hyde,* Hyde's make-up is designed

to suggest that he is a cross between a man and a spider. See James B. Twitchell's analysis in his *Dreadful Pleasures: An Anatomy of Modern Horror* (New York: Oxford University Press, 1985), pp. 245–246.

38 Though not strictly horror images in the terms of my theory, Francis Bacon's paintings often evoke descriptions as horrifying because they suggest virtually *formless* mounds of human flesh. See his *Lying Figure With A Hypodermic Syringe*.

39 In her *Powers of Horror: An Essay on Abjection* (New York: Columbia University Press, 1982), Julie Kristeva also uses Douglas's work to discuss horror. However, the topic of her book does not quite coincide with the topic of this book. This book is narrowly concerned with the genre of art-horror; Kristeva's theorizing is probably meant to encompass this as well as much else. For her, it seems that horror and abomination are metaphysical elements which she connects with an abstract conception of the female (specifically the mother's body), and which she believes we would be advised to acknowledge. I do not know whether Kristeva's meanderings are even intelligible; however, I will not pause to examine them, for her project is of a scope that is probably not ultimately germane to this investigation; it is much larger.

40 Considering the opening distinctions in this section, a question may arise at this point concerning the reason why the monsters of fairy tales do not raise horror responses from either the human characters they meet or in their readers. But aren't these creatures categorical violations? It seems to me that there are at least three possible answers to this puzzle, though as yet I am uncertain which I prefer. First, we might argue that these creatures are not categorical violations in fairy tales and myths. Second we might take note of the way in which fairy tales characteristically begin with formulas like "Once upon a time." Perhaps this functions to remove them from the rules of *prevailing* categorical schemes. Lastly, it may the case that categorical transgression is only one of several necessary conditions for impurity. If this is so, the discovery of further conditions might reveal why horrific monsters are impure whereas fairy-tale monsters are not.

41 Indeed the very sight of a horrific creature may kill. See Arthur Machen's "The Great God Pan."

42 In Sigmund Freud's celebrated essay "The 'Uncanny,' " he notes that the relevant German concept attached to this term signals a disclosure, revelation, or exposure of what is ordinarily alien, hidden, repressed, concealed, or secreted by our familiar ways of seeing. This view, at least in a minimal way, corresponds to our notion of the importance of categorical transgression in the production of art-horror. The horrific creature is one that is ill-adjusted to our cultural schemata, and those categories, in a sense, might be thought to exclude and to perhaps obscure the recognition of the kinds of possibilities such creatures represent. However, I must also admit that I'm a bit uncomfortable with putting the matter this way. For it seems to me more apt to say that in general our cultural categories ignore— rather than repress, hide, or suppress—the kinds of conceptual possibilities represented by horrific creatures. Undoubtedly, the notion of the return of the repressed has some applicability to horror; the question is whether it applies comprehensively to every manifestation of art-horror. My sense is that it does not. But more on the issue of repression and the relation of the theory propounded here and rival psychoanalytic theories appears in later sections of this book. Freud's essay is anthologized in *Studies in Parapsychology*, ed. Philip Rieff (New York: Collier Books, 1963), pp. 19–62.

43 I owe the counterexamples in the two paragraphs above to Ed Leites who called them to my attention at a symposium on philosophy and film at the Museum of the Moving Picture in Astoria, Queens, in 1986.

44 Recently, Cheshire Calhoun has challenged the notion of cognitive emotions by denying that beliefs are constituents of emotions. Instead of beliefs, she argues that "seeing the

world as . . . " *experiences* are what we should be talking about. I don't think that even if Calhoun is right, the consequences for this book will be troublesome. I see no problem with recasting what I have said about the spectator's beliefs and/or thoughts with respect to horrific monsters in the language of "seeing-as." On the other hand, I am not completely convinced that by advocating the "seeing-as" experience as a constituent of emotions, Calhoun has ceased to be a cognitivist; "seeing-as" seems to me to be a cognition on any reasonably broad view of cognition. See "Cognitive Emotions?" in *What is an Emotion?*, ed. Cheshire Calhoun and Robert Solomon (New York: Oxford University Press, 1984), pp. 327–342.

45   As well, it also seems advantageous to advance this theory of horror in its strongest form in order to encourage discussion and the production of more (perhaps countervailing) evidence. That is, progress in the study of art-horror is most likely to progress if strong conjectures are initially introduced, if only to be ultimately refuted.

46   Cronenberg has said that in *The Fly,* he wanted to illustrate his experience of the death of his father. His father had a cancer that in its later stages was apparently quite repulsive. However, Cronenberg never lost sight of the human he knew and loved, despite the deterioration of his father's flesh. The fly figure he created replicates the conflicting emotions of disgust and care that Cronenberg presumably felt toward his declining father.

47   Thus, Superman is a monster, but not a horrific monster, on our account. Ditto: Mighty Mouse.

48   Joseph Margolis has discussed the importance of the distinction between an entity versus an event theory of horror with me in several very helpful conversations. However, he might not agree with my attempts at resolving this issue.
      Also, interestingly, Aristotle in his *Poetics* may be translated as applying a notion of horror in his analysis of tragedy, and there it will be a matter of events not, entities. However, Aristotle is not considering what we think of as art-horror. Rather, he has in mind is the representation of what we call *natural horror*.

49   In my discussion of art-horror from the perspective of an object (as opposed to an event) theory, I noted that on the border of that genre were similar fictions, like *Psycho,* that lacked reference to the supernatural; so too there are neighbors to the stories of supernatural events discussed above. Here, the incongruous events to which the audience's attention is riveted find their origin not in transgressions of nature, but in psychological and criminal perversity. Examples of this variation include Lord Dunsany's "The Two Bottles of Relish," Roald Dahl's "Man From The South," and many of the episodes of TV programs like those in such series as *Alfred Hitchcock Presents* and *Thriller Theater.*

50   Sigmund Freud, *The Interpretation of Dreams,* trans. James Strachey (New York: Avon Books, 1965), pp. 327–28.

51   Recall Hume's notion that the fantastic beasts of mythology are recombinations of elements previously experienced in perception. David Hume, *Treatise on Human Nature,* I, 1, 3.

52   Sigmund Freud, *On Dreams,* trans. James Strachey (New York: The Norton Library, 1952), p. 46.

53   The distinction between temporal and spatial fission is an elaboration of Robert Rogers, *A Psychoanalytic Study of the Double in Literature* (Detroit: Wayne State University Press, 1970).

54   The real boyfriend is hanging on some kind of ray-gun meat hook in an alien spaceship whose interior resembles that of a large icebox.

55   *I Married A Monster From Outer Space* belongs to a subgenre of space-possession films including *Invasion of the Body Snatchers* (both versions), *Creation of the Humanoids, Man from*

Planet X, Invaders From Mars (both versions), *Phantom From Space, It Came From Outer Space, Killers From Space* etc. Depending on the specific context of the film, the possessed earthlings in these films can be examples of either spatial or temporal fission. For an interpretation of *Invasion of the Body Snatchers,* see my "You're Next" in *The Soho Weekly News,* Dec. 21, 1978.

56 Carmilla may not represent an absolutely pure case of fusion since at times she is described as a dark figure that may be an animal. Thus, she may be a shape-changer, but I think the text is somewhat ambiguous.

57 At the same time, the distinction between fission and fusion can be useful to the critic as a means of penetrating the symbolic organization of the fantastic being in question in such a way that the thematic oppositions that the creature's biology prefigures are clarified.

58 James has prepared for this denouement by emphasizing the *"poysonous Rage"* and *"venomous"* aspect of the witch in the opening of the story.

59 One also suspects that one could also generate a horrific being by miniaturization. There is a story in the movie *Stephen King's Cat's Eye* where the troll monster is all the more horrifying for being tiny, insofar as this allows him to endanger the child heroine by being effectively invisible to adults (but luckily not to cats).

60 See William Morton Wheeler, *Ants: Their Structure, Development and Behavior* (New York: Columbia University Press, 1910), pp. 246–256. "Leiningen versus the Ants" was made into a movie called *The Naked Jungle* by Byron Haskin.

61 These tropes may not be mutually preclusive and the list may not be exhaustive; however, I think that it does supply a useful characterization of a number of the most recurrent structures of horrific imagery.

62 Of course, I do not mean to suggest that the Beast can only be conceived as a wolf-man. Among other things, he has been depicted as an ogre (in *Popular Tales of the Olden Time,* 1840), as a wildboar-man (by Edmund Evans, 1874), as a sabre-toothed panther (Eleanor Vere Boyle, 1875), and as a minotaur (W. Heath Robinson, 1921).

Also, in discussing illustrations, it may be useful to address what some readers may regard as a lacuna in my theory thus far. I have claimed to develop a theory that ranges across art forms; however, my examples have come primarily from fictional literature, motion pictures and theater. Thus, the question may arise as to whether my approach can assimilate the fine arts.

Fictional literature, motion pictures, and theater in our culture are, standardly though not necessarily, narrative arts replete with characters. On the other hand, it might be thought that fine art is essentially nonnarrative, and, as a result, an approach like mine that relies so much on narrative and character would not fit it trimly.

However, the presupposition of this objection is misguided. Much fine art is narrative, and in works that show characters responding to monsters the application of my account advances as it would with a narrative film. In Barclay Shaw's illustration *Martian Way,* two futuristic humans uncover an enormous eye in a cage. The fingers on the hand of the human nearest to us are frozen in the kind of paralysis of fear found in the examples from literature and film above.

Moreover, much of the fine art that would count as horrific serves, of course, as illustrations for books and magazines, and as advertisements for motion pictures. These often function as capsule narratives—showing the monster or the maniac lowering over some victim whose expression exemplifies horror (See, for example, John Newton Howett's cover for the August–September 1937 issue of *Horror Stories*). Also, where such illustrations do not show victims, but only monsters, they are nevertheless grounded in the responses of the characters in the fictions they illustrate.

Undoubtedly, however, there is horrific imagery in fine art which is not connected to the reaction of a fictional victim or character. Perhaps, Mark Leatherdale's photo *Gargoyle/ Devil* is an example of this. In such cases, it seems to me that we can take advantage of the theory of horror developed through this study of horror in narrative contexts, and identify an image as horrific, even if it lacks a mediating character, just in case the viewer of the picture regards the creatures in it as meeting the criteria for art-horror stated above.

63 For a discussion of the "indiscernible method" in philosophy, see Arthur Danto, *The Transfiguration of the Commonplace* (Cambridge: Harvard University Press, 1981).

64 Another interesting context where the issue of "indiscernible monsters" can arise is comedy. In films like *Teen Wolf, Teen Wolf Two, My Demon Lover,* and *Abbott and Costello Meet Frankenstein* (etc., etc.), the audience regards creatures made-up exactly as they might be in a horror film as risible rather than hair-raising. Moreover, the characters in these films generally appear to regard these monsters as violations of nature, as abnormal, as disturbances of the cosmic order. Thus, if such comedies are not to be thought of as counterexamples to my theory, some explanation must be supplied.

Such an account begins by noting that these comedies are parodies of horror films; a measure of comic distance has been has been introduced between the fictional world and the audience. Often this operates in such a way as to refocus the audience's attention from the monster to the ridiculous reactions of characters to the monsters. In the Teen Wolf films, characters may respond to the monster as one would to the creature of a horror film; however, the audience knows this is inappropriate because the Teen Wolf is really a sterling fellow; the Teen Wolf does not fulfill the requirement that the monster be genuinely fearsome. A character who doesn't know this and who responds as if the Teen Wolf were the Wolfman becomes a comic butt in virtue of his misperception of the situation vis à vis the audience's superior knowledge.

The Abbott and Costello films also refocus attention on the character's response for comic effect. Specifically, Costello's reactions are exercises in hyperbole. The monsters in these films are dangerous enough; but they relinquish pride of place to Costello's virtuoso apoplexies.

65 The first chapter—"The Gothic Romance" by Frederick S. Frank—of Marshall Tymn's *Horror Literature: A Core Collection and Reference Guide* (N.Y.: R.R. Bowker Company, 1981) begins the history of horror in 1762.

66 Crane Brinton, "Enlightenment," in *The Encyclopedia of Philosophy* (New York: Macmillan Publishing Co, Inc. and The Free Press, 1967), Vol. One, p. 519.

67 Quoted in *The Philosophy of the Enlightenment* by Ernst Cassirer (Princeton: Princeton University Press, 1951), p. 135.

68 Brinton, p. 520.

69 Often a correlation is made between the flourishing of the horror genre and the Romantic movement, which movement, of course, is a reaction to the Enlightenment. This is a suggestive idea and should not be rejected completely. However, it is important to realize that it does not always square neatly with the ideas of the Romantics themselves. When in the introduction to his *Lyrical Ballads,* Wordsworth complains about frantic novels, one takes it that he has, among other things, horrific gothics in mind. He, at least, would appear to question whether these works are really part of a visionary company.

70 Speaking of the genre of the fantastic, which has interesting relations with horror and which will be discussed in Chapter Three, Todorov says it is "nothing more than the uneasy conscience of the postivist nineteenth century" (*The Fantastic*, p. 169). Also with reference to the fantastic, Louis Vax maintains that "the period of unbelief allowed for the emergence of fantastic literature in its strictest sense" (in "L'art de faire peur," *Critique,* I

[Nov. 1957], p. 929); while Maurice Levy maintains that "The fantastic is a compensation that man provides for himself, at the level of imagination, for what he has lost at the level of faith" (*Le roman gothique anglais 1764–1824* [Toulouse: Association des publications de la Faculte des lettres et sciences humaines, 1968], p. 617). And Georges Bataille, in a more general vein, claims that "Those arts which sustain anguish and the recovery from anguish within us, are the heirs of religion" (*Literature and Evil* (London: Calder and Boyars, 1973), p. 16. This view of the genre also corresponds to the self-understanding of the genre of such authors as H.P. Lovecraft.

71   This is a conjecture about the rise of the horror genre in the eighteenth century. I do not mean to claim that there was no art-horror before the eighteenth century. I have restricted my theorizing to works from the eighteenth century to the present, following what I take to be the consensus of authorities in the field concerning the life span of the genre. There may in fact be examples of art-horror prior to the coalescence of the genre; there are certainly forerunners of various sorts as well as important transitional works like *The Monk* by M.G. Lewis. It is the task of criticism to identify earlier works of art-horror, to establish that they are examples of art-horror (rather than merely incomplete predecessors thereof), and to explain how within the cultural context from which they emerge the monster, in these fictions, would have been identified as unnatural within presiding conceptual frameworks. Whether this can be done or not—I have no fixed conviction in the matter— is something to be determined by further research.

2   Metaphysics and Horror, or relating to Fictions

1   Kendall Walton, "Fearing Fictions," in *Journal of Philosophy*, vol. 75, no. 1, (January 1978).

2   For further examples of this sort, see Colin Radford, "How can we be moved by the fate of Anna Karenina?," in the *Supplementary Volume of the Aristotelian Society*, 49, (1975).

3   Samuel Taylor Coleridge, *Biographia Literaria*, in *Selected Poetry and Prose of Coleridge*, ed. Donald Stauffer (New York: The Modern Library, Random House, 1951), p. 264.

4   Coleridge, *Biographia Literaria* p. 264.

5   In his "Meditation IV; *Of the True and the False*," Descartes maintains that we can, in certain cases, will our beliefs. This supposition is later roundly challenged by Spinoza and Hume.

6   Of course, in the context of the argument concerning fiction in general and horror fiction in particular on the matter of the possibility of willing belief, this is not really an acceptable retort by the proponent of the willing suspension of disbelief. For like the proposition "5+7=1492," the propositions "It is not the case, that Dracula does not exist" and its equivalent "Dracula does exist" are such that we know they are false. So if we cannot will "5+7=1492" on the grounds that it is false, then, analogously, we cannot will "Dracula does exist."

7   If anyone thinks there is a problem here because I am speaking of beliefs rather than disbeliefs, one could change the example to a disbelief—"Nonwhites are not the equals of whites"—and the argument will run the same course.

8   See Descartes, Meditations I.

9   My arguments against the idea of the willing suspension of disbelief stress that there does not seem to be any evidence for the performance of any act of will. But perhaps buying a ticket to a monster movie or deciding to read a horror novel will be advanced as evidence of the relevant act of will. In other words, reading the novel or viewing the film as fictions are the relevant acts of will. But then suspending disbelief becomes a matter of knowingly

reading or viewing a fiction. But in the context of the argument at hand, the willing suspension of disbelief was supposed to mark a process over and above knowingly reading or viewing a fiction. If it is not such an "added" process, then it is hard to see how it will resolve the paradox of fiction as stated so far. Knowingly reading *The Exorcist* as a fiction will not neutralize our beliefs that the demon in Regan, as well as Regan herself, do not exist. Of course, one could stipulate that the willing suspension of disbelief just is the process of knowingly reading a fiction. But then it is hard to see how the notion can usefully figure as an answer to the paradox of fiction. It is just a way of reinstating the problem, even if it finds a harmless meaning for the phrase *suspension of disbelief.*

Also, another attempt to salvage the suspension of disbelief view in the face of my arguments might go like this: we suppose that for ordinary suspension of disbelief, our settled beliefs must be under fire from countervailing evidence; I suppose that there is no countervailing evidence with respect to fictions. But perhaps someone might claim that with movies, for example, the countervailing evidence is supplied by the images of the film themselves. Since these are only fictional images to begin with, we are skeptical about whether what they portray is true. But if this is the countervailing evidence, we wonder how the belief that is being contested—say, that Rodan is aloft—ever came to be acquired. The fictional images themselves will have to be simultaneously the source of our belief and our skepticism. And it is extremely difficult to see how this will be worked out. Rather, I would want to say that the images of Rodan present us with the idea of Rodan, a creature whose existence is not something we are even prone to countenance. Thus, if ever we realize that the only evidence we have for his existence is the film image, we do not suddenly think that one of our beliefs is being challenged. For we never had the belief in the first place.

Again, one might say that viewing a movie fiction knowingly just is what the willing suspension of disbelief amounts to. But this kind of stipulative definition will not supply the proponent of the suspension of disbelief with the kind of mental process required to dispel the putative contradiction between our genuine emotional response to horror fictions and our knowledge that the horror fiction does not portray existing creatures and events. Suspension of disbelief redefined as knowing the fiction is a fiction merely reinstates the putative contradiction.

10 The Green Slime example was, I believe, first introduced in Kendall Walton's classic "Fearing Fictions," *Journal of Philosophy.*

11 At this point, some readers have asked for whom Charles is pretending and why. On the model of a child who is playing by himself and who is pretending to be a superhero, we might answer that Charles is pretending for himself for the fun of it.

12 See Kendall Walton, "Fearing Fictions"; and "How Remote Are Fictional Worlds From The Real World?," in *The Journal of Aesthetics and Art Criticism,* vol. 37, no. 1, (Fall 1978). The use of the concept of make-believe in these articles is an extension of Walton's use of the concept of make-believe to deal with general questions of representation. See his "Pictures and Make-Believe," *Philosophical Review,* vol. 81, no. 3 (July 1973), and his "Are Representations Symbols?," *The Monist,* vol. 58, no. 2 (April 1974).

13 Kendall Walton, "Fearing Fictions," p. 11.

14 Kendall Walton, "Fearing Fictions," p. 24.

15 Walton finds a related puzzle in German, where he says that, with the exception of the case of fiction, the use of the indicative always signals that the speaker is committed to the truth of the statement. Walton also explains this exception in terms of the speaker's game of make-believe. However, native speakers of German tell me that in German, as in English, if the context is ambiguous the *fictional* prefix will be used.

There are also two other puzzles that Walton believes his theory can resolve. The first is the case in which a reader, who does not like happy endings, gets caught up in a story so that he wants the heroine to be rescued despite her principled aversion to such plotting. Personally, I don't think this is much of a puzzle nor that we need Walton's theory to resolve it. Surely, one can be opposed to a certain kind of plot in principle and still get caught up in it just as in principle one might be opposed to smoking and yet savor the taste of a fine tobacco when one finds oneself in a social situation where in order to be polite one accepts a ritual cigar.

The last puzzle to which Walton applies his theory involves the question of how we can enjoy suspense fictions that we have already read. That is, if we know that the Green Slime is going to be emulsified in the last chapter, how is it that we can pick up the story for another reading and still be wrapped up in it? On Walton's view, this is not a problem because we are simply playing yet another game of pretense—albeit with the same props. I will discuss the resolution of this puzzle in the next chapter where I deal with the relation of horror to suspense.

16   For an example of this sort of theory see John Searle's "The logical status of fictional discourse," in his *Expression and Meaning* (Cambridge: Cambridge University Press, 1979). Also, see Richard Gale, "The Fictive Use of Language," in *Philosophy,* vol. 46, (1971).

17   For a systematic example of a speech act theory, see John Searle, *Speech Acts* (Cambridge: Cambridge University Press, 1969).

18   Walton, himself, does not claim such an advantage for his theory; so the preceding remarks should not be taken as pertaining to Walton. Rather, I am attempting to foreclose the temptations to make this move not because Walton has attempted it, but because I have noticed that sometimes in conversation people tend to conflate the pretend theory of emotion with pretend theories of fictional assertion.

19   Another way of defending the attribution of pretend emotions to spectators—one proposed to me by Mary Wiseman—is to maintain that it is not an attempt to offer a phenomenology of the spectator but instead to offer an explanation of what must really be going on if the spectator's response is to be logically coherent. Maybe a helpful analogy here is the distinction between what is really going on organically in a medically illiterate person, such as myself, and what I think and feel. But I'm not sure that accounts of psychological states can be sharply distinguished from the self-awareness and reflexive convictions of the subjects as cleanly as might be the case with certain medical states. Moreover, the pretend theory might not be the only theory that can offer the kind of explanation that will render the spectator's response logically coherent. And, if a rival theory can not only propose this kind of explanation, but also do it while neither postulating "theoretical" pretend states nor doing violence to the phenomenology of art-horror, that theory would be superior, all things being equal, to the pretend theory. And, obviously, that is just the sort of rival theory I will attempt to develop in what follows.

20   If this indeed is the way Walton's theory is supposed to go, I find it implausible. Using the example of fear, might obscure the difficulty here. But if we think in terms of the emotion of grief at the end of Robert Bolt's *A Man For All Seasons,* it is not because we have been betrayed or beheaded or had a friend betrayed or beheaded, make-believedly or otherwise.

21   My point here in this section is dialectical. I wish to undercut the persuasiveness of one of the paradigm cases in the argument that emotions always require beliefs, viz., the case in which emotion dissipates when we learn a story is concocted. I wish to contest this case by showing that it is probably more complicated than it may appear—indeed, complicated in a way that might lead us to refrain from generalizing from it. Specifically, I wish to

suggest that the possible element of resentment in such cases may account for our predicted losses of sympathetic affect when learning that we have been victims of a cock-and-bull story. Also, I have attempted to advance a scenario in which it seems plausible that we could learn a story was a fiction and in which our emotional response is not diminished. The conclusion I am reaching for is that in some cases learning something is a fiction may diminish emotional response for reasons unconnected with learning it is a fiction, while in other cases, learning a story is a fiction will not alter emotional response. My dialectical point is that we have not been convinced that the absence of existence beliefs does clearly always correlate to absence of emotions. On the other hand, I am not, at this juncture, arguing for a general theory of my own. I am not claiming that in all cases when emotions dissipate with respect to cock-and-bull stories, resentment is always the cause; sometimes, I may simply lose interest or become bored when I learn the story is made-up (of course, contrariwise, I may also say while weeping: "Damned good story even if it is made-up"). Nor, it should be added, am I claiming that there are no emotions that require existence beliefs. I am only challenging the general theory that emotions always require existence beliefs as that thesis is advanced on the shoulders of dubious examples of cock-and-bull stories. For dialectical purposes, all I need to be committed to in the argument so far is that in some cases emotions may not be attached to existence beliefs, that knowing a story is not the case does not preclude emotional response, and that the cock-and-bull story paradigm does not conclusively support the thesis that emotions require belief because the dissipation of sympathetic affect predicted by these cases could be explained equally well in terms of our becoming resentful.

In summary, my claim here is not that there may be no emotions whatsoever that require existence beliefs. I have only disputed the claim that all emotions require existence beliefs. Moreover, I have tried to show that generalizing from the paradigm case of the cock-and-bull story to what is required of all emotions is not as straightforward as is usually supposed.

22 Walton says precious little about these quasi-fears. My own suspicion is that if more were said about these quasi-fears, it is likely that they would turn out to be what we would ordinarily take to be genuine fears. And, in that case, the pretend theory could only proceed by smuggling genuine fear in through the back door, which, of course, would completely undermine the purpose of the theory of pretend emotions. It is difficult, to advance this suspicion with utter confidence, however, since Walton does not tell us much about quasi-fear, and certainly not enough to make it easy to see how exactly it differs from real fear.

On page 13 of "Fearing Fictions," Walton says "It is arguable that the purely physiological aspects of quasi-fear, such as the increase of adrenaline in the blood, which Charles could ascertain only by clinical tests, are not part of what makes it make-believe that he is afraid. Thus one might want to understand 'quasi-fear' as referring only to the more psychological aspects of Charles's condition: the feelings or sensations that go with increased adrenaline, faster pulse rate, muscular tension, etc."

However, what Walton is calling "the more psychological aspects" of this quasi-state are explicitly things like sensations. And, these sensations, as I argued in the first chapter, can appear as constituents in many different psychological states. So how does Charles know on the basis of these sensations that his quasi-state is one of quasi-fear rather than one of quasi-excitement or quasi-indignation? In virtue of being aware of the cognitive states that give rise to these sensations? But then it sounds to me that Charles's state is simply a genuine state of fear. Or, to put the matter differently, it seems to me that quasi-fear is just plain fear. That is, it has all the elements of fear; so it is fear.

Walton might reject this by explicitly adopting an account of the emotions that would block this argument. But the burden of proof is on Walton. Moreover if this argument cannot be deflected, then it would seem correct to say that Charles knows to engage in pretend fear because, at stage one in his reaction, he is really afraid. So, at the very least, Walton's notion of pretend fear presupposes (rather than replaces) genuine fear.

That is, either quasi-fears have cognitive components or they don't. If they don't, then it is difficult to understand how they help Charles to realize that he should adopt pretend-fear rather than some other make-believe state. On this alternative, then, there is a gaping lacana in Walton's theory. On the other hand, if quasi-fear has a cognitive component, then it is a genuine emotion. And if it is a genuine emotion, then the theory is at best redundant and, more likely, self-defeating. The only way out of this dilemma for Walton, that I see, is for him to develop an alternative theory of the emotions to the one presumed in this book.

Walton seems to need quasi-fear in his theory in order that Charles will know what pretend-emotion is appropriate with respect to the fiction. However, it seems to me that if we are skeptical about the notion of quasi-fear, and suppose, given what Walton has told us, that Charles knows pretend fear is appropriate because he is initially in a state of geniune fear, then it is hard to see how embracing pretend fear can solve the paradox of fiction in the light of how Walton sees that problem. In the next section, I will explore an alternative way of solving the paradox of fiction.

23 I originally developed the thought theory as the result of discussions with Kent Bendall and Christopher Gauker and defended it in talks at the University of Warwick, The Museum of the Moving Image and LeMoyne College. Eventually, a version of it was incorporated in the essay that is the basis of this book: "The Nature of Horror," in the *Journal of Aesthetics and Art Criticism,* vol. 46, no.1 (Fall, 1987). Upon reading my essay, Richard Shusterman alerted me to a series of articles by Peter Lamarque which had developed a thought theory of fictional characters that was far more advanced and detailed than the one I had been working with; Lamarque had already had a clear conception about that toward which I was only groping. I have, in consequence, benefited greatly from Lamarque's work and a great deal of what follows is derived from his published work. See: Peter Lamarque, "How Can We Fear and Pity Fictions?," *British Journal of Aesthetics,* vol. 21 , no. 4, Autumn, 1981; Lamarque, "Fiction and Reality," in *Philosophy and Fiction,* ed. by Peter Lamarque, (Aberdeen: Aberdeen University Press, 1983); and Lamarque, "Bits and Pieces of Fiction," in the *British Journal of Aesthetics,* vol. 24, no. 1 (Winter 1984)

24 At one point, Walton suggests that one of the values of fictions and our make-believe interactions with it is that it enables us to practice with emotional crises. This notion is particularly ill-suited for his favorite example—horrific fiction. For one hardly needs to practice the way in which one will respond to the Green Slime. That would be like practicing on a nonexistent musical instrument; you'd never get to play it. Ditto Dracula, the Werewolf of London, his American counterpart, and the rest of the horrific bestiary.

25 The following discussion of the thought content toward which the emotion of art-horror is directed is heavily indebted to Peter Lamarque's "Fiction and Reality," and his "How Can We Fear and Pity Fictions?"

26 Gottlob Frege, "On Sense and Reference," in *The Logic of Grammar,* ed. Donald Davidson and Gilbert Harman (Belmont, California: Dickenson Publishing Co., 1975), p. 120. In a footnote appended to this statement, Frege notes that it would be convenient to have a special term for signs that have only sense. He opts for "representations," though that, it seems to me, would at this point be confusing since in current philosophical discourse that term can be applied to signs with reference as well as sense. But it is interesting to note that Frege's primary examples of signs without reference are *fictional representations* — the words of a play and the actor himself. This suggests that we might think of the genus to which fiction belongs as that of signs without reference. With fiction, we contemplate the sense of the text without concern for the truth value of what is literally conveyed by the text.

27 Frege, "On Sense and Reference," p. 117.

28 Lamarque, "How Can We Fear and Pity Fictions?"

29 John Searle, *Speech Acts*, p. 30.

30 An alternative way of speaking to propositional content talk here might be to adopt the notion of "situation type," as introduced by John Perry and Jon Barwise. This may be very useful in the context of art-horror, for the representations that we are discussing are not merely literary texts (to which the notion of a proposition neatly fits, though, of course, one should not think of propositions as sentences), but also pictorial representations, and situation types, ostensibly, are abstractions that can be used to classify pictures as well as utterances (e.g., the illustration on p. 59 of *Situations and Attitudes*). Using the idea of situation types, we might identify the relevant content of our thoughts with respect to horror fictions in terms of the abstract situation types we use to classify the "assertions" made in the representation, where these "assertions" are understood to be about fictions and not about the real world. We will say that our thought contents are to be identified and individuated with respect to the situation types that classify the representations in the fictions. To carry this analysis in detail would require elaboration, including extensively supplementing the approach to fiction that Barwise and Perry suggest on pp. 284–285. Though an eminently worthwhile research project, this is beyond the scope of the present book. For references, see Jon Barwise and John Perry, *Situations and Attitudes* (Cambridge, Massachusetts: The MIT Press, 1983).

It should also be noted that with the theory advanced in the text above the content of our thoughts with respect to fictions will generally have to be relativized to the texts we are reading and to the spectacles that we are viewing. The reason for this is that particular fictions can add or substract properties from even well-known horrific beings. For example, in Patrick Whalen's *Monastery*, we suddenly learn how vampires react to radioactivity, something that is a nonstandard part of the vampire myth. Because a given fiction can vary the properties of even an often repeated myth, it is best to think of the appropriate perimeter of the reader's thought as restricted to the text at hand. Whether there are features of a given myth which, so to speak, cross all the members of a subgenre and which need not be stated or implied by given fictions is a task for criticism to decide. If there are such cross-fiction presuppositions, they might be legitimate constituents of the reader's thoughts. However, without that knowledge, the more conservative strategy of identifying the legitimate compass of the reader's or viewer's with what is said or implied in the fiction seems the best course.

31 Bijoy Boruah, *Fiction and Emotion* (Oxford: Clarendon Press, 1988). This book was released while my own was in press. It deserves detailed study, but I have not had the opportunity to treat it in any depth. The cursory paragraph above, however, is a promissory sketch of the way in which I would defend the thought theory against Boruah's imagination theory.

32 This, of course, actually involves saying something about our relations to protagonists in all kinds of fictions, not just horror fictions.

33 Indeed, these considerations alone may suggest an argument to the effect that it is never necessary to postulate character-identification in describing our responses to protagonists. For if such central instances of our response to protagonist—such as suspense, sympathy, pathos, the laughter directed at comic butts, and so on—do not require the invocation of character identification to, for example, explain the intensity of our response, then we may demand to know why in whatever cases remain—if any do—we are compelled to invoke character-identification. That is, we will be entitled to ask what explanatory advantage character-identification affords, since we can be moved quite intensely by the plight of characters in many cases where there can be no question of identification.

34 Of course, if one said at this point is that what one means by identification is simply sharing parallel emotive evaluations, then the argument would be over. But I take it that this move

would amount effectively to an abandonment of any conception of identification that involved the fusion of identities.

35   Of course, there is a typical variation in which the protagonist's concern might be called altruistic. If the monster is chasing her lover, and the protagonist is struggling to save him, it may be plausible to infer—if she is not just driven by adrenaline—that her emotional state is altruistic. But even in this case, the audience's emotional state is different; it is more altruistic—since the audience is concerned not only for the heroine's lover but for the self-sacrificing heroine herself

36   A related motive for the belief in character-identification might be that its proponents think that the only explanation that we could have for our *intense* response to characters is that we identify, because we could only muster such an intense response for ourselves. However, this just flies in the fact of the facts. Feeling suspense with respect to a character would not seem to be plausibly explained in terms of identification. But it is quite often intense. Moreover, if intensity of response can be explained for cases like suspense without reference to character-identification, perhaps we should be suspicious about its postulation anywhere else

   Of course, another motive for thinking that the postulation of character-identification is necessary is the underlying belief that we could not respond with intensity unless we really believed that we were endangered by monsters. But this, of course, would return us to the sort of illusion theory rejected in the preceding section.

37   Hearing my arguments against identification, some listeners, like Berenice Reynaud, have commented that they believe that the relevant process of identification is not with characters but with the "position of knowledge of the story itself," by which they may mean something like the implied narrator. So when the shark in *Jaws* attacks an unwary swimmer, we are not identifying with the character, but with the some position of knowledge which the story itself or the implied narrator is said to have. A theory like this on identification would avoid the asymmetry problems that I have emphasized. However, it has problems of its own. Namely, why postulate identification with "the knowledge position of the story itself?" Why not just say that we know the shark is attacking the swimmer while the swimmer is unaware of this? What pressure from the data compels us to hypothesize either that there is such a "knowledge position" or that we undergo a process of "knowledge identification?" We can say everything we need to say in terms of what the audience knows without multiplying theoretical posits like knowledge positions and identification. Of course if you are pretheoretically committed to the notion of identification, such posits deal with the asymmetry problems, logically speaking. But the lack of any other motive for postulating these processes seems to me more of a rationalization of identification than a defense of it. Indeed, positing this process of identification violates the ontological principle of economy; it is unmotivated by any data that I can discern.

3   Plotting Horror

1   I have already discussed plots of this sort in my "Nightmare and the Horror Film: The Symbolic Biology of Fantastic Beings," *Film Quarterly*, vol. 34, no. 3 (Spring 1981). In that essay, I called the plot the discovery plot. For reasons that will become evident, I have not only changed the name of the plot structure, but I have also developed a much more complicated account of horror plotting than what is found in that essay. The present section on horror narration is meant to supersede my earlier speculations on the topic in a way that incorporates the strengths of that analysis while supplementing its oversimplifications.

2   Here I am making a point about onset; King's *It* is not straightforwardly an instance of a

complex discovery plot; it might be better thought of as a discovery plot, though one in which the process of discovery is iterated.

3 Often the characters and the audience come to discover the existence of the monster together. However, as noted above, it can be the case that the audience's realizations about the existence and nature of the monster can be phased in ahead of comparable realizations on the part of characters. In this case, one might wish to distinguish two lines of discovery in the narration—that of the audience, on the one hand, and that of characters on the other (And to further complicate matters, it is also the case that different characters or groups of characters can also discover the existence of the monster independently of each other.) Nevertheless, these different lines of discovery will tend to converge upon the decisive manifestation of the monster, the point at which the central protagonists become utterly convinced of the monster's presence. This point is crucial even for audiences already apprised of the monster's existence because they have been drawn into suspense over whether or not the human characters will discover the monster.

4 The importance of the detailed attribution of horrific properties to the monsters when they are offscreen and unseen may be relevant to explaining why horror movies, like mystery movies, appear to flourish most successfully after sound comes to film. Neither genre is a major genre of silent film. With mystery stories the reason for this is evident; a great deal of the impact of a detective story depends on talk—particularly on the detective's retelling of the course of events in his summing up at the end of the film. But all this talk becomes quite cumbersome when it is spelt out on the intertitles of silent film. Or, for that matter, think of all the intertitles that would be required to set forth the dialogue required by a courtroom mystery drama. Clearly, that amount of spoken language is more easily accommodated in an unbroken flow of information in a sound film; and this suggests why it is that mystery films only come into their own with sound.

However, I would argue that a similar point can be made with respect to horror films. Language, spoken language, is one of the most effective ingredients in a horror film. And I would guess that the genre's primary success in sound film rather than silent film, has less to do with the absence of sound effects in the silents than with the presence of all that dialogue about the unseen monsters in talkies. Bela Lugosi is not all that frightening to look at; but by the time Van Helsing finishes lecturing on vampires and what they can do, we are ready (we have been readied) to greet Dracula's advance with a shudder.

5 This play of ratiocination may not only be enacted by characters; the audience may also be piecing together clues. And where the audience has more clues available to it than do individual characters, its hypotheses may be in advance of those of the characters.

6 For a discussion of this device, see Harold Schechter, *The Bosom Serpent: Folklore and Popular Art* (Iowa City: University of Iowa Press, 1988).

7 Rotating the head 180 degrees is a feature of orgies of the sort associated with black sabbaths; it is a practice Satan putatively indulges when sodomizing witches.

8 This analysis of the plot structure of the play *Dracula*, like many of the plot explications in this section, is somewhat abbreviated. I have foregone the detailed, formal analyses of the plots of the examples in this section, since my aim is to convey an overall sense of the way in which these plots work and of the wide range of exemplifications of these plots. To give blow-by-blow narratological analyses of each of my examples would not only be daunting, but might in fact be counter-productive to the goal of giving a general outline of the relevant plot functions. I do, nevertheless, think that persuasive, precisely detailed, formal analyses of these examples can be supplied. I also think that the abstract schemata that I've sketched and filled in, albeit with often cursory observations, will be instrumental in developing more exact analyses of the texts and films in question, as well as many others.

9 Father Brennan is a bit different than a number of the discoverers that we've encountered so far. He seems to have been in on the original demonic plot to a certain extent, but then to have recanted. So it is not clear how much of what he tells Thorn about Damien is the result of what he has discovered as opposed to what he knew as a co-conspirator. In this respect, we might want to call him a discloser, rather than a discoverer. And we might want to call this variation the disclosure movement or disclosure function, rather than the discovery movement. I have not added this refinement to the account above, for it seems to me that the discovery function and the disclosure function appear to have pretty much the same role in terms of the overall narrative. However, future research may profit from exploring this and other subtle refinements in the plot structures outlined above.

At this point in my work, I regard the plot structures in this chapter as first approximations of basic horror structures. It is my intention that these first approximations will be used by other scholars as jumping-off points for the discovery of further plot structures (such as any I may have overlooked) and more fine-tuned analyses of the structures that I have identified. I regard my work here, and in other parts of this book, as provisional. I have attempted to make my theories about horror plots clear enough so that they can be profitably criticized for their shortcomings by others in a way that will extend research in the field. I don't think of these plot structures as the last word in the matter, but hope that they will stimulate and, through their clarity, even facilitate continued discussion, even where that discussion supersedes what is offered herein.

10 As many readers will recall, Jenning's decapitation is a stunning piece of cinema. As Jennings bends over to pick up the ritual knives, the brake of a truck is released and it rolls downhill until it hits an obstacle. This causes a piece of plate glass to slide off the back of the truck and it neatly severs Jenning's head from his trunk. This is shot in extremely graceful, even exquisite, slow motion. *The Omen*, like many horror films in the present horror cycle, orchestrates a series of cinematically spectacular deaths—grand guignols for the delectation of the audience. These scenes involve ingenious complications and breathtaking cinematic precision—e.g., Father Brennan's impalement. Often the momentum of such films seems toward increasingly ornate scenes of death and destruction—as if each later sequence were out to top the earlier ones. You can see this, for example, in the sequel to *The Omen*, the murders in the *Dr. Phibes* series, and the successive killings in the original *Halloween* and *Friday the 13th*.

In its taste for the spectacular—and in its proclivity toward escalating the spectacle—the recent horror film is part of a larger trend in contemporary cinema toward the fetishization of effects. Many films nowadays have replaced the "production numbers" of yesteryear with what I call "destruction numbers"—car chases, murders, shoot-outs and so on—of ever-increasing cinematic pyrotechnics. This is particularly evident in horror films, which supply obviously convenient pretexts for dazzling effects and feats of cinema. Perhaps it is no accident that at a period in which social commentators find intimately identified with spectacle, the horror film should reign supreme.

Similarly, the drift toward spectacle has also engulfed Broadway theater, which appears bent on mounting show after show on a scale many hitherto would associate with Hollywood. And, in the midst of this theater of effects, the current, biggest spectacle of them all is *Phantom of the Opera*.

11 It should also be remarked that the complex discovery plot is not unique to the horror genre. It can be found in other types of fantasies such as what I call the beautific/beatific (as opposed to the horrific) fantasy genre: e.g., *Close Encounters of the Third Kind* has a complex discovery plot quite reminiscent of films like *Jaws*, though what is discovered and confirmed to exist in the former film is an object of reverence rather than revulsion. Crime and detection thrillers might also employ this plot structure. Thus, the complex discovery plot is only a characteristic device of horror texts; it is not an essential device of

the genre. Nevertheless, as a characteristic device, it may still have a great deal to tell us about the genre.

12 For a more detailed account of *King Kong*, including discussion of its narrative structures and their generic sources, see my *"King Kong:* Ape and Essence" in *Planks of Reason,* ed. Barry Keith Grant (Meteuchen, New Jersey: The Scarecrow Press, 1984).

13 Of course, the vast majority of these possible plots will never be realized in practice because they would involve more iteration than the even the most avid horror buff could stand.

14 The overreacher (usually Dr. So-and-so), especially in this phase of the story, is generally quite megalomaniacal, a quality commented upon, for instance, by the dizzingly vertical labrotory sets in the Universal film productions of *Frankenstein* and *Bride of Frankenstein.*

15 Though I believe that the above aptly describes many of the most famous overreacher stories, allowance needs to be made in terms of this movement in the plot for the fact that some overreachers have as the point of their experiment bringing into existence a monster whose purpose is to wreck havoc. One thinks here of the creation of the robot in the classic film *Metropolis* by Fritz Lang. Since the robot is supposed to cause destruction, one should not say that this is an instance of the experiment going awry. To accommodate mad scientists and magicians who create in order to destroy, this movement in the overreacher plot might be best conceptualized as "the dire consequences of the experiment." However, as I have already noted, in the best examples of this plot, I think these dire consequences usually result in narrative contexts where the overreacher's expectations have been frustrated in putatively unforeseen ways.

16 See the preceding footnote for an alternate description of this plot function.

17 Sometimes elements of this "figuring out" are left up to the reader, as in Clive Barker's "Rawhead Rex," where we understand more about the significance of the stone Venus than the protagonist does (although he does do some on-the-spot ratiocination in the heat of confrontation).

18 Eric Rabkin, *Narrative Suspense* (Ann Arbor: University of Michigan Press, 1973).

19 Edmund Husserl, *The Phenomenology of Internal Time-Consciousness* (Bloomington: Indiana University Press, 1964). On page 76, Husserl writes: "Every primordially constitutive process is animated by protentions which voidly constitute and intercept what is coming, as such, in order to bring it to fulfillment."

20 Roland Barthes, "Structural Analysis of Narrative," in *Image-Music-Text* (New York: Hill and Wang, 1977). The quotation above comes from page 119.

21 For a fuller account of erotetic narration, see my *Mystifying Movies* (New York: Columbia University Press, 1988). Also see my "The Power of Movies," in *Daedalus,* vol. 114, no. 4, (Fall 1985).

22 One consequence of this analysis of suspense is that it enables us to discuss the relation between suspense and mystery. Mystery and suspense seem to be closely related phenomena. Often, mystery fictions are treated automatically as examples of suspense fiction. But does the preceding theory of suspense really capture the quiddity of mystery? In a very broad sense, of course, it does. A mystery will have a macro-question—will the criminal be caught or not? Presumably the apprehension of the criminal will be a moral good which, due to the ambiguity of the evidence, seems unlikely. But this application of the suspense formula does not aptly chacterize what is special about mystery, or, at least, what is called classical detective mystery by people like John Cawelti (see his *Adventure, Mystery and Romance* [Chicago: University of Chicago Press, 1976]).

The missing feature is that of the puzzle, which is the central element of the classical detective mystery. My solution to this problem is to claim that the classical detection fiction, while loosely in the realm of suspense, is better conceived of as a category unto itself, which in its most important respects is distinct from suspense. In distinguishing suspense from mystery I am making a distinction analogous to that made in the analysis of crime literature by Todorov when he divides thriller stories from detective stories. (See his "The Typology of Detective Fiction," in his *The Poetics of Prose* [Ithaca: Cornell University Press, 1977].

Given this formula, we can zero-in on the difference between suspense and mystery by considering the structure of the suspense question versus that of the classical mystery question. The suspense question has two competing answers. But the typical mystery question—who did it?—has as many answers as the fiction has suspects. The bulk of the mystery fiction is devoted to introducing an inventory of ambiguous leads and to a review of all the suspects who might have committed the crime. But the culprit, whose revelation we anticipate, is not unmasked until a scene near or at the end of the fiction.

To a limited extent the character of our anticipation is suspense at this point—we wonder whether the criminal will be found out or not. But at the same time, our anticipation is less focused on an outcome and more focused on a *solution,* a solution to the whodunit puzzle. Moreover, this puzzle can have many more than two alternative answers—it has as many potential answers as there are suspects. Thus, at the end of the film *The Thin Man,* everyone at the dinner table might be the culprit; the detective weighs the evidence in regard to each of them in a *tour de force* of speculation. But our anticipation is not structured in terms of two possible outcomes but is distributed over a handful of possible solutions. In *Murder on the Orient Express,* we have approximately ten alternative solutions before the investigator's summing-up, the quintessential moment in the classical detective genre.

Thus, though overlapping in some respects, the suspense fiction and the classical mystery might better be considered as distinct forms whose difference can be stated by reference to the different structures of their animating questions. In suspense, the animating question calls forth two contrasting outcomes, whereas in a mystery, the key question asks for a solution which is not limited to two contrasting answers but has as many different potential answers as there are suspects.

23 This approach to suspense was originally advanced in my "Toward a Theory of Film Suspense," in *Persistence of Vision,* no. 1 (summer 1984). Since that time, I have found that this approach correlates in significant ways with certain research in cognitive psychology. See especially: Paul Comisky and Jennings Bryant, "Factors Involved in Generating Suspense," in *Human Communications Research,* vol. 9, no. 1 (Fall 1982), pp. 49–58. In this article they see suspense as a function of uncertainty and of the audience's disposition to like the imperiled protagonist. Though they write of the disposition to like the protagonist rather than of the morality of the situation, it is clear from the way in which they framed their experimental material about the character (he is an *antisocial* recluse, or he is a *good* man, or he is a *fine* individual) that moral considerations are at the root of the experimental subjects' dispositions.

24 The recent film *Predator* seems to me to be essentially yet another reworking of "The Most Dangerous Game."

25 See Comisky and Bryant, "Factors Involved in Generating Suspense," p. 57.

26 Also, the human protagonists in horror stories are generally marked as virtuous, in contrast to the morally loathsome monsters. Thus, the probable destruction of the humans becomes suspenseful insofar as a moral wrong is implied by the prospective destruction of the *virtuous* human characters. On the role of virtues in securing the moral evaluation of the suspenseful situation see my "Toward a Theory of Film Suspense."

Comisky and Bryant do not speak of virtues in their characterization of suspense. But, it seems to me, that their account of the audience's pro-disposition toward the protagonist is intimately connected to the possession of what I call virtues. For research into the formation of said dispositions see: D. Zillman, "An Anatomy of Suspense," in *The Entertainment Functions of Television*, ed. P.H. Tannenbaum (Hillsdale, New Jersey: Erlbaum, 1980); D. Zillman, J. Bryant, and B.S. Sapolsky, "The Enjoyment of Watching Sport Contests," in *Sports, Games and Play*, ed. J. Goldstein (Hillsdale, New Jersey: Erlbaum, 1978); and D. Zillman and J.R. Cantor, "A Disposition Theory of Humor and Mirth," in *Humour and Laughter*, ed. A.J. Chapman and H.C. Foot (New York: Wiley, 1976).

27   This is a common device in suspense. Just as it looks like the representative of the forces of good has a chance, some complication—like forgetting the keys—is introduced in order to rev up the suspense machine one more time. In Clive Barker's "Rawhead Rex," when it appears as though the protagonist, Ron, has an advantage with his talisman, the mad deacon Declan jumps him, thereby momentarily, changing the odds in his master Rawhead's favor.

28   The talk of likelihoods or probabilities above refers to the likelihood that the audience assays for the alternative outcomes of scenes relative to each other *before* one outcome is actualized in the narrative. Moreover, I am talking about the probability of the outcomes as they are presented by the fiction, not as they would be in similar situations in life. That is, the probability of any human body—zombified or otherwise—actually withstanding a point-blank shot from a 30–30 is low; though, in *Night of the Living Dead*, given what the fiction says of the ghouls' physical make-up, such survival is plausible.

Also, I should add that I am categorically excluding from the audience's estimate of the relative probabilities, their knowledge of such desiderata of popular fiction as that the heroine is generally rescued just in the nick of time or that the hero usually doesn't get killed.

This talk of relative probabilities, I think, concretizes the essential truth of Alfred Hitchcock's emphasis—in *Hitchcock/Truffaut* (N.Y.: Simon and Schuster, 1967)—on the importance of the audience's having knowledge for suspense (as opposed to shock) to succeed. What I think the audience needs knowledge of is the relative likelihoods of the alternative outcomes of scenes.

Furthermore, the idea of probability that I have in mind in the characterization of suspense above is a nontechnical one. For a reader or spectator to believe that x is probable or improbable is not for the audience member to assign x some ranking or value in terms of the probability calculus. Rather it is for the audience to believe that if x is probable then x is likely to occur, or can be reasonably expected to occur, given all the available, permissable evidence advanced in the fiction. Nor does this imply that the audience is in its seat actively calculating probabilities of either the technical or nontechnical sort. I see two cars—headed at each other, three feet apart and each traveling over eighty miles per hour—and I immediately form the belief that a crash is likely, indeed, highly likely. Similarly, when the buzz saw is an inch away from the heroine's neck, and the hero is still in an anteroom battling with six fulgurating ninjas, I, *sans* conscious calculation, presume that the heroine's moments, in all probability, are numbered.

29   Throughout the preceding discussion of suspense, I have moved freely between examples from film, literature, and theater. The obvious reason for this is that I am attempting to sketch a general theory of suspense, one whose general outline should apply across media. This, of course, is not meant to say that different media may not have different resources and conventions for putting suspense in operation. For example, I think that there are certain differences in the formal means of literary suspense and film suspense that make attempts at bald extrapolation from the former to the latter problematic. In literary suspense, for instance, I have found that suspense is often narrated by going into the mind

of the characters to give us a direct, elaborate, and extended account of what the characters feel and of what they think their prospects are. That is, characters' thoughts, directly presented, supply us with assessments of the likelihood or improbability of various outcomes, as well as of the loathsomeness of their horrific nemeses. Moreover, these expatiations upon the inner assessments of characters can be sustained in detail in the midst of an action scene in literature. However that kind of portrayal of a suspenseful scene in film (perhaps by means of voice-over narration) is awkward and uncinematic, at least with respect to the prevailing norms of the action film.

30   For a more detailed exposition of the analysis and defense of suspense outlined above see my "Toward a Theory of Film Suspense."

31   Tzvetan Todorov, *The Fantastic* (Ithaca, New York: Cornell University Press, 1975).

32   One way that I am deviating from the letter of Todorov's account is that I am counting an explanation as supernatural (or, at least, not naturalistic) if it resorts to the invocation of sci-fi entities *as well as* if it resorts to supernatural entities. This corresponds to my conviction that the monsters in sci-fi are often not different in kind to those of horror stories. In order to sustain this insight, if it is an insight, I will take any explanation that depends on the existence of monsters not countenanced by science to be one that is opposed to a naturalistic explanation.

33   Todorov, *The Fantastic 33*.

34   The idea of a "loophole" here is inspired by M.R. James who in describing the mechanics of ghost stories says "It is not amiss sometimes to leave a loophole for a natural explanation, but I would say, let the loophole be so narrow as not to be quite practicable." See the introduction to his anthology entitled *Ghosts and Marvels*. Obviously, with a fantastic fiction as opposed to a ghost story, the naturalistic loophole has to be wide enough to trip up a naturalistic explanation.

35   Douglas Gifford, *James Hogg* (Edinburgh: The Ramsay Head Press, 1976), p. 145.

36   Gifford makes the case for these optical deceptions in *James Hogg*, pp. 149–51.

37   The phrase "justified sinner" may be intentionally ambiguous here. On the one hand it refers to a religious doctrine to which Wringhim subscribes: viz., that those predestined to be of the elect are justified sinners (those who will be saved despite their sins). On the other hand, under a naturalistic interpretation, Wringhim's projection of the *doppleganger* figure justifies (i.e., self-justifies) Wringhim in the face of all the accusations that can be brought against him.

38   Todorov, *The Fantastic*, p. 44.

39   Quoted in Todorov, *The Fantastic*, p. 38. The italics are Todorov's.

40   That is, these examples are what philosophers call referentially opaque contexts. From the statement "I believe that JFK was eight feet tall," one cannot infer that "JFK was eight feet tall." This is a feature of all the that-clauses introduced by propositional attitudes which Todorov reviews.

41   When I speak of "eyewitness certainty" in this section, I do not have in mind the kind of certainty that Descartes sought. Rather, I am thinking of the kind of eyewitness certainty manifested when I say that "I see the workmen in the backyard." In normal discourse, I can be certain of this eyewitness observation if certain criteria are met, even if for Descartes I cannot be certain that I am not afflicted by delusions served up by an evil deceiver.

This variety of certainty requires that I have a clear, unoccluded view of the objects of my perception, that I have enough time to recognize them and that I am close enough to identify them, along with the caveat that I am not in some unusual physical or psychological state that might impede my perception. This is the kind of eyewitness certainty that we trade on in everyday life. The criteria of eyewitness certainty are embodied in ordinary discourse, and they may come to the fore particularly on certain occasions, such as that of courtroom testimony. My thesis is that in cinema, the filmmakers can exploit our everyday intuitions about eyewitness certainty—and our informal grasp of what would stand up as eyewitness testimony before the law—in order to engender "fantastic hestitation" by deploying the means of cinematic narration—both visual and aural—in such a way that the representation of supernatural beings and events are problematized insofar as they fall short of meeting the criteria of eyewitness certainty.

42 I think the shot of the panther in this scene, though very brief, is sufficient to satisfy us that we've now got the kind of evidence by observation that we've wanted all along— though, of course, in some cases, the very brevity of such an observation, given the editing in certain films, might undermine our faith in opting for a supernatural hypothesis. That is, in certain instances, a glimpse might be too short to be reassuring; it might be just another way for the filmmaker to render the facts of the matter visually obscure and ambiguous.

43 This implicit distinction, though rooted in the epistemic practices of the culture at large, is made salient in the film itself in part by introducing the conflict of naturalistic and supernatural interpretations.

44 Earlier I noted that examples of the pure fantastic were rare in cinema. However, the discussion above concerning the availability of cinematic devices and conventions for the propagation of "fantastic hesitation" indicates that there are no technical or formal obstacles to implementing the pure fantastic in film. What then accounts for the fact that such exercises are very infrequent? My own *guess* is that the answer here probably has to do with the prospective market for such films.

Often it is a very young audience; it may have a positive preference for the supernatural. Also, many fantasy films are also action films, suggesting that their audiences have a taste for chases and debacles. The pure fantastic is less likely to accommodate this taste than the fantastic-marvelous, since in order to do so would generally appear to demand the production of a supernatural being for the purposes of confrontation. And this, of course, would frustrate the aims of the pure fantastic.

Undoubtedly, there are ways of handling this problem, such as substituting real violence with pyrotechnical cinematic spectacle (which, nevertheless, stays in the bounds of ambiguity), in the manner of the end of *The Innocents*. However, then, it may just be the case that, usually, movie audiences are more attracted by the prospect of having their supernatural hypotheses gratified immediately by the film than by the prospect of suspended judgment. In short, I suspect that answering our question—even if my attempts are all faulty— requires learning something about the kind of audiences that are typically drawn to horror and fantasy films.

4   Why Horror?

1 Frank McConnell, *Spoken Seen,* (Baltimore: Johns Hopkins University Press, 1975), p. 76.

2 Robin Wood, "Sisters," in *American Nightmare* (Toronto: Festival of Festivals Publication, 1979), p. 60

3 John and Anna Laetitia Aikin, "On the Pleasure Derived from Objects of Terror; with Sir Bertrand, a Fragment," in their *Miscellaneous Pieces in Prose* (London, 1773), pp. 119–37. John Aikin's sister also published under the name Anna Laetitia Barbauld.

In this article, it is true that the Aikens are not writing precisely about what I have called horror in this text; however, their questions are prompted by the kinds of writing that will give rise to the horror genre.

4   David Hume, "Of Tragedy," in *Of the Standard of Taste and Other Essays,* ed. John W. Lenz (Indianapolis: Bobbs-Merrill, 1965), p. 29. This essay was first published in 1757 in Hume's *Four Dissertations.*

5   John and Anna Laetitia Aikin, "An Enquiry into those Kinds of Distress which excite agreeable Sensations; with a Tale," in *Miscellaneous Pieces in Prose,* pp. 190–219.

6   Edmund Burke, *A Philosophical Enquiry into the Origin of our Ideas of the Sublime and Beautiful* (Notre Dame: University of Notre Dame Press, 1968), pp. 134–35. Burke's treatise was first published in 1757

7   H.P. Lovecraft, *Supernatural Horror in Literature* (New York: Dover Publications, 1973). Versions of this monograph were published in 1927 and 1945. The text is influential in two senses. First, it supplies certain norms concerning the effects and methods of horror fiction which were to be important to the many horror writers who followed in Lovecraft's footsteps. Second, its historical approach to the subject seems to me to be imitated in most attempts to give a general approach to horror. That is, in contradistinction to the present book, most of Lovecraft's text is concerned to narrate the history of the horror genre; and, it strikes me, that this narrative approach to elucidating the genre is the standard way of examining it. See, for example, Stephen King's interesting *Danse Macabre.* (New York: Berkley Books, 1987).

8   Lovecraft, *Supernatural Horror In Literature,* p. 16.

9   Lovecraft, *Supernatural Horror in Literature,* p. 14.

10 In his introduction to *Hardshell* in the *Night Visions* anthology series, Clive Barker offers a predictably un-Lovecraftian explanation of the source of the horror genre's attraction. In implicit opposition to the more mystical bent of Lovecraft, Barker sees the address of horror from an earthly viewpoint. Horror stories dramatize "our confrontation as spirits with the brutal business of physicality," something the recognition of which we are said to avoid assiduously. The major problem I see with Barker's approach, as a general characterization of horror, is that it fails to explain why, if horror compels due to its presentation of repressed knowledge about bodily deterioration, it must do so with all the supernaturalist trappings that are essential to the genre. On the other hand, Barker's introduction is very informative about his own conception of horror fiction as *stories of the body.* For this conception patently underwrites his immensely original contributions to the genre as a writer, anthologist, filmmaker, and connoisseur.

11 Lovecraft, *Supernatural Horror in Literature,* p. 15.

12 Undoubtedly, there would be some disagreement among commentators about whether the audience for horror is best described as "sensitive."

13 Indeed, many horror stories with their urge to explain everything would appear to ape materialistic sophistication.

14 Rudolf Otto, *The Idea of the Holy: An Inquiry into the Non-Rational Factor in the Idea of the Divine and its Relation to the Rational,* trans. John W. Harvey (London: Oxford University Press, 1928).

15 Otto, *Idea of the Holy,* pp. 12–24.

16 Otto, *Idea of the Holy,* p. 26.

17 In John Coyne's *The Hunting Season,* at one of the nodal points of disclosure, we read: "April swallowed hard at the sight of the small creature, the strange alabaster girl-child lying on the dirty sheets. Yet she couldn't look away. The child repelled and fascinated her."

18 Philip C. Almond, *Rudolf Otto: An Introduction to His Philosophical Theology* (Chapel Hill: University of North Carolina Press, 1984), p. 69.

19 See Almond, *Rudolf Otto* pp. 80–81, for an account of the way in which daemonic dread falls short of numinous experience.

20 Though I shall not pursue the matter at length, I would also want to deny that the attraction of art-horror can be developed on an analogy with the sublime. Rather than protract the argument, I will primarily fall back upon the authority of Kant, our leading architect of the concept of the sublime. In section 48 of the "Analytic of the Sublime," from his *The Critique of Judgement* Kant writes: "There is only one kind of ugliness which cannot be represented in accordance with nature without destroying *all aesthetic satisfaction,* and consequently artificial beauty, viz. that which excites *disgust.* For in this singular sensation which rests on mere imagination, the object is represented as if it were obtruding itself for our enjoyment, while we strive against it with all our might. And the artistic representation of the object is no longer distinguished from the nature of the object itself in our sensation, and thus it is impossible that it can be regarded as beautiful." Emphasis added. Here Kant argues that any aesthetic satisfaction is inimical to disgust. I am not completely sure this is right; however, it at least suggests an initial reason to suspect that art-horror cannot be assimilated to Kant's notion of the sublime, which is about the best characterization we've got of it. This, of course, is not decisive. I cite Kant in order to bypass what would be an extremely detailed exposition of the sublime for the purpose of showing it ill suits art-horror. Like Kant, though perhaps for different reasons, I think that the element of repulsion required in art-horror precludes the kinds of response engendered by either the mathematical or the dynamical sublime.

   Edmond Burke, as is well known, offers a somewhat different account of the sublime. For him terrifying objects can cause sublime delight just in case we are not in harm's way of said objects. Burke does not consider how disgust might figure in this picture. But here I think that Kant's observations are relevant. For if we are disgusted by an object, we are, in Burke's idiom, pained by it—genuinely pained by it—and so it does not correlate to the kind of distance Burke maintains the sublime requires. As Kant suggests, disgust stands in the way of the sublime. This is not a direct criticism of Burke's notion of the sublime. Rather, it is a consideration that should warn one against trying to assimilate art-horror to the Burkean sublime.

21 One wonders whether when the attractions of horror are contrasted to materialism and positivism, we are supposed to think that something like a taste for rationalistic explanation ought to be included in the latter. For if this is the case, then it is hard to see how the contrast can be maintained since so much horror fiction—in its internal momentum—imitates rationalistic explanations. That is, though the explanations horror fictions provide are customarily downright silly, they nevertheless ape the forms of rational explanation. Thus horror would not appear to provide an escape hatch from rationalizing explanations since to a large extent it often celebrates, or at least exploits, the form of such explaining.

   Another variation on the instinctual theme is to say that horror fictions enable us to entertain some sort of primordial play with death. In his "Aesthetics of Fright" (*American Film,* vol. 5, no. 10 [September, 1980]), Morris Dickstein analogizes consuming horror fiction with fairground attractions as if this provided an explanation related to the death instinct. He writes: "Horror films are a safe, routinized way of playing with death, like going on the roller coaster or parachute jump at an amusement park. There is always *some* chance however remote, that the car will jump the tracks—otherwise the thrill would be gone—but this death trip is essentially vicarious." This analogy, however, is perfectly insane and explains nothing. There is no risk of death in watching horror movies, no matter what chagrined parents might say. What could Dickstein possibly be thinking about?

22 The notion that horror attracts simply because it is emotionally invigorating is frequently advanced. For example, see Frank Coffey's introduction to his anthology *Masters of Modern Horror*.

23 An argument somewhat along these lines seems to be developed by Edmund Burke in his *Enquiry*. In his discussion of the sublime, which he associates with objects of terror, he thinks that the pain that would ordinarily accrue to such objects is relieved by the fact that we do not feel imperiled by them. For Burke, the relief of pain, in turn, causes delight. As well, Burke posits a rationale for seeking this kind of delight. Just as our body needs exercise, lest it atrophy, so our *finer feelings* need exercise. Seeking out the objects of the sublime (like the gigantic, the obscure, the dark, etc.) given circumstances where these properties are not threatening to self-preservation, keeps our finer feelings from stagnating.

The problem with this account is, of course, that it does not give us any reason why horror would be sought out in particular; wouldn't any sort of object of terror do? This, in a way, is not a fair criticism of Burke, since it was not his intent to offer an analysis of horror. But this is a problem for anyone who would wish to extend a Burke-type analysis to horror. Moreover, it is not clear that we should accept Burke's analogy of bodily exercise with emotional exercise. And, even if we did, we should want to ask if every emotion is deserving of the justificatory exercise he advocates. Considering the stupendous unlikelihood of our ever encountering a horrific monster, what purpose is served by our exercising the finer feeling of art-horror?

24 In *The Paradox of Cruelty* (Middletown, Connecticut: Wesleyan University Press, 1969), pp. 63–84, Philip Hallie offers a theory of horror that involves not only fear and disgust but attraction, specifically, attraction to the horrific creature or, in Hallie's terms, the victimizer. For Hallie, horror involves imaginatively inhabiting not only the position of the victim (which brings fear and repulsion into play), but also the position of whoever terrorizes the victim. Melmoth the Wanderer is Hallie's preferred example. Now I think that Philip Hallie does say a great deal that is useful about *this type of horror*. But he is speaking about a type or subgenre of horror when he notes (and insightfully interprets) the way in which such monsters seduce their audience. For not all of the monsters in the horror genre are seductive; many (The Blob?) cannot be seductive even if they are very, very powerful. Thus, the notion that the attraction of the horror genre is rooted in the attracting power of the monsters—though a useful observations for subgenres involving figures such as Dracula—is not theoretically adequate for horror in general.

25 That is, something like a psychoanalytic take on the imagery of the horror genre is often internal to given works of horror, e.g., the film *The Forbidden Planet*.

26 See my, "Nightmare and the Horror Film: The Symbolic Biology of Fantastic Beings," in *Film Quarterly*, vol. 34, no. 3 (Spring, 1981). An expanded version of this appeared in Udena Publications's *The Anxious Subject: Nightmares and Daymares in Literature and Film*, ed. Moshe Lazar (Malibu: Udena Publications, 1983).

27 Ernest Jones, *On the Nightmare* (London: Liveright, 1971).

28 Jones, *On the Nightmare*, p. 78.

29 See Sigmund Freud, "The Poet in Relation to Daydreaming," in the anthology *Character and Culture*, ed. Philip Rieff (New York: Collier Books, 1963).

30 The main character, Parkins, is introduced as effeminate ("henlike") and the maids "giggle" in a suggestive way when he announces he plans to have a male roommate in a few days. He summons the spirit—who is, in fact, an unwanted sleeping partner—inadvertently by *blowing a whistle*. This whistle, in turn, has been unearthed at an archaeological site. Given the kinds of associations that psychoanalysis warrants, then, it at least seems plausible to

conjecture that the spirit might be interpreted as a figure of Parkins's repressed homosexual desire.

31   Jones, *On the Nightmare*, p. 79.

32   John Mack, *Nightmare and Human Conflict* (Boston: Little Brown, 1970).

33   The importance of the infantile delusion of the omnipotence of thought for such fictions is discussed by Freud in his "The 'Uncanny,' " in *Studies in Parapsychology*, edited by Philip Rieff (New York: Collier Books, 1963), pp. 47–48.

34   One psychoanalytic counter-attack to my argument might be that since horrific creatures in my account must involve disgust, then psychoanalysis will always be relevant, because psychoanalysis claims that all disgust has its origin in such processes as repression. Obviously, we should want to derail such a counterargument by denying that the causes of disgust are solely in the province of psychoanalysis. Just as not all fear of being devoured is traceable to childhood fantasies of being devoured by a parent, not all disgust is traceable to the operation of psychoanalytic mechanisms. Note how in earlier sections of this book, via Mary Douglas, disgust could be elucidated without reference to psychoanalysis.

35   Freud, "The 'Uncanny,' " p. 55.

36   Freud, "The 'Uncanny,' " p. 51. What I think Freud believes must be added to meeting this necessary condition in order to render his characterization of the uncanny sufficient as well is that what is repressed be connected to either infantile complexes or primitive beliefs.

37   See Rosemary Jackson, *Fantasy: The Literature of Subversion* (London: Methuen, 1981).

38   Jackson, *Fantasy*, p. 4. Note that Jackson speaks of fantasy here and not horror. Nevertheless I feel entitled to criticize her formula with respect to horror because I believe that on her view—given her examples—horror is a subcategory of fantasy and, therefore, the formula is supposed to fit it.

39   Jackson, *Fantasy*, p. 48.

40   There is another variant of the repression hypothesis that is becoming popular. This construes the horror fiction as a drama of reenacted repression. Terry Heller writes: "We can follow the hints offered by Andrew Griffin and Christopher Craft and hypothesize that the horror thriller offers a reenactment of repression. By bringing readers into carefully controlled contact with symbolic representations of the culturally forbidden and affirming that control, the horror thriller becomes one of a culture's instruments of repression. The reader of Lovecraft or Brown becomes better at repressing the forbidden by meeting it again in another identity—the implied reader—and repeating original acts of repression. Henry James, Edgar Allan Poe, and others, including filmmakers such as Val Lewton, have helped to make us aware that horror images are most effective when minimally specified because the reader is then encouraged to read his own personal versions of cultural repressions into the images. . . . Now we may further hypothesize that works that encourage this kind of reading will be more greatly valued because the individual reader will be enabled to reenact his personal repressions. Both Lovecraft and Brown give the reader opportunities to meet the repressed and to reassert the power of identity over it. The power of choosing ourselves as personalities in whole bodies is one of humanity's major accomplishments; it is something that, on the whole, humans do well. The main visible result of this activities is a rich variety of human cultures. It would seem natural then, to take pleasure in 'doing it again.' " (From Terry Heller, *The Delights of Terror: An Aesthetics of the Tale of Terror* [Urbana: University of Illinois Press, 1987], pp. 72–73.) See also: Christopher Craft, " 'Kiss Me with Those Red Lips': Gender and Inversion in Bram Stoker's *Dracula*," in *Representations: 8* (Fall 1984); and, Andrew Griffin, "Sympathy for the Werewolf," *University Publishing*, 6 (1979).

The idea here seems to be that with horror fictions we reenact repressions that we have already undergone in the process of acculturation. That is, the plot of a horror thriller introduces the monster—a figure of repressed psychic material—only to (in general) obliterate every vestige of the return of the repressed by the end of the fiction. As we participate in the story as readers, we reenact the suppression of this psychically troubling material. In turn, repression, on this view, seems to be pleasurable, and, therefore, having the opportunity to repress once more what is culturally unacknowledged again gives us pleasure. Thus the paradox of horror is dissolved by showing that the manifestation of the horrific, though horrifying, affords a pretext for indulging pleasurable repression which more than outweighs the reader's discomfort.

This hypothesis posits that repression is pleasurable. I have no idea whether this is correct, though it sounds suspicious. It does not seem to be the standard view of repression. Nevertheless, it may be true; whether it is is beyond the scope of a book like this.

However, it is important to stress that this view apparently contradicts the standard account of how repression figures in promoting pleasure with respect to horror. In the standard account, repression is not pleasurable. What is pleasurable is the lifting of repression. Therefore, it would appear to be ill-advised—without further explanation—to attempt to combine the repression-reenactment account of horror with the standard repression hypothesis. That is, repression can't be pleasurable and unpleasurable at the same time. Only one—if either—of these hypotheses can be right; which one—if either—is to be preferred is a debate for psychoanalytic critics and theorists. Since I have questioned the standard repression hypothesis above, and since I, on admittedly personal and introspective grounds, question the notion that repression is pleasurable, I shall not enter this debate.

41 Hume, "Of Tragedy," pp. 33–34.

42 Hume, "Of Tragedy," p. 35.

43 With respect to some genres, like tragedy, the pleasure that the Aikins believe we have derives not from the distressful situation itself but from our response to the distressful situation. That is, we are distressed by the tragic event, and then we take pleasure in noting that we are the kind of morally concerned persons who are shaken by such events. Pleasure in the objects of terror seem more mysterious to them. For they do not see what it is about our terrified response and what having that response indicates about us that would give us satisfaction. This difficulty prompts them to search for an account of the pleasures of distressful, fictional events—of the terrifying variety—in terms of such narrative elements as suspense.

Interestingly, in a recent paper entitled "The Pleasures of Tragedy"—in *American Philosophical Quarterly*, vol. 20, no. 1, January 1983—Susan Feagin opts for a similar view of the pleasures of tragedy. The pleasure derived here, she believes, is a *metaresponse*, a satisfaction with the fact that we react sympathetically to tragic events. Later in the text we will take up the question of whether or not Feagin's idea of a metaresponse might not be useful in dealing with at least some aspects of the paradox of horror.

44 J. and A.L. Aikin, "Of the Pleasure derived from Objects of Terror," p. 123–24.

45 The special fermata over the discovery/disclosure of the monster in horror narratives is also in evidence in some of the most standardly employed expositional strategies in movies. For example, with respect to point of view editing in horror films, J.P. Telotte writes: "one of the most frequent and compelling images in the horror film repertoire is that of the wide, staring eyes of some victim, expressing stark terror or disbelief and attesting to an ultimate threat to the human proposition. To maximize the effect of this image, though, the movie most often reverses what is a standard film technique and, in fact, the natural sequence of events. Normally an action is presented and then commented upon with reaction shots; the cause is shown and then its effect. The horror film, however, tends to

reverse the process, offering the reaction shot first and thus fostering a chilling suspense by holding the terrors in abeyance for a moment; furthermore, such an arrangement upsets our ordinary cause-effect orientation. What is eventually betrayed is the onset of some unbelievable terror, something which stubbornly refuses to be accounted for by our normal perceptual patterns." Though I do not agree with the analysis—in terms of identification—that Telotte appends to this description, the description itself is an apt one of a recurring cinematic strategy in horror films, and it suggests the way in which this editing figure reflects, in the form of a "mini-narrative," the larger rhythms of discovery and disclosure in horror plotting. See J.P. Telotte, "Faith and Idolatry in the Horror Film," in *Planks of Reason,* ed. Barry Keith Grant (Metuchen, New Jersey: The Scarecrow Press, 1984), pp. 25–26.

46　In claiming that the pleasures derived from horror are cognitive in the broad sense—of engaging curiosity—I am attempting to explain why the genre often engages us. I am not attempting to justify the genre as worthy of our attention because its appeal is cognitive. Nor by saying that it is cognitive, in the special sense of engaging curiosity, am I even implicitly signaling that I think it superior to some other genres whose appeal might be said to be exclusively emotive.

47　"Ideally" here is meant to take note of the fact that not all such horror fictions are successful.

48　This is not said to retract my earlier claim that with disclosure-type narration our fascination fastens primarily on the way in which our curiosity is orchestrated. However, in order to be orchestrated and to have that orchestration rewarded, the monster will ideally be capable of some independent source of fascination. And that source of fascination, I conjecture, is its anomalous nature.

49　David Pole, *Aesthetics, Form and Emotion* (New York: St. Martin's Press, 1983), pp. 228–229.
　　In composing the last stages of this book I was pleasantly surprised to learn that the late David Pole had reached a number of the same conclusions about disgust and horror that I advanced in the opening part of this book in his essay "Disgust and Other Forms of Aversion" (in *Aesthetics, Form and Emotion*). Much of this correspondence in approach is explicable by the fact that both Pole and I rely very heavily on the researches of Mary Douglas. Pole explicitly cites Mary Douglas's book *Implicit Meanings,* a text that I also independently consulted in the construction of my theory. (See Mary Douglas, *Implicit Meanings* [London: Routledge & Kegan Paul, 1975]).
　　There are, however, some differences between Pole's view and my own. He considers horror in the actual contexts as well as aesthetic ones, whereas my focus is narrowly on art-horror. Also, whereas I am only concerned with the way in which entities, specifically beings, are horrifying, Pole is interested in horrifying events as well as entities. Nevertheless, both of us take disgust to be a central element in horror, and both see the disgust and fascination of horrific things to be grounded in their categorically anomalous nature.
　　But there is one point of strong disagreement between Pole and myself. Pole thinks that every instance of horror involves self-identification of the audience with the object of horror. When the horrific is manifested we incorporate it through some process of identification such that it becomes part of us, (p. 225). The gesture of being horrified, then, is seen as an extrusion or expulsion of that which is disgusting, which has been incorporated. The model of being horrified here is that of vomiting.
　　I find this hypothesis dubious. In previous sections I have argued against the notion of identification. Also, I have maintained that if identification amounts to admiring or being seduced by horrific creatures like Dracula, then, even in this loose sense, identification is not definitory of all our encounters with horrific beings. That is, identification in this psychologically inoffensive sense is not a comprehensive feature of art-horror.

Undoubtedly, an advocate of Pole's position would respond to this objection by noting that Pole includes under the rubric of *self-identification* being interested in or fascinated by the object of horror. But to view identification (even "self-identification"), interest, and fascination in the same light distorts all of the concepts in this cluster beyond recognition. I do not have to identify with everything that interests me; nor need I be fascinated by everything with which I identify (for I might not be fascinated by myself). In any case, the extension of the concept of identification to subsume interest is clearly strained. Therefore, I question the viability of the identification/fascination/interest characterization of horror, which, of course, also challenges the extrusion/vomiting model of the horrific response as an adequate, general theory.

Moreover, Pole appears to me to want us to think of disgust exclusively as a process in which we imaginatively swallow the object of our loathing and then spit it out. But with regard to horror, it is hard to imagine swallowing something as big as Mothra or even something the size of the Creature from the Black Lagoon. And in any case, not all disgust, it seems to me, is connected with oral incorporation, e.g., the aversion to funestation (something that comes into play with many monsters, such as zombies).

50 In her article, "A Strange Kind of Sadness," Marcia Eaton postulates that in order to appreciate distressing fictional events we must somehow be in control. As Gary Iseminger points out—in his "How Strange A Sadness?"—that the idea of control here is a bit ambiguous. However, if the control that Eaton has in mind is self-control (rather than control over the events in the story), then adoption of the thought theory of fictional response with respect to horror could explain how we have this control, by virtue of the fact that we are knowingly only responding to the thought that some impure creature is devouring human flesh. Indeed, perhaps the very notion that I am merely *entertaining* this thought implies the requisite self-control. See Marcia Eaton, "A Strange Kind of Sadness," in *The Journal of Aesthetics and Art Criticism*, vol. 41, no. 1 (Fall 1982); and, Gary Iseminger, "How Strange A Sadness?" in *The Journal of Aesthetics and Art Criticism*, vol. 42, no.1 (Fall 1983).

In his "Enjoying Negative Emotions in Fictions," John Moreall also cites the importance of control in enjoying fictions. He seems to suggest that such control enables us to vicariously feel the pleasure that the characters when they are angry or sad (p. 102). But I am not convinced that it is correct to say of the victims in horror fictions that they can feel pleasure in the state they are in. Perhaps some examples of anger and sadness have pleasureable dimensions. But surely not all the emotional states of fictional characters have such a dimension—surely, for example, horror does not. See John Moreall, "Enjoying Negative Emotions in Fiction," in *Philosophy and Literature*, vol. 9, no. 1 (April 1985).

51 If I am statistically wrong about the pervasiveness of disclosure narration in the genre, then I would probably want to rename the second part of my view *the special theory* of the appeal of horror. For I think the account of the appeal of disclosure narration offered above is right for that "special" group of horror narratives even if that group does not represent the most common formation in the genre. Needless to say, however, at present, I still am of the opinion that the drama of disclosure—in the ways discussed earlier in the book— is the most commonly practiced form in the genre.

52 See Iseminger, "How Strange A Sadness?," pp. 81–82; and Marcia Eaton, *Basic Issues in Aesthetics* (Belmont, California: Wadsworth Publishing Company, 1988), pp. 40–41.

53 Interestingly, I think that psychoanalytic accounts of horror also turn out to be co-existentialist, for the disgust and fear that the imagery elicits is the price that must be paid in order to have repressed wishes manifested without censorship.

54 Some informal evidence for this might include: 1) that within the fantasy movie cycles of the last decade and a half, there is an easy movement from the dominance of horror entries

like the *Omen* series, to space odysseys, like *Star Wars*, to benign fantasies like *E. T.*, *Splash*, *Cocoon*, to sword and sorcery quests, like *The Never Ending Story*, *Willow*, *Labyrinth*, *Legend*, *Princess Bride*, *Dark Crystal*, etc. 2) that popular writers like King can move from horror to sword and sorcery without losing their following

55 Feagin, "The Pleasures of Tragedy;" and Marcia Eaton, *Basic Issues in Aesthetics*, p. 40.

56 Fredric Jameson, "Magical narratives: romance as genre," *New Literary History*, 7, 1 (Autumn 1975), pp. 133–63.

57 Some readers may be surprised that I have not reviewed the possibility of some sort of catharsis explanation—after the fashion often attributed to Aristotle's analysis of tragedy—of the pleasures of horror. Such an approach sees the aesthetic pleasure of distressful representations to be a matter of having our negative emotions relieved. Stated one way, this kind of theory is quite absurd. The pleasure in a given genre is located in getting rid of certain negative feelings that we have. But we only have these feelings because a given instance of the genre has engendered the relevant displeasure in us in the first place. And this hardly makes the interest we have in the works in the genre plausible. For it would make no sense for me to put my hand in a vise simply for the pleasure of having my pain relieved when the vise is loosened.

Of course, a catharsis theorist might avoid this attempted refutation by analogy by claiming that the negative emotions relieved are not those engendered by the fiction itself but rather are negative emotions that have built up over the course of everyday life. The cathartic effect, then, would be the evacuation of these pent-up emotions. But if this is the way that catharsis is thought of, then it will clearly have no application to art-horror. For horror of the sort found in horror fictions has no correlate in ordinary life and, therefore, cannot be pent-up in the course of everyday events. This is entailed by the fact that we don't encounter monsters in everyday life; so we are not accumulating the requisite sort of negative emotion to be relieved upon attending to horror fictions. This indicates that catharsis cannot possibly be the correct model for art-horror; whether it is relevant to the discussion of other negative, aesthetic emotions is an issue beyond the scope of this book.

58 Perhaps this is one reason why when you read political criticism of horror fictions, you will sometimes encounter, with the self-same fiction, one critic finding it emancipatory and the other finding it repressive. That is, because the fiction is really vague and indeterminate with respect to any political point, each critic can read his or her own *parti pris* into it. I, however, would at least leave open the *possibility* that a politically vague and indeterminate horror fiction might have no ideological point, admitting, as well, the *possibility* that empirically based reception studies might reveal that even though vague, a given fiction, in a specific social context, in fact, did have ideological repercussions. Of course, we should also be willing agree that empirically based reception studies might indicate that the horror fiction in question had no such effects.

59 One might want to deal with the objection in this paragraph in another way: viz., by expanding the list of the ideologically suspect themes and, then, claiming that any horror fiction will fall into at least one of these categories. Such a claim, however, cannot be evaluated until someone produces the list in question.

60 Barry B. Longyear's novella *Enemy Mine*, as well as its film adaptation by Wolfgang Petersen, both include horrific elements and are opposed to racial bigotry and oppression. John Sayle's movie *Brother From Another Planet*, though perhaps not a full-blooded case of horror, is also anti-racist.

61 Tim Underwood and Chuck Miller, eds., *Bare Bones: Conversations on Terror with Stephen King* (New York: McGraw-Hill Book Company, 1988), p. 9.

62 King, *Danse Macabre*, p. 39.

63 King, *Danse Macabre*, p. 48.

64 E.g., Steven Neale, *Genre* (London: British Film Institute, 1980).

65 In the introduction of *Madame Crowl's Ghost*, M.R. James gives an instructive recipe for these first two movements: "Let us, then, be introduced to the actors in a placid way; let us see them going about their ordinary business, undisturbed by foreboding, pleased by their surroundings; and into this calm environment let the ominous thing put out its head, unobtrusively at first, and then more insistently, until it holds the stage."

66 Max Gluckman, *Custom and Conflict in Africa* (Glencoe, Illinois: Free Press, 1965). See also, Gluckman, "Rituals of Rebellion in South East Africa," in his *Order and Rebellion in Tribal Africa* (Glencoe, Illinois: Free Press, 1963).

67 Though perhaps the first of the quotations by Stephen King above might suggest a way to begin such an account.

68 It should be noted that the safty-valve model of inversion rituals has been challenged by many anthropologists and other social scientists. See T.O. Beidelman, "Swazi Royal Ritual," in *Africa*, 36, 1966; Peter Rigby, "Some Gogo Rituals of Purification: an Essay on Social and Moral Categories," in *Dialectic in Practical Religion*, ed. Edmond Leach (Cambridge: Cambridge University Press, 1968); Roger Abrahams and Richard Bauman, "Ranges of Festival Behavior," in *The Reversible World: Symbolic Inversion in Art and Society*, ed. Barbara Babcock (Ithaca: Cornell University Press, 1978). Thus, one cannot rely on the anthropological authority of the safety-valve model with respect to rebellion rituals to strengthen the case vis à vis horror, since this model has been questioned within anthropology itself.

  Moreover, the newer anthropological models of inversion rituals do not seem adaptable to horror. They involve the notion of the social conflicts of a given community being accommodated (rather than resolved). However, this requires a community with a rich set of relations—such as totemic ones—that can be inverted and so on. But horror fictions are not made within such communities; the fusion figures in the genre do not play with recombining totemic figures that stand for different social formations due to a shared myth. Such fusion figures may be made to stand for certain social relations within a given horror fiction. But they do not have antecedent, communal recognition outside given works. This, one assumes, may be a function of the fact that horror fictions are the product of mass society, not folk society. Mass society may lack the necessary, shared, totemic-type symbolism for such rituals of rebellion. And, that may provide yet another reason not to think of horror fictions in general as analogous to rebellion rituals (though, needless to say, one could attempt to make a horror fiction that, in pertinent respects, analogized certain of the forms and functions of rebellion rituals).

69 Even if—and that's a big *if*—this is the right way of putting what happens in horror plots. My worry here is: in what sense, if a horrific being really challenged a classificatory category, could killing it be conceived of as reinstating the category? The appearance of the monster in and of itself, at least in the fiction, should count against the relevant classificatory scheme; a dead monster is a dead counterexample, but a counterexample none the less.

70 If the value commitment of a given horror fiction were identified as "killing innocent people is bad," and this was said to be political, I would regard it as trivial insofar as all political interest groups will to agree to it.

71 "Books" here refers to copies not titles.

72 A tendency toward returning to the sympathy for the monster theme appears increasingly in recent horror fiction, e.g., Barker's *Cabal* and Terence J. Koumaras's *Eye of the Devil*.

In Robert R. McCammon's bestseller *The Wolf's Hour,* lycanthropy is enlisted in the war against Fascism.

73 Obviously another fear appears to be lurking in the fifties' sci-fi cycle, viz., the anxieties of the nuclear age. A number of the monsters of this cycle seem to be reflections of worries about the effects of radiation on genetic material—the blue roses of Brookhaven effect.

74 Jack Sullivan, "Psychological, Antiquarian and Cosmic Horror, 1872–1919," in *Horror Literature: A Core Collection and Reference Guide,* ed, Marshall B. Tymm (New York: R.R. Company, 1981), p. 222.

75 Ann Douglas, "The Dream of the Wise Child: Freud's 'Family Romance Revisited in Contemporary Narratives of Horror," *Prospect,* 9 (1984), p. 293. Though I am not always convinced by Douglas's psychoanalytic interpretations of this subgenre, I think that her general characterization, as cited, of the source of interest in the cycle—minus the implication of anxieties about the atomic bomb—is accurate.

76 Since I am willing to take the "social anxiety model" as affording the basis of an explanation of why horror may command attention at certain historical junctures, it may be wondered why I did not consider such an explanation as a generic account of the appeal of horror. That is, if we suppose that people are interested in horror because it provides imagery that speaks to their anxieties in some cases, why not say that this is an enduring source of attraction of the genre? I have two reasons for doubting this: 1) horror appears and is consumed in times that are not marked by social crisis and anxiety; horror has its own audience even when it is not a reigning popular form; 2) the reflection of social anxieties alone does not seem to me to be compelling enough a draw; lectures on social problems are not known for their mass appeal; something else must be in place, like the possibility of fascination, before the reflection of social anxieties have their supplemental effect. And, of course, it is that supplemental effect that is crucial for accounting for why, though horror has been with us continuously since its inception, it is only at certain junctures that large scale cycles emerge.

Moreover, if it is not clear already, I should explicitly state that I do not think that the social anxiety model—either as applied to horror cycles or to the genre as a whole—can be reduced without remainder to either the psychoanalytic or the ideological theories of horror reviewed earlier. For the relevant social anxieties in a given set of historical circumstances need not be repressed, nor psychosexual, nor need their manifestation either subvert or reaffirm the reigning social order.

77 On the intertextuality of the contemporary horror film, see especially: Philip Brophy, "Horrality—The Textuality Of Contemporary Horror Films," reprinted in *Screen,* vol. 27, no. 1 (January–February 1986) pp. 2–13.

78 The connection with post-modernism sometimes seems virtually explicit in the work of (genre relative) avant-gardists like John Skipp and Craig Spector. For example, see their *Dead Lines.* There is a kind of literary adventurousness about this book; it is not pure slice 'em and dice 'em.

79 For an attempt to correlate certain themes of the postmoderns, such as Michel Foucault, with the imagery of the contemporary horror film see Pete Boss, "Vile Bodies and Bad Medicine," *Screen,* vol. 27, No. 1, (January–February 1986) pp. 14–24.

80 Citizens other than those of the United States buy into this myth as well.

81 For the record, though it is not of material consequence to my account of the present horror cycle, let me say that I think that, overall, it is a good thing that the myths of the social system of Pax Americana have been contested. At the same time, this does not imply a valorization of the contemporary horror cycle. The cycle is a fact, one which I have tried

to explain. That it is a fact and that the fact has an explanation does not imply that the cycle is good as such. When it comes to questions of the goodness of contemporary horror, I would think that it is only really plausible to speak of the goodness of individual works rather than of the goodness of the whole cycle as a block.

Concerning my reservations, alluded to above, with regard to the philosophical claims of the postmodernists, see Noel Carroll, "The Illusions of Postmodernism," *Raritan, VII,* 2 (Fall 1987), p. 154.

Index